Drugs and Society

VOLUME 3

Oxycodone – Youth Culture

Marshall Cavendish Reference
New York

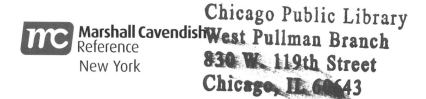

Marshall Cavendish
99 White Plains Road
Tarrytown, New York 10591

www.marshallcavendish.us

Library of Congress Cataloging-in-Publication Data
Drugs and society
p. cm.
Includes bibliographical references and index.
ISBN 0-7614-7597-4 (alk. paper set) -- ISBN 0-7614-7598-2 (alk. paper vol. 1) -- ISBN 0-7614-7599-0 (alk. paper vol. 2) -- ISBN 0-7614-7600-8 (alk. paper vol. 3)
1. Drugs of abuse. 2. Drug abuse. 3. Pharmacology. I. Marshall Cavendish Corporation. II. Title.

RM316.D765 2005
362.29--dc22

2004063775

Printed in Malaysia

09 08 07 06 6 5 4 3 2

Consultants
Michael J. Kuhar, PhD, Charles Howard Candler Professor of Pharmacology, Emory University, Atlanta, Georgia
Howard Liddle, EdD, Director, Center for Treatment and Research on Adolescent Drug Abuse, University of Miami Medical School, Miami, Florida

Marshall Cavendish
Editorial Director: Paul Bernabeo
Production Manager: Michael Esposito

The Brown Reference Group
Project Editor: Wendy Horobin
Editors: Paul Thompson, Selina Wood
Designer: Seth Grimbly
Picture Researcher: Clare Newman
Illustrators: Darren Awuah, Stefan Morris, Mark Walker
Indexer: Kay Ollerenshaw
Managing Editor: Bridget Giles
Senior Managing Editor: Tim Cooke
Editorial Director: Lindsey Lowe

Photographic Credits
Front Cover: PhotoDisc: Nick Rowe, background; **Corbis:** Hutchings Stock Photography, insert

Brookhaven National Laboratory: 755; **Corbis:** Tony Arruza 690, Bettmann 667, 820, Bojan Brecelj 745, Steve Chenn 801, Jim Cummins 726, Najlah Feanny 806, Jon Feingersh 811, Franz-Marc Frei 769, Zach Gold 763, Robert Holmes 850, Jeremy Horner 735, Scott Houston 683, Hutchings Stock Photography 710, Ed Kashi 845, 873, Douglas Kirkland 852, Bob Kirst 689, Rob Lewine 737, James Leynse 871, W. Wayne Lockwood M.D. 687, Jim McDonald 825, Mark Peterson 767, Reuters 660, 804, 823, Chuck Savage 885, Jerome Sessini/In Visu 733, 862, Ariel Skelley 866, Joseph Sohm/ChromoSohm Inc. 721, Tom Stewart 679, Tom Wagner 842, David H. Wells 701, Larry Williams 649, Alison Wright 694, Bo Zaunders 883; **Corbis Royalty Free:** 665, 713, 742; **Corbis Sygma:** Scott Houston 739; **DEA:** 765; **Getty Images:** 839; **Library of Congress:** 718; **PDFA:** Ogilvy & Mather 709; **PHIL:** 808; **PhotoDisc:** Keith Brofsky 702; **Rex Features:** Action Press 864, Burger/Phanie Agency 657, 792, Raphael Cardinael 775, Tim Clark 655, Image Source 681, Ojala 771, Phanie Agency 788, 877, Sakki 736, Sipa Press 675, 794, 835; **Still Pictures:** Jean Jean 853; **Topham Picturepoint:** 880, Bob Daemmrich/The Image Works 697, 707, 723, 799, Eastcott/Momatiuk/The Image Works 715, Esbin-Anderson/The Image Works 816, Jeff Greenberg/The Image Works 783, Colin Jones 752, Pressnet 859; **U.S. Department of Defense:** 870; **USDA:** Peter Manzelli 831, Ken Hammond 827.

Contents

Volume 3

Articles in Volume 1

Articles in Volume 2

Oxycodone

Oxycodone is a prescription opiate used for the treatment of moderate to severe pain. It has been abused as an alternative to heroin, particularly among younger users who may have access to it in the home.

Opium yields a number of alkaloids, including morphine, codeine, papaverine, and thebaine. Thebaine itself has little analgesic effect, but it is a precursor to several important compounds, including the semisynthetic opiate oxycodone.

Oxycodone is typically made into the salt form, oxycodone hydrochloride, a white, odorless crystalline powder that is highly soluble in water and slightly soluble in alcohol. Its half-life in serum following oral administration is quite short, ranging from 3 to 4 hours, which also corresponds to the duration of its analgesic action.

As with other opiates, the most dangerous potential side effect of oxycodone is respiratory depression by direct action on the brain stem respiratory centers. Oxycodone also depresses the cough reflex, constricts the pupils of the eyes, and produces some degree of nausea, vomiting, and slower digestion. Headache, dry mouth, constipation, somnolence, itching, sweating, dizziness, and weakness are also reported by a small percentage of patients.

KEY FACTS

Classification
Schedule II (USA), Schedule I (Canada), Class A (UK), Schedule I (INCB). Opioid.

Street names
Cotton, hillbilly heroin, kicker, O.C., oxy, oxycotton

Short-term effects
Analgesia (pain relief), euphoria, nausea and vomiting, slowed breathing, constipation. Risk of overdose if OxyContin is crushed and injected.

Long-term effects
Tolerance to the analgesic effect and physical dependence. Withdrawal symptoms include muscle spasms, gooseflesh, restlessness, insomnia, diarrhea, and vomiting.

Oral 5-milligram oxycodone formulations have been available in the United States since the 1950s, typically combined with a coanalgesic agent such as aspirin (Percodan) or acetaminophen (Percocet, Tylox, Roxicet). In large doses, however, aspirin and acetaminophen can be toxic to the liver, stomach, and kidneys. Since the 1990s, single-entity oxycodone products have been available as 5-milligram tablets (Roxicodone, Percolone, OxyIR) and liquid formulations (Oxyfast). These products removed the potential for aspirin or acetaminophen toxicity, but the problems of frequent dosage persisted because of the short half-life of oxycodone.

OxyContin is the brand name of a 12-hour slow-release formulation of oxycodone, available in 10-, 20-, 40-, 80-, and 160-milligram dosage forms. Controlled-release oxycodone is effective in the control of pain caused by cancer, osteoarthritis, major surgery, and degenerative spine disease.

The clinical usefulness of OxyContin, however, has been obscured by its abuse liability, especially in its highest dosage forms. OxyContin abusers either crush the tablets and ingest or snort it, or dilute it in water for injecting. Oral and nasal routes of administration are more common because extra purification steps are required to prepare OxyContin for injection. Regardless of the route of administration, crushing or diluting the tablets disarms the timed-release action of the medication and causes a quick, powerful high, which is liked by users and often preferred to the high produced by heroin, although it is of shorter duration. In some areas of North America, the use of heroin has been overtaken by the abuse of OxyContin.

F. LERI

SEE ALSO:
Morphine • Opiates and Opioids • Prescription Drugs • Withdrawal

Paraldehyde

Paraldehyde was one of the earliest sedatives to enter medical use. Its effects are similar to those of the barbiturates and benzodiazepines that have replaced its use in surgery and the treatment of agitation and seizures.

Paraldehyde entered medical usage as a sedative in the late nineteenth century. It provided a safer alternative to the bromide salts and chloral hydrate that until then had been the alternative sedatives to alcohol and opium. Paraldehyde was notably useful in calming mentally ill patients whose condition made them agitated or aggressive, and it made the use of physical restraints redundant in most cases. Other applications included the induction of sleep and the treatment of alcohol withdrawal.

In common with other central nervous system depressants, paraldehyde works by increasing the affinity between gamma-aminobutyric acid (GABA) and its receptors. These receptors dampen the neural activity stimulated by glutamate receptors, so paraldehyde has a calming and sedating effect.

Alcohol withdrawal

For many years, paraldehyde was the treatment of choice for alcohol withdrawal. In a landmark article about Alcoholics Anonymous in *The Saturday Evening Post* of March 1, 1941, Jack Alexander described the aroma of paraldehyde in the psychiatric ward of Philadelphia General Hospital as resembling a mixture of alcohol and ether. The aroma would be due to paraldehyde on the patients' breath.

Paraldehyde forms when three molecules of ethanal (acetaldehyde, CH_3CHO) condense together in the presence of sulfuric acid. Despite the suggestion in its name, it is an alcohol rather than an aldehyde.

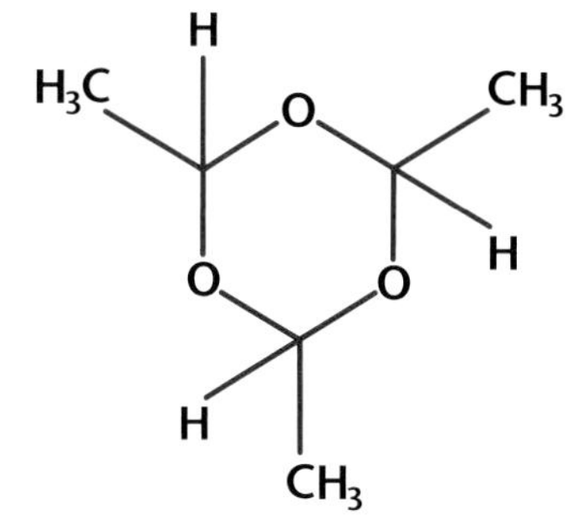

The role of paraldehyde in alcohol withdrawal was to reduce the incidence and severity of seizures by stimulating the GABA system—a role now overtaken by benzodiazepines. Such intervention is necessary because the GABA receptors of chronic heavy drinkers become desensitized to compensate for the constant presence of alcohol in the brain.

Once alcohol levels start to fall during withdrawal, the blunted GABA system fails to provide sufficient regulation for excitatory nerve impulses, and seizures can result. Paraldehyde provides the necessary stimulation of GABA activity in the place of alcohol and must be withdrawn gradually as the GABA system slowly returns to a healthy level of activity.

Disadvantages

Paraldehyde has a strongly unpleasant odor and taste, which are problematic because much of the drug leaves the body through the lungs. Paraldehyde is an irritant, so injection sites often became inflamed and painful. For this reason, paraldehyde was usually given as a mixture with vegetable oil to be swallowed or deposited in the rectum by syringe. Above all, there is potential for creating paraldehyde dependency in those who are treated with the drug.

The introduction of barbiturates displaced paraldehyde from most applications in the first decade of the twentieth century. In the late twentieth century the introduction of benzodiazepines and major tranquilizers further reduced the need for paraldehyde. Even so, its use continued in a minority of psychiatric hospitals until the end of that century.

Paraldehyde is no longer available for prescription in the United States, where it is a Schedule IV controlled substance. It continues to be a raw material in the manufacture of certain plastics.

M. CLOWES

SEE ALSO:
Alcohol • Alcoholism Treatment • Barbiturates • Benzodiazepines • Chloral Hydrate • Delirium Tremens • Gamma-aminobutyric Acid • Withdrawal

Parenting

Parents play a vital role in a child's developing attitudes and behaviors as he or she grows up. Positive actions and consistent messages against drug use can have a significant impact in preventing teenagers from getting involved with drugs.

Drug use is a complex of behaviors shaped by a variety of factors, both internal and external. It is determined in part physiologically; it is determined in part by learned behaviors, from family, neighborhood, and societal models; and it is determined by opportunity. Each of these pathways may be influenced by parenting, as parents are typically the suppliers of genetic traits for tolerance and personality, the primary moderators of social learning, and the gatekeepers to childhood and adolescent opportunities and experiences.

Parenting before birth

Physiologically, parents can influence their children's drug use in two ways—genetically and prenatally. Studies of twins, separated at birth and raised in different environments, have demonstrated that twins are more likely to share tendencies to addiction than unrelated persons are, which is evidence that at least some of the influences underlying addiction are hereditary. Genetic studies have identified some of the genes that carry the predisposition to abuse alcohol and to become addicted. In these cases, individuals carry genes that raise levels of liver enzymes in the presence of alcohol, causing nausea, flushing, and rapid heartbeat, making it generally unpleasant to continue drinking. This ability to assimilate alcohol has been found to vary by ethnicity, with some groups—in particular, Japanese, Chinese, and Jews—more likely to react negatively to alcohol and therefore less likely to abuse it. Some personality traits are also genetically determined, and substance use is frequently associated with personality traits of impulsivity, risk taking, and high levels of anxiety, depression, or obsessive-compulsive behavior. Molecular biologists have found variations in a particular gene that acts on gamma-aminobutyric acid (GABA), an inhibitory neurotransmitter. People with a certain form of this gene are 40 percent more likely to become alcohol dependent than those with other variations. The variation of the gene is determined by heredity.

Prenatally, the mother's drug or alcohol use can cross the umbilical cord and be found in the fetal blood in concentrations similar to those in the mother's blood. Because of the fetus's smaller size and immature liver, it cannot process the alcohol as fast as the mother can, and so it is more subject to damage from it. Historically, there have been references to harmful effects on infants from mothers' drinking as far back as the ancient Greeks. Modern research has more closely documented this link between maternal alcohol use and a specific pattern of malformations and disabilities called fetal alcohol spectrum disorders, consisting of the more severe fetal alcohol syndrome and the less severe fetal alcohol effects. Damage to fetal brain and central nervous system development is most likely to occur from maternal drinking in the first trimester of pregnancy, when these systems are undergoing the most rapid growth. No "safe" level of alcohol use has been determined. The most common symptoms of fetal alcohol spectrum disorders include mental retardation or severe learning disabilities, growth retardation both before and after birth, dental malformations, microcephaly (small head), and specific facial characteristics. Worldwide, the incidence of fetal alcohol spectrum disorders is estimated to be approximately two out of every thousand births.

A great deal of research has been done since the 1980s on the potential fetal harm from other drug use, including heroin, cocaine, crack cocaine, marijuana, and methamphetamine. While the popular media presented horrific stories of epidemics of "crack babies" in the mid-1990s, research attempting to document the short-term and long-term effects of maternal use of crack and other drugs has been much more equivocal. Some studies found cocaine- and crack-exposed babies to have lower birth weights, smaller heads, and increased rates of behavioral problems, including inability to focus and inability to ignore distractions, which can impede their progress in school settings. Babies exposed to marijuana in the uterus may show problems in reacting normally to visual input. They may also, in preschool and early school years, have more behavioral problems and difficulty with tasks of visual perception, language comprehension, and memory, which may lead to problems in decision making and sustaining attention. The impact of prenatal drug use is, however, difficult to disentangle from the impact of parenting skills of drug-using parents. Many studies have demonstrated that the responsiveness, monitoring, and management skills of drug-using parents are lower than those of other parents, which could cause the infants to "learn" to be unresponsive, or to not learn important skills, such as language, during critical periods when the brain is most receptive to learning these skills. It is also difficult to assess how many infants are actually born under the influence of drugs, as mothers are not usually asked at birthing if they have used drugs. The truthfulness of their responses in such a situation would be dubious, as some drug-using pregnant women have been incarcerated in the United States for child endangerment, and others have lost their children to social welfare programs.

Children learn many of their behavior patterns from their parents. Providing strong, positive role models through close family involvement can be a key factor in preventing future drug use in adolescence.

Parents as teachers

Learning occurs both verbally and schematically. Infants learn by watching what goes on around them. They remember sequences of actions, and they remember objects and people associated with those sequences. Later, as they acquire language, they become able to learn verbally—taking in information, integrating it with what they already know, and remembering it—but they retain the primary ability to learn purely by watching and reenacting, physically or mentally, what they have seen. Parents influence childhood and adolescent drug use by the verbal messages they give and by the behavioral models they provide through their actions. These messages and models interact with the child's personality, genetic makeup, and environmental opportunities and consequences, and they can be positive or negative in nature, enhancing or reducing the likelihood of youth substance use. They are consistently found by research to be one of the most powerful predictors of adolescent drug use and addiction.

One way in which parents provide a message that increases the likelihood of youth substance use is to model the use of substances themselves. It is difficult to determine how many adolescents who report substance use on standardized surveys have parents who also are substance users, as such questions are not included in most surveys. Tobacco research has found that those adolescents who report that their parents smoke cigarettes are themselves more than twice as likely to be smokers, and are also more likely to use other drugs. Most adults occasionally drink alcohol, providing another strong model for youth behavior, since alcohol is the predominant substance of abuse used by both adults and youth.

Parents can also give verbal messages. Those who give clear verbal expectations to their children about not using alcohol and other drugs are significantly less likely to have children who use those drugs. Some surveys have found that approximately 65 percent of parents report that they do not think it wrong for teenagers to drink alcohol as long as they do not drink and drive.

Another way in which parents can give messages is by reflecting on the meaning and intent of media messages. Adolescents are exposed to more alcohol advertising and product placement messages than any other age group, through the Internet, television, movies, and magazines. Parental intervention in explaining the commercial intent of these messages can reduce the likelihood of youth substance use.

Parental management

Parents also impact youth substance use through their family management styles. Adolescents who are integrated into the family, who have regular responsibilities, who are involved in decision making, rewarded for meeting expectations, and given consistent and appropriate consequences for not meeting stated expectations, are less likely to be involved in drug use and other delinquent behaviors. Similarly, those children whose parents monitor their whereabouts are less likely to be substance users. It is believed that as children grow and interact with their social environment, they develop the ability to self-regulate their behavior. Different theories of learning suggest that this happens in different ways, but all developmentalists recognize that children must somehow internalize the rules that govern their world in order to successfully negotiate it and that parents are the primary provider of rules.

Behavioral theory states that children learn by interacting with their environment and getting positive or negative reinforcement for their actions. Positive reinforcement is something that increases the likelihood of the behavior being repeated, while negative reinforcement reduces the likelihood that the behavior will be repeated. Parents are the main delivery system of reinforcement in the child's early life; parents and schools are the main delivery systems of middle childhood and adolescence. Children whose parents establish clear rules for behavior, consistently reinforcing positive behaviors with positive reinforcement and negative behaviors with negative reinforcement, increase the likelihood that their children will grow up to be rule followers. For example, a child may be told by a parent that smoking is not allowed, and the punishment for smoking will be "grounding," or confinement to the house for a week. If that child is caught smoking, the consequences levied by the parent directly influence whether or not the child will smoke again. If the parent grounds the child for a week, the child will be less likely to smoke again. If, instead, the parent does not ground the child but only gives another verbal warning, then the likelihood that the child will smoke again will not be reduced. Inherent in this theory is the necessity of the parent monitoring the child's behavior in order to reinforce it. The less the parent monitors what the child does, where the child goes, and with whom, the more likely it is that the child will become influenced by other systems of reinforcement in the environment. Hence, research has consistently found that parental monitoring is associated with reduced substance use, and reduced parental monitoring is associated with other persons, frequently peers, becoming more influential in determining behavior.

Social learning theories state that children learn by watching and listening to adults, and then rehearsing what they see and hear until they internalize the behaviors. Children model their behavior after those to whom they feel attached; again, in most cases in early childhood, these are the parents. Where the parent models are not strong, the child may model after peers or other adults whose behavior is different and more attractive than that of the parents. In current Western society, media such as television and movies offer role models that show alcohol and drug use to be attractive and associated with monetary, physical, or sexual rewards. Parents can act as interpreters of these messages, indicating their commercial intent and explaining that drinking alcohol does not imply that the drinker will be beautiful, thin, and drive a very expensive sports car; or they can reinforce the messages by appearing to believe that the behaviors shown are acceptable and the message realistic.

Messages and monitoring are equally as important as behavior management. Appropriate messages, increased monitoring, and behavior management that does not seek to control the child so much as to train the child to cognitively monitor his or her own behavior are all associated with reduced levels of substance use in adolescence.

R. GEALT

SEE ALSO:
Adolescents and Substance Abuse • Children • Family Environment • Peer Influence • Pregnancy and Fetal Addiction • Prevention • Protective Factors • Risk Factors • School and Drugs

PCP

PCP is a dissociative drug that was tested as a human anesthetic before becoming a street drug. It has potential for causing powerful hallucinations and occasional psychotic behavior in patients and recreational users.

Pharmaceuticals company Parke, Davis developed phencyclidine in the 1950s as a safer alternative to barbiturates for human anesthesia. Its alternative name, PCP, is an abbreviation of the chemical name for phencyclidine: 1-(1-*p*henyl*c*yclohexyl)*p*iperidine.

An alternative anesthetic was desirable because of the tendency of barbiturates to suppress breathing at anesthetic dosages. Early clinical trials indicated phencyclidine to be an effective anesthetic for use alone or with a reduced dosage of barbiturate. Furthermore, it produced its effects without hindering respiration. By the end of the 1950s, Parke, Davis had patented phencyclidine and created the Sernyl brand of phencyclidine anesthetic.

Anesthetic properties

Human trials revealed PCP to produce a state of anesthesia in which the patient was conscious but unaware of pain, free of distress, and unable to move voluntarily. This condition was called a cataleptoid state at the time of early trials, but later became known as dissociative anesthesia. In this state of anesthesia, the patient's conscious mind is isolated from signals from the body that supports it. Complete unconscious sedation for surgery can be achieved by increasing the dosage above that for dissociative anesthesia or by additional use of other medications. However, the state of untroubled, pain-free wakefulness was considered potentially useful for childbirth and some surgical procedures.

Negative effects

Phencyclidine revealed itself to be far from ideal for anesthesia in 1957, during the first trials on humans. The principal problems with phencyclidine were due to patients emerging from anesthesia in distressed and agitated states, sometimes suffering from delusions, hallucinations, or psychotic episodes. Slow elimination caused these symptoms to last for several hours and sometimes days. Over time it became clear that these side effects made PCP unsuitable for human use, and Parke, Davis withdrew Sernyl in

KEY FACTS

Classification
Schedule II (USA), Schedule I (Canada), Class A (UK), Schedule II (INCB). Dissociative hallucinogen.

Form
As the hydrochloride salt in powders, pills, capsules, or solutions. Impregnated into or sprinkled over leaves of kitchen herbs, marijuana, or tobacco for smoking.

Street names
Angel dust, embalming fluid, peace pill, rocket fuel, wack. Mixed with marijuana: crystal supergrass, killer weed, KJs (killer joints, krystal joints). Mixed with crack: space base. PCP is also sold as other drugs, notably as pure THC (tetrahydrocannabinol).

Short-term effects
Mild doses cause euphoria, increased breathing and heart rate, sweating, nausea, and vomiting. Moderate doses numb physical and emotional pain and can cause out-of-body sensations and other hallucinations. Delusions of extreme physical strength are common, as are anxiety, aggression, lack of reasoning, paranoia, and psychotic behavior. Speech becomes garbled. Some users fall into an unresponsive state of catatonia. High doses kill by stopping heart and lung functions.

Dangers
Self injury is likely owing to failure of judgment and the inability to feel pain. Accidents are the principal cause of death through PCP use. Paranoia, aggression, and feelings of strength can exacerbate problems in encounters with law enforcers. Potential exists for irreversible brain damage and changes in behavior and mental capacity. Pregnant users risk fetal brain damage leading to mental retardation of their children.

1965. Having failed for humans, phencyclidine reappeared in 1967 as Sernylan, a veterinary anesthetic that persisted on the market for over a decade.

PCP use in the 1960s

As far as is known, the first wave of recreational PCP use occurred in 1967 and was based around the Haight Ashbury district of San Francisco. The reception of PCP on the drug scene was mixed, since it was nearly impossible to judge the outcome of any given PCP experience. The most usual format was in pills that took full effect after around 30 minutes, by which time the user was committed to the effects of whatever dose he or she had taken.

Users seeking the euphoria of a light dose often became overwhelmed by sinister and powerful hallucinations with distortions of their own body images. Some believed they had died, some had hallucinations of traveling through a dark tunnel toward a light—a typical near-death hallucination. Inevitably, many recreational users also suffered the psychoses that occurred in clinical trials.

While a few recreational users enjoyed the feeling of mind separating from body and the profundity of hallucinations on PCP, the widespread opinion was that it was an unpredictable and risky drug. Upbeat street names such as peace pill and angel dust failed to boost the popularity of PCP in the recreational drug community, and its bad reputation practically killed off its street use by the end of the 1960s.

PCP JARGON

The nature of PCP's subjective effects varies greatly, depending on dosage and user sensitivity. Various terms have arisen to describe different states of PCP intoxication, and four of these terms have been adopted by researchers.

"Buzzed" refers to a mild stimulant high that occurs at low doses and does not interfere with senses or actions. "Wasted" is the state when coordination and senses start to fail; the user has odd sensations, such as the feeling of walking on spongy ground. "Ozoned" is when the still-conscious user can hardly move or communicate sensibly. "Overdosed" is when the user loses consciousness; in this context, the term usually refers to having taken too much PCP to be able to enjoy its psychoactive effects.

1970s to 1990s

Undaunted by failure in the 1960s, drug dealers began to reintroduce PCP in the early 1970s. This time the emphasis was on PCP-containing solutions and powders that could be injected, snorted, or mixed into materials for smoking. These methods deliver the drug to the brain much more quickly than swallowing a pill that has to break down in the stomach and be absorbed into the bloodstream, so the full effects were felt in three minutes or less, compared with half an hour or more for a pill.

The change in format made it easier to reach the desired level of high by taking multiple small doses and waiting for effects. In theory, this change might have improved sales by making the drug seem more controllable. Also, the euphoric rush of a small dose would be greater as its effects took hold more rapidly. In practice, the reputation of PCP was so bad that few people would knowingly buy it when more reliable highs were available from other drugs.

In another ploy, dealers sold PCP under the guise of another street drug with a better reputation. The most frequent ruse was to sell PCP as "pure" tetrahydrocannabinol (THC), the main active compound in cannabis products. Alternatively, PCP was soaked into poor-quality marijuana or dried leaves of other plants with no psychoactivity to then be sold as marijuana leaves. Some PCP was sold as hallucinogens such as LSD, psilocybin, and mescaline, or mixed with the authentic products as a cheap but potent filler. Only a small proportion of the all PCP in street trade was sold as PCP itself. As a result, many casualties of the PCP trade took the drug in the belief that it was another substance whose effects were familiar to them, and subsequently became overwhelmed by the potent effects of PCP.

Dealers made such efforts to market PCP because it is potent yet cheap and easy to make, and hence has great potential for making profit. When Parke, Davis withdrew the drug in 1978, clandestine factories were already capable of supplying the street.

Despite the initial unpopularity of PCP, some people became regular users of the drug. Its

MEDIA FRENZY

Lurid reports of bizarre and dangerous behavior caused by drug use are standard media fare. It is no surprise that PCP is a good target for such reporting, since it has a well-documented ability to cause psychotic states in clinical trials.

In 1980 the *Journal of Psychedelic Drugs* published a study by John Morgan and Doreen Kagan of media coverage of PCP. The authors found 323 articles on PCP in a selection of U.S. newspapers between 1958 and 1979. Of this total, 247 articles appeared in 1978; a fall to 42 articles in 1979 showed that the main swell of media interest in PCP had passed by that year.

The flood of PCP horror stories followed in the wake of interviews with R. Stanley Burns in the journal *Emergency Medicine* (1976) and on the television show *60 Minutes* (October 23, 1977). Burns was coauthor of a clinical report on PCP in 1975, but it was in the subsequent interviews that he mentioned murders, suicides, and accidental deaths by burning and drowning while under the influence of PCP. Burns formed a corporation offering PCP-related advice and treatment with Steven Lerner, who contributed PCP horror stories in the *60 Minutes* interview, and Ronald Linder. Lerner went on to make several appearances in topical television programs and to act as a PCP consultant to popular television dramas.

Many of the PCP-related horror stories that went into print featured different locations and people but were substantially similar, suggesting that a single story had become distorted by retelling. The story that recurred most often was that of a person—usually male—who gouged out his or her own eyes while in custody after arrest. Some versions specified a male Baltimore college student, in one case the son of a Massachussetts member of Congress, who had been arrested for indecent exposure.

In their report, Morgan and Kagan identified a police case from 1971 that they suggested to be a possible origin of the oft-cited PCP story. The subject of this case was Charles Innes, a college dropout living in Baltimore who was the son of a state legislator from Massachusetts.

During a police raid at his home, Innes swallowed a drug that was later identified as LSD. No test for PCP was performed. Four days later, Innes was arrested after an incident of public nudity and subsequently blinded himself in jail. Innes claimed he had taken PCPA (para-chlorophenylalanine), a street drug completely unrelated to PCP despite the common initials. On this basis, it seems feasible that the most popular "PCP" story of the late 1970s was in fact a retelling of an old story related to a different drug.

popularity peaked in the 1980s but declined into the mid 1990s as a result of users perceiving the potential of PCP for causing long-term brain damage. Clinical tests suggest that long-term PCP use might indeed cause neurological problems with symptoms such as poor memory, depression, and psychosis.

Current status

Reports suggest that PCP is enjoying a new lease on life on the recreational drug scene. In 2001 the U.S. National Institute on Drug Abuse (NIDA) listed PCP as an emerging drug after an upsurge in PCP-related deaths and emergency room (ER) admissions. Similarly, the Drug Abuse Warning Network (DAWN) reported a 28 percent increase in ER admissions from 1995 to 2000, followed by a 42 percent increase from 2000 to 2002. Other data indicate that the major use of PCP is among early adolescents, who usually lose interest in the drug by the end of their teens. Nevertheless, the proven contribution of PCP to accidental deaths and the possible risk of cumulative brain damage through long-term PCP use are cause for concern.

M. Clowes

See also:
Crime and Drugs • Cutting Drugs • Illicit Manufacturing • Ketamine • PCP Analogs

PCP Analogs

PCP analogs are chemical relatives of phencyclidine that share at least some of its psychoactive properties. The analogs include medical anesthetics, illicit drugs, and experimental compounds for research into the brain and addiction.

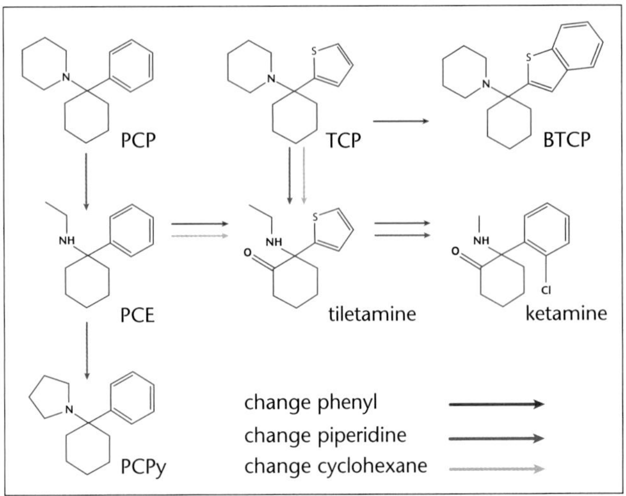

When a chemical compound has clear physiological or psychoactive effects, the testing of related compounds is a routine approach to studying how the parent compound works and searching for new compounds with better therapeutic effects or fewer side effects.

One reason for the study of PCP analogs is that this otherwise useful anesthetic has an ability to cause psychotic and catatonic states that are hard to distinguish from symptoms of schizophrenia. Hence, many related compounds have been produced in the search for an anesthetic that is less likely to cause such disturbances.

The search for alternative anesthetics led to the development of eticyclidine (PCE), rolicyclidine (PCPy), and tenocyclidine (TCP)—all of which are now INCB Schedule I drugs—as well as ketamine and tiletamine. Ketamine is still used as a human and veterinary anesthetic, and tiletamine is used in conjunction with a benzodiazepine as an anesthetic for large animals. All these drugs have similar effects to PCP and have also been manufactured illicitly for sale as recreational drugs.

General patterns

The structural unit responsible for activity, or pharmacophore, seems to be cyclohexylamine with an aromatic ring attached to the same carbon atom as carries the nitrogen atom. At least 30 variants on this structure have been sold as street drugs, and the potencies of these variants follow certain trends.

An increase in activity occurs when a thienyl group replaces the phenyl group of PCP, as is the case for TCP. Activity drops when there are additional groups on the phenyl group, such as the chloro (Cl–) group in ketamine. The strongest effects occur when the nitrogen atom is part of a ring system such as piperidine (as in PCP) or pyrrolidine (as in PCPy). If a straight hydrocarbon chain replaces a ring, the loss of potency is least for an ethyl group (C_2H_5–), as in PCE and tiletamine. Compounds with other numbers of carbon atoms have reduced potency.

Experimental drugs

PCP affects many neurotransmitter systems. Its characteristic interaction is with sites near NMDA glutamate receptors, but it also interacts with dopamine, serotonin, and norepinephrine systems—targets for cocaine and other stimulants—as well as with acetylcholine, endorphin, and sigma receptors.

PCP analogs vary greatly in their interactions with different types of receptors, and some have effects that are not typical of PCP. In particular, BTCP has interactions that resemble those of cocaine. This PCP analog can quell a dependent's craving for cocaine without creating a habit. As such, it has potential for use in treating dependency. On the other hand, it is also possible that clandestine chemists will find other PCP analogs that they can manufacture as cheap but powerfully addictive substitutes for cocaine.

M. Clowes

SEE ALSO:
Agonists and Antagonists • Analogs • Drug Receptors • Ketamine • Opiates and Opioids • PCP

Peer Influence

It has long been thought that adolescents may be pressured into using drugs through the influence of friends in their social peer group. Alternative theories propose that teenagers choose to take drugs to conform with a group's ideology.

Adolescence is a time when teenagers begin to identify more closely with friends than with their parents. They declare their independence through shared styles of clothing, activities, or experimentation with substances.

One of the most enduring and pervasive theories on drug initiation is that of peer pressure, the idea that children start taking drugs because of pressure from their peers. This article will examine this theory and some aspects of how it may affect drug use.

Developmental theories suggest that the most powerful influence on shaping our personality and nature comes from our parents. It is our parents, in particular our mothers, who share and guide our early experience, our first steps, first words, and so on. However, parental influence tends to wane temporarily as a child enters adolescence. During adolescence, parents and children become more psychologically and physically distant from each other: physically distant because the adolescent spends increasing amounts of time away from the family and the family home, usually with friends of his or her own age; psychologically distant as the parent's and adolescent's range of interests diverge. In developmental terms, this distancing is part of the normal process of growth and maturation. It creates opportunities for an adolescent to extend his or her ideas and to try new experiences away from adult influence or judgment. However, peer pressure has acquired negative connotations; the media and popular literature are full of discussions about peer pressure and advice on how to save the adolescent from the insidious force that comes from peers.

Why do adolescents start using drugs?

There is no definitive answer to this question, as there are a number of reasons that adolescents start to use drugs, from curiosity and rebellion to the environment and coping with problems, or any combination of these elements. What is known is that about 50 percent of drug use, legal and illegal, begins between the ages of 15 and 18 years. Some of these factors can help explain why adolescents start using drugs.

Environment. One could argue that those brought up in areas of multiple deprivation, little money, and few prospects of employment, education, or a good future are at an increased risk of drug use and abuse. Drugs can offer an escape from the despair and boredom that these adolescents experience and can even offer a career path as a dealer—after all, the risks may be high but so too are the profits. While there may be more people from deprived areas who choose this path, the evidence suggests that drug users span the full spectrum of social class and demographic area. Many of the traditional boundaries between the affluent and the deprived are falling as drug use becomes more egalitarian. For example, crack and heroin use was far more prevalent in deprived areas in the 1980s, while Ecstasy and cocaine use was common in the more affluent areas. Subsequently differences between the social classes may lie less in the range of available drugs and more in the resources that people possess to alleviate the worst effects of drugs; for example, those with greater finances do not need to commit crimes to feed their habits, and those with more social support are less likely to become addicted or to stay addicted for as long.

Coping with problems. Another commonly given reason for drug use is that it is used as a "crutch," that is, it is used to help cope with trauma. Researchers have also found that initiation of drug use generally occurs during major changes in a person's life, for example, moving from junior to senior high school, or going to college, or getting a job. There would also appear to be a significantly large group of adolescent drug users who come from families where there is either little stability or there is active conflict leading to separation or divorce. Drug-using adolescents also appear to be low achievers; however, that could be a consequence rather than a cause of drug use. Also, while coping may provide a plausible explanation of maintenance and even escalation of drug use, it has limited utility as an explanation of initiation.

Curiosity and experimentation. Adolescence is a time of discovery about oneself and the outside world. Research has shown that it is a pivotal time cognitively as attitudes move from the childlike to the mature. For example, research on attitudes toward alcohol has found that, prior to age 12, attitudes tend to be negative, viewing alcohol as something to be avoided. However, after the age of 12, these attitudes change to become positive and more like those of an adult. As part of these changes, adolescents will experiment to discover what they enjoy. Thus, they may try smoking, drinking, and perhaps drugs.

Rebellion. Since adolescence is a time for experimenting, part of that experimentation can involve testing the boundaries and rules of society. Part of growing up involves finding out who we are in relation to others, that is, in what ways we are the same and in what ways we differ. Adolescence is the time where conformity is eschewed in favor of rebellion and a declaration of uniqueness, characterized by clothes, music tastes, speech, and behavior. Since the adolescent believes that he or she has now "invented" life, sex, and values, the teachings and warnings of adults regarding certain behaviors, such as those involving sex and drugs, may be ignored in favor of the new mores. This cycle has repeated for generations, the only difference now being that the menu of substances that can be used to express rebellion has greatly increased, from legal substances such as alcohol and tobacco to illicit drugs.

Peer pressure

As stated above, peer pressure has been one of the most frequently invoked reasons for the initiation of drug use. The question is how to define peer pressure and whether this pressure is emotional or physical. What is known is that adolescents and, for that matter, humans of all ages are influenced by their peers. Fashion is an obvious manifestation of peer influence. How else could one explain some of the clothes worn or hairstyles sported in the past? Although we may cringe now when we see old photographs, the styles seemed not only fine at the time but we may have felt differentiated from and excluded by our friends if we had not followed the fashion. Much of youth fashion and culture is bound up with experimentation and rebellion and is a fairly harmless part of the process of maturing. The mechanism that drives it is, ironically, conformity. While rebelling and stating their uniqueness, most adolescents are aware of the very strict boundaries that govern inclusion in their selected group. However, this is mostly an informal process. Would that kind of influence be enough to initiate drug use, or is there a more powerful and insidious force at work among adolescents? Some researchers suggest a different explanation.

Peer pressure or peer preference?

Alternative theories suggest that, rather than being pressured by peers, adolescents instead exercise choice, and that a better explanation may be "peer preference." Adolescents choose the groups to which they want to belong. If that group takes drugs, then part of the admission cost may be to indulge in the same behavior. One can observe that there are usually a number of adolescent fashions in vogue at any given time. The followers of each of these fashions usually have a dress code, a musical taste, and a set of behaviors. To gain membership in such a group usually requires the individual to adopt some of the characteristics of the others. If part of the behavior of the group entails drug taking, then that may be a consideration that is addressed as part of the admission process.

Of course neither of these theories, peer pressure or preference, are mutually exclusive. Just because one has chosen a particular group does not mean that the group cannot or will not exert some influence on its members. This is especially true during early to middle adolescence, when the group may still be trying to define itself, and what is considered acceptable behavior within the group may be changing. The group may grow more daring or extreme in its behavior and there may be influence on more reticent members to participate. The theory of peer preference, while plausible, also assumes that there are a number of groups from which to choose, an assumption that may be correct in larger urban environments but not in small communities.

Parental involvement in a teenager's life can be a key factor in building resistance to peer pressure about taking drugs and other negative behaviors.

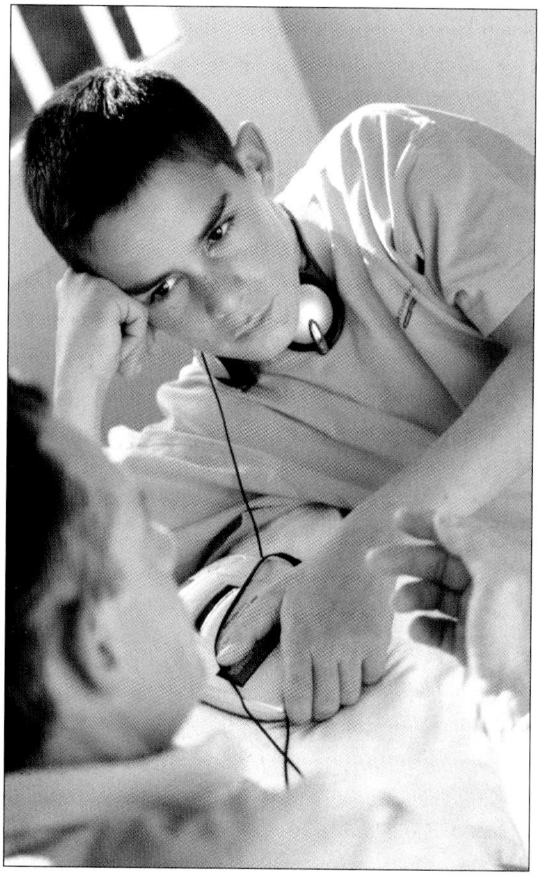

Combating peer influence

Assuming that peer influence is indeed a major cause of initiation into drug use, what measures can be taken to minimize its effect? Most commentators would suggest that the process of inoculating against peer pressure should begin when the child is very young. Two basic ingredients are required: strong values and a good sense of self as an independent and valuable person. These ingredients are dependent on the main caregivers, usually the parents. Discussing drugs (including alcohol) at an early age is advisable—parents should take responsibility rather than simply leaving drug education to schools. Parents also need to be aware of and monitor their own alcohol and drug use, since adolescents are extremely sensitive to parental substance use.

Parents also need to help their children to value their own choices and opinions. If teenagers are to resist peer influence, then they need to feel confident that their own decisions are correct for them. This requires an ongoing process starting at a young age: expecting adolescents to make difficult choices when they have never before had the opportunity is almost certainly unrealistic.

Harnessing peer influence for prevention

Drug education is beginning to take advantage of the putative power of peer influence. For many years psychologists and educators have recognized that the status of the educator is as important as the message that is delivered. Advertisers rely on the same principle when paying celebrities to endorse their products. More recently, this same strategy has been used in drug prevention programs. However, rather than celebrities, it is adolescents themselves who deliver the message.

Much of the information in drug prevention programs had previously been delivered by teachers and the police, knowledgeable educators of high status. However, evaluations of these programs suggested that they were not very effective. Reasons given for the lack of effectiveness concerned the message and, perhaps more important, the message giver. Adolescents felt that some of the messages being delivered were exaggerations because the information conflicted with their personal or vicarious experience. For example, one approach was to emphasize the dangers to health from drug taking. These messages were at odds with the fact that most adolescents had taken drugs or knew someone who had taken drugs with no ill effects. Therefore the message, however otherwise accurate, often fell on deaf ears. The second problem was the message carrier. While the police and teachers may have impeccable credentials to deliver factual information, there was a generation gap that further called their credibility into question.

One solution was to recruit recovering drug users to teach drug education. Their credibility was not in question and they were usually closer in age to the adolescents they were teaching. Unfortunately this strategy was not as successful as had been hoped. The problem with this aproach was that few adolescents saw themselves as people who would succumb to addiction.

Finally, two solutions suggested themselves—change both the message and the deliverer of the message. Changing the message consisted of being pragmatic; if young people are going to take drugs, despite being warned of the dangers, then perhaps they need to be taught about harm reduction, that is, how to make drug taking safer. This part of the solution has not been universally adopted, as it is viewed by some as condoning, if not actually encouraging, drug use. However, it does allow the topic of social norms to be discussed—how common drug use actually is and what sort of quantities are being used. This important information is omitted from a "just say no" type of program. The second component of the solution is much less controversial —peer-led drug education.

Adolescents can be selected and trained to deliver a program of drug education. This strategy should avoid the problems of credibility so redolent when adults in authority deliver the program. The success of the strategy depends very much on the selection process. For this approach to be a success, the peer educators delivering the program must be malleable enough to deliver the program as designed. They need to have good communication skills and must be drug free themselves. To be taken seriously by their peers, they need to be respected by them. This is not an easy process but it is one that has proved to be very effective. A number of studies have shown that giving adolescents the opportunity to help and learn from each other encourages feelings of self-worth and efficacy in resisting pressures to take drugs. Not having adults conduct sessions also allows adolescents to discuss their attitudes and experiences more openly. Another finding is that acting as a peer leader can transform the school performance of some teenagers who may have been underachieving or feeling alienated from school life.

Overall effect of peer influence

Peer influence is apparent in all aspects of one's life. It can be particularly strong in adolescence when youths are still trying to discover who they are. Peer influence can also provide a positive effect on drug use, not only in peer education; a minority of adolescents use illegal drugs so most groups in fact support abstinence. Although peer pressure has been cited as a main cause of drug use, peer preference suggests an opt-in system whereby adolescents choose those who will influence them.

J. MCMAHON

SEE ALSO:
Adolescents and Substance Abuse • Dependence • Education • Parenting • Prevention • School and Drugs • Self-esteem • Vulnerability • Youth Culture

Penalties and Punishments

Possession and trafficking of illegal drugs carry stiff penalties for anyone caught using or dealing substances. In the United States, drug offenders comprise more than half of the prison population.

For as long as history has been recorded, society has sought effective ways to reward positive, or "prosocial," behavior and to punish negative, or "antisocial," behavior. The method of establishing these rewards and punishments varies across centuries and across cultures but is consistently found in both ancient and modern literature, art, and historical records.

The United States has two categories of offenses within its three primary enforcement systems (federal, state, and local). The two categories are felonies and misdemeanors. The differences between federal, state, and local arrests, sentences, and incarceration are determined by evaluation of several factors, including jurisdiction, severity of offense, and the primary law enforcement agency responsible for the arrest.

Convictions and offenses may be violent or nonviolent, but approximately 54 percent involve drug offenses. In fiscal year 2000 the United States Department of Justice spent $5.3 billion in the investigation and prosecution of criminal offenses. Criminal behavior and substance abuse are co-occurring problems that cost society billions of dollars in lost revenue, justice expenditures, and health care–related costs.

A person may be sentenced to probation for a variety of offenses. Probation is considered an alternative to incarceration and provides monitoring for offenders while they are living in the community and serving their sentence. Parole is used for people who have been incarcerated for some period of their sentence and will complete their sentence while living in the community.

Sentencing policy in the United States

The idea of punishing people for the illegal use of alcohol and drugs is not new to society. Beginning in the 1920s with the start of Prohibition, extensive legal, political, and social strategies have been explored with varying levels of success. Other types of criminal behavior, including both nonviolent and violent offenses, are also often associated with some form of alcohol or drug use. Data collected in the Arrestee Drug Abuse Monitoring (ADAM) program on alcohol and other drug use by arrestees demonstrates that 57 percent of males reported consuming alcohol and 54 percent reported consuming cocaine in the 72 hours prior to arrest.

In 2002, state and federal courts convicted a combined total of nearly 1,051,000 adults of felonies. State courts convicted an estimated 1,114,000 adults and federal courts convicted 63,217 adults (accounting for 6 percent of the national total). In 2002, 69 percent of all felons convicted in state courts were sentenced to a period of confinement: 41 percent to state prisons and 28 percent to local jails. Jail sentences are for short-term confinement (usually for a year or less) in a county or city facility, while prison sentences are for long-term confinement (usually for more than a year) in a state facility. State courts sentenced 31 percent of convicted felons to straight probation with no jail or prison time to serve. As well as being sentenced to incarceration or probation, 36 percent or more of convicted felons also were ordered to pay a fine, pay victim restitution, receive treatment, perform community service, or comply with some other additional penalty. A fine was imposed on at least 25 percent of convicted felons.

The U.S. Department of Justice is the umbrella organization under which most policy, sentencing, and reform efforts originate. Among other things, the department is responsible for law enforcement, courts, prosecutions, juvenile justice, and corrections. Within the Department of Justice there is an Office of Legal Policy, which has a mission to plan, develop, and coordinate the implementation of major legal policy initiatives of high priority to the department and to the administration. The office also provides legal advice and assistance to the attorney general and to other Department of Justice components. The office further functions as a focal point for the development and coordination of departmental policy. Essential to accomplishing the goals of the president of the United States, the department must assume a proactive leadership role in developing and implementing legal policy initiatives.

Sentencing policy

The official policy at the federal level of law enforcement is to seek out major drug suppliers and traffickers and prosecute those offenses. These prosecutions are aimed at removing large quantities of illicit drugs from the streets. These large cases are generally handled on the federal level, and smaller amounts and less serious cases are handled at the state and local level. The goal of drug laws is to punish drug offenders and in some cases introduce and provide drug treatment through the various levels of corrections. According to the Bureau of Justice Statistics National Judicial Reporting Program, 195,183 people were convicted in state courts of drug trafficking in 1998. That same year, 119,443 were convicted of drug possession.

Penalties for possessing a drug are determined by the drug's classification under the Controlled Substances Act. However, the introduction of mandatory sentencing for drug offenses, aimed at habitual offenders, has removed discretionary sentencing from judges. Instead, the power to influence sentences has passed to prosecutors, who may reduce sentences according to plea bargains, usually for information that leads to the conviction of others. This measure has resulted in situations in which high-level offenders who plea bargain receive comparatively lower sentences than first-time offenders, who may be incarcerated for possessing minimum quantities of drugs simply because they have no information to trade. The mandatory sentencing policy also increases the levels of fines and lengths of prison terms substantially for each subsequent offense, until after "three strikes" the offender automatically receives the maximum sentence, even if caught with a minimal amount of the drug. The quantity of drugs is the major factor in determining the sentence; for example, a drug "mule" carrying more than 12 pounds (5 kg) of cocaine will receive a minimum sentence of 10 years and a fine of up to $4 million for a first offense. Another feature of current drug sentencing policy is "truth in sentencing," whereby convicted individuals serve their full sentence instead of being eligible for early release. Whether such rigid strategies for drug offenses act as a deterrent is a hotly debated issue. A 1997 study by the Rand Corporation found that neither mandatory sentencing nor truth in sentencing had any significant effect in reducing drug crime or the number of arrests in states that used one or both strategies.

This airport worker, caught smuggling drugs and weapons in Miami, would automatically face strict mandatory sentences for both types of offense.

While first-time offenders face imprisonment for possession of heroin, cocaine, or amphetamines, they are less likely to be sent to prison for possessing a small amount of marijuana. Possession of an ounce or less of marijuana is a misdemeanor offense, and twelve states have reduced simple possession of marijuana to the equivalent of a traffic violation. However, estimates from the Bureau of Justice Statistics show that in mid-2002, approximately 8,400 state prisoners were serving time for possessing marijuana. About one-half of the total number were incarcerated for a first offense.

One of the biggest discrepancies in drug sentencing policy arises with powder cocaine and crack. In 1988 Congress established a special sentencing exception for crack even though it is exactly the same drug as powder cocaine and has the same effects. A dealer caught with 5 grams of crack receives the same punishment as one caught with 500 grams of powder. Simple possession of crack incurs a minimum sentence of five years. The Drug Enforcement Administration (DEA) reportedly made 10,518 cocaine- or crack-related arrests during fiscal year 2003. This number represents approximately 39 percent of the total arrests reported by the DEA. In 2002 cocaine or crack was involved in 37 percent of all federal drug arrests. Of the 25,609 federal drug offense cases during 2002, powder cocaine was involved in 23 percent and crack cocaine was involved in 20 percent.

The penalties for trafficking in other drugs increased after their abuse became seen as a growing problem. The Department of Justice reports that Ecstasy (MDMA) was involved in 153 Organized Crime Drug Enforcement Task Force (OCDETF) investigations during 2002. The number of arrests by the DEA for Ecstasy-related offenses declined between 2001 and 2002. The number of OCDETF indictments filed in which an Ecstasy trafficking offense was reported in the indictment also declined between 2001 and 2002. In response to the Ecstasy Anti-Proliferation Act of 2000, the U.S. Sentencing Commission increased the recommended guidelines for trafficking sentences involving Ecstasy. Effective November 1, 2001, the sentence for trafficking 800 or more Ecstasy pills increased by 300 percent, or jumped from 15 months to 5 years. Similarly, the penalty for trafficking 8,000 or more pills increased by nearly 200 percent, jumping from 41 months to 10 years. According to the DEA, the number of arrests for GHB (gamma-hydroxybutyrate)-related offenses increased from zero in 2002 to nine in 2003. The number of GHB-related investigations by the DEA increased from eight in 2002 to 19 in 2003.

Alternative sentencing models

Due in part to the large numbers of offenders incarcerated for drug-related offenses, overcrowding, and increasing budgets, federal, state, and local authorities have begun to explore creative and cost-effective models for sentencing nonviolent drug offenders. Incarceration of drug-using offenders costs between $20,000 and $50,000 per person per year. The capital costs of building a prison cell can be as much as $80,000.

One of the most successful of these alternatives has been the institution of drug courts. The first drug court was implemented in 1989 in Miami, Florida. An important force behind the drug court movement was the Violent Crime Control and Law Enforcement Act of 1994, which started federal support for planning, implementing, and enhancing drug courts for nonviolent drug offenders. Between 1995 and 1997 the Department of Justice, through its Drug Courts Program Office, provided $56 million in funding to drug courts. A drug court rehabilitation course typically costs between $2,500 and $4,000 annually for each offender.

A drug court can be defined as a special court given the responsibility to handle cases involving drug-addicted offenders through an extensive supervision and treatment program. Drug courts vary somewhat from one jurisdiction to another in terms of structure, scope, and target populations, but they all share three primary goals: to reduce recidivism; to reduce substance abuse among participants; and to rehabilitate participants. As of September 2004, there were 1,212 drug courts operating in all 50 states, the District of Columbia, Puerto Rico, Guam, and two federal districts. Another 476 drug court programs were in the planning stages. Drug court participants undergo long-term treatment and counseling, sanctions, incentives, and frequent court appearances. Successful completion of the treatment program results in dismissal of the charges, reduced or set aside sentences, lesser penalties, or a combination of these.

Juveniles

The numbers of juveniles involved in the legal system is increasing at a steady rate. In 1974 the Office of Juvenile Justice and Delinquency Prevention was established as a separate entity within the Department of Justice. The purpose of the office was to provide federal assistance to states working to combat juvenile delinquency and child victimization. Many programs and community initiatives have been developed through the leadership of this office. These unique programs include Support for

Drug Communities, Juvenile Mentoring, Truancy Reduction, and Safe Schools, among others.

There are over 3,600 juvenile residential facilities in the United States that house over 110,000 juvenile offenders. Approximately 13 percent of the total are female offenders. Much like their adult counterparts, these juvenile offenders commit a variety of violent and nonviolent offenses for which they are incarcerated. These offenses range all the way from truancy to murder and often include alcohol- or drug-related offenses. Similar to adults, the number of minorities in juvenile custody is disproportionate to the percentage of minorities in the general population. In particular, black youths have the highest custody rate nationally. An estimated 38 percent of American youths are minorities, but they make up 62 percent of American youths in custody.

A small percentage of youthful offenders end up being sentenced to state prisons. These young offenders are typically 17 or older, minorities, males, and convicted of crimes of a violent nature that were committed against another person.

In 2001 law enforcement agencies in the United States made an estimated 2.3 million arrests of persons under the age of 18. According to the Federal Bureau of Investigation (FBI), during the same period juveniles accounted for 17 percent of all arrests and 15 percent of all violent crime arrests.

Punishment

The United States has gone through several stages in its approach to incarceration. The first known penitentiary was built in Philadelphia, Pennsylvania, in 1790 and was known as the "Walnut Street Jail." The penitentiary system, also known as the "Pennsylvania System," used the primary methods of isolation, solitary confinement, repentance, and Bible reading as a means of controlling prisoners. During the late 1880s there was a brief effort at reform in major penal institutions that included the practice of indeterminate sentences. Offenders were able to earn or lose time toward their release by their own behavior. This reform was the beginning of many of the practices used today, such as parole, vocational training, education, and rehabilitation as an alternative to punishment alone.

Between 1935 and 1945 the movement shifted back to a punitive model, and the primary goal of enforcement institutions was to maintain security and keep convicted offenders off the streets. The treatment era was characterized by the use of therapeutic models of treatment for offenders. Group and individual therapy, substance abuse education, behavior modification, and other types of treatment came into use. Overcrowding and the financial strain of operating major prisons led to community correctional centers being established in many states, which still operate today. These are essentially halfway houses for convicted felons who are leaving prison. Many act as safe places where drug offenders who have undergone treatment can maintain their drug-free status before returning to their communities.

Currently the United States has the second highest incarceration rate in the world. The total prison population has more than doubled since 1984, largely as a result of the increases in arrests and convictions for drug-related offenses. As of June 30, 2002, the nation's prison and jail population exceeded 2 million for the first time in its history, and during 2003 the number peaked at 2.2 million. On December 31, 2003, 2,085,620 prisoners were held in federal or state prisons or in local jails. This represented an increase of 2.6 percent from the year 2002. By the end of 2003 a total of 6.9 million adults were on probation, in jail or prison, or on parole. These numbers represent approximately 3 percent of all U.S. adult residents, or 1 in every 32 adults.

More than 90 percent of the 26,234 people convicted for federal drug felony offenses (trafficking or possession and dealing) in 2002 received a prison sentence; the remainder were put on probation. The average length of sentence was 76 months. Of the 1,113 convicted at misdemeanor level for simple possession of drugs, 223 were imprisoned for an average of 20 months. The remainder were fined, were given probation averaging 15 months, or received a mixed sentence.

D. E. BIRON

SEE ALSO:
Arrestee Drug Abuse Monitoring Program (ADAM) • Controlled Substances • Crime and Drugs • Drug Control Policy • Drug Courts • Drug Trafficking • Enforcement of Laws • Financial Consequences • Legal Controls • Organized Crime • Prison Drug Use and Treatment

Pentazocine

Pentazocine is a synthetic opioid drug that is used as a painkiller and is abused for its mood-altering effects. To prevent the drug from being used intravenously, many pentazocine formulations are made with a built-in antidote.

Pentazocine belongs to the class of drugs called opioid analgesics (narcotic painkillers). It is a synthetic benzomorphan compound that has effects similar to morphine. Narcotic drugs act at specific sites on nerve cells in the brain and spinal cord called opioid receptors, which reduce the sensation of pain. There are different types of opioid receptors, and most narcotic painkillers act at the mu-receptor to cause their effects. Pentazocine has a weaker effect through the mu-receptors and, if taken with a drug that fully activates mu-receptors (for example, morphine), it will compete and can antagonize the effects of the more powerful drug. This effect can cause withdrawal symptoms in patients dependent on drugs that act via the mu-receptors.

Pentazocine is used for the relief of moderate to severe pain. The analgesic effect occurs with very small doses (as low as 25 milligrams) and lasts for approximately three hours, necessitating repeated doses for long-term pain management. It is most commonly taken by mouth, though preparations for injection are available for hospital use. Another property of the drug is that it causes sedation, which can be useful in patients prior to surgery.

Beyond the clinically useful analgesic properties of pentazocine, it has characteristic adverse effects. These include some of the typical side effects of opioid drugs, such as changes in mood, excessive sedation, nausea, and depression of breathing. Hallucinations and thought disturbances are occasionally seen with pentazocine use, effects possibly due to the drug acting at the sigma-receptor.

Pentazocine, like other narcotic analgesic dugs, has a known abuse and dependence liability due to its mood-altering effects. However, the liability for drug dependence is reportedly less than with patients taking morphine, and consequently, withdrawal symptoms are generally less severe. It is commonly abused in the pill form, but injection of the contents of crushed pills is another method of taking the drug. For this reason, certain pill formulations of pentazocine (Talwin NX) include small doses of naloxone, an opioid antagonist (antidote). If taken by mouth, the antagonist is not absorbed and therefore does not interfere with the painkiller. However, if the pills are crushed and injected intravenously, naloxone can counteract the effects of pentazocine. These preparations are designed to reduce the drug's abuse potential. Pentazocine is often abused in combination with certain stimulants (such as Ritalin) or antihistamines to enhance the effects on mood, giving a greater rush to the user. Known on the street as "poor man's heroin," these drugs in combination reportedly mimic the effects of heroin taken with cocaine.

J. DERRY, A. KAPUR

KEY FACTS

Classification

Schedule IV (USA), Schedule I (Canada), Class B (UK), Schedule III (INCB). Opioid.

Street names

One and ones, poor man's heroin, T's and B's, T's and R's, Talwin

Short-term effects

Analgesia (pain relief), sedation, changes in mood (for example, euphoria), respiratory depression

Long-term effects

Tolerance to the analgesic effect, physical and psychological dependence (after repeated use, but less than with morphine), withdrawal symptoms if drug is abruptly stopped

SEE ALSO:
Agonists and Antagonists • Morphine • Naloxone • Opiates and Opioids • Withdrawal

Pentobarbital

Pentobarbital is a barbiturate, one of a class of sedative drugs that are also effective in preventing seizures and treating anxiety. It is a central nervous system depressant, with behavioral effects similar to those of alcohol.

The barbiturates were introduced at the turn of the twentieth century for use as sleep-inducing agents. The popularity of pentobarbital was related in part to its accompanying feelings of relaxation and euphoria. With the introduction of benzodiazepines, barbiturate use declined markedly, and pentobarbital is now rarely used to aid sleep.

As an intravenous medication, pentobarbital is used for induction of surgical anesthesia due to the extremely rapid loss of consciousness. Pentobarbital also reduces brain metabolic activity and decreases brain swelling after injury, leading to its use by neurosurgeons to help the brain recover after a severe trauma. Pentobarbital is used by addicts for its antianxiety and euphoric effects, or as a "downer" by polydrug abusers to reduce the anxiety and unpleasant side effects of repeated stimulant use.

KEY FACTS

Classification
Schedule II (USA), Schedule IV (Canada), Class B (UK), Schedule III (INCB). Sedative-hypnotic.

Street names
Abbots, barbs, downers, nembies, Mexican yellows, yellow jackets

Short-term effects
Relaxation, euphoria, decreased inhibitions, coordination problems, sleepiness progressing to coma

Long-term effects
Physical dependence, requiring higher doses for the same effect. Erratic behavior and social isolation. Risk of fatal overdose

Use and abuse

Barbiturates work by enhancing the action of the inhibitory neurotransmitter GABA at its receptor on brain neurons. Pentobarbital acts as a central nervous system depressant, slowing reaction times, dulling the senses, and causing "drunken" incoordination and slurring of speech before inducing sleep. Tolerance develops quickly and contributes to the addictive potential. A typical adult oral dose of pentobarbital for sleep induction is 100 milligrams, though abusers may take several pills once tolerance develops. The respiratory depressive effect persists, hence the risk of a dangerous overdose increases with prolonged use. Street addicts will sometimes dissolve the contents of the capsule in water and inject pentobarbital intravenously, a dangerous practice since the drug passes quickly through the blood-brain barrier: an overdose can kill within minutes. Pentobarbital is often taken together with other depressant drugs, including the opiates and alcohol, which increases the likelihood of respiratory depression. Barbiturate intoxication also impairs the memory, so users may forget that they have taken it and take additional doses. The drug is metabolized in the liver, and prolonged use induces the liver to synthesize more enzymes, leading to faster breakdown and contributing to tolerance.

Dependence on the drug manifests initially as insomnia, but later can result in a severe withdrawal syndrome beginning 8 to 12 hours after the last dose, consisting of anxiety, muscle twitches, tremors, nausea and vomiting, delirium, and seizures. These symptoms last up to 5 days and can be fatal. Pentobarbital addiction is usually treated by decreasing the dose by 10 percent per day. Alternatively, it can be replaced by substituting phenobarbital, a longer acting barbiturate, which prevents withdrawal but no longer causes a "high," and gradually reducing the dose.

L. J. Greenfield, Jr.

SEE ALSO:
Amobarbital • Barbiturates • Secobarbital • Sedatives and Hypnotics

Pharmaceutical Industry

Many of the drugs that people abuse started out as therapeutic drugs to alleviate symptoms such as pain and depression. Developing drugs is expensive, but the market for pharmaceuticals is enormous and still growing.

The pharmaceutical industry's origins lie in the use of herbal potions and wound dressings by "wise women" and "medicine men" in early human society. The earliest written references to a trade in drugs are from the Sumerian culture of Mesopotamia (modern Iraq) where the opium poppy, known as *hul gil,* the "joy plant," was cultivated; opium, the dried resin secreted from incisions made in the unripe seed pod, was exported to Egypt.

By the classical period in the Mediterranean basin (500 BCE–400 CE), a professional class of physicians and apothecaries were trading proprietary concoctions for the cure of various ills. The decline of the Roman Empire inhibited development, although the rise of Islamic medicine preserved classical works on pharmacy through the European Dark Ages. These works provided a basis for renewed research into drugs in early modern Europe. Around 1527, the apothecary and scientist Paracelsus is credited with inventing laudanum, a solution of unrefined opium dissolved in concentrated alcohol obtained via the recently invented pot-still distillation process.

The commercial history of the early pharmaceutical industry is one of individual entrepreneurs marketing patent or proprietary medicine. Patrick Anderson's "Scotch Pills" were widely sold in Britain from the 1630s, and an opium solution, "Sydenham's Laudanum," was first marketed in England in 1680. Many patent medicines contained high levels of poisons such as antimony and mercury. Nonetheless, self-medication was cheaper than consulting a physician. Rising prosperity led to manufacturing and marketing improvements and increased sales of laudanum, popular sedatives, and restoratives such as Dr. Solomon's brandy- and herb-based "Balm of Gilead" and the many brands of "digestive" pills.

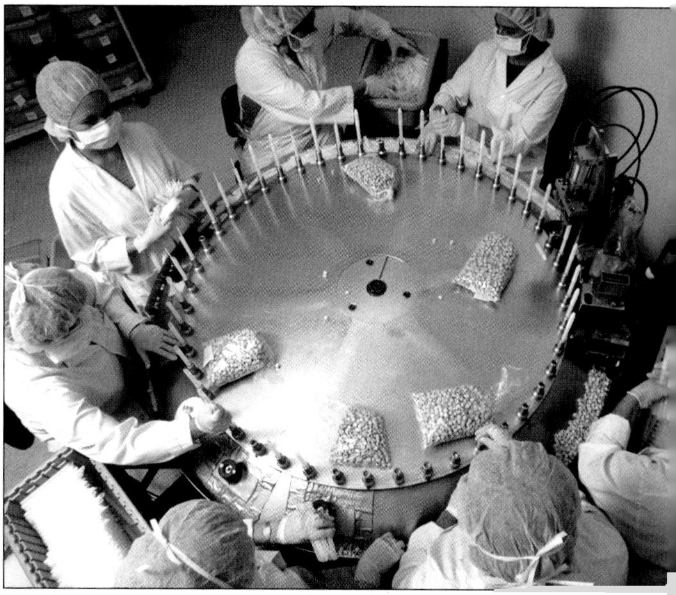

The market for drugs is huge. In 2000 more than $317 billion was spent on pharmaceutical products globally, nearly half of this by U.S. consumers.

Development of pharmaceutical chemistry

Infusions of cinchona tree bark and raw opium poppy resin were known to be effective treatments for malaria and pain before it was understood that such plant products contained active drug compounds, which could be purified to give more reproducible effects. Advances in analytical chemistry in the late eighteenth century stimulated efforts to isolate pure drugs, and in 1803 the German pharmacist Friedrich Sertürner discovered that a single alkaloid chemical was the active ingredient of opium, comprising 9 to 15 percent of unrefined opium. He named it morphine, after Morpheus, the Greek god of dreams.

In 1820 two French chemists, Pierre-Joseph Pelletier and Joseph-Bienamié Caventou, purified quinine from the bark of the cinchona tree. Within a few years pure quinine was available to treat malaria. In 1856 William Perkins, an 18-year-old English chemist, attempted to synthesize quinine in the laboratory. Perkins failed to synthesize quinine but he did synthesize "mauve," the first water-fast synthetic textile dye and the catalyst for the rapid expansion of a chemical dye manufacturing industry.

The nineteenth-century dye industry was the progenitor of the modern pharmaceutical industry. It recruited highly trained chemists into the first industrial research laboratories and had close links to university laboratories, particularly in Germany. In 1889 the German medical researcher Paul Ehrlich noticed that the synthetic dye methylene blue stained microscopic malaria parasites inside human blood cells. He reasoned that because the dye stained the parasites, it might also kill them. In 1891, in the first clinical trial of the first synthetic drug ever used in humans, Ehrlich cured two patients of malaria with methylene blue. German dye manufacturers such as Friedrich Bayer began to diversify into profitable new pharmaceutical ventures, recruiting research teams to develop new drugs such as synthetic antimalarials, using methylene blue as a prototype compound.

Aspirin and the modern pharmaceutical industry

Around 400 BCE the Greek physician Hippocrates prescribed extracts of the white willow tree, *Salix alba,* for the relief of pain and fever, particularly in pregnant women. In 1828 Johan Andreas Buchner purified an extract of willow bark and named it "salicin." By 1859 the chemical structure of salicylic acid was derived by Hermann Kolbe of Marburg University. His student, Friedrich von Heyden established a business in Dresden, manufacturing salicylic acid to reduce fevers and relieve rheumatic stiffness and pain.

Salicylic acid has an unpleasant taste and causes stomach irritation. To improve the prototype, in 1897 a Bayer chemist, Felix Hoffmann, synthesized acetylsalicylic acid, a derivative with reduced side effects, effective as an analgesic, anti-inflammatory and fever-reducing drug. Bayer registered this compound in 1899 as aspirin. Aspirin was originally marketed as a powder but was quickly formulated by Bayer into a stamped tablet, to standardize dosage and prevent adulteration. Aspirin remains the most consumed drug in history, more than 100 billion tablets being taken per year.

Two interesting twists that were to exert significant influence on the twentieth-century pharmaceutical industry can be added to the story of aspirin. Aspirin was not only a major commercial and medical success, it was seen as a demonstration of the scientific and industrial might of an increasingly nationalistic Germany in a politically unstable world. During World War I (1914–1918) both the United Kingdom and the United States seized German assets, including Bayer's New York aspirin factory and its patents, licences, and trademarks. The bitterness this caused contributed to the exacerbation of normal commercial rivalries in the postwar pharmaceutical industry, which became organized on a decidedly nationalistic and somewhat cartelized lines. In 1986, 61 years after their confiscation, Bayer AG of Germany paid $800 million dollars for the right to use their name and the "aspirin" trademark in the United States to Sterling Drug.

The second twist is that Bayer's management was initially cool toward Hoffmann's work on aspirin and much more interested in another of their research laboratory's discoveries, diacetylmorphine, which was seen as a promising treatment for coughs in an era when lung diseases such as pneumonia and tuberculosis were the leading causes of death. Thought to be nonaddictive, indeed useful in suppressing morphine addiction and withdrawal symptoms, this compound was marketed with the brand name "Heroin." Unfortunately, heroin itself proved to be dangerously addictive and rapidly became the most notorious illegal narcotic in history.

The age of chemotherapy

The truly important age of pharmaceutical advancement was ushered in by Paul Ehrlich's discovery of Salvarsan in 1909. Marketed by Hoechst, Salvarsan was the first effective cure for syphilis, a hitherto incurable degenerative venereal disease transmitted by the bacteria-like spirochete *Treponema pallidium.* Sulphonamide, the first of the class of drugs now referred to as "antibiotics," was developed in 1934 by May & Baker, a British subsidiary of the French pharmaceutical combine Rhone-Poulenc.

World War II (1939–1945) forced the pace of drug development, particularly the search for effective antimalarials such as mepacrine and paludrine. Chloroquine, a novel synthetic derivative of quinine, was to play a major role in the eradication of malaria from Europe and North America in the early 1950s.

There were spectacular advances in disease treatment. The most famous was penicillin—a "miracle" drug effective against a broad spectrum of bacterial infections, including wound infections,

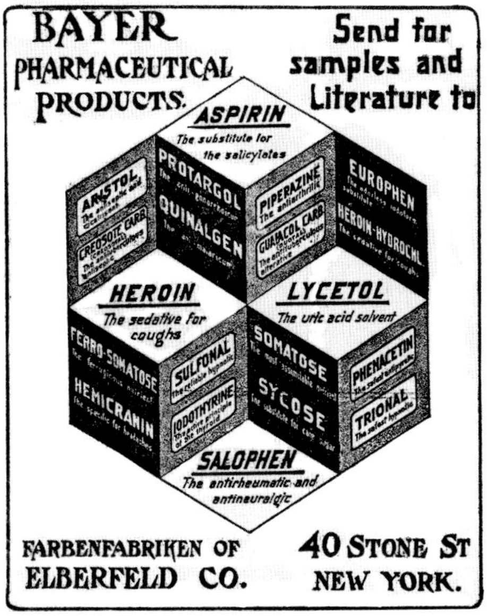

An early advertisement for two of Bayer's most famous products—aspirin and heroin.

venereal diseases, and respiratory tract infections. Several British and American firms, now household names, owed their early success to penicillin sales. The 1950s saw the development and mass production of new classes of antibiotics, such as tetracycline, chloramphenicol, and erythromycin, all major medical and commercial successes. With the development in the 1950s of effective combination antibiotic treatments for tuberculosis, using drugs such as rifampicin, streptomycin, and isoniazid, many once common diseases nearly disappeared from the developed world. By 1970 the United States surgeon general declared that infectious disease was no longer a significant health problem in the United States.

Sedatives, stimulants, and the relief of depression

The commercial success of the sedative-hypnotic barbiturates, such as veronal (introduced in 1903) and phenobarbitol (introduced in 1912), encouraged development of new sedatives and sleeping pills. Stimulant drugs such as the amphetamine benzedrine were also developed and introduced in the 1920s and 1930s, initially for the treatment of asthma and lung congestion. These were widely used by all sides during World War II to counter exhaustion in fighting men.

Problems with addiction and recreational use (also a problem with amphetamines) led to a gradual replacement, in the 1960s, of barbiturates with non-barbiturate "tranquilizers," such as diazepam (Valium) and chlordiazepoxide (Librium). Although heavily prescribed and extremely profitable to their manufacturers (principally Hofmann-LaRoche), by the end of the 1970s the side effects and dependence induced by tranquilizers reduced their popularity, although they remain the most widely prescribed mood-altering drugs in the United Kingdom.

Research to find safer antidepressants led to the discovery of the specific serotonin reuptake inhibitors (SSRIs). Marketed by Eli Lilly in 1987 as Prozac, SSRIs have proven very successful in relieving anxiety and depression. The wide prescription of Prozac, particularly in the United States, has ensured its commercial success, but it remains to be seen if the SSRI drugs will avoid following the same path as the barbiturates and tranquilizers from enthusiastic reception to ultimate disillusion.

Regulation of pharmaceutical products

Morphine was first marketed as a painkiller and cure for opium addiction. Its sale was completely unregulated. However, its use as an anesthetic and for dysentery treatment during the U.S. Civil War (1861–1865) led to the creation of the so-called army disease—morphine addiction—suffered by half a million veterans. By 1890 the United States had started to legislate to control narcotic drugs, initially by imposing a tax on opium and morphine sales. In 1905 the U.S. Congress banned the sale of opium and in 1906 passed the landmark Federal Pure Food and Drug Act. This law required all pharmaceutical products and patent medicines to have an accurate description of their complete contents on the label.

The 1906 act was concerned solely with drug purity but was amended in 1937 to impose product safety standards. These required analysis of product toxicity to be submitted to the Food and Drug Administration (FDA) before approval for marketing could be granted. Further regulation was introduced in the 1960s in both Europe and the United States following the thalidomide scandal. Thalidomide, a sedative-hypnotic with no advantage over existing products, was introduced in Europe but not the United States, where it had not been licensed. It caused severe birth defects after prescription to pregnant women for morning sickness. The 1962 Harris-Kefauver amendment to the Pure Food and Drug Act introduced stringent new standards of pharmacologic and toxicological testing before any drug could be tested in humans and required that proof of superior efficacy be demonstrated for new drugs.

Globalization of the pharmaceutical industry

The FDA system of approval has been copied throughout the world and has driven consolidation of the pharmaceutical industry. The costs of research and development (R&D) and regulatory compliance have driven companies into mergers and acquisitions. In order of sales in 2001, the "Big 10" drug companies are Pfizer (U.S.), GlaxoSmithKline (U.K.), Merck (U.S.), AstraZeneca (U.K.), Johnson & Johnson (U.S.), Bristol-Myers Squibb, (U.S.), Novartis (Switzerland), Aventis (France), Pharmacia (U.S.), and Abbot (U.S.). These corporations sell 47 percent of all drugs, and the top 20 corporations have 66 percent of global sales, totaling $450 billion and growing at around 11 percent annually.

In 2002 the United States spent $122 billion on pharmaceutical drugs out of total health costs of $1.3 trillion. This amount represents 9 percent of total health expenditure, 2.6 percent of gross domestic product, or around $700 per person. Japan spends around $450 per person annually on pharmaceuticals, the United Kingdom around $200. The developing world, including China and India, spends less than $20 per person annually. The prospects for further expansion of the pharmaceutical industry in the twenty-first century seem assured.

Problems and challenges

Individual drug companies face a less certain future. It has proved impossible to predict whether scientific ideas can be translated into safe and effective medical treatments. More than 75 percent of the 5,000 candidate drugs under current development will fail to be approved for marketing, and even approved drugs are sometimes recalled following new revelations of risks to users. Drug companies are spending an average of $800 million and 15 years on each drug that reaches the market. Patent protection from legal copying of a drug by "generic" manufacturers with no R&D costs is limited to 20 years from the date of filing the first patent application. As a result of these costs and time frames, despite increased research expenditure, companies are experiencing diminishing returns and are thus introducing fewer new drugs.

Conditions remaining without cures are more complex than those tackled at an earlier stage in the industry's development. A major problem is the new wave of infectious disease. In 1984 a new disease was recognized, the acquired immunodeficiency syndrome (AIDS), caused by the rapidly mutating human immunodeficiency virus (HIV) transmitted through blood products and sexual contact. A huge effort by the pharmaceutical industry has succeeded in delivering new antiviral drugs that delay the onset of severe manifestations of the infection.

Antiretrovirals have saved many lives, but they have severe side effects and have to be taken for the rest of the patient's lifetime. Compared with the antibiotic miracle cures of the past, this is a partial success. Furthermore, the ethics of a situation in which HIV-positive Westerners have access to expensive drugs while poor Africans and Asians frequently do not, are now hotly debated. In a more educated and skeptical world, laboratory success has not brought the public admiration that was accorded to the early pioneers of the pharmaceutical industry.

These factors have contributed to a crisis in the pharmaceutical industry. If highly successful drugs emerge from 5 percent of research projects, then a company needs to support 20 projects to ensure profitability. The model breaks down, however, if the rate of success falls and costs per project rise, as has occurred. Attempts to pass increasing development costs on to consumers have led to media criticism and political opposition, notably in the case of HIV therapy costs in Africa. It remains to be seen whether scientific advances into genomic medicine, bioinformatics, and computerized chemistry can be combined with changes in the business model, such as the trend toward "biotech start-up" companies, thereby renewing the smaller flow of curative drugs and the confidence of the industry.

D. E. ARNOT

SEE ALSO:
Analogs • Classification of Drugs • Controlled Substances • Narcotic Drugs • Psychotropic Drugs

Pharmacokinetics

For drugs to work in the body, they must overcome a number of physiological barriers to reach their site of action. The study of how drugs are taken into, metabolized by, and eliminated from the body is called pharmacokinetics.

Pharmacokinetics is the study of how drugs are taken into the body (absorption), distributed among body tissues (distribution), broken down or changed by body organs (metabolism), and eliminated from the body (excretion). These factors differ markedly between drugs and are critical determinants of how drugs behave in the body. The ultimate effect of a drug depends on its interaction with receptors, which are proteins in the cell membrane with sites where the drug binds tightly, changing the shape of the protein and resulting in chemical or electrical signals within the cell. These factors will be considered in more detail below. However, the ability of the drug to reach its receptor, and how long it stays there, can be equally important in determining a drug's effect. For example, heroin and morphine are both drugs that act on opioid receptors in specific areas of the brain, causing narcotic effects including pain relief, sleepiness, euphoria, and respiratory depression. They differ only by the presence of two acetate (CH_3CO) groups on heroin that make it more lipid (fat) soluble. The increased lipid solubility helps heroin cross cell membranes, enabling rapid transport across the blood-brain barrier. As a result of this pharmacokinetic property, high drug levels occur quickly in the brain and produce the rush desired by addicts, which may increase its addictive potential relative to morphine. Understanding the pharmacokinetics of a drug is key to knowing how abusers will get it into their bodies and how it will behave when it gets there.

Routes of administration

Use of mind-altering substances like alcohol, opium, cocaine, and marijuana has occurred since prehistoric times, and a variety of methods have been devised for taking in these and more recently discovered substances. Specific routes of administration are used for individual drugs, often defined by social customs that vary over time. Psychotropic substances were initially discovered by chewing, eating, or drinking natural products, and this mode is still used for both traditional, unrefined substances (for example, peyote, coca leaves, betel nuts) and highly purified pharmaceuticals.

Smoking of tobacco, opium, and marijuana dates back 2,000 to 4,000 years. Burning the drug-bearing plant matter suspends microscopic organic particles in air, where they can be inhaled into the lungs and rapidly absorbed through the thin alveolar lining into

For administration routes other than intravenous, drugs have to pass through a number of biological membranes before they reach the blood plasma. Once in the plasma, they are taken to their site of action or can be transferred to other extravascular body fluids that surround the target receptors. Waste products and metabolites are removed from the body by excretion.

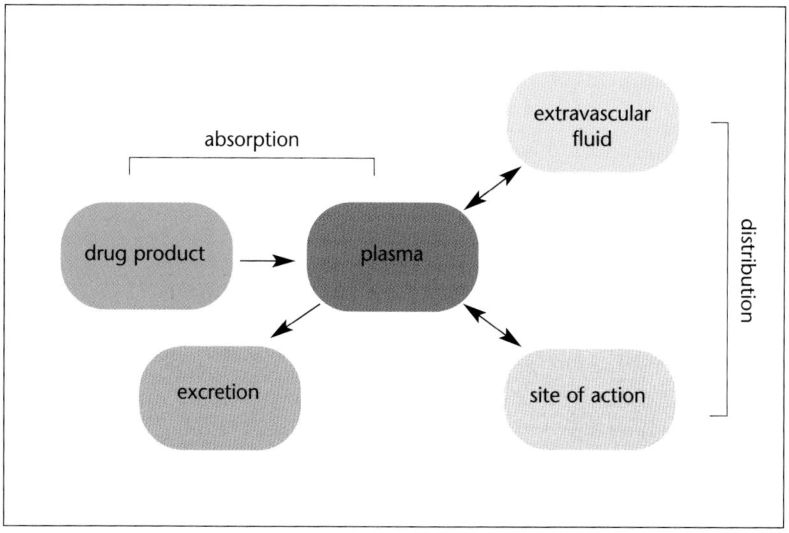

lung capillaries. Smoking is an efficient method for getting drugs into the bloodstream; nicotine reaches the brain within eight seconds of being inhaled. However, smoking also generates more than 4,000 gaseous and particulate compounds, including tar (composed of aromatic hydrocarbons that are often carcinogenic), carbon monoxide, nitrogen oxides, hydrocarbons, sulfur-containing compounds, ketones, alcohols, and aldehydes. Inhalation can also be used for volatile hydrocarbons (such as toluene) that are used as solvents for plastic glues (sniffing glue, or "huffing"), a dangerous practice that can be fatal if the user loses consciousness, can no longer pull away from the source of fumes, and suffocates.

The mucous membranes lining the nasal passages are another available site for drug absorption, traditionally used for cocaine, heroin, and tobacco (snuff), and more recently for crushed tablets of methylphenidate (Ritalin) or slow-release oxycodone (OxyContin). Snorting the crushed tablets defeats the slow-release mechanisms that make these drugs effective for chronic use and that limit their abuse potential. Users who snort drugs avoid the social stigma of injection and the fear of acquiring syringe-borne diseases such as HIV/AIDS and hepatitis. However, repeated snorting can damage mucous membranes and cause severe nosebleeds.

The hypodermic syringe was invented by Thomas Wood in 1853 and rapidly gained popularity as a means of introducing drugs into the body. The tip of the needle can be placed under the skin for subcutaneous injection (known as "skin popping" when heroin is injected in this fashion), into a muscle for intramuscular injection, or directly into a vein. Absorption from subcutaneous and intramuscular injections occurs over minutes to hours, hence most injection drug users prefer the intravenous route. Veins have relatively thin walls relative to arteries, and will collapse unless venous return of blood to the heart is blocked. A rubber constriction band is used above the injection site to allow the veins to fill with blood so that the drug can be injected. Repeated injections cause the major veins to collapse and sclerose (harden), forcing addicts to seek new sites and creating tracks of injection scars along the veins of the arms or legs.

In 1999 opiates accounted for 83 percent of substance abuse treatment admissions in the United States for injection drug abuse, followed by amphetamines (11 percent) and cocaine (5 percent). Substances must be in liquid form and are usually placed in a spoon with water and heated over a flame to help the drug melt or dissolve. A small wad of cotton is used as a filter for particulate impurities, but cellulose, talc, and other substances frequently end up in the lungs and other tissues of injection drug users. Although most diseases, including hepatitis and HIV, could be prevented by sterile needle exchange or cleaning injection paraphernalia with bleach, sharing needles is still rampant, and injection drug abuse accounted for 36 percent of HIV cases in the United States in 2000.

Absorption

Drugs are poorly absorbed across the multiple cell layers of skin but are more readily exchanged across the mucous membranes lining the gastrointestinal, nasal, and respiratory passages. Drugs that are lipid

Drugs administered orally will survive the harsh environment of the stomach longer if they are weak acids (HA), as this will prevent them from splitting into ions (H^+ and A^-) until they have crossed the mucosal barrier. Once in the neutral pH of the plasma, the drug ionizes and becomes trapped until it reaches its site of action.

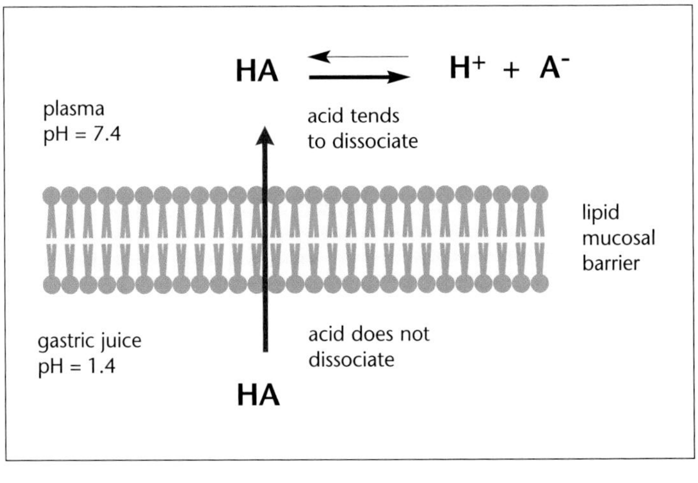

soluble can be absorbed by passive diffusion across mucous membranes. However, many drugs are weak acids or bases that exist in solution in equilibrium between ionized (charged) and non-ionized (neutral) forms. The non-ionized form distributes fairly quickly across lipid mucosal membranes, while ionized forms do not. The distribution between charged and uncharged forms depends on the pH at which H^+ ions dissociate from the drug, known as the pKa. For a drug that is a weak acid (HA) with a pKa of 4, the drug will exist primarily in the non-ionized state in the acid environment of the stomach (pH 1.4), promoting transport across the stomach mucosal membrane (*see* diagram at left). When that drug crosses into the blood plasma, the neutral pH (pH 7.4) favors dissociation to H^+ and A^-, trapping the drug in the plasma and promoting absorption of the drug from the stomach. Some drugs are transported across the mucosal membrane by specific molecules known as carriers, either by energy-dependent processes (active transport) or by using the electrochemical gradient generated by cellular ion pumps (facilitated diffusion). These carriers exist to aid absorption of essential amino acids and nutrients, and many drugs are sufficiently similar in chemical structure to these compounds that they can use the same transport mechanisms.

Oral ingestion is the most common and convenient method of drug administration for conventional pharmaceuticals, but some drugs are poorly absorbed by this route, destroyed by stomach acid, or metabolized extensively by the liver just after absorption ("first pass effect"). Drugs in solution are readily absorbed after subcutaneous or intramuscular injection, while intravenous injection bypasses the absorption process and leads directly to the next phase of pharmacokinetics, drug distribution.

Distribution

Once the drug enters the bloodstream, it initially travels with venous blood toward the heart, where it makes a pass through the lungs before being distributed via the arterial system to body tissues. A large proportion of the cardiac output of blood is directed to the major organs, including the brain, liver, and kidneys, while distribution to muscles, skin, and fat is slower. Blood passes through smaller and smaller end arteries until it reaches capillaries, where only a single cell layer separates the drug-containing plasma from the end-organ tissues. Blood is a mixture of cellular elements (red and white blood cells, platelets) and soluble proteins; the latter contain binding sites for many drugs. The binding of drugs to plasma proteins limits the distribution to tissues, since only the unbound fraction ("free drug") is available to distribute across cell membranes into tissues. The lipid solubility and pKa are important in determining how drugs partition into different organs; highly lipid-soluble drugs accumulate in fat stores, and to a lesser extent in the brain and liver, where the concentrations of lipid membranes are high. In obese people, the fat content of the body can exceed 50 percent of body weight, and drugs such as the highly lipophilic barbiturates may accumulate in the fat within minutes to hours after administration. In fact, redistribution of such drugs from the brain or heart into fat stores is the initial means of terminating their actions in these tissues, since it lowers end-organ drug concentrations rapidly.

Distribution of drugs into the brain is different from other end organs, because the cells lining brain capillaries are joined by tight junctions, creating the blood-brain barrier (BBB). The more lipophilic the drug, the more likely it will pass through this barrier. Specific uptake transporters also assist in getting some drugs across the BBB. Other proteins, particularly the P-glycoprotein, actively transport some drugs out of the brain. Brain infections (for example, meningitis or encephalitis) or tumors can increase the permeability of the BBB. A similar but less restrictive barrier is present in pregnant women between the uterus and the placenta that feeds the developing fetus; this barrier is easily permeated by lipid-soluble drugs. Hence, many drugs taken by pregnant drug users are also exposed to the fetus, and dependence on such drugs as cocaine, opiates, barbiturates, or benzodiazepines can result in withdrawal symptoms after delivery.

Metabolism, clearance, and elimination

Drugs are eliminated from the body either unchanged or after modification by various enzymes, most often in the liver. Charged or polar compounds (which have no net charge but have a positive and a negative orientation) are more easily excreted than those with high lipid solubility. The kidney is the chief organ for excretion of drugs and their metabolic products. Drugs unabsorbed after oral ingestion are excreted in the feces, along with some drug metabolites excreted by the liver into the bile. Some drugs are secreted into breast milk, which can expose the nursing infant to their toxic effects. Inhalants can be excreted through the lungs into the exhaled air.

The kidneys excrete body waste products, toxins, and drugs by three processes: filtration of the blood in capillary structures called glomeruli, followed by active secretion of ions and charged drug metabolites in the proximal renal tubule, and finally passive reabsorption of sodium ions and water in the distal tubule. Multidrug transporters assist in the excretion of many drug metabolites. In the case of drug overdose, weak acids or bases are sometimes given to make the urine more acid or alkaline, which traps the drug in the excreted fraction and hastens elimination. The speed at which a drug is removed from the body is known as the clearance rate.

More lipophilic drugs require biotransformation to more polar and less biologically active forms before they can be excreted by the kidneys. These reactions are performed by several classes of liver enzymes. Phase I reactions create a new functional group on the drug, which can then actively combine with other compounds to produce water-soluble conjugates. Many of these reactions are mediated by a large family of enzymes known as the cytochrome P450 system. Phase II conjugation reactions link a functional group on the drug (or its Phase I metabolite) to water-soluble compounds, including glucuronic acid, sulfate, glutathione, amino acids, or acetate. The most important of these enzymes is uridine diphosphate glucuronosyltransferase (UGT), which adds a glucuronate group to oxygen, nitrogen, or sulfur atoms on a number of compounds. The conjugates are usually biologically inactive and readily excreted in the urine. There is significant variation in the degree of metabolism and hence the rate of drug elimination between individuals, likely

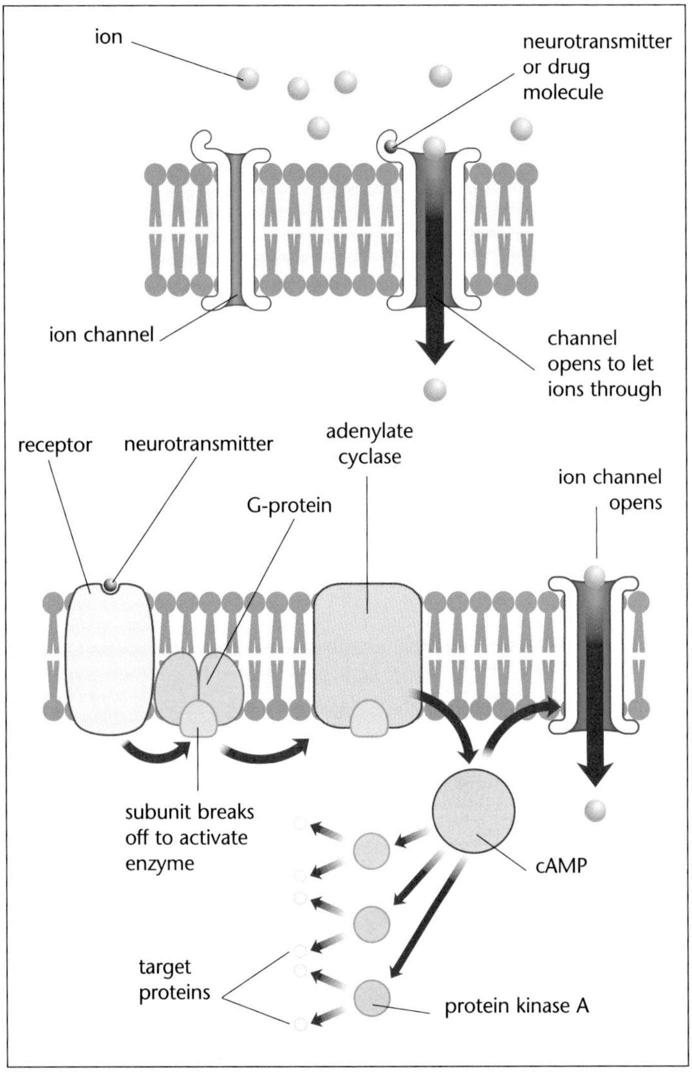

Drugs can bind to the receptors for endogenous neurotransmitters that activate ion channels (top) or to G-protein–coupled receptors (bottom). The latter are coupled to second messenger systems such as adenylate cyclase, which makes cyclic AMP (cAMP). This in turn activates protein kinase A molecules, enabling these molecules to phosphorylate a number of other target proteins, thus propagating the initial signal many times over.

due to genetic differences (polymorphisms) in the enzymes involved. Some of these enzymes differ among individuals by single nucleotide changes in the genes encoding them, known as single nucleotide polymorphisms (SNPs). Such differences may lead to the development of individualized drug therapies based on a person's genetic makeup.

Pharmacodynamics

Pharmacodynamics is the study of the biochemical and physiological mechanisms of drug actions. These actions result from the binding of drugs to receptor proteins in the brain, heart, or other organs. The receptors for many drugs are also receptors for neurotransmitters (chemicals that nerve cells secrete to transmit electrical signals from one cell to the next) or hormones (chemicals secreted by endocrine glands into the bloodstream to regulate body functions) and mimic, enhance, or inhibit the function of those signaling molecules. For example, benzodiazepines, barbiturates, alcohol, and inhaled anesthetics bind to and enhance the function of the GABA type A receptor, a chloride channel activated by the inhibitory neurotransmitter gamma-aminobutyric acid (GABA). The opiates bind to several classes of opioid receptors, which are the target of endogenous opioid peptides that generate chemical signals called "second messengers" in their target cells. Other drugs act elsewhere in signaling systems, binding to neurotransmitter transporters, the enzymes that synthesize or degrade them, voltage-gated ion channels that mediate electrical signaling, or other enzymes that mediate or modify intracellular chemical signals. Hence, drug receptors are binding sites that affect cellular biochemistry and physiology in a number of different ways. A schematic view of some of these mechanisms is shown in the diagram on page 672.

Drugs that bind to the same sites as endogenous transmitters and hormones can have several possible effects. Those that mimic the endogenous agent are called agonists. Such drugs may be equally effective in activating the receptor as the actual transmitter (full agonists), or less effective (partial agonists). A drug may have no efficacy at all, but it can block the action of the endogenous neurotransmitter when it binds to the transmitter's binding site, making it a competitive antagonist. Other drugs known as allosteric agents affect receptor function without affecting the transmitter binding site, since they bind at different sites on the receptor molecule. Allosteric agents can either enhance or inhibit the function of the receptor by changing its shape or activity. For example, the benzodiazepines allosterically enhance $GABA_A$ receptor function at a benzodiazepine binding site distinct from the place where GABA binds (*see* diagram below). The benzodiazepines are considered agonists at this site. Drugs that bind to the benzodiazepine site and have no effect are termed benzodiazepine antagonists. A third class of allosteric agents binds to the benzodiazepine site and inhibits $GABA_A$ receptor function; these are called inverse agonists. The most prominent example of inverse agonists are certain beta-carbolines, benzodiazepine-like compounds that bind to the benzodiazepine site on the $GABA_A$ receptor and inhibit its chloride channel function. Another class of drugs, which includes picrotoxin and penicillin, block the $GABA_A$ channel directly.

While some membrane ion channels are activated by binding neurotransmitters or hormones, others

The $GABA_A$ receptor has a number of sites where other chemicals can attach that can change the shape or activity of the receptor, inhibiting or enhancing its ability to send signals.

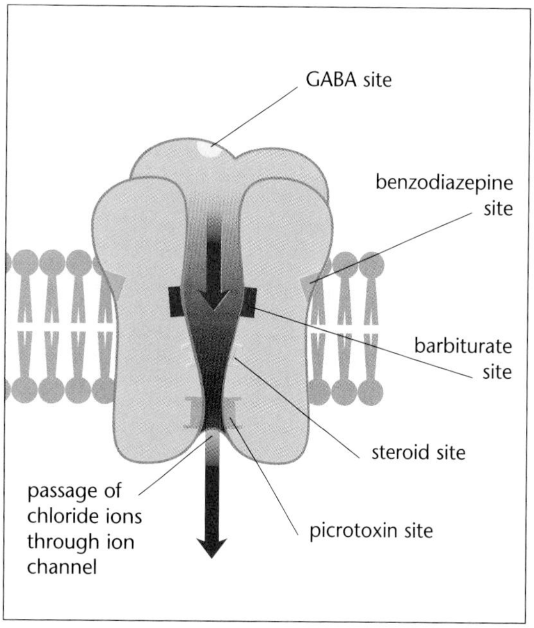

are activated by changes in the voltage across the membrane. These are also the targets of some drugs. The local anesthetics bind to voltage-gated sodium channels that are opened when the neuron's membrane potential is depolarized, preventing the neuron from firing action potentials. Part of the effect of cocaine is as a local anesthetic, though it also acts at adrenergic (norepinephrine emitting) nerve terminals to block reuptake of norepinephrine, increasing the amount of that transmitter in the synaptic junction. The barbiturates enhance $GABA_A$ receptor function but also inhibit voltage-gated sodium channels, blocking repetitive action potentials. Other drugs target channels that carry potassium or calcium ions.

Besides operating ion channels, neurotransmitters can also trigger chemical signaling in the target cell. Some receptors interact with GTP-binding proteins ("G-proteins"), resulting in activation of intracellular second messenger systems, like the enzyme adenylate cyclase that makes cyclic AMP from the energy molecule, ATP (*see* diagram, p. 672). Cyclic AMP then activates another enzyme called protein kinase A that attaches phosphate groups to certain target proteins, altering their function. A large number of kinases, phosphatases (enzymes that cleave off the phosphate groups), and other signaling proteins have complex and interacting pathways with multiple targets for drug action. In some cases, ions themselves act as second messengers after entry through voltage or transmitter-gated channels; most notably, calcium can activate a variety of kinases and phosphatases. As noted above, some drugs can interact at multiple binding sites and have several mechanisms of action.

Pharmacokinetic and pharmacodynamic tolerance

Repeated or continuous exposure to a drug often results in tolerance, defined as decreased drug effect with same amount of drug. Along with tolerance, some drugs also induce dependence, a state in which failure to take the drug results in a withdrawal syndrome. Tolerance can result from several different mechanisms. Pharmacodynamic tolerance results when receptors produce a smaller signal for the same drug concentration. This can be due to desensitization, which can occur when the receptor is modified (for example, the beta-adrenergic receptor undergoes phosphorylation) or enters an inactive state (as occurs with many ion channel receptors). Heterologous desensitization occurs when a second messenger system shared by several receptors becomes less responsive, such that any receptor that works through that system is affected. Long-term drug exposure can also change the number or type of receptor molecules expressed by the target cell by changing the pattern of receptor processing at the protein or RNA level; receptor proteins may be degraded more quickly, or the number of mRNA molecules encoding the receptor may be reduced. Drugs such as cocaine and methamphetamine that act at presynaptic terminals can cause depletion of the endogenous neurotransmitter, making subsequent doses less effective; this process is called tachyphylaxis. In addition to these mechanisms, a drug may also cause pharmacokinetic tolerance by increasing the synthesis of enzymes that metabolize it in the liver, increasing the number of transporters that keep it out of the brain, or increasing processes that assist in its excretion. All of these mechanisms have the same final result—increased drug doses are needed to achieve the same effect.

Tolerance and dependence can result from several of these mechanisms at once. For example, chronic alcoholics metabolize alcohol much more quickly than naive subjects due to induction of alcohol dehydrogenase in the liver. However, they also develop decreased sensitivity to high alcohol concentrations that would be fatal to people who had never used alcohol before. Similar mechanisms apply to the opiates and barbiturates. The escalation of drug doses is not just more expensive for the addict; it also increases the risk of death. For barbiturates and opioids, tolerance to the somnolence, incoordination, and euphoric effects may be greater than tolerance to respiratory depression, making fatal overdose more likely with chronic use.

L. J. GREENFIELD, JR.

SEE ALSO:
Agonists and Antagonists • Blood-Brain Barrier • Brain Physiology and Function • Central Nervous System • Drug Receptors • Metabolism • Neurotransmission • Pharmacology • Research, Medical • Sensitization • Tolerance • Toxicity

Pharmacology

Pharmacology is the science dealing with the interactions between chemicals and systems in the body. Understanding how substances react is vital to the way that drugs are used and the effects they will produce, both good and bad.

The science of pharmacology is extremely broad. Pharmacology deals with numerous aspects of drugs, including their history, where they come from, how they are made, their physical and chemical properties, the effects of drugs (biochemical or physiological), how drugs work, how they are handled by the body, what diseases they affect, and what other uses there may be for the drugs. Since drugs may be defined as any chemical or even biological agent that can affect a living organism, the general area of pharmacology extends well beyond humans. However, this review will be restricted to the area of pharmacology as it relates to people.

While most interest in pharmacology centers on drugs that are useful in the prevention, diagnosis, or treatment of human diseases, the pharmacological study of drugs is also relevant to the areas of household and industrial health as well as drug abuse. The former area deals with drugs that may play a role in environmental pollution as well as potential poisonings that could occur at home or at work. The latter area, drug abuse, deals with the inappropriate use of drugs that are taken illegally or in excess for their pleasurable effects.

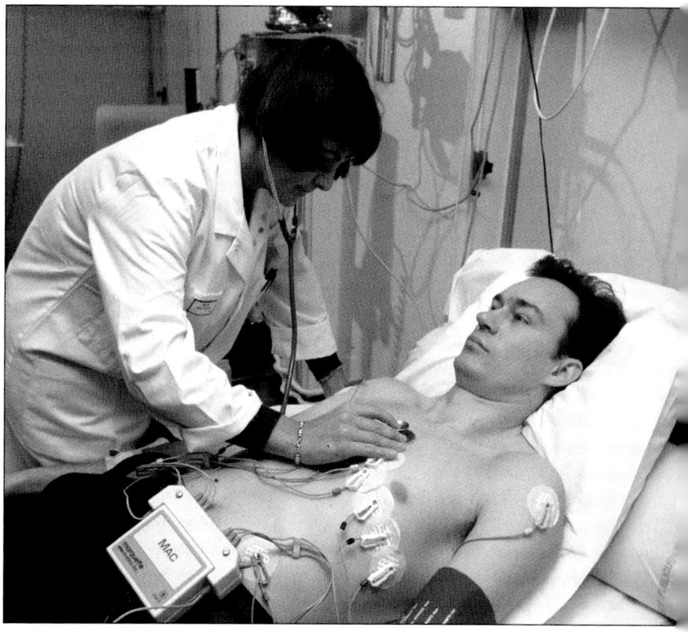

Before drugs are allowed to be used by the public they are carefully assessed to determine whether they have any harmful effects on the body.

Aspects of pharmacology

There are many subdivisions of pharmacology. These include pharmacokinetics, pharmacodynamics, clinical pharmacology, and toxicology. While there is a certain amount of overlap among these areas, conceptually they help us understand the intricate nature of the complexities of pharmacology.

The area of pharmcokinetics deals with how drugs are handled by the body. Much of pharmacokinetics is described by the acronym ADME, which stands for absorption, distribution, metabolism, and excretion. In examining the absorption of a drug, the scientist is interested in how and how much of a drug that a person consumes actually gets into the bloodstream and tissues. When a drug is given intravenously, all of what is given gets into the bloodstream. However, most drugs are taken orally, in which case the drug must be absorbed across the lining of the stomach or other parts of the gastrointestinal tract, that is, the small or large intestine. Once the drug is inside the body, it is then carried around the body through the bloodstream to the various tissues and organs of the body. This process is called distribution. While in the bloodstream or in the tissues, a drug may be altered by the body. This process, called metabolism, usually happens through enzymes changing the chemical nature of the drug. The metabolism of drugs may be quite variable. Some drugs undergo quite extensive metabolism within the body, while others may not be metabolized at all. Finally, the body must excrete or dispose of the drug or its metabolites (breakdown products). The usual route of excretion is into the urine or feces. However, other routes of excretion may include exhaling the drug or metabolites through the lung or sweating, that is, excretion through the skin.

While pharmacokinetics may be viewed as answering the question of what the body does to the drug, the area of pharmacodynamics is concerned with the issue of what the drug does to the body. Again, the drug itself may affect the person, or it may be a metabolite of the drug that has the major effect on the person. In many circumstances, it is both the drug and its metabolites that have pharmacodynamic effects on people. In order to understand the pharmacodynamics of drugs, the researcher relies heavily on a variety of other sciences, such as physiology and biochemistry. For example, two pharmacodynamic effects of narcotic analgesics such as morphine or oxycodone are pain relief and constipation. Understanding these effects requires insight into the physiology of both pain and gastrointestinal peristalsis, or movement of food through the stomach and intestines.

When the pharmacokinetics and pharmacodynamics of a drug have been determined, it is then important to study the interrelationships between these two areas, called pharmacokinetic-pharmacodynamic interactions, sometimes abbreviated as PK/PD. For example, it can be useful to understand what concentrations of a drug in the bloodstream (pharmacokinetics) produce certain effects on the body (pharmacodynamics). This sort of information is crucial in determining what doses of drugs are appropriate to prescribe.

Variations in effect

When dealing with the pharmacology of drugs in humans, the area of clinical pharmacology is crucial. The same drug may have different effects on men than on women, the elderly than on the young, and on people of different races, such as Caucasians or Asians. In addition, if a drug is metabolized or excreted by the liver or kidneys and those organs are not functioning properly, the dose of the drug may have to be altered, or perhaps the drug cannot be used at all. The absorption of a drug may be very different if the drug is taken on an empty stomach or with food. Numerous questions such as these are studied by the clinical pharmacologist. Understanding all these potential factors is important before a drug can safely be given to a particular population. Thus, even though a drug may be approved for adults, it is usual to study at a minimum its clinical pharmacology in children before the drug is given to children.

Unexpected effects

One of the greatest concerns in the use of drugs in humans is the area of side effects, or adverse reactions. The study of toxicology, frequently considered an area of pharmacology, concerns understanding the effects of drugs other than the intended therapeutic ones. Before a drug is given to a human, it is studied fairly extensively in animals to determine the toxicology profile, usually in two species of animals. While the toxicology in animals is not necessarily predictive of what the adverse effects will be for people, it does give some insight into which organ systems may be most affected by the drug, as well as the types of side effects that may occur in humans. If a drug is very toxic in animals, it may never even be tried in humans. Specific areas of toxicology that are studied in animals include embryotoxicity and genotoxicity. There is concern for all drugs that they do not alter the patients' genes, or in the case of pregnant women, adversely affect the fetus. Ultimately, the toxicology of any drug must be studied in humans to be certain it is safe in humans. When an adverse reaction is common, it can usually be noticed very quickly when the drug is given to people. However, some adverse reactions to drugs occur very infrequently. These reactions can be extremely difficult to detect and may not become obvious until even thousands or tens of thousands of patients have been treated with the drug.

Thus, the purpose of pharmacology is to help understand both the intended use of a drug as well as the potential problems or side effects of a drug. Pharmacological studies are usually the first to be carried out in humans during the prolonged process of drug testing. These studies are of immense importance in the decision-making process to determine which drugs will ultimately be useful in the detection, prevention, or treatment of disease.

M. NADEL

SEE ALSO:
Adverse Reactions • Classification of Drugs • Metabolism • Pharmacokinetics • Toxicity

Pharmacy Drugs

Many people think that drugs that can be bought without a prescription are legal and safe to use. Although this may be true when used properly, these drugs are still dangerous if abused or taken in excess.

Pharmacy, or over-the-counter drugs (OTC), are substances that are sold without a prescription and can be easily bought at pharmacies, drugstores, gas stations, and grocery stores across the country. Because of their legal status and easy accessibility, there is a heightened risk of self-medication and intentional abuse of OTC drugs. Abuse of OTC drugs is becoming an increasing problem among teenage and young adult populations.

Individuals who self-medicate or intentionally abuse OTC drugs commonly misperceive that because OTC drugs are so prevalent and legal, they are also safe. Abuse of these types of drugs, however, can lead to a variety of serious health problems, including death. Preventive methods like supply control are usually not successful because it is difficult to restrict OTC drugs. The Internet is becoming an increasingly important source of information on how to abuse certain types of OTC drugs to get high. The Internet is also becoming a key source for the legal purchase of OTC drugs through online pharmacies, even among teenagers and young adults. As a result, restricting access to these drugs is very difficult.

Medications that are abused

Although the majority of OTC users are responsible users, a small number of users do intentionally self-medicate and abuse. Three of the commonly cited reasons include weight control, weight loss, and getting high.

Commonly abused OTCs related to weight control or weight loss include laxatives, ipecac, and diet pills. Abuse of laxatives entails taking laxatives too frequently or using multiple types at once. Many abusers, mostly misguided dieters and individuals with eating disorders, believe abuse is safe because of the legal status and easy accessibility of these drugs. Misguided dieters include those individuals who do not have eating disorders but still use laxatives with the idea that it will prevent weight gain. Laxatives are available at any grocery store or convenience store, and this availability offers unlimited opportunities for self-medicating. Self-medicating can become very dangerous when an individual is using the drug for the wrong reasons, or is intentionally overusing the drug.

Two types of commonly abused laxatives include stimulant-type and bulk agents. Stimulant-type laxatives are more likely to be abused than bulk types and include products like Ex-Lax, Correctol, and Feen-a-mint. Bulk agents include products such as Metamucil and Colace. Individuals who abuse either type of laxative often do not understand the effects of laxatives. For example, many abusers believe that taking laxatives will move food through the body faster, preventing calorie absorption. However, calorie absorption occurs in the small intestine, and laxatives only stimulate the large intestine. Any weight loss that does occur is actually related to the loss of water. This weight is usually regained when the body rehydrates itself, but a person who continually abuses laxatives can suffer from severe dehydration.

Dehydration is not the only negative health risk associated with laxative abuse. Other negative effects include deterioration of the colon, bleeding (which may result in anemia), impaired bowel function, electrolyte abnormalities, abdominal pain, tremors, kidney damage, and, in severe cases, death. Laxative abuse is also habit forming. If an individual continually uses laxatives the body may become dependent on the drug to function properly.

Ipecac abuse is another way individuals may attempt to control or lose weight. Ipecac is sold as a product that induces vomiting and is used by those who have ingested poison or overdosed on medication. To induce vomiting, ipecac stimulates the central nervous system and stomach. Individuals with eating disorders abuse ipecac as a way to facilitate purging. Once again, abusers may believe that using ipecac is harmless because it is so easy to buy. However, abuse of ipecac can lead to serious health complications, including seizures, shock, blackouts, high blood pressure, respiratory complications, dehydration, electrolyte abnormalities, hemorrhaging, cardiac arrest, and death.

Another commonly abused OTC drug related to weight control and weight loss is diet pills. Diet pills, like the previously mentioned OTC drugs, are easily accessible and are sold at grocery, health food, and convenience stores. Diet pills are composed of stimulants such as ephedrine, caffeine, and phenylpropanolamine, which stimulate the central nervous system. Although diet pills are used as an appetite suppressant to facilitate weight loss, they are also used and abused for a number of other reasons. For example, diet pills are often used by adolescents in high school and young adults in college as a way to stay awake and study. Truck drivers also use diet pills to stay awake, and athletes often use them to improve energy and strength.

As with laxative and ipecac abuse, there are a number of negative health effects associated with prolonged use and abuse of diet pills. These effects include seizures, heart palpitations, high blood pressure, dizziness, anxiety, insomnia, paranoia, menstrual irregularities, cardiac arrest, and death.

Cold remedies

OTCs commonly abused for psychedelic effects are cough and cold medicines. Abuse of cough suppressants or syrups usually involves adolescents looking for a cheap and legal alternative to more serious drugs. Although there are no formal statistics kept on the rate of cough-suppressant abuse, it is a very dangerous form of drug abuse because it occurs in unpredictable waves. Most drug abuse among young people usually follows a trend pattern. However, information about abusing cold remedies is mostly passed from student to student, school to school, by word of mouth. As a result, it is very difficult to predict where it is becoming a problem. Most towns are not aware that this type of drug abuse is a problem until a number of students experience hallucinations or overdose while at school.

Two common cough and cold medicines include Robitussin cough syrup and Coricidin cold-relief pills. Cough and cold medications are sold in a variety of forms, including tablets, capsules, lozenges, and syrups. Just like other commonly abused OTC drugs, cough and cold medicines are cheap and easily accessible. Teenagers abuse these types of medicines for the ingredient dextromethorphan (DXM). DXM is used in more than 125 over-the-counter medicines. It is a synthetic drug related to opiates and is chemically similar to morphine. It was approved by the FDA in 1954 and in the 1970s was put in cough medicines as a substitute for codeine.

Taken in appropriate doses, cough suppressants containing DXM have no serious negative side effects, but in large doses its effects mimic PCP or ketamine. Desired effects include sensory enhancement, heightened perceptual awareness, hallucinations, and perceptual distortion. Street names include skittles, Triple Cs, and robo, and using DXM is often referred to as "robotripping," "dexing," or "robodosing." Negative effects of DXM include confusion, blurred vision, slurred speech, loss of coordination, paranoia, high blood pressure, impaired judgment, loss of consciousness, irregular heartbeat, seizure, panic attacks, brain damage, addiction, coma, and death. Abusing DXM can result in serious negative health effects; however, a number of these are the result of abusing a combination of drugs. Using in combination can occur in two ways. A user can mix cough syrup use with alcohol or other drugs, which increases the dangers. There is also increased physical danger with the mix of medicines in the syrup itself. For example, many cough and cold medicines also contain acetaminophen. Acetaminophen is a painkiller, commonly found in Tylenol. Consuming large quantities of acetaminophen can cause liver damage and, in severe cases, liver failure.

Since there are no legal restrictions on DXM, it is very difficult to regulate. A wide variety of cough medicine is available in a range of stores, and DXM is therefore very easy to acquire. In areas across the United States most directly affected by cases of youth abuse of DXM, drug stores are putting DXM products behind the counter so people must request them. Another technique designed to prevent the purchase of this type of drug by youth involves packaging. The manufacturers of Coricidin increased the package size of their products containing DXM to make them more difficult to steal. However, there is another easy source: the family medicine cabinet. Many teenagers do not need to step out of

More than 700 medicines that were previously available only by prescription can now be bought over the counter. Global sales of these products totaled $47 billion in 2001. More than three-quarters of Americans take OTC remedies to deal with minor ailments, saving them $20 billion a year in doctors' fees, prescription costs, and time lost from work.

the house to find an OTC medicine that contains DXM. The powdered form of DXM is also available through a variety of sources.

Painkillers

Analgesics for the relief of headaches and moderate pain, particularly those containing codeine, are another abused OTC product. Codeine converts to morphine in the body, giving the characteristic opiate high. Because the amount of codeine in these products is low, large quantities are taken to produce the desired effect. Other ingredients in these formulations include aspirin or acetaminophen, which can both cause organ damage or overdose when taken in large quantities. Restrictions are sometimes placed on how many can be bought without a prescription, but this does not prevent people from going from shop to shop or ordering online to build up a supply. Taking OTC drugs at the same time as prescription drugs can also be dangerous.

Conclusion

Not all abuse of OTC drugs is related to getting high. The factor that links all forms of OTC drug abuse is the incorrect belief by many abusers that these drugs are safe because of their legal status and easy accessibility. Many abusers may be ill informed about the real effects of OTC drug use and abuse, especially DXM abuse; techniques of abuse are often passed around by word of mouth.

Prevention of OTC drug abuse is clearly very difficult. The most important tool in preventing OTC drug abuse is education. For example, if abusers of laxatives were educated on proper use, they would know that laxatives do not prevent calorie absorption. In terms of DXM abuse, the role of the Internet poses a serious problem. Web sites that educate people about negative effects also inform readers about exceeding the appropriate dosage to experience a high. Online pharmacies are also very difficult to regulate, especially when the drug of concern is legal. With potential abusive drugs within easy reach, increasing awareness and education among teenagers, young adults, parents, and teachers should be considered the primary defense in the prevention of OTC drug abuse.

E. J. FARLEY, D. J. O'CONNELL

SEE ALSO:
Adolescents and Substance Abuse • Drug Use, Life Patterns • DXM • Elderly • Multiple Addiction • Pharmacy Drugs • Women and Drugs

Phenethylamines

Phenethylamine is a simple compound that occurs in a multitude of plants and animals. Its chemical derivatives include neurotransmitters as well as natural and synthetic substances used in medicine and abused for recreation.

A phenethylamine molecule consists of a phenyl ring (C_6H_5–) linked to an amino group (–NH_2) by a chain of two carbon atoms, each with a pair of hydrogen atoms attached. Diverse chemical groups can replace one or more hydrogen atoms on any of the eight carbon atoms or the nitrogen atom of this molecule. Such substitutions form a myriad of compounds that qualify as phenethylamines or, more precisely, as derivatives of phenethylamine.

Phenethylamines form and participate in the life processes of plants and animals. They pass through food chains as one species ingests another and absorbs them, and their ultimate fate is to be excreted or destroyed by enzymes. Enzymes that destroy phenethylamines in humans and other animals include monoamine oxidases (MAOs) and catechol-ortho-methyltransferases (COMTs).

Neurotransmitters

The phenethylamine structure is present in three of the principal chemicals that convey signals between neurons in humans and other animals. These are the neurotransmitters dopamine and norepinephrine, and the neurohormone epinephrine.

Dopamine is phenethylamine with hydroxy groups (–OH) in place of hydrogen atoms at the 3 and 4 positions of the phenyl group. Norepinephrine has a further –OH group at the beta position of the

The diagram of phenethylamine below has labels in parentheses that identify positions where chemical groups can substitute hydrogen atoms to form phenethylamine derivatives. The *1* position of the phenyl group is occupied by ethylamine and cannot be substituted. The two hydrogens on the nitrogen (N) atom can be substituted. Dopamine, norepinephrine, and epinephrine are examples of natural phenethylamines; the hydroxy groups at the *3* and *4* positions of the phenyl ring specify them as catecholamines.

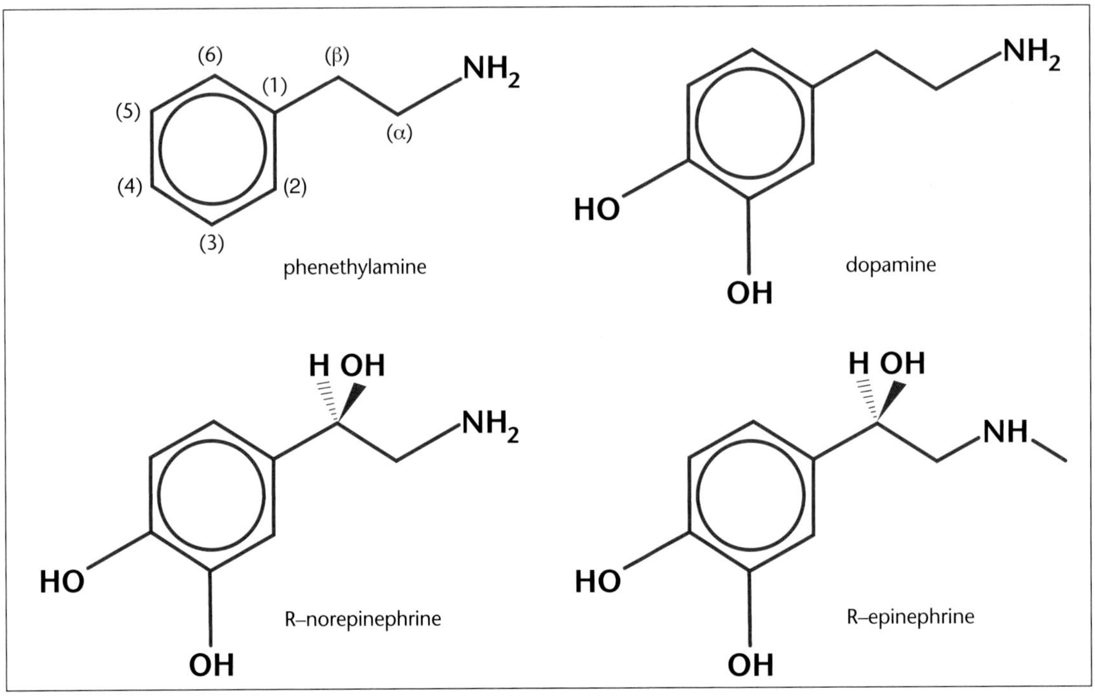

ethylamine chain, and epinephrine is similar to norepinephrine but has a methyl group in place of one of the hydrogens on the amino group.

Dopamine, epinephrine, and norepinephrine stimulate neural activity when they attach to receptors that fit them. The consequences of that stimulation in the brain include exhilaration, alertness, anxiety, paranoia, and outright psychosis. The same compounds have stimulant effects in the body that include increased heart rate and blood pressure, and dilation of the pupils and airways.

Many other phenethylamines have effects on the mind and body because of their structural similarity to neurotransmitters. Some phenethylamines directly mimic the effects of such compounds by stimulating receptors that respond to them; some act indirectly by causing the release of natural neurotransmitters. Alternatively, phenethylamines can reinforce the effects of neurotransmitters by blocking the entities that deactivate them. These entities are reuptake channels that return neurotransmitters to storage vessels in neurons, and enzymes that convert neurotransmitters into inactive compounds.

Chocolate contains phenethylamine, up to around 2 percent by weight. The presence of this compound has been cited as a potential contributor to the mood-elevating property of chocolate, but it is likely that enzymes destroy phenethylamine before it has a chance to work its effects in the brain.

Structure and activity

The physical shape of a molecule plays a key role in its drug activity, as does the presence or absence of charge variations around a molecule. Polar molecules have regions of positive and negative charges that attract other polar molecules by electrostatic forces; they have much less affinity for nonpolar molecules such as those that constitute the lining of the small intestine and the blood-brain barrier.

Groups such as $–OH$ and $–NH_2$ tend to contribute polarity. Molecules that have such groups have difficulty entering the bloodstream when swallowed, and even more difficulty getting into the brain from the bloodstream. The polarity of these groups reduces when methyl groups replace hydrogen atoms to form $–OCH_3$, $–NHCH_3$, or $–N(CH_3)_2$ groups. Such modifications improve absorption into the bloodstream of such drugs and can also increase their activity in the brain. They also hinder enzymes that attack polar groups, so they keep the compound active for longer.

The dependence of activity on structure also makes for differences in the drug activities between isomers—compounds that have the same chemical formula but different structures. In some cases, a small difference in structure can have major consequences for drug activity.

The effect of isomerism is perhaps easiest to understand for positional isomerism, whereby the same chemical groups attach to different parts of a core structure. The presence of the phenyl ring in phenethylamines offers plenty of scope for positional isomerism, and changes in the positions of groups attached to this ring cause enormous variations in the therapeutic or recreational properties of drugs.

Stereoisomers

Stereoisomerism is the existence of pairs of mirror-image molecules that are distinctly different. It has consequences for drug activity because nature tends to use only one of the pair of possible molecules, so the drugs that correspond to the natural isomer are more active than their mirror-image counterparts.

Stereoisomerism becomes a possibility when chemical groups replace one or more hydrogen atoms on the carbon atoms of the ethylamine chain. A carbon atom attached to four different chemical groups is a source of asymmetry that leads to the existence of mirror-image pairs.

The formation of stereoisomeric pairs can be visualized by considering the successive addition of four different groups to a carbon atom. Once the first two groups are in place, the second two can be added in either of two distinct configurations. Each configuration results in a different stereoisomer, denoted *R* or *S* according to the arrangement of chemical groups around the carbon atom in question.

Another naming system uses *d* (dextro) and *l* (levo) to distinguish between stereoisomers according to how they rotate the plane of polarization of light that has passed through a polarizing filter. The interaction with light is the reason that this type of stereoisomerism is sometimes called optical activity. The rotation of polarized light as it passes through a solution provides a useful means of testing for and identifying the stereoisomers present.

Stimulant phenethylamines

A number of natural and synthetic phenethylamines increase alertness, chattiness, and euphoria without causing hallucinogenic or psychedelic effects. These are the stimulant phenethylamines, as typified by amphetamine. Members of this group increase heart rate and blood pressure; they also relieve congestion and symptoms of asthma by dilating the airways, and their ability to reduce appetite gives them potential as antiobesity drugs.

The negative properties of the stimulant phenethylamines include their potential for causing dependency and psychosis. Malnutrition can also occur as a result of prolonged appetite suppression, and they can cause strokes or heart attacks in people who are vulnerable to such diseases. Because of these negative effects most stimulant phenethylamines appear in the strictest schedules of drug legislation. A few exceptions have recognized uses in the treatment of breathing difficulties, obesity, and attention deficit disorder.

Stimulant phenethylamines typically have no additional substituents on the phenyl ring of phenethylamine, but they are otherwise close relatives of dopamine, epinephrine, and norepinephrine. The absence of hydroxy groups on the ring is crucial to their activity, since their polarity prevents molecules that carry them from crossing the blood-brain barrier. Also, the absence of ring hydroxy groups makes these compounds less attractive targets for destruction by COMT enzymes, so they remain active for longer.

One of the principal stimulant phenethylamines is ephedrine, an active principal in the traditional Chinese medicine ma huang. This substance is present in the stems of the ephedra shrub, and it is largely responsible for the effectiveness of ma huang in treating congestion and asthma as well as providing energy by burning fat deposits. Ephedra also contains pseudoephedrine, which produces a milder effect similar to that of ephedrine.

Ephedrine and pseudoephedrine both have a phenethylamine core with methyl groups attached to the nitrogen and beta-carbon atoms, and a hydroxy group on the alpha carbon. The alpha and beta carbons are both sources of stereoisomerism, so two pairs of mirror-image isomers are possible. Both compounds

This diagram represents an ephedrine molecule docked to matching regions in a receptor. The strength of the interaction has three major sources. First, there is an affinity between the hydrophobic phenyl ring of ephedrine and a hydrophobic region in the receptor. Second, there is hydrogen bonding at the hydroxy group. Third, there is ionic attraction between a negatively charged region in the receptor and the positive charge of the nitrogen.

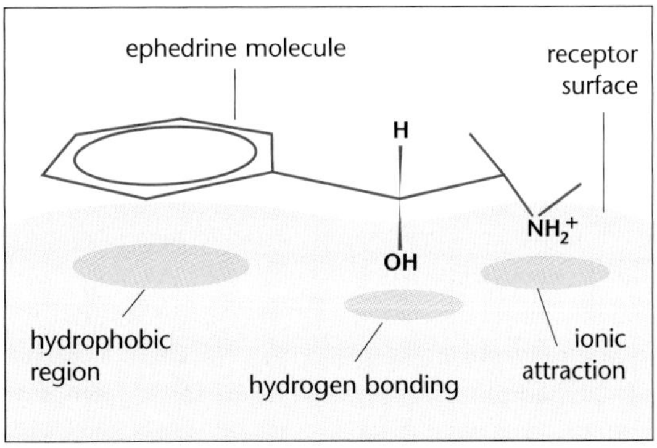

have *S* configurations at the alpha carbon, and the difference of configuration at the beta carbon is what separates ephedrine and pseudoephedrine.

Ephedrine has the *R* configuration at the beta carbon, as do the natural forms of epinephrine and norepinephrine. This resemblance makes for a good interaction at receptors. Pseudoephedrine has the *S* configuration and is much less active. Nevertheless, its reduced cardiovascular side effects make it safer for use in decongestant medicines.

Ephedra also contains small amounts of norephedrine and norpseudoephedrine, which differ from their parent compounds by having no methyl groups on their nitrogen atoms. These are also stimulants. Norephedrine also has the name cathine, which stems from its presence as the main active compound in *Catha edulis* (khat), a stimulant shrub.

Ephedrine, pseudoephedrine, and cathine all have pronounced effects on breathing and heart rate, but they have relatively little effect in the brain. The polarity of their beta-carbon hydroxy groups is sufficient to ensure they stay mainly on the blood side of the blood-brain barrier.

Psychostimulant phenethylamines

Amphetamine and methamphetamine are close chemical relatives of the ephedra stimulants, but they lack the polar hydroxy group. Chemical reduction of either ephedrine or pseudoephedrine produces methamphetamine and is the main clandestine source of this drug; the same reaction converts cathine into simple amphetamine.

This removal of the hydroxy group has two consequences. First, it produces compounds that get into the brain with relative ease; second, these compounds have chemical structures more closely related to that of dopamine. Thus, it is no surprise that these compounds produce their characteristic rush by interfering with the normal functioning of dopamine neurons in the brain.

The amphetamines have mirror image isomers because they have methyl groups at the alpha carbon. Their *dextro* or *S* forms are responsible for the amphetamine rush, while the *R* isomers are much less potent. Careful reduction of natural ephedra stimulants produces the desired *S* isomer of methamphetamine rather than its less effective *R* isomer counterpart.

Seen here in his laboratory, Alexander "Sasha" Shulgin synthesized more than 200 phenethylamines between the mid-1960s and the withdrawal of his DEA license in 1994. He also tested many of these compounds on himself and a group of scientists to evaluate their psychoactivity. Some people call him the "godfather of Ecstasy" despite the fact that MDMA was synthesized many years before Shulgin started his research. Shulgin's purpose was to explore the potential use of phenethylamines in psychotherapy.

Cathinone is a psychostimulant phenethylamine that accompanies cathine in khat. It has a ketone group at the beta position, and this again is less polar than the hydroxy group in cathine. Hence, cathinone has similar psychoactive effects to amphetamine.

Just as cathinone is the substance that would result from the oxidation of cathine, methcathinone or ephedrone is the oxidation product of ephedrine or pseudoephedrine. Methcathinone became a drug of abuse in the former Soviet Union, where it was prescribed as an antidepressant, but it does not have much history of recreational use elsewhere.

Psychedelic phenethylamines

While stimulant phenethylamines tend to have plain phenyl rings, psychedelic phenethylamines have diverse substituents for hydrogen atoms on the phenyl ring. These chemical groups provide the principal cause of psychedelic effects. Substituents on the ethylamine chain modulate the potency and length of action of phenethylamines. The presence of one or two methyl groups at the nitrogen atom usually removes psychedelic activity.

Mescaline. The natural prototype of the psychedelic phenethylamines is mescaline, and it is one of the benchmarks for comparisons of the action of psychedelics. Mescaline gets its name from mescal, a peyote cactus that contains it, and its chemical name is 3,4,5-trimethoxyphenethylamine.

The presence of three methoxy groups on the phenyl ring of mescaline makes its molecular shape significantly different from that of phenethylamine. A consequence of this change is that mescaline and related phenethylamines interact with serotonergic neurons—those that respond to serotonin. These interactions are responsible for psychoactive effects ranging from hallucinations to the "loved-up" empathogenic state associated with Ecstasy and its analogs. Serotonergic neurons can also cause nausea and vomiting when these drugs are taken.

DOM. The mid-1960s saw synthetic psychedelics start to emerge from research laboratories. Some of these compounds revealed themselves to be extremely potent; an example is DOM, also named STP after an unrelated gasoline additive. This amphetamine derivative proved to be an effective hallucinogen at doses of a few milligrams, compared with the hundreds of milligrams in mescaline doses.

The amphetamine core of DOM makes stereoisomerism possible, and U.S. pharmacologist Alexander Shulgin (1925–) made and tested the two stereoisomers for psychoactivity. He found that the *R* isomer produced hallucinogenic effects, while the *S* isomer was inactive as a hallucinogen. This result contrasts with the pattern for stimulant phenethylamines, whose *S* isomers are more active. It suggests that the two types of phenethylamines act at different receptors that have different geometries.

Other hallucinogens. Intrigued by the potential for self-exploration during mescaline experiences, Shulgin embarked on a search for similar or superior psychoactivity in other phenethylamines. He generated several series of compounds that varied by positions of chemical groups and lengths of alkyl chains, and he substituted such entities as bromo (–Br), iodo (–I), methyl (–CH_3), and methylthio (CH_3S–) groups onto the phenyl ring.

In 1991, Shulgin and his wife, Ann, published the results of this work in *PiHKAL: A Chemical Love Story,* where "PiHKAL" is an acronym of "phenethylamines I have known and loved." The first part of *PiHKAL* is semi-autobiographical, but the second half lists the synthesis and testing of 179 phenethylamines. Some of these compounds proved to have neutral or unpleasant psychoactive effects; others became popular recreational hallucinogens. The latter group includes DOM and Nexus (2C-B).

Entactogenic phenethylamines

Shulgin produced a third class of phenethylamines whose effects differ from those of both the stimulant and the hallucinogenic phenethylamines. The prototype of this group is the 1960s "love drug" 3,4-methylenedioxyamphetamine, or MDA; the *N*-methyl derivative of this drug is MDMA, the active component of genuine Ecstasy. The characteristic chemical group of these compounds is the methylenedioxy (–O–CH_2–O–) bridge between the 3 and 4 positions of the phenyl ring.

In common with the stimulants and in contrast to the hallucinogenic phenethylamines, the more active forms of drugs in this group are the *S* isomers. Also, these compounds have pronounced stimulant effects that suggest some similarities to the amphetamines. However, the effect of these drugs is characterized by heightened contentment and empathy for others, which are the opposite of the typically "edgy" amphetamine effects. The term *entactogen* was coined for these drugs and refers to their ability to make users feel more in touch with themselves and others. Drugs in this class also have a mild hallucinatory action that contributes to their popularity for use in club environments.

M. CLOWES

SEE ALSO:
Amphetamines • Dopamine • Ecstasy • Ecstasy Analogs • Ephedrine • Epinephrine • Mescaline • Neurotransmission • Nexus • Norepinephrine

Placebos

Placebos are medications used to test the efficacy of new drugs. Despite the fact that placebos do not contain an active ingredient, some patients claim relief from their symptoms, which suggests that expectations play a role in a drug's effects.

A placebo is a substance or treatment believed to be inert or to have no known therapeutic effect. A placebo could be a sugar or starch pill or even "fake" surgery. Currently the only known and accepted use for a placebo is in research experiments; when a new drug (medicine) is being tested for efficacy, or a drug that has an established use is being tested for a new condition, then placebos are used. A drug is usually tested by administering it to people suffering from the condition that the drug has been designed to cure. If, after taking the drug, the subjects show an improvement in their condition, the drug is deemed to be effective. In fact, it is not that simple.

When designing experiments, scientists attempt to control the environment as much as possible in order to eliminate other possible explanations. According to this principle, if all possible alternative explanations are eliminated, then the one that is left must be true. So, if people are given a drug and they get better, what other explanations might there be? One explanation could be that the condition would have improved in time, without medication. One way to control for this outcome might be to give a second group of subjects a placebo. If all subjects, those taking the drug and those taking the placebo, improve, then the explanation is probably that drugs are not required. If only the subjects who are given the drug improve, then the drug is probably effective for this condition. This is the most common use of the placebo, to test the effect of other drugs.

In the 1950s researcher H. K. Beecher coined the phrase "placebo effect" to describe a strange phenomenon. In a number of studies, he noted that a substantial number of subjects given a placebo were improving in a similar manner to those given the real drug—people were getting better even though they had not been given any active medication. Over the years, a number of explanations have been suggested for this phenomenon.

One explanation was that the subjects improved because they were never actually clinically ill. Since they suffered from an imaginary illness, an imaginary cure would suffice. Opponents of this theory point to the finding that the phenomenon has been observed with visible illnesses; for example, it has been found that warts can react to a placebo ointment. Hence, some suggest the effect may be produced by chemicals, such as endorphins, being released in the body. Indeed, there is an ongoing debate over whether or not antidepressants have any pharmacological effect or whether they have a placebo effect. Finally, others have suggested that the healing process is more than just the administration of a pill and that the effect, whatever it may be, could be triggered by the climate of caring that surrounds the patient. Whatever the explanation, healing appears to be based on the deception that the subject is taking beneficial medication. Thus, the person believes that he or she will get better. This finding also has relevance for the abuse of alcohol and other drugs.

Chemical effects and learned behaviors

Until the end of the 1960s, it was widely believed that alcohol and other drugs had certain predictable effects and that those effects were purely a function of the chemical properties inherent in the drugs. These are known as the pharmacological effects. However, in 1969 researchers McAndrew and Edgerton published a book called *Drunken Comportment.* This cultural and anthropological study demonstrated that people of different cultures and nations consumed alcohol in different ways, experienced different effects, and behaved differently (the "drunken comportment" of the book's title). It would appear that the differences between the groups were cultural; for example, some cultures became more violent, while others became more friendly. McAndrew and Edgerton argued that the effects of alcohol must owe more to cultural learning than to pharmacological effects. Indeed, when the behaviors were examined, only three universal effects, called the "three S's," were found: impaired gait (staggering), impaired speech (slurring), and drowsiness (sleeping); all other effects were learned.

THE BALANCED PLACEBO EXPERIMENT

The balanced placebo experiment is an elegant and powerful experimental design that allows researchers to distinguish between the pharmacological (purely chemical) and the learned or psychological effects of alcohol. The design of the experiment is quite straightforward. If 100 people were taking part in the experiment, 50 of them, chosen at random, would be told that they would be given alcohol (conditions 1 and 2). The remaining 50 would be told that they would be given a soft drink (conditions 3 and 4). Of the first 50, half would be given an alcoholic drink (usually vodka and orange juice) and the other half would be given a placebo, a drink that looks and smells like an alcoholic drink but contains no alcohol—usually a glass of orange juice that has had vodka rubbed on the rim of the glass. The second group of 50 are treated the same—half are given straight orange juice and the other half are given vodka and orange juice.

All subjects are then given some task to perform, for example, filling in questionnaires or watching films. Researchers observe the subjects and take measures to gauge the effect. If all subjects who have consumed alcohol (conditions 1 and 3) behave similarly and different from those subjects who did not consume alcohol (conditions 2 and 4), then any effect or behavior can be explained by the pharmacological effect of alcohol. However, if all subjects who believe they have consumed alcohol (conditions 1 and 2) behave similarly, and different from those subjects who believe they have consumed a soft drink (conditions 3 and 4), any effect or behavior is then explained by the mere belief of drinking alcohol and not by any pharmacological effect.

Researchers in the 1970s and 1980s became interested in this "learning" explanation of intoxication and started to investigate it using a design called the balanced placebo experiment (*see* box above). Using this experiment, they found that learning explained the majority of intoxicated behaviors; for example, aggression, sexual arousal, and social facilitation could all be explained by the placebo effect of alcohol. Researchers studying alcoholism found that some firmly held views such as the priming effect (if an alcoholic takes one drink, then loss of control and drunkenness will inevitably ensue) and craving were again culturally learned behaviors. Thus, new questions were asked about the validity of viewing alcoholism as a disease. The learned effects of alcohol have been found to be powerful motivators to initiate and continue drinking and indeed appear to have a greater influence on relapse in dependent drinking than the effects of alcohol itself. It has been found that people drink to achieve the effects that they expect, and that this is true of both social and dependent drinkers. Among the commonly expected effects are:

- Global positive change (things are generally better after a drink)
- Sexual enhancement (more attractive to opposite sex, more sexually accomplished)
- Social facilitation (can mix better at social functions)
- Relaxation, both physical and emotional
- Assertiveness
- Aggression.

Finally, it should be obvious that the placebo effect applies as well to other recreational and illicit drugs. Thus, much of the effect of drug use that people experience is learned, much of it depends on the individual's metabolism, and the rest is governed by pharmacology. An examination of the effects of drug use must therefore take into account the individual and the environment as well as the drug.

J. MCMAHON

SEE ALSO:
Addictive Behavior • Conditioning • Cultural Attitudes • Disease Theory of Addiction • Reinforcement • Violence

Plant-Based Drugs

Plants have been used to treat diseases in all cultures for centuries. As well as treating illnesses, plants have been and continue to be used in their natural as well as manufactured forms for their hallucinatory, stimulative, or sedative effects.

The natural world contains many drug-producing plants. People in the West and other societies often use these drugs in social situations, for medicine, or as part of their cultural rituals. This article covers a variety of such naturally occurring drugs.

Many plants contain natural substances that affect the brain's chemistry; these substances may have a stimulating, sedating, or hallucinatory action. Once these properties are discovered, people with access to such plants make use of them in various ways.

In Western society, for example, there are several well-known legal and illegal drugs that are derived from plants. For example, alcohol is a product of the fermentation of yeast and sugar; the stimulant caffeine comes from coffee beans; the powerful pain-killer morphine is from the opium poppy; and tetrahydrocannabinol (THC) in marijuana is found in hemp leaves. Alcohol and caffeine are used by millions of people every day, marijuana is smoked illegally, and morphine is an important analgesic used in medicine.

There are many more plant-based drugs that are not widely used in modern Western society but that were used in the past or were used by other cultures. A wide range of natural substances work as drugs in the body because the chemical messengers in the human brain are sometimes similar to compounds found in plants. For example, nicotine in tobacco is a poison used by the plant to deter pests, but it also reacts with acetylcholine receptors in the brain because its chemical structure is similar to acetylcholine, a natural body chemical.

Fly agaric mushroom

Amanita muscaria, known more commonly as fly agaric, is a brightly colored mushroom that contains several hallucinogenic substances and organic poisons. It is around 6 inches (15 cm) tall and has a distinctive appearance, with a bright red or yellow-orange cap covered with white spots. The main psychoactive effects of eating Amanita mushrooms are from muscimol, which is metabolized by the body from ibotenic acid in the mushroom. A few mushroom caps at first produce nausea, then a dreamy relaxed feeling, and finally hallucinations for several hours. However, some people also find the experience distressing. *Amanita muscaria* is legal to pick and grows widely over the Northern Hemisphere.

Several cultures use *Amanita muscaria* in their religious rituals, including Siberians, Native Americans, and the Sami of Scandinavia. In these rituals, the hallucinogenic dreams are often interpreted as visions. The Western name, fly agaric, comes from a traditional use of the mushroom in flypaper.

Yopo

The seeds from the yopo tree (*Anadenanthera colubrina*) contain a powerful psychoactive drug, which tribes in Colombia, Venezuela, and parts of Brazil use to make a hallucinogenic snuff called *yopo*.

The story book appearance of fly agaric is deceptive; if eaten these mushrooms are very poisonous.

Typically, the seeds are dried, ground, and then snorted through a bamboo tube. The main active chemical in the snuff is dimethyltryptamine (DMT). A regular dose of around 30 milligrams of DMT has a similar hallucinogenic effect to LSD, but DMT begins to wear off after only half an hour. Many plants containing DMT can be grown legally, although its purification is illegal.

Yopo is relatively unknown but has been popular among native South Americans for centuries. For example, almost one in five Mayans regularly took *yopo*. Many tribes in South America also use similar plants to make other snuffs.

Hawaiian baby woodrose

Seeds from the clambering vine Hawaiian baby woodrose (*Argyreia nervosa*) contain several hallucinogenic chemicals called ergot alkaloids. Of these psychoactive alkaloids, the main active chemicals—chanoclavine, lysergol, ergotmetrine, and ergine—are all members of the lysergic acid amide (LSA) family of chemicals, which are closely related to LSD. Ergot alkaloids naturally occur in several plants. Hawaiian baby woodrose, like many bright red or yellow-orange plants that contain LSA, can be grown legally. The seeds of Hawaiian baby woodrose were not traditionally used as a psychoactive drug, although in recent times they have become popular for their LSD-like effects.

Absinthe

Wood from the absinthe (*Artimisia absinthium*) shrub, more commonly known as wormwood, is a main ingredient of the alcoholic beverage absinthe. Called green fairy, or *la feé verte* in French, this drink is also flavored with licorice, fennel, and aniseed, and it gets its distinctive green coloring from chlorophyll in the wood. In addition to its alcohol content, wormwood contains a psychoactive drug, thujone, that has a similar effect to the active chemical tetrahydrocannabinol (THC) found in marijuana. The combination of thujone and alcohol can result in extreme intoxication, while excessive use is associated with addiction, hallucination, and mental deterioration. It is illegal to sell absinthe in the United States, although it is legal to possess the drink.

A French doctor named Pierre Ordinaire invented the recipe for absinthe in 1792. Soon after, the Swiss distiller Henri-Louis Pernod acquired the recipe and began large-scale commercial production. Absinthe was a popular drink throughout the nineteenth century, and was often drunk to excess by artists such as Edouard Manet (1832–1883) and Vincent Van Gogh (1853–1890), who believed it helped their creativity. Because of worries about its adverse health effects (thujone is toxic and can cause seizures), many countries banned absinthe at the beginning of the twentieth century.

Ergot

Claviceps purpurea, more commonly known as ergot, is a fungus that infects grains such as rye and some wild grasses. Because the fungus is both toxic and psychoactive, it causes an unpleasant disease called ergotism in cattle and humans. Symptoms include a burning sensation, convulsions, hallucinations, and black, gangrenous limbs, all of which originate from a large amount of ergot alkaloids in the fungus. Ergot is also an abortifacient (causes abortions).

The main chemicals ergotamine, ergotine, and ergotoxine are derivatives of lysergic acid and are also collectively termed lysergic acid amides (LSA). Similarly to LSD, these alkaloids induce hallucinations, while ergotamine constricts the body's blood vessels, causing gangrene.

In the European Middle Ages, there were periodic plagues from ergot infestation of crops. Other than causing gangrene and hallucinations, ergotism is accompanied by a burning feeling, which led to its name *ignis sacer*, or "holy fire." In modern times, ergot is used to treat migraines and is the main ingredient used to illegally manufacture LSD.

Ma huang

Ephedra equisetina, or ma huang, is a Chinese herb that has several pharmacological effects. The active chemicals in ephedra are ephedra alkaloids, of which the most important is ephedrine.

Usually taken as an ingredient in traditional Asian medicine, ephedra has a stimulating effect that is stronger than caffeine but weaker than amphetamine. Ephedra also suppresses appetite and is a natural decongestant. Asian medicine has used ephedra for over five thousand years to treat asthma and weight problems. In more recent times, ephedra has been sold as "herbal Ecstasy" preparations, which have a recreational use similar to Ecstasy (MDMA) and amphetamines. Ephedra has now been banned by the U.S. Food and Drug Administration because of its recreational use as a stimulant and unreliable claims about its medicinal properties.

Kola nut and guarana

Both the kola nut and guarana are natural sources of the stimulant caffeine, and are used by some cultures in a similar way to coffee in the West. Kola nuts grow on the *Kola vera* tree, a North American member of the cocoa family; guarana seeds come from the guarana shrub, which is native to Brazil. Coffee beans typically contain 1 to 2 percent caffeine, while the kola nut has around 2 to 3 percent and guarana 4 to 8 percent. Caffeine stimulates the central nervous system and is used to stay alert; too much can cause nervousness, irritability, and sleeplessness.

At one time the kola nut was an ingredient in American colas, although now it is replaced by synthetic flavorings that mimic its taste. Meanwhile, South American tribes have used guarana for thousands of years as a stimulant in many foods and drinks. Today guarana is used in many energy drinks and is a main ingredient of guarana soda, a popular beverage in Brazil.

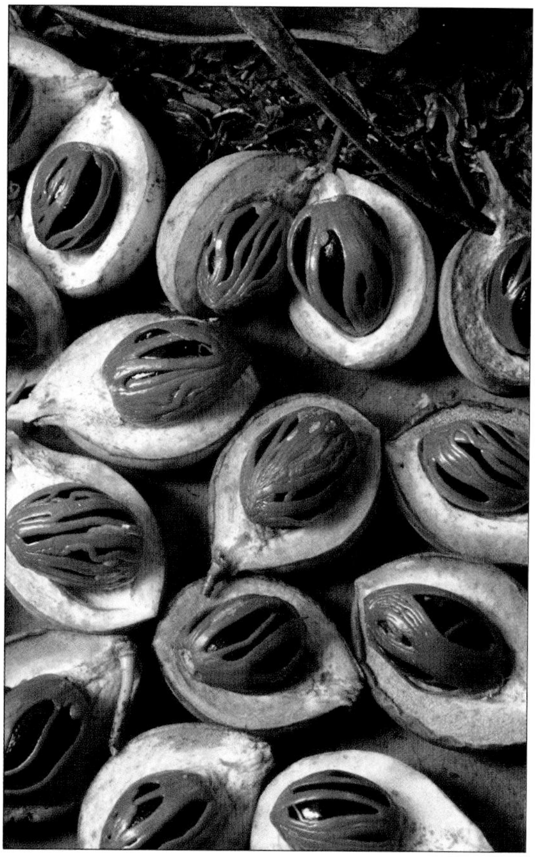

The common culinary spice nutmeg is also a hallucinatory drug when taken in large amounts of more than one pound.

Mimosa

The sweet-tasting flowers of the Chinese herb mimosa (*Albizia julibrissin Durazz*), or he huan hua, are used in traditional Asian medicine for their calming effects. Commonly referred to as Chinese herbal Prozac, mimosa flowers are used as an anti-depressant, to relieve anxiety, and as a sleeping aid. Although there is little research on the pharmacology of the flowers, their sedative action is thought to be from quercitrin, a drug found in the flowers. Another compound, tetracosanoic acid, is also present, but its effects are currently unknown.

Nutmeg

Myristica fragrans, the common nutmeg, is a tree native to the Indonesian spice islands. When dried and ground, the seeds are called nutmeg. Around 10 to 20 ounces (280–560 g) of nutmeg produces an intense hallucinogenic effect that is often accompanied by vomiting, diarrhea, and an extremely dry mouth. Its effects start after a few hours, last for up to a day, and are usually described as very unpleasant. The main psychoactive chemical in nutmeg is myristicin, also called methoxysafrole. European and North American cooks have used nutmeg as a spice since the sixteenth century in cakes, savory dishes, and mulled wine. Its psychoactive effects have been well documented for most of its modern history. Some cultures use nutmeg as a medicine; a Hindu pharmacopoeia mentions it as a treatment for fever, asthma, and heart disease.

Reed canary grass

Phalaris arundinacea, more commonly known as reed canary grass, is a tall, reddish green grass that grows on marshy land and contains small amounts of the psychoactive chemical dimethyltryptamine (DMT). There is too little DMT in the grass to have a direct

The flowers of mimosa are used in traditional Asian medicine to relieve insomnia, depression, and anxiety.

effect, although it can be chemically extracted, then snorted in its pure form. Pure DMT is illegal, but legislation against the plants is impossible because they are common around the world.

Reed canary grass is sometimes used in traditional South American brews called ayahuasca, which are drinks that have hallucinatory effects. The plant has been used as a source of illegally obtained DMT.

Kava

The roots of the kava shrub (*Piper methysticum*), a pepper plant from the islands of the South Pacific, are dried and ground to make a mood-altering herbal remedy. Typically, the powdered roots are boiled in water and taken as a drink, although kava can also be eaten in its natural form or as tablets. Its main pharmacologically active chemicals are kava lactones, which produce relaxation and sharpen the senses.

One of the properties of kava is the relief of anxiety; it is also a muscle relaxant. Kava is one of the most popular herbs bought from health food stores in the United States.

Pacific islanders have grown kava for thousands of years, using it at social gatherings, religious ceremonies, and in many other ways. More recently, kava has been sold in the West as a health food remedy for a variety of ailments. Kava is banned in some countries, such as the United Kingdom, because of safety concerns.

Diviner's sage

Salvia divinorum, or diviner's sage, is a shrub native to southern Mexico. It is probable that the native Central Americans used *Salvia divinorum* in religious rituals. The leaves of the plant contain a powerful psychoactive chemical called salvinorin. Salvinorin is a drug that is traditionally imbibed by chewing pairs of leaves, although the plant can also be dried and smoked. Salvinorin is a powerful hallucinogen, which when smoked lasts for around half an hour; if it is chewed, its effects last longer. Users do not become tolerant to salvinorin. However, many people find the hallucinations unpleasant and choose not to repeat the experience.

N. LEPORA

SEE ALSO:
Belladonna Alkaloids • Betel Nut • Coca Leaf • DMT • Jimsonweed • Marijuana • Mescaline • Psilocybin and Psilocin • Tobacco

Potentiation

Potentiation is the enhancement of the physiological activity or psychoactivity of one substance as a result of the action of other substances. Potentiation can occur through a wide variety of mechanisms as a drug passes through the body.

The term *potentiation* applies to a diversity of mechanisms that enhance the effects of a substance that is either psychoactive or physiologically active in some other way. Targets for potentiation include hormones and neurotransmitters naturally present in humans, as well as synthetic or natural substances taken for recreational or therapeutic purposes.

In the case of a psychoactive drug, effects such as distorted perception, euphoria, drowsiness, or social disinhibition are manifestations of cascades of nerve impulses that originate when the drug binds to receptor sites on neurons. Potentiation occurs when one or more secondary substances increase the availability of a drug at an active site. Alternatively, a potentiating agent can enhance the interaction of the drug with its receptor so as to make a given concentration of a substance more effective.

Improved absorption

The path of a drug through the body starts with the administration method, such as injection, sniffing, smoking, or swallowing. In all cases but injection, the drug must pass through a tissue membrane in order to reach the bloodstream. This is the first opportunity for potentiation to occur.

In the traditional use of coca, leaves from the plant are chewed and mixed together with ash in a wad. The ash provides alkalinity that frees the cocaine base from its salts. When the user squeezes the wad between cheek and gums, cocaine freebase passes through the lining of the cheek more readily than cocaine salts would. Hence, ash potentiates the effect of cocaine from coca leaves by keeping it in a form that favors its absorption into the bloodstream.

Cytochrome P450 inhibition

After absorption, drugs have to contend with enzymes that catalyze their bioconversion into substances that often have no activity. This assault is part of the process that helps prevent accumulations of potentially toxic compounds. Nevertheless, such enzyme action can hinder the effects of psychoactive drugs if enzyme activity eliminates a compound before enough of the drug crosses the blood-brain barrier to produce effects.

Substances that inhibit enzyme-mediated destruction of active compounds potentiate by increasing the length of time an active compound stays in the body. The same mechanism also increases the maximum drug concentration when gradual absorption of a drug from the intestine is at least as fast as the rate of elimination of the drug.

One of the major families of enzymes that destroy drugs are the cytochromes P450, or CYPs. The different members of this family are identified by codes such as 3A4 and 2C19. The CYPs reside mainly on cells in the liver and small intestine. These locations are ideal for eliminating drugs from the bloodstream and even from the contents of the intestine before they reach the bloodstream.

The nature of enzyme action provides a basis for potentiation because an enzyme molecule can only process one molecule at a time. Also, each type of

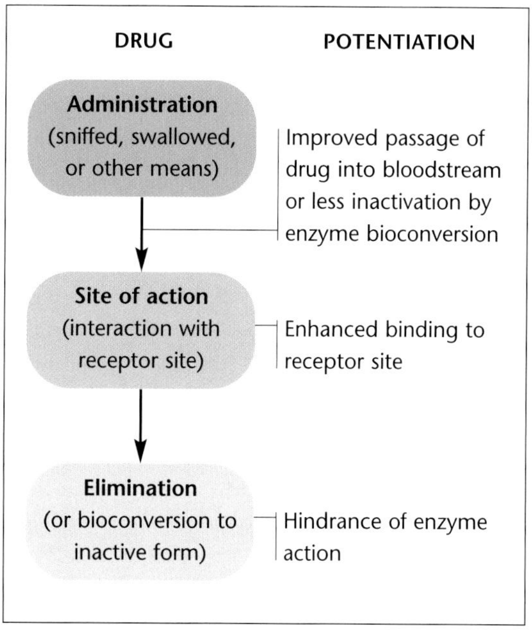

CYP enzyme promotes a specific bioconversion reaction in a given type of chemical compound. Thus there can be competition between different substances that degrade under the influence of a given enzyme, and one substance can impede the degradation of another by monopolizing an enzyme. A curious example is the potentiation of certain drugs by grapefruit juice, which is due to the presence of a compound called bergamottin in grapefruit. Bergamottin degrades by the action of CYP3A4 and CYP1A2; these enzymes also catalyze the degradation of benzodiazepines, cannabinoids, cocaine, codeine, fentanyl, methadone, and various tricyclic antidepressants. A glass of grapefruit juice contains enough bergamottin to interrupt normal metabolic processes, thus distorting the effects of both prescription and nonprescription drugs. The activity of some drugs can be inhibited by eating broccoli.

Another CYP enzyme, type 2D6, degrades drugs such as amphetamines, methadone, morphine, and oxycodone. Substances that potentiate these drugs by inhibiting CYP2D6 include cocaine, antidepressants, antipsychotics, and HIV drugs.

Monoamine oxidase inhibition

Recreational drugs such as amphetamines, phenethylamines, and tryptamines all belong to a class of compounds called monoamines. Such substances are prone to degradation by enzymes called monoamine oxidases (MAOs); there are two broad classes of these enzymes—MAO_A and MAO_B.

MAO_A occurs in dopamine and norepinephrine neurons as well as in the liver and gut. MAO_B occurs in serotonin neurons and on blood platelets. Hence, these enzymes can attack monoamine drugs in the gut before they are absorbed, in the bloodstream as they circulate, and in the brain where they act.

A class of drugs called MAO inhibitors (MAOIs) reduces the activity of MAOs by binding to the site where monoamines attach in the first stage of their bioconversion. Drugs such as phenelzine (Nardil) form permanent bonds to MAOs, and their inhibition is irreversible. Thus the body must produce new MAO molecules after MAOI treatment has finished before normal MAO activity returns. Other MAOIs form reversible bonds with MAOs, so their effect gradually wears off as they detach from MAO molecules and the body eliminates them.

The clinical use of MAOIs is in the treatment of depression, since they boost the activity of neurotransmitters such as serotonin and norepinephrine, whose reduced activities are implicated in depression. However, MAOIs can sometimes cause dangerous potentiation of recreational and therapeutic drugs by knocking out an enzyme system that degrades both the drugs and the neurotransmitters they cause to be released.

Some natural compounds are able to inhibit MAO activity and have traditional use together with natural extracts that contain psychoactive monoamines. An example of such a concoction is ayahuasca, which contains MAO-inhibiting harmine and psychoactive DMT and is a tool in shamanic rituals in South America. Harmine is essential for the brew's effects, since MAOs would otherwise destroy much of the DMT (*N,N*–dimethyltryptamine) before it had a chance to produce effects in the brain.

Potentiation at GABA receptors

A broad class of central nervous system (CNS) depressants reduces anxiety and can induce sleep by potentiating gamma-aminobutyric acid (GABA)—a neurotransmitter that has a calming effect on brain activity. Substances that act in this way include benzodiazepines, barbiturates, and alcohol.

This potentiation mechanism differs from others in that it occurs directly at the receptor. When CNS-depressant molecules attach to sites on GABA receptors, they induce changes in the shape of the receptor that are favorable for stronger interactions with GABA molecules. Hence such drugs strengthen the effects of a given concentration of GABA.

There is a risk of fatal overdose when two different types of CNS depressants work together. This is particularly true for mixtures of alcohol and barbiturates. Both depressants have different bonding sites on GABA receptors, and one drug amplifies the potentiation caused by the other. In this way, doses that would be tolerable for either drug on its own can be fatal in combination.

M. CLOWES

SEE ALSO:
Alcohol • Barbiturates • Benzodiazepines • DMT • Gamma-aminobutyric Acid • MAOs and MAOIs • Phenethylamines • Tryptamines

Poverty and Drugs

Poverty and its consequences have a cyclical relationship to drug and alcohol abuse, for once someone is in the cycle, it is very difficult to break out. Support services for drug users are often uncoordinated and hard to access.

Substance abuse and alcohol abuse are major factors that contribute to a downward economic spiral for some people. Continuing patterns of self-destruction for many adolescents and adults can result in poverty, homelessness, and untreated physical and mental illnesses. These individuals struggle on the margins of society where basic needs may go unmet. Substances offer temporary respite from the reality of a life of poverty and addiction.

Definition of poverty

Definitions of poverty vary; the official measure of poverty used by the U.S. Government Office of Management and Budget Policy defines poverty by using a formula that considers cash income before taxes (excluding capital gains or non-cash benefits such as public housing, Medicaid, and food stamps), and the number of people living in a household. People or families living below established thresholds are considered to be living in poverty. For example, in 2004, the poverty threshold for an individual under 65 was $9,310. The poverty threshold for a family of four was $18,850.

Factors contributing to poverty

Factors contributing to poverty include race and ethnicity, being a single mother, having limited education, and unstable, seasonal, or part-time employment. In 2002, African Americans saw the only significant increase in rates of poverty, with 23.9 percent living in poverty. Single mothers and their children represented 50 percent of all families living in poverty. Of these children, those under six live in poverty at five times the rate of a six-year-old living with both parents. Overall, children represent a disproportionate share of Americans living in poverty, since 35 percent live in poverty but represent only 25.5 percent of the total population. In contrast, the poverty rate for non-Hispanic whites was lower than any racial group, accounting for 45 percent of people living in poverty, though this group represents 68 percent of the total population.

Employment can lift people out of poverty, yet 37.9 percent of people living in poverty are employed. Of these impoverished workers around 11 percent hold full-time jobs, the other 27 percent hold only part-time or seasonal employment. These data reflect the U.S. government's welfare reform from open-ended entitlement under Aid to Families with Dependent Children (AFDC), in which recipients received benefits if they met income and other criteria, with work not being mandatory. Legislation introduced during the Clinton administration—the Personal Responsibility and Work Opportunity Reconciliation Act (PRWORA)—requires those who can work to do so. Under TANF (Temporary Assistance to Needy Families) there are specific time limits on receiving benefits. The work requirement and a strong economy in the 1990s led to a dramatic decrease in welfare rolls.

Relationship between poverty and drug use

Substance abuse is a nationwide problem and is a pervasive and significant problem among welfare recipients. Attempts to determine prevalence rates have been undertaken at both federal and state levels, with federal reports indicating that 10 to 30 percent of people live in poverty and struggle with substance or alcohol abuse. Some states report that as many as 50 percent of welfare clients are affected by substance abuse problems.

Researchers have found evidence of higher drug use among the most economically disadvantaged families. After adjusting for sex, age, race, and education and after matching respondents on community characteristics, substance use was higher in welfare recipients, thus establishing a strong association between poverty and drug use.

Changes in the welfare system are too recent to understand how those changes will affect recipients with substance abuse problems. Substance users on welfare face several barriers to self-sufficiency (defined as earning enough money to live above the poverty level), including lack of job skills, education and vocational skills, lack of prior work history often

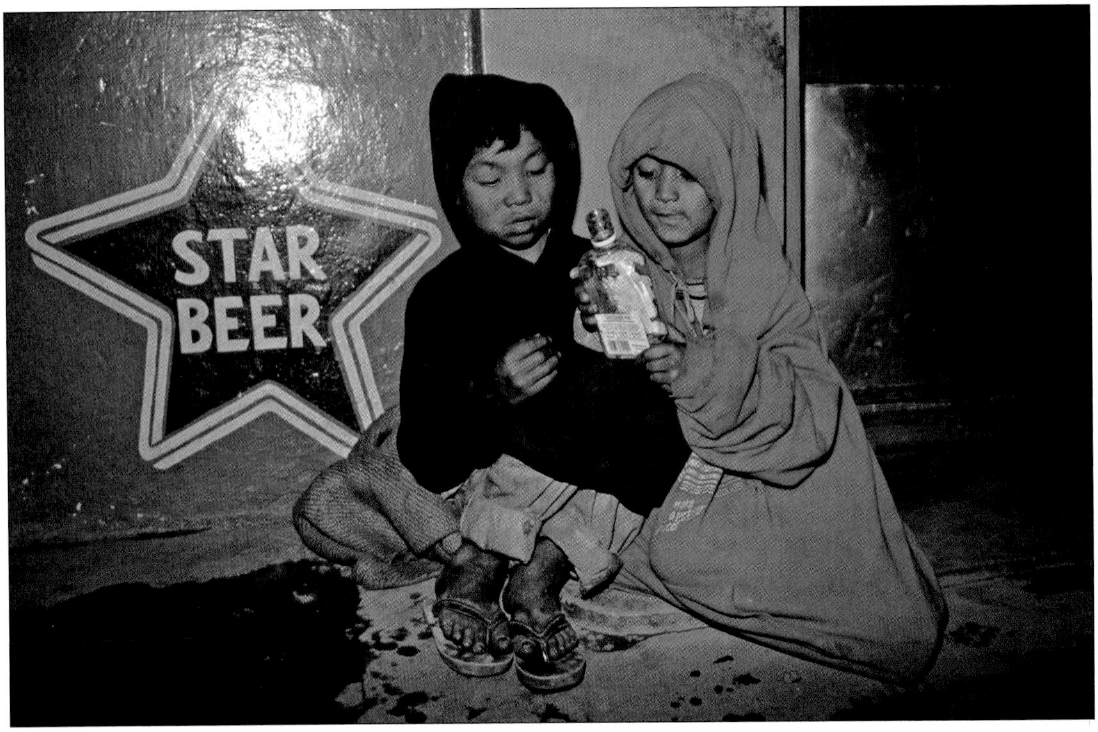

Street children in Nepal drink alcohol they have found while scavenging. Homelessness may lead children to substance use to reduce the pain of their circumstances, adding to their health, social, and welfare problems.

associated with having a criminal record, language problems, reliable transportation, and child care. In addition, the number of those in need of substance abuse treatment far exceeds the number of available treatment slots. Yet substance abuse treatment has been demonstrably effective for welfare recipients preparing for job training and placement. The Center for Substance Abuse Treatment reports a 60 to 76 percent increase in employment among recipients following treatment, and earning power is positively associated with time in treatment. One study found recipients' income six months after treatment to be 33 times higher than before. Among federally funded treatment programs, drug use has been reduced by 50 percent a year after treatment, but effective programs are at a premium.

Substance use and homelessness

It is a widely accepted belief that alcoholism is a major contributor to homelessness. Recent estimates suggest that one-half to three-quarters of homeless adults have coexisting alcohol, drug, and mental disorders. These problems often go unrecognized. Also, homeless adults have higher rates of chronic physical disorders, injuries, and victimization.

Crack cocaine has become a particularly destructive force in the lives of homeless people. This inexpensive drug offers a brief escape from life on the street and may also lead to criminal activity, mismanagement of funds, eviction, and employment- and relationship-related issues that can contribute to homelessness. Its use has also been associated with increased high-risk sexual activities, including prostitution, infrequent condom use, and multiple sex partners, resulting in increased risk of acquiring human immunodeficiency virus (HIV).

Women are estimated to comprise one-third of the homeless population in the United States. The majority of these women have children, and one-third have substance abuse problems. They are usually high school dropouts under 35, of minority race or ethnicity, who have experienced multiple episodes of homelessness. The homeless youth population is estimated to be approximately 300,000 each year, with 2.8 million U.S. young people reporting a runaway experience during the previous year. The majority of runaways come from economically disadvantaged families who are no longer able to support them. Because of their age, homeless young people face a multitude of difficulties with few legal means to earn money. Legal barriers to education include guardianship and residency requirements, locating proper records, and lack of transportation. The result is lost educational and vocational opportunities, and these adolescents may resort to exchanging sex for food, clothing, and shelter. Thus, they are at increased risk of contracting sexually transmitted illnesses.

Many homeless adolescents suffer from severe anxiety and depression, poor health and nutrition, and low self-esteem. These people have been found to have higher rates of substance abuse than those in shelters or living at home. Rates of substance use vary widely depending on age, gender, ethnicity, and current living circumstances. Substance abuse rates are highest among older, male Caucasian youths. Researchers have found a relationship between serious drug and alcohol use and the prevalence of other risky behaviors such as physical victimization and criminal activities. Runaway and homeless young people who abuse drugs are at particular risk for suicide. Other analyses indicate that the length of time a youth spends being homeless is positively associated with risk for the development of an alcohol or substance abuse disorder.

A well-documented connection exists between a young person living in foster care and becoming homeless as an adult. Three in 10 of the nation's homeless adults are former foster children. Factors associated with increased risk for these people becoming homeless adults include out-of-home placement, physical or sexual abuse (or both), parental substance abuse, and residential instability.

Substance abuse treatment

For a variety of reasons, treatment for people who are homeless and suffer from substance abuse problems has proved to be largely ineffective. These individuals present special challenges, including psychological problems, and basic needs for food, shelter, clothing, income, and social support, which make it difficult for service providers to package the services needed. These psychosocial interventions are often ineffective due to high drop-out rates. Research on out-of-treatment homeless drug users reveals multiple treatment failures and profound addiction.

Homeless women and young people

Homeless women with substance or alcohol issues, or both, have many complicated life circumstances and are less likely to receive treatment, particularly specific and targeted interventions, and perceive a lack of support from social service agencies. Women with children face an additional dilemma when making decisions about whether to seek treatment. While they are at risk of losing their children if they continue to abuse drugs, they also risk losing their children if they bring their addiction to the attention of treatment providers. Service providers must work to reduce barriers to treatment as well as improve facilities for women with children.

Homeless adolescents face many challenges and limited service options. Advocates for this population call for increased services, including specialized substance abuse treatment, youth-only shelters, aggressive outreach strategies, improved access, and better coordination of social services. Prevention services, such as educational outreach programs and assistance in locating job training and employment, as well as transitional living programs within child welfare agencies, are needed to better prepare foster children and those in other types of out-of-home placements for the transition to independent living.

Overall barriers to service

Regardless of age or gender, there is disparity in access to medical and substance abuse treatment for people living on the margins of society. Multiple barriers exist whereby people with drug problems must navigate an often confusing and disconnected social service network to meet their needs, including physical and mental health care, substance abuse treatment, child care, transportation, and housing.

J. SCHROEDER

SEE ALSO:
Adolescents and Substance Abuse • Causes of Addiction, Psychological and Social • Crime and Drugs • Prostitution • Social Services • State Agencies • Suicide • Treatment

Pregnancy and Fetal Addiction

Drug use during pregnancy poses distinct risks to a developing baby. Not only can the baby suffer a wide range of cognitive and physical abnormalities, it may also spend the early weeks of its life with symptoms of drug withdrawal.

Everything that a pregnant woman eats, drinks, smokes, or otherwise puts into her body goes into her unborn baby's body, too. As in the mother, every substance has an effect on the baby's brain and body. The difference between the mother and the baby, however, is that the baby's brain and body are still developing. While the mother may be destroying a couple of million used brain cells, the baby may never get the chance to develop them.

Drug use during pregnancy is the single most preventable cause of birth defects, mental retardation, and developmental disorders in the United States today. Despite knowledge of the risks, as many as 1 in 5 pregnant women drink alcohol and, in some areas of the country, nearly 1 in 4 pregnant women smoke cigarettes. Undoubtedly, drug use during pregnancy is a significant public health problem.

Risks for drug users becoming pregnant

The ages of childbearing and the ages of greatest risk for alcohol and other drug abuse are nearly the same (ages 15 to 44). Alcohol and most drugs of abuse affect judgment and decrease inhibitions. Some drugs, for example, cocaine, can actually stimulate sexual desires. These combined effects set the stage for unplanned and unprotected sexual encounters, leading to pregnancy. Women who are addicted to alcohol and other drugs are at an increased risk of being involved in prostitution or using sexual favors to get drugs. They are also at greater risk for contracting sexually transmitted diseases (STDs), including HIV, and for being victims of physical and sexual abuse.

Problems of addiction during pregnancy

Addiction to alcohol and drugs is no different for the pregnant woman than it is for anyone else. A woman will often reduce her drug use once she finds out she is pregnant, but the addictive properties of the drug will usually prevent her from quitting completely without treatment. Addicted pregnant women often suffer from inadequate nutrition, medical problems such as pancreatitis, hepatitis, toxemia, numerous infections, and anemia. All place the unborn baby at increased risk for problems with growth and development.

Prenatal care

Prenatal care is the most effective strategy for intervening in the life of the pregnant addicted woman. Unfortunately, many addicted women do not seek prenatal care until late in the pregnancy, if at all. Pregnant substance users are often suspicious of becoming involved with the health care system for fear that they will lose custody of their children or that they will be identified to the authorities as a drug user.

Some women who do seek prenatal care are never identified as drug users until pregnancy complications develop or until the baby's delivery because health care providers have not asked about drug or alcohol use. Many pregnant users will time visits to clinics around their drug use so as to test negative if blood or urine samples are required. All women receiving prenatal care should be asked about their history of drug and alcohol use, their partner's history, and their family's history. Even if a woman states that she is not currently using any drugs or alcohol, she may relapse into drug use again during the course of the pregnancy; therefore, she should be asked about use at every prenatal visit.

It is in the health interests of both mother and child that a woman should try to stop using drugs during pregnancy. Treatment can take the form of accessing outpatient clinics or therapeutic communities, or pursuing methadone maintenance for opioid addicts. Pregnancy can often be a way to persuade a female drug user into treatment, although many feel that there is a lack of understanding by medical staff about their addiction and social or welfare problems. Psychosocial counseling should ideally be carried out by experienced professionals who can support the pregnant user and encourage her to attend medical appointments.

Effects of various drugs on the unborn baby

Just as different drugs have different effects on the user, drugs have various effects on the unborn baby. Drugs can affect the baby either directly, by destroying tissue and cells, or indirectly, by interfering with the mother's body and its ability to provide the growing baby with blood, oxygen, and adequate nutrition. The severity of these effects is not necessarily dependent on the amount of the drug used or at what point in the pregnancy the drug was used—and not all babies exposed to drugs will experience these effects. However, most pregnant drug abusers use a number of different substances, increasing the risks that the baby will experience harmful effects from those drugs.

Alcohol. Alcohol affects the growth and development of the brain and central nervous system. As a result, babies are at increased risk for problems with their growth in the mother's womb and will be born small for their gestational age. These babies are prone to heart abnormalities and bone (skeletal) malformations, particularly of the head. The terms *fetal alcohol syndrome* (FAS), *alcohol-related birth defects* (ARBD), and *alcohol-related neurodevelopmental disorder* (ARND) have been defined to describe the physical and neurological effects of prenatal alcohol use on the child. The box on page 698 provides more specific information on these effects.

Amphetamines. Also known as "speed," amphetamines speed up the development process but do not allow the baby to grow and the brain to develop normally. The result is a higher rate of miscarriages and stillbirths. Babies born to women who use amphetamines during their pregnancy are usually born prematurely and are small. These babies also tend to have small heads, an indicator of an underdeveloped brain.

Cocaine. The effects of cocaine on the baby are similar to those of amphetamines. For these babies there is a significantly higher rate of miscarriage, stillbirth, and premature births. Additionally, there is a high risk of the placenta separating from the mother's uterus, reducing or cutting off the blood

Drinking and smoking present risks to a developing baby. Research has shown that even low levels of fetal alcohol can cause intellectual difficulties and behavioral problems later. Women who smoke during pregnancy are likely to continue after the birth, further exposing the baby to the harmful effects of tobacco.

FETAL ALCOHOL SYNDROME (FAS)

Fetal alcohol syndrome (FAS), a term coined in 1973, describes a pattern of physical and neurological features associated with children born to mothers who drank alcohol during pregnancy. In 1996 the definition of FAS was refined into five categories of alcohol-related effects. This was necessary because not all children born to women who drank during pregnancy demonstrated all of the signs of FAS, but had some. Conversely, there were children who demonstrated all of the signs of FAS, but the mother's drinking during pregnancy could not be confirmed. In order to help researchers and clinicians speak the same language, the following categories of alcohol-related birth effects were defined:

Category 1: FAS with confirmed maternal alcohol exposure

- Heavy regular or episodic (binge) drinking by mother during pregnancy
- A pattern of facial abnormalities: small head, small eyes, skin folds at corners of eyes, flat midface, short and flat nose, thin upper lip, and no ridge (philtrum) between the nose and the upper lip
- Growth retardation: low birth weight, slow growth or weight gain over time, disproportional weight-to-height ratio
- Central nervous system (CNS) abnormalities such as small head size and abnormal brain structures or neurological symptoms of CNS impairment such as poor motor skills, hearing loss, and poor eye-to-hand coordination.

Category 2: FAS without confirmed maternal alcohol exposure

- The same pattern as Category 1 except mother's drinking during pregnancy is unknown.

Category 3: Partial FAS with confirmed maternal alcohol exposure

- Maternal drinking during pregnancy
- Some facial features described in item 2 above
- And any of the following:
  Growth retardation, as in item 3 above,
  CNS abnormalities, as in item 4 above, or
  behavior or learning problems that cannot otherwise be explained.

Category 4: Alcohol-Related Birth Defects (ARBD)

- Maternal drinking during pregnancy
- One or more birth defects (bone deformities, heart, kidney, vision, or hearing defects).

Category 5: Alcohol-Related Neurodevelopmental Disorder (ARND)

- Maternal drinking during pregnancy
- CNS abnormalities, such as those in Category 1, or
- Behavior or learning problems that cannot otherwise be explained.

supply to the baby. This results in a lack of oxygen to the baby and can result in a stroke or bleeding in the baby's brain, causing permanent brain damage. As with amphetamines, babies born to mothers who used cocaine during their pregnancy are small, and will experience some level of drug withdrawal.

Heroin. Heroin directly affects the chemistry of the brain, both in the mother and the unborn baby. The baby will experience growth retardation in the womb and may be born prematurely. These babies also tend to be very small and have small heads. These babies will experience severe withdrawal symptoms that may require medical detoxification from the drug, similar to an adult who is in withdrawal from heroin.

Marijuana. A mother who smokes marijuana during pregnancy exposes her unborn baby not only to the brain-altering chemicals in the drug but also to oxygen depletion as a result of inhaling the smoke. These babies tend to be born prematurely and are very small. They may experience shakes and tremors, tend to have respiratory problems, and will be prone to infections and colds.

Sedatives. This family of drugs depresses the central nervous system, slowing everything down. The result for the unborn baby is growth retardation in the womb, small size, and very little activity. Because sedative drugs take a long time to be eliminated from the body, withdrawal symptoms may not appear until the baby is one to three weeks old. Until withdrawal begins, the baby will sleep more than other babies and will be hard to wake. The baby will not be very active and will not want to eat as often as it should, resulting in a condition called "failure to thrive," which can lead to the death of the infant.

Tobacco. The primary risk of smoking during pregnancy is the lack of oxygen to the baby caused by the reduction of oxygen in the mother's lungs. This is caused in two ways: first, smoking reduces the ability of the mother's lungs to absorb oxygen and to release carbon dioxide; and second, tobacco smoke contains carbon monoxide, which replaces oxygen in the bloodstream and starves the body of oxygen. This lack of oxygen prevents the baby's brain from developing and functioning properly. It also causes problems in the development of the lungs and circulatory system (heart and blood vessels), leading to respiratory problems and heart defects in the baby. These babies are more prone to die from Sudden Infant Death Syndrome (SIDS) within the first year of life.

Problems during delivery

The most common problem during delivery of the baby for women who use drugs is premature delivery. Because labor is unexpected, women may wait until the labor is very advanced before they go to the hospital, and may deliver the baby before proper medical help is available. Additionally, there is an increased risk of breech presentation, meaning that the baby has not turned in the mother's womb to be delivered in a normal position, head first. In breech presentation, the baby's leg, arm, or buttocks enters the birth canal first, making it difficult for the baby to be delivered without medical help. Without quick and proper medical intervention, the baby is at high risk for birth trauma, such as broken bones, dislocation of joints, or even death. In some drug users the placenta may separate prematurely from the mother's womb or rupture, depriving the baby of oxygen from the mother's bloodstream.

Another common problem, especially among marijuana users, is meconium staining. Meconium is the first bowel movement that a baby has after birth. Meconium staining is caused by the baby eliminating the meconium while still in the mother's womb. When this happens, the meconium may float around in the amniotic fluid and can be aspirated (inhaled) into the baby's lungs at the time of delivery. This is very dangerous and may be fatal.

Postnatal care

Most women and babies are hospitalized for 24 hours after a baby is born, unless there are medical complications. Hospitals do not systematically conduct drug screens on mother or baby, and even if they did, the drugs might not be detectable. The drug-exposed baby usually goes home with the mother, and drug-withdrawal symptoms may not appear for several days. Depending on the severity of the symptoms, the mother may return to the hospital or go to the pediatrician because the child is not feeding properly or is showing symptoms of withdrawal.

Addicted newborns

Normal newborn babies are able to interact with their caregiver and their environment from the time they are born. They respond to faces and voices, they can comfort themselves by drawing their hands to their mouths and sucking, and they can follow the movement of an object with their eyes for short periods. These skills improve as they get older. The amount of time spent crying increases during the first 6 to 8 weeks after birth, then crying time decreases as they get older. Similarly, the length of time they sleep at one time increases as they get older.

Drug-exposed newborns do not interact well with their environment or their caregivers. They may be sensitive to light or noise, will avoid looking at their caregivers, and may become agitated and cry when being held or even touched. They go from sleeping to crying with no intervals between, and they are unable to comfort themselves. They do not have a regular sleep-wake cycle and may sleep for only short periods (1 to 2 hours) at a time. When they are awake, they are crying.

These babies have a lot of feeding difficulties. Some problems are caused by the excessive crying, which causes gas to build up in the baby's stomach, causing pain. For some babies, there is a lack of coordination of the suck and swallow reflex. The baby may suck constantly but is unable to swallow the formula or breast milk. This excessive sucking when not feeding also leads to gas in the stomach, causing pain and crying. Often the mother will think that the baby is hungry because of the constant sucking and will overfeed the baby, leading to frequent vomiting and diarrhea.

These types of problems will continue until the baby is 4 to 6 months of age, making caregiving very difficult and exhausting. These babies do not bond well with their caregivers, and the reverse is also true. When mothers (or caregivers) do not bond with their babies, the baby is at an increased risk for child neglect and abuse.

Managing withdrawal

Symptoms of drug withdrawal in newborns depend on the type of drug, how recently the unborn baby was exposed, and how much was used over time. How long a drug stays within the body depends on the drug and the body's metabolism of the drug. Infants have a slower metabolism rate than do adults, have less blood volume, and lack certain enzymes that break down the substances in their blood; drugs will therefore stay in their bodies for longer periods of time and may not be detectable using standard drug-testing procedures. Because of this, withdrawal symptoms may not occur for 1 to 3 days for drugs such as alcohol, cocaine, and heroin, or as long as 1 to 3 weeks for barbiturates or sedative-type drugs.

Withdrawal symptoms can be categorized according to the body system in which they are manifested. As all drugs affect the central nervous system (CNS), withdrawal also affects the CNS. Common CNS symptoms include agitation, high-pitched crying, stiffness of the legs, arms, neck, and back, tremors or jitteriness, overactive reflexes, and small seizures or sudden jerks of legs or arms. The withdrawal symptoms related to the autonomic nervous system (the system that regulates involuntary actions in the body) include sweating, sneezing, yawning, rapid breathing rate, and poor body temperature regulation. Vomiting, diarrhea, lack of coordination of sucking and swallowing when feeding, excessive sucking, excessive feeding, and stomach and intestinal gas are all withdrawal symptoms related to the gastrointestinal system.

Treatment of withdrawal depends on the severity of the symptoms. Medical professionals who are familiar with drug withdrawal in infants use a monitoring system in which they rate the severity of symptoms at regular intervals. If the symptoms persist and the infant fails to feed properly, medical intervention is required. Two medications commonly used to detoxify babies are tincture of opium and phenobarbital. For opiate-type drugs, such as heroin, tincture of opium is given in very small quantities every four hours for 2 to 3 weeks, gradually reducing the amount administered over time. For alcohol, cocaine, and sedative-type drugs, phenobarbital is administered every 8 hours in small doses, gradually decreasing the dose over 1 to 2 weeks. Even with medical detoxification, the symptoms of withdrawal can last 4 to 6 months.

Management of withdrawal symptoms requires recognition of the baby's needs. Because the baby reacts negatively to stimulation (light, noise, touch), the child needs to be kept in a dark, quiet environment. Sometimes white noise (soft music or the hum of an electric motor, or even a vacuum cleaner running in another room) can soothe the baby, as he or she was accustomed to muffled noises while in the womb. Likewise, the baby in the womb is accustomed to the movement of the mother, so slow rocking, swinging in an infant swing, or car rides can be comforting to the baby experiencing withdrawal. The stiffness of a baby's arms and back prevent a baby from being able to pull its arms to its face to suck on its fists, making the baby unable to comfort itself. One comforting measure is to swaddle the baby by wrapping a blanket tightly around its body, with its arms wrapped against the body.

Problems with vomiting and diarrhea can be reduced by feeding the symptomatic baby frequent feedings of small amounts, burping often. Use of a pacifier is recommended to comfort the baby and to alleviate the gas built up by excessive sucking. The caregiver should be prepared to deal with the baby's short sleep cycles, but should try to get the baby to sleep at regular intervals and to extend those intervals as normal babies do. Finally, the caregiver needs to recognize when she or he is losing

Children born with fetal alcohol syndrome suffer brain damage, growth problems, and have distinct facial characteristics. With a caring and supportive environment, many of the difficulties they face can be overcome.

patience with the baby, and should have another adult available to lend a hand or provide breaks from caregiving responsibilities.

Long-term outlook for addicted babies

Research continues to be done to determine the long-term effects of prenatal exposure to alcohol and other drugs. Drug-exposed babies who experienced muscle stiffness as a symptom of withdrawal may have some delays in the development of fine and gross motor skills (reaching, grasping, rolling over, sitting on their own), but they usually catch up to normal children by 6 months of age. The same is true for their physical growth, particularly babies who are born prematurely. Most premature babies will remain small during the first year, but tend to grow normally after that. Language skills should develop normally, unless there is severe mental impairment or hearing loss.

Long-term negative effects of prenatal drug exposure are manifested mainly in the child's intellectual functioning and behavior. There is a higher rate of mental retardation (IQ less than 70) in children prenatally exposed to drugs. The majority of these children, however, are not mentally retarded, but may experience other learning problems.

Current research has shown that brain structures and brain functioning in children prenatally exposed to cocaine and methamphetamines are different from those of normal children. These affected brain structures are those that enable children to control their impulses and to sustain attention to tasks. These changes in the brain may be the reason that many drug-exposed children are diagnosed with attention deficit hyperactivity disorder (ADHD) and conduct disorder.

Finally, children who were prenatally exposed to drugs, including tobacco, are at greater risk of developing substance use disorders as they grow older. They are more likely to experiment with substances of abuse at earlier ages, and to become addicted. This behavior may produce the next generation of drug-exposed babies.

M. D. REYNOLDS

SEE ALSO:
Children • Social Services • Treatment • Withdrawal • Women and Drugs

Prescription Drugs

Almost everyone has taken a prescription drug at some point in his or her life. While millions take these drugs safely, some drugs are potentially addictive. Misuse can lead to intentional or unintentional dependence.

Prescription drugs come in many forms and can successfully help people cope with ailments ranging from severe pain to insomnia to attention deficit disorder (ADD). While prescription drugs can increase the quality of life for many people if taken responsibly, if misused or abused they can also pose a very serious health problem. Consequences of misuse and abuse include overdose, addiction, and even death. The misuse of prescription drugs has always caused concern, but the rapid increase in the rate of prescription abuse by young people has alarmed practitioners, policy makers, and the general public alike. What are the problems, and how alarmed should we be?

Many factors must be considered when trying to understand prescription drug misuse and abuse. The belief that a pill exists for every illness or problem is pervasive in modern society. Reliance on prescription drugs for a wide range of physical and psychological ailments easily creates an opportunity for misuse and abuse among users. There are unintentional and intentional pathways to prescription drug misuse and abuse. Many people with legitimate prescriptions may begin using their medications properly. Yet prolonged self-medicating behaviors may lead to unintentional physical dependence. In 2003 Rush Limbaugh, the radio personality, admitted that he had developed an unintentional dependence on prescription painkillers. When he announced to the public that he was addicted, he claimed his addiction arose out of a legitimate prescription given for serious back pain. As his tolerance grew, he began to self-medicate by increasing his dosage of OxyContin and other drugs and, as a result, became addicted. The intentional abuse of painkillers with the objective of getting high is a serious problem among the young. Understanding the pathways into prescription drug abuse, how it varies by age, race, and gender, and the various negative consequences are key to fully grasping the effects of prescription drug abuse. It is also an important factor in creating effective preventive, educational, and treatment programs.

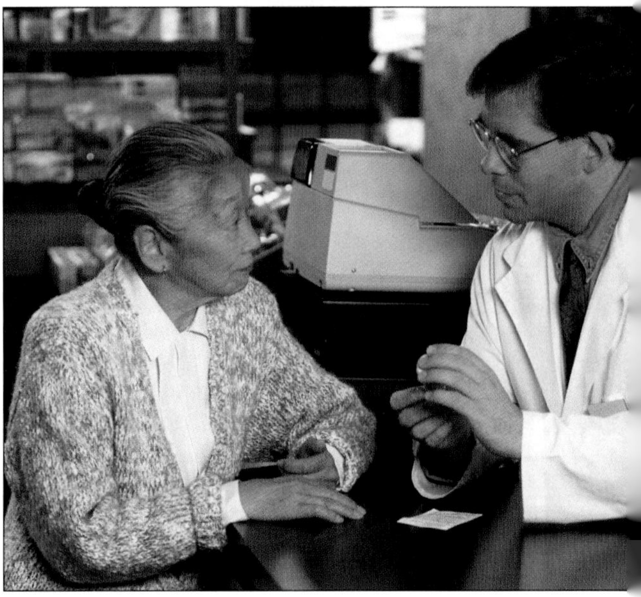

Advice on side effects and the proper use of drugs is available from the pharmacist. The elderly are often unaware of the potentially addictive effects of some prescription drugs.

Prescription drugs of abuse

There are a number of categories of substances that fall under the category of prescription drugs. The most abused are stimulants, depressants, and painkillers.

Stimulants. Stimulants, such as amphetamines, are prescribed for numerous conditions, including depression, ADD, obesity, and narcolepsy. Stimulants can increase alertness, attention, and energy. Common prescription names include Ritalin, Adderall, and Dexedrine. Prolonged use of these medications can develop a tolerance to the drug and tolerance can lead to taking higher doses. This pattern of prescription use can lead to addiction.

Depressants. Central nervous system depressants are commonly used to treat sleep disorders, tension, panic attacks, and anxiety. Two categories of depressants are barbiturates and benzodiazepines. These types of medicines slow brain activity, resulting in a calming effect for the user. Though both types are depressants, drugs considered tranquilizers are mainly of the benzodiazepine family, and drugs considered sedatives are mostly barbiturate preparations. Common prescription names include Xanax and Valium. Long-term consequences are similar to those of stimulants, in that a person is at risk for developing a tolerance, which then can lead to addiction.

Painkillers. The pain relievers most at risk of abuse belong to the narcotic analgesic family of drugs derived from opium poppies. Opioid drugs elevate dopamine levels in the brain and trigger feelings of pleasure. Drugs derived from opioids are used to relieve moderate-to-severe chronic pain. Common brand names include OxyContin, Vicodin, Percocet, Darvon, and Demerol. Users of narcotic analgesics can develop a tolerance over a prolonged period of use. This tolerance may lead to higher dosage, which in turn may lead to addiction. Opioid drugs have the ability to elevate dopamine levels in the brain, but prolonged use or misuse has the potential to permanently change the brain in fundamental ways. Among the various painkillers, OxyContin (also called "hillbilly heroin" owing to its initial emergence as a serious health problem within rural areas across the United States) has been receiving greater attention due to dramatic increases in abuse.

Size of the problem

Uncovering and learning what types of prescription drugs are being abused and misused is very difficult. Prescription drug abuse is not always easy to detect. For example, it may not be obvious that someone is physically dependent until he or she runs out of medication and begins to experience withdrawal symptoms. However, national surveys and various research studies focusing on prescription drug abuse have elucidated the extent of this type of substance abuse within the United States. In general, the majority of research studies reveal that the population most likely to abuse prescription drugs includes the elderly, whites, females, and, increasingly, adolescents and young adults.

According to the 2003 National Survey of Drug Use and Health (NSDUH) report, roughly 6.3 million (2.7 percent) of people aged 12 or older were current users of prescription drugs for nonmedical reasons. Of this group of users, 4.7 million reported using painkillers, 1.8 million reported using tranquilizers, 1.2 million reported using stimulants, and 0.3 million reported using sedatives.

More specifically, regarding nonmedical use of painkillers, lifetime use among respondents aged 12 and older significantly increased, from 29.6 million in 2002 to 31.2 million in 2003. Vicodin, Lortab, and Lorcet, as a group, had the largest increase in use (12.1 million to 15.7 million), followed by Percocet, Percodan, and Tylox (from 9.7 million to 10.8 million), hydrocodone (from 4.5 million to 5.7 million), OxyContin (from 1.9 million to 2.8 million), methadone (from 0.9 million to 1.2 million), and Tramadol, an opioidlike analgesic (from 52,000 to 186,000).

NSDUH findings for 2003 reveal important age differences in prescription drug abuse. For example, among respondents aged 12 to 17 who reported past-month illicit drug use (11.2 percent), 4.0 percent

Self-reported use of prescription drugs for nonmedical reasons (age 12 and above).

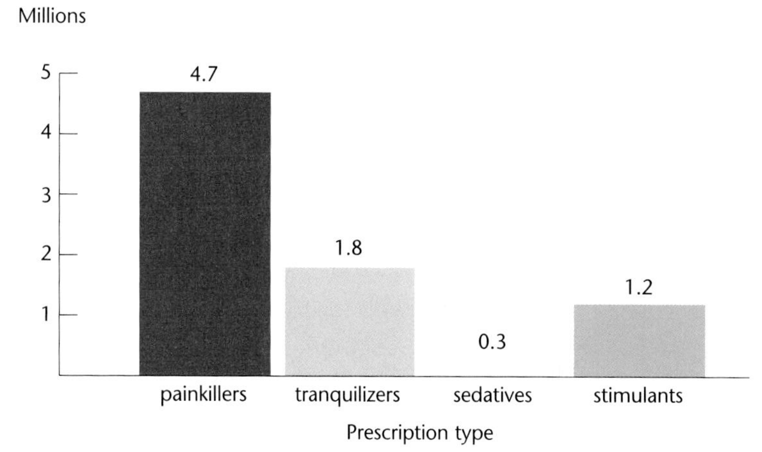

Source: National Survey on Drug Use and Health, 2003

reported using prescription drugs for nonmedical reasons, while 7.9 percent reported monthly marijuana use. The highest rate of general illicit drug use was that of young adults aged 18 to 25 (20.3 percent). Nonmedical use of prescription drugs was reported by 6 percent of young adults and, similar to the younger age group, this type of drug use was second only to marijuana (17 percent). Among the 5.6 percent of adults aged 26 or older who reported current illicit drug use, 1.9 percent reported prescription drug use, while 4.0 percent reported marijuana use. Nonmedical use of prescription drugs did not significantly change from the past year for young people aged 12 to 17 or those aged 26 and above; however, past-month use of painkillers increased for young adults (18 to 25 years old) from 4.1 percent in 2002 to 4.7 percent in 2003.

The abuse of painkillers is an important topic to address. According to the NSDUH, painkillers had the highest number of new users in 2002, with 2.5 million new users versus tranquilizers with 1.2 million, stimulants with 761,000, and sedatives with 225,000 new users. Painkillers are thus considered a growing source of potential abuse.

Other than age, 2003 NSDUH findings do not reveal many other significant demographic differences. Although other research studies have revealed that females are more likely than males to abuse prescription drugs, NSDUH finds no gender differences in the rate of any nonmedical prescription use (2.7 percent for males against 2.6 percent for females). However, there are other equally important national surveys to compliment those conducted by the NSDUH. Another commonly cited resource is the Drug Abuse Warning Network (DAWN).

DAWN collects information on drug-related hospital emergency room episodes. DAWN defines a drug episode as an emergency room visit related to the use of an illegal drug (or combination of drugs), or the nonmedical use of legal drugs (specifically for patients aged 6 to 97 years old). A drug mention is defined as the mention of a substance (up to four) during an emergency room episode. In terms of nonmedical use of legal drugs, DAWN records emergency room episodes that involve the intentional abuse of prescribed or legally obtained pharmaceuticals. However, these numbers do not account for accidental overdoses. Recent findings have revealed important implications in the use of painkillers in relation to emergency room episodes.

Amphetamine abuse significantly increased in emergency room visits from 2001 to 2002 (18,555 to 21,644). Benzodiazepines represented 9 percent of overall emergency room mentions (105,752) and did not change significantly from 2001 to 2002.

DAWN has shown a long-term increase in opioid mentions since 1995, being driven largely by oxycodone preparations (for example, OxyContin) and hydrocodone (Vicodin). However, these drugs are not always reported alone. Many of the various prescription drugs discussed are also reported in combination with other drugs or medications. For example, three-quarters of emergency room visits that involved the mention of oxycodone and hydrocodone also mentioned other drugs.

From 1995 to 2002 the mentions of hydrocodone (Vicodin) increased 160 percent, mentions of oxycodone combinations (OxyContin) increased 560 percent, and mentions of unspecified nar-

Long-term trend in emergency room mentions of hydrocodone and oxycodone.

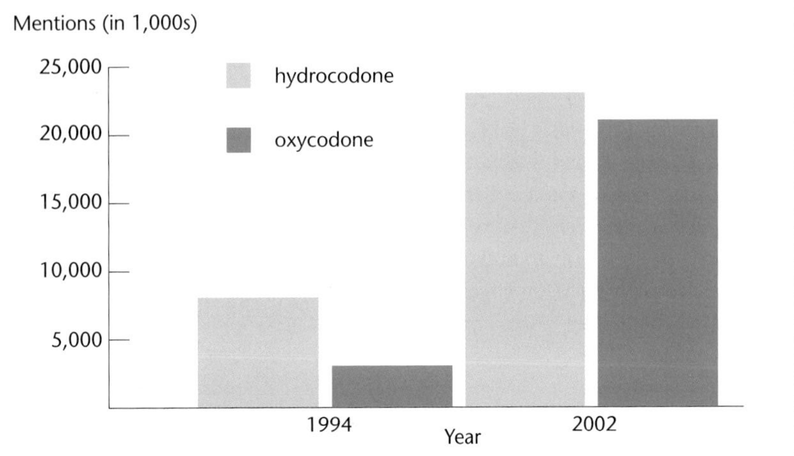

Source: Drug Abuse Warning Network, 2003

cotic analgesics increased 341 percent. These findings have alarmed both medical practitioners and law-enforcement officials alike.

There have been many reports in the media concerning the abuse and misuse of oxycodone and, in some respects, this attention is warranted. According to DAWN findings, hydrocodone mentions used to be twice as high as oxycodone; however, this gap has shrunk significantly since the 1990s, with the rate of oxycodone dramatically increasing. For example, there were only 4,000 mentions of oxycodone in 1994; in 2002 there were 22,000, an increase of 450 percent. In 1994 there were 9,300 mentions of hydrocodone, and in 2002 there were 25,000, a 170 percent increase. However, attention should not be completely focused on oxycodone abuse, because hydrocodone remains the more popular painkiller drug of choice, and overall depressants are the most commonly abused prescription drug.

In terms of demographic comparisons focusing on prescription drug use alone, DAWN findings are similar to NSDUH findings in that no racial or ethnic differences are discussed. According to DAWN 2003 findings, the only mention in terms of significant gender differences refers to a higher rate of amphetamine episodes in males than females (10 versus 7). There were no other significant gender differences in emergency room episodes.

Drugs and the elderly

An important and underexamined population that is extremely vulnerable to prescription drug abuse is the elderly. Although reports on nonmedical prescription drug use among young people have increased steadily since the 1990s, the population most likely to misuse prescription drugs is the elderly. The elderly (aged 65 and above) consume one-third of all prescription drugs, although they represent only 13 percent of the population. National surveys may not detect the amount of prescription drug abuse among this population is because the elderly are difficult to monitor. Some refer to prescription drug abuse among the elderly as an invisible epidemic because the phenomenon is largely undiagnosed and undertreated. This is becoming an increasing concern because adults aged 65 and older are the fastest-growing sector of the American population.

DOCTOR SHOPPING

Doctor shopping involves a person feigning an illness or pain to obtain a prescription. A person feigning an illness will visit as many doctors as possible to get numerous prescriptions and build up a large supply of a drug. If these prescriptions do not go through insurance companies, doctor shopping is very difficult to detect. Many doctors may not be aware that they are one of many writing a pain reliever prescription for the same person.

Common risk factors for prescription abuse among the elderly include social isolation, chronic physical illness, being female, having a history of psychiatric hospitalization, and past alcohol abuse. Benzodiazepines and opiates are the most commonly abused prescription drugs among the elderly. Prescription drug abuse causes unique and serious complications for the elderly. As a result of the fragile medical conditions of most elderly populations, abuse of prescription medications increases the likelihood of serious negative health consequences and, in turn, emergency room visits.

Prevention and treatment

There are many components involved in preventing prescription drug abuse. These components include monitoring the medical community, educating the public and prescription drug users, adequately monitoring prescription use, and the early detection of misuse.

From the perspective of education and detection, it is the primary health care physicians, pharmacists, and nurse practitioners who become the first line of defense in preventing prescription drug abuse. General practitioners should critically evaluate the need to prescribe strong medication. There are many people suffering from severe or chronic pain who legitimately need narcotic pain relievers; however, there is still a large population of people who may not need them. Once a prescription is written, general practitioners and nurse practitioners should closely monitor their patients' use. Pharmacists also have the opportunity to advise users on how to use the medication appropriately. They also have the ability to detect prescription fraud by being watchful for altered or false prescription forms.

However, most prevention techniques may fail when the doctor is intentionally writing unnecessary prescriptions for nonexistent medical problems. There are many doctors who are misled by dishonest patients who are "doctor shopping", and there are other doctors who sell prescriptions for money. Prescription drug abuse is difficult to enforce because a large proportion of prescription abusers are getting their drugs legitimately through a doctor's prescription. A key prevention technique entails ensuring that doctors are writing prescriptions for patients who rightly deserve them.

Another important component of prevention is raising public awareness of the dangers of misusing and abusing prescription drugs. In 2001 the National Institute for Drug Abuse (NIDA) and the Federal Drug Administration (FDA) joined forces to create a new initiative to educate the public about prescription drug abuse, specifically abuse of oxycodone. Educational programs aimed at the public are extremely important as research reveals that people from all walks of life are susceptible to abuse.

For those who are already abusing prescription drugs, there are various types of treatment options available today. Treatment may vary depending on the type of prescription drug that is being abused, but two common treatment techniques include behavioral and pharmacological treatment. The first step in treatment is usually detoxification, ridding the body of the drug and managing any withdrawal symptoms.

Behavioral treatments educate abusers about how to function without the drug, how to manage cravings, and how to avoid or deal with relapse. Behavioral treatments may include group, family, or individual counseling. Pharmacological treatments, on the other hand, treat addiction with medications. These medications can decrease the physical signs of withdrawal and counteract the effects of the drug on the brain. There are no medications that treat stimulant addiction, so behavioral treatment is used. Owing to the potentially serious negative consequences of detoxification, treatment for depressant addiction should always begin with closely supervised detoxification. Successful detoxification is usually followed by behavioral treatments, such as cognitive behavior therapy or counseling. Opioid or painkiller addiction can be treated with various types of medications, depending on the patient. Medications include methadone and naltrexone. The FDA added another drug, buprenorphine, to the list of treatment medications for opioid addiction in 2002.

For the elderly, behavioral treatment and counseling are two of the most important ways of treating prescription drug abuse. One of the risk factors for prescription abuse among this population is social isolation. Important elements of treatment for this vulnerable population include the creation of a network of friends and family who will visit on a regular basis and increasing the opportunity to socialize with peers who are healthy. Physical withdrawal for the elderly is obviously a complex treatment conducted on a case-by-case basis, considering the myriad health problems faced by this group.

Final note

Prescription drug abuse is an important issue to address across many different types of populations. Gender is obviously a complex yet important factor in understanding prescription drug abuse and will require more critical attention and analysis. Although risk factors that lead different populations to abuse prescription drugs may vary, an important line of defense for the general public—for both those who intentionally and unintentionally abuse—is the primary physician. Not only does the general public need increased awareness and education about the dangers of prescription drug abuse, but so do doctors.

In addition, abuse of oxycodone receives a huge amount of attention from the media, government, and medical practitioners. Oxycodone abuse has been increasing and is a legitimate problem that needs to be addressed; however, caution should be taken in not abandoning attention toward the many other prescription drugs that are also being abused at higher rates.

E. J. FARLEY, D. J. O'CONNELL

SEE ALSO:
Adolescents and Substance Abuse • Drug Use, Life Patterns • Elderly • Multiple Addiction • Pharmacy Drugs • Women and Drugs

Prevention

Some young people present a greater risk for drug addiction than others. However, a combination of preventive measures and legal controls can have a significant impact in reducing levels of drug use in teenagers and young adults.

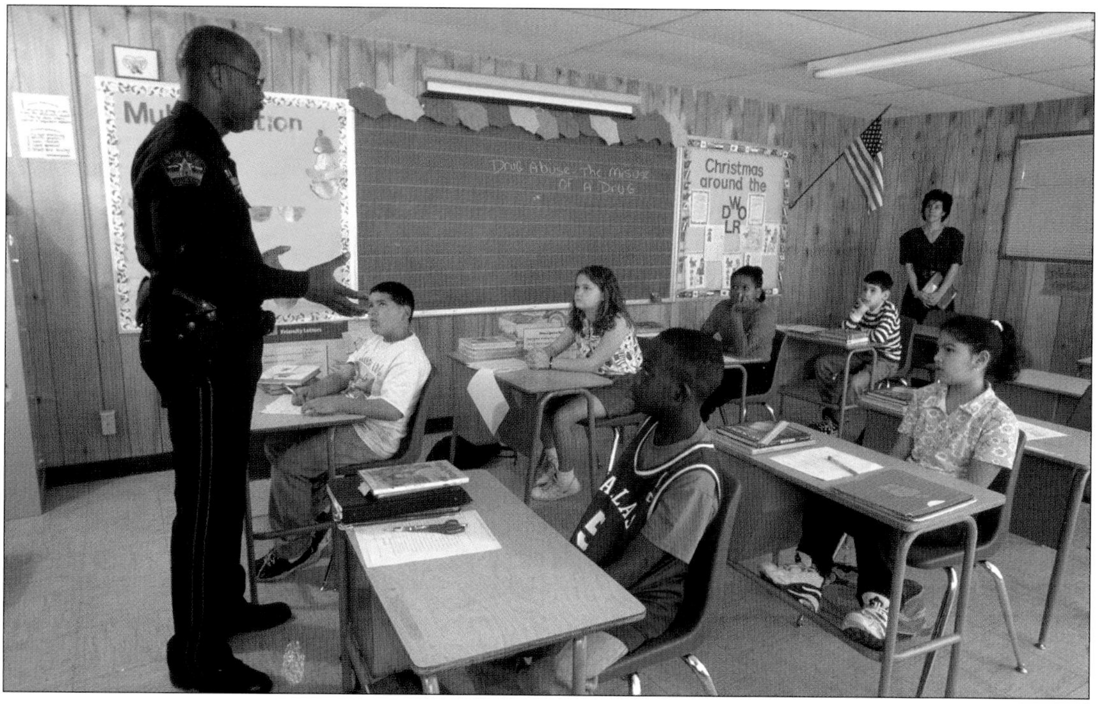

Teaching children and young adults about the dangers of drugs is an essential component of the curriculum in most schools. While this approach does have an effect, research has shown that the message that drugs are harmful must be reinforced every few years if its impact is not to diminish.

Work in prevention is designed to stop substance use problems before they begin. When applied to young people, the goal of prevention is to sustain their abstinence from alcohol and other drugs. For adults, the goal can be safe or moderate use, as is the case with alcohol; restricted medical use, as with prescription drugs; or abstinence, as with illicit drugs. The field of public health commonly refers to prevention at this level as primary prevention.

Primary prevention is usually differentiated from intervention, or secondary prevention, which is focused on early detection and reduction of substance use problems that have already begun. The goal is to prevent further use. In turn, tertiary prevention focuses on preventing any further progression of alcohol and other drug problems and reducing problems associated with established patterns of substance use or addiction. When used alone, the term *prevention* refers to primary prevention, usually with children and teenagers in mind.

A fundamental decision is whether to target high-risk individuals whose characteristics are predictive of future substance use problems or to apply broad-based strategies that will reduce substance use by the general population. A mix of both is needed, but population-level approaches should predominate. High-risk individuals are more likely to experience problems due to substance use, but they constitute a relatively small percentage of the population. Those at lower risk are less likely to experience problems, but given their far greater numbers, they will usually generate more cases than do the high-risk individuals.

Risk and protective factors

Developing an effective prevention program first requires an understanding of the multiple factors that contribute to patterns of substance use. Prevention experts often distinguish between risk factors, which make substance use more likely, and protective factors, which inhibit substance use.

Risk and protective factors can be classified according to the social ecological level at which they operate: individual, interpersonal, institution, community, or society. Prevention programs seek to reduce the influence of risk factors while augmenting the influence of protective factors.

Many risk and protective factors operate at the individual level. Key risk categories include genetic predisposition; personality traits, including impulsivity, need for stimulation, rebelliousness, and emotional stability; behavioral problems, including aggression and other high-risk behaviors; learning disabilities; poor problem-solving skills; weak social skills; and low self-esteem.

There are other individual-level factors more directly tied to substance use. Teenagers are less likely to use alcohol, tobacco, and other drugs when they know basic facts about their serious negative consequences, especially short-term effects; believe that substance use would jeopardize their personal health and safety; and perceive substance use as being inconsistent with their own values or self-image. Young people who know how to turn down peers who encourage them to experiment with substance use are also at less risk.

At the interpersonal level can be found family and peer group factors. Key protective factors include strong and nurturing family bonds, coupled with parental involvement in their children's lives, clear rules of conduct that are consistently enforced, and parental monitoring of children's activities and their peers. In contrast, a disorganized home environment greatly increases risk, especially when one or both parents are substance abusers, mentally ill, or physically or verbally abusive.

Association with peers engaging in deviant behavior, especially substance use, greatly increases risk. Recent research also has underscored the perception of broader social norms as a critical factor. Investigators have repeatedly shown that many teenagers tend to overestimate how many of their peers use alcohol, tobacco, or other drugs. Such misperceptions are associated with greater substance use.

At the institutional level, a key protective factor for young people includes a strong bond with school, which promotes identification with teachers and contributes to academic success. Such bonds are greater when the school has an orderly and safe environment and when teachers communicate high expectations and provide emotional support. Schools that fail to enforce rules related to substance use put students at greater risk. Teenagers with strong ties to religious organizations are also less likely to engage in substance use.

Communities present greater risk when they are economically disadvantaged. Other negative factors include high crime rates, a high density of alcohol outlets, an active drug trade, and gang activity. Community disorganization and a large number of transient residents also increases risk, while greater social capital—formed by a rich mix of neighborhood institutions and community-sponsored activities—provides a higher level of protection.

Protective communities make available after-school programs for young people. These programs offer opportunities for teenagers to work with adult mentors, receive academic tutoring, and develop protective knowledge, attitudes, and skills, while also providing a structured environment during after-school hours, a time of especially high risk for substance use when parents work and children are left unsupervised.

Broad societal factors are also important to consider, including cultural norms, economic conditions, and public policy. Media influences are especially noteworthy. Advertising for alcohol, tobacco, and prescription drugs normalizes substance use, and even abuse in the case of alcohol. Entertainment films and television programs reinforce this message by persistently depicting illegal or abusive substance use without portraying the negative consequences of this behavior.

Prevention programs

Substance use prevention programs can be broadly conceived as attempting to increase the strength and impact of protective factors while decreasing the strength and impact of risk factors. Determining which factors are the most critical and how best to address them has been the subject of intensive study since the 1970s.

The years following the 1970s have seen a marked change in the direction of substance use prevention. Early school-based health education programs focused on providing young people with knowledge about positive and negative health behaviors. Educators believed that this knowledge, combined with students' self-interest, would lead to healthy decisions to avoid substance use. Research eventually made clear that this approach, when used alone, is of marginal value.

Another early approach was affective (or emotional) education, which was based on studies showing a relationship between initiation of substance use and self-esteem, attitudes, and personal values. These programs focused on activities designed to promote a positive self-image, interpersonal skills, and improved decision making by clarifying personal values and analyzing the consequences of substance use in light of those values. Research on this approach generated disappointing results.

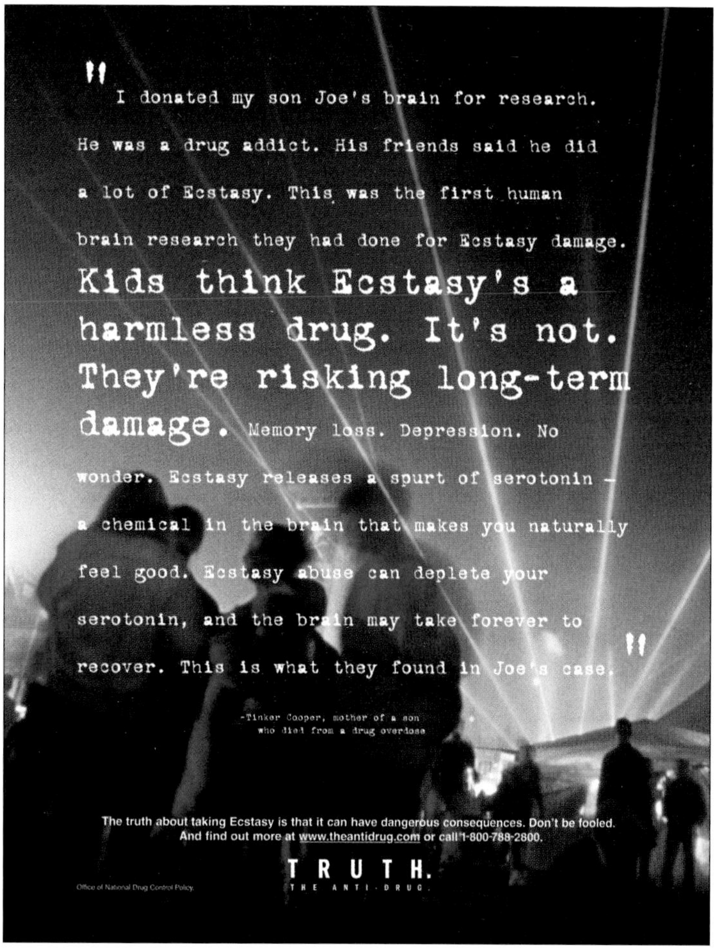

Prevention through advertising campaigns often focuses on reversing misconceptions of the effects of drugs and the level of use by young people. Scare tactics can have a negative effect if they exaggerate what teenagers experience in their own environment, but concentrating on actual facts in a consistent manner can get the message across.

Attention then turned to the social pressures that prompt teenagers to use alcohol, tobacco, and other drugs. This next generation of programs focused on social-skills training so that students could recognize and successfully resist both overt and covert pressure to engage in substance use, especially peer pressure. To motivate students to apply these skills, these programs also included information on the immediate, rather than long-term, consequences of substance use and corrected students' misperceptions of peer substance use norms. Such programs often culminated in students making a public commitment to apply their new skills outside the classroom and to remain substance-free. Selected programs targeting preteens and young adolescents have produced short-term success in reducing cigarette and marijuana use but appear to have been less successful in reducing alcohol use. Without refresher programs in later years, the positive effects of these education programs have proved to be short-lived, often lasting only one or two years.

Over time, prevention experts began to realize that educational programs would continue to have limited effect if they failed to take environmental context into account. In retrospect, it was unwarranted to expect teenagers to say "no" to substance use if their environment continued to say "yes." It is not enough to rescue individual teenagers from the dysfunctional environments in which they are growing up. Also needed are efforts to diminish risk factors and enhance protective factors in the environment.

Environmental management

Environmental management is a term used to describe a wide range of prevention strategies that focus on changing the physical, social, economic, and legal environment in which young people make decisions about substance use. One of the clearest lessons from the field of public health is the value of environmental change in reducing mortality and morbidity due to high-risk behavior, including substance use. The principal vehicle for creating environmental change is policy development and stricter enforcement at the institutional, community, and societal levels.

Consider the case of youth alcohol use. The National Institute on Alcohol Abuse and Alcoholism (NIAAA), a U.S. federal agency that funds alcohol research, issued a report in 2002 with evidence-based recommendations on how to curb heavy drinking and its consequences among college and university students. All five recommendations were examples of environmental management:

Increased enforcement of minimum legal drinking-age laws. Laws to increase the minimum legal drinking age have been a major success in the United States, with substantial decreases reported in alcohol consumption and alcohol-related traffic accidents. This is the case even though enforcement of the age restriction laws has been patchy. More important, studies show that increased enforcement can substantially reduce sales to minors. By extension, NIAAA urged college and community officials to apply a variety of measures to prevent underage drinking, including, among others, cracking down on false age identification (fake IDs), eliminating home delivery of alcohol, and keg registration.

Implementation and enforcement of other laws to reduce alcohol-impaired driving. The best available estimate is that nearly 80 percent of alcohol-related fatalities among U.S. college students are the result of traffic accidents. In response, NIAAA stated that campus and community officials should call for state laws that will lower the legal limit for adult drivers to 0.08 percent BAC (blood alcohol concentration), set legal BAC limits for drivers under age 21 at 0.02 percent BAC or lower, and permit administrative license revocation after DUI (driving under the influence) arrests. NIAAA also recommended greater enforcement of existing laws, including the use of sobriety checkpoints and targeted patrols.

Restrictions on alcohol retail outlet density. The density of alcohol outlets is related to alcohol consumption and alcohol-related problems, including violence, other crime, and health problems. NIAAA noted in its report that restrictive local alcohol control policies and local zoning and land-use planning ordinances have been shown to reduce alcohol outlet density and consumption.

Increased prices and excise taxes on alcoholic beverages. The effect of price on alcohol consumption is well documented. Studies have shown that when the price of alcohol is increased many alcohol-related problems, including fatal traffic accidents, go down. Price variations especially affect young people, even

Enforcement of measures to control underage drinking or drug use is an effective strategy in reducing consumption. If students know that they will be prosecuted for trying to buy alcohol under age or for drunk-driving offenses, they will be less likely to take risks that will lead to arrest.

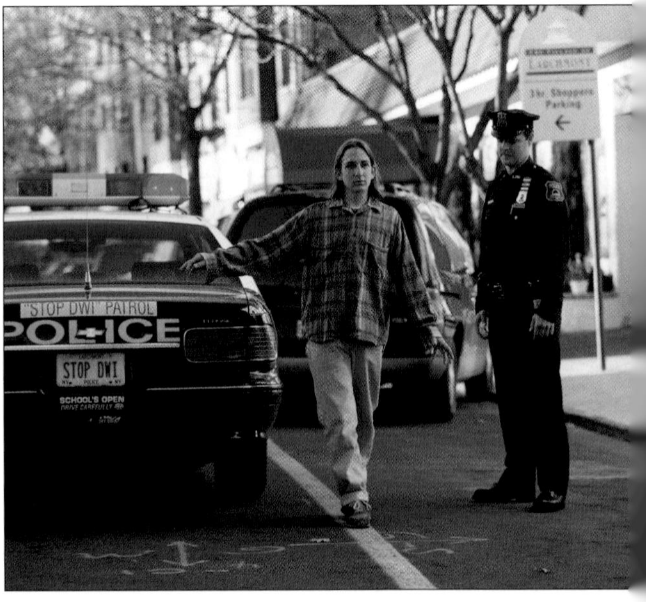

heavy drinkers. Price increases can come about by raising alcohol excise taxes. Another tactic is to work out cooperative agreements with local merchants to institute minimum pricing or to restrict or eliminate low-price drink specials.

Responsible beverage service (RBS) policies. RBS involves several policies to reduce alcohol sales to minors and intoxicated patrons at bars and restaurants, including checking for false age identification, serving alcohol in smaller standard sizes, limiting the number of servings per alcohol sale, restricting sales of pitchers, promoting alcohol-free drinks and food, eliminating last-call announcements, and cutting off sales to patrons who might otherwise become intoxicated. Studies suggest that such policies—reinforced by training for both managers and staff and by compliance monitoring—can reduce inappropriate alcohol sales significantly.

Environmental management can be applied to address other risk and protective factors, including efforts to offer and promote social, recreational, extracurricular, and public service options that do not include substance use and to create an environment that supports health-promoting norms. On campus, examples of specific ideas include providing greater financial support to student clubs and organizations that are substance free, expanding hours of operation for the student center, bolstering academic standards, and increasing faculty-student contact through revised advisory programs.

Prevention planning

A prerequisite to a successful program is a systematic planning process. Key steps include: a thorough analysis of the problem, including an examination of the physical, social, economic, and legal environment that drives substance use; outcome-driven strategic planning that outlines goals and objectives, specific activities designed to achieve those objectives, and the resources and infrastructure needed to support each activity; and a process and outcome data collection plan for evaluating the outlined program. Community mobilization involving coalitions of civic, religious, and government officials is now widely recognized as a primary means of organizing and implementing effective prevention.

In the United States, for example, the Community Prevention Trial (CPT) was implemented for five years in three small towns in California and South Carolina, with three additional communities serving as matched control sites. Community coalitions pushed for several environmental change strategies: responsible beverage service (RBS), zoning restrictions to reduce alcohol-outlet density, stricter enforcement of underage drinking laws to reduce youth access, and enhanced anti–drunk-driving enforcement, which included monthly sobriety checkpoints and use of passive alcohol sensors. Results included reduced alcohol sales to minors; a 6 percent decline in self-reported alcohol consumption; a 51 percent decline in self-reported driving after drinking; a 6 percent drop in single-vehicle nighttime traffic accidents (a proxy for alcohol-impaired driving); fewer drivers with BACs of 0.05 or higher; and a 43 percent decline in emergency room–reported assault injuries.

For Communities Mobilizing for Change (CMCA), part-time local organizers in seven small communities in Minnesota and Wisconsin worked with citizen groups in each community to identify and implement a variety of formal and informal policy initiatives that would make it more difficult for young people to obtain alcohol from both social and commercial sources. The organizers led their group through a multistage development process: conducting a needs assessment; forming a core leadership group; developing a strategic plan; building community awareness and support; implementing the action plan; institutionalizing the campaign; and evaluating campaign activities and outcomes. In CMCA communities, alcohol retailers increased age-identification checks and reduced sales to minors, while 18- to 20-year-olds were less likely to try to purchase alcohol, less likely to frequent bars, less likely to drink, and less likely to provide alcohol to other teens. Arrests for impaired driving also declined significantly among 18- to 20-year-olds.

W. DEJONG

SEE ALSO:
Adolescents and Substance Abuse • Binge Drinking • Biopsychosocial Theory of Addiction • Drug Abuse Resistance Education (DARE) • Education • Intervention • Legal Controls • Peer Influence • Protective Factors • Risk Factors • School and Drugs • Vulnerability

Prison Drug Use and Treatment

Despite the fact that the majority of prisoners in U.S. jails have drug problems, little is done to cure them of their addictions. One reason for this situation is reversals of policy that have alternately provided or discontinued treatment.

When you consider that there is a relationship between drugs and crime, there must be a relationship between drug use and prisoners. Movies and television shows often portray prisoners using drugs while incarcerated. Actually, drug use in prison, while not as open and dramatic as depicted on television, is a constant problem, affecting everything from institutional violence to drug treatment programs to family visits. Research has shown, however, that it is a problem that can be reduced by active efforts by prison staff. Knowing something about the relation between prisoners and drug use can also be seen as a way to achieve a more effective use of prison resources.

Drug use and prisoners

According to the Bureau of Justice Statistics, 33 percent of state prison inmates were under the influence of drugs when they committed their offenses. When alcohol is considered, a full 52 percent of inmates were under the influence of a mind-altering substance at the time of their offenses. These numbers do not consider the debilitating effects of long-term addiction to drugs and alcohol. The state of Pennsylvania assesses all of its inmates for drug addiction problems and finds that 92 percent need some form of substance abuse treatment. Yet a 1997 national survey of prison inmates found that only 32 percent had participated in drug or alcohol treatment during their current sentences. Further, most of those who did participate (28 percent) only reported involvement in a drug education or self-help program. Only 7 percent received treatment in a dedicated residential program unit, while another 5 percent received counseling from a drug treatment professional. Thus, while more than 90 percent of prison inmates in Pennsylvania demonstrate a need for treatment, most do not get it, and most of those who do receive treatment get only limited and nonprofessional help.

We know that many inmates are drug abusers, but how many actually continue their use in prison? This is an important question because treatment professionals agree that you cannot effectively treat people who are currently practicing their addictions. While virtually everyone agrees that drug use in prison is a problem, numbers on the extent of users are extremely difficult to determine; drug use in prisons is severely punished when discovered, so inmates understandably do not talk about it. In the mid-1990s the Pennsylvania Department of Corrections began an extensive program to curtail drug use in its prisons. As part of the study, the department conducted hair sample drug tests on approximately 1,000 inmates. It found that 10.6 percent tested positive for some type of drugs. Breaking it down by drug type, 9.3 percent were using marijuana, 2.3 percent were using cocaine, and less than 1 percent were using opiates. Obviously, one out of ten inmates using drugs while incarcerated is a serious problem, for a variety of reasons.

As well as the obvious problem of people continuing their addictions to drugs inside prison, drug use can have consequences for inmates, prison guards, and relatives on the outside. Drugs come into the prison in various ways: they are passed to inmates during visits, thrown over the walls packed in tennis balls, hidden in objects and mailed in, stashed in hollowed-out heels of shoes worn to sentencing, and brought in by correctional staff. Once inside, the drugs enter into a black market that has a unique manner of functioning. Because inmates do not generally have access to cash, drugs must either be traded for commissary goods, or outside arrangements must be made. Sometimes inmates will have a friend or relative on the outside pay a friend of their inmate dealer. Other methods involve sending money to the prison commissary account of an inmate dealer. All of these methods present possible problems for an inmate user: commissary orders can be lost, contacts on the outside can be missed, and people asked to send money may not do so. In an environment where resources are scarce, even small deals that have gone wrong can create serious

Although cigarettes are addictive, they are not seen as a problem in prisons, but rather as a way to reduce tensions. However, they are a valuable commodity and can be used to trade for harder drugs among inmates.

problems. Such drug deals often lead to violent acts and contribute to escalating cycles of violence within the prison walls. Also, prison gangs are often involved in the prison drug trade, and their well-documented willingness to use violence as a tool feeds the connection to violence behind the walls.

Regarding treatment, the violence created by the prison drug trade makes it very difficult for inmates to change their behavior. If inmates do not feel safe walking down the halls or going to meals or classes or the exercise yard, they are likely to rely on the familiar patterns of criminal thinking and thus are not receptive to drug treatment. Drug use in prison therefore has both direct and indirect detrimental effects on both individuals and the prison environment.

Drug use in prisons does not have to be taken for granted. Knowing that 10 percent of inmates were using drugs, Pennsylvania set out to eliminate or at least curtail drug use in its prisons. A focused intervention beginning in 1996 dramatically increased the number of cell searches. K-9 dog units were used to sniff cells, common areas, and vehicles entering the grounds, for drugs. Scanning equipment was installed in visiting rooms, and more background information was required of visitors, resulting in an increase in the number of people denied visits. A new phone system was installed that allowed staff to monitor inmate telephone calls. Finally, the state increased its use of urinalysis among inmates from just under 30,000 in 1995 to over 100,000 in 1998. The results were both dramatic and far reaching. Hair analysis found that drug use declined from 10.6 percent in 1995 to 2.3 percent after 1998. Interestingly, most of the decline was in marijuana use, which fell from 9.3 percent to 0.8 percent. Use of cocaine and opiates declined but by a much lesser margin. The difference was probably caused by two factors: those addicted to these more powerful drugs were willing to go to greater lengths to obtain them; and cocaine and opiates are easier to smuggle, as much smaller amounts are needed to have an effect. Drug use in prisons, though highly problematic, is a problem that can be reduced through active interventions by correctional systems.

Juveniles, drugs, and incarceration

Reliable data on drug use in juvenile institutions are difficult to obtain, mostly because juvenile facilities tend to be smaller and are more likely than adult facilities to be short-term. A lot is known, however, about drug use by juveniles prior to their incarceration. According to the FBI, there were 116,781 juveniles arrested for drug abuse violations in 2002. As with adults, however, this is only part of the story. According to the Arrestee Drug Abuse Monitoring Program (ADAM), 60 percent of male and 46 percent of female juvenile arrestees sampled in 2002 tested positive for drug use. These numbers are actually higher than for adults, indicating that being under the influence may have a more detrimental effect—in terms of getting arrested—for juveniles than for adults.

Looking at the percentage of arrestees who are under the influence of drugs at the time of offense is useful, but another way to look at the numbers is to compare the drug use patterns of juvenile arrestees to that of the general population. The chart below shows past-year drug use by teenagers aged 12 to 17 and whether they have ever been in a juvenile detention facility. As can be seen, those who have been in detention have a much higher likelihood of past-year drug use. Other research has shown much the same relationship in adult populations. While this tells us that drugs are a problem in relation to crime, it also provides an opportunity for treatment. One of the problems with fighting any disease is gaining access to the affected population. The chart clearly shows that juvenile justice practitioners are in constant contact with juveniles suffering from substance use disorders and therefore have access to the affected population. With the use of substance abuse treatment, this "problem" can become part of the solution.

COMPARISON OF DRUG USE BETWEEN IMPRISONED AND NONIMPRISONED TEENAGERS

	Been in detention	Never been in detention
Any illicit drug	42%	21%
Marijuana	32%	15%
Cocaine	10%	2%
Heroin	10%	0%
Hallucinogens	12%	3%
Inhalants	8%	4%
Prescription drugs	21%	8%
Abuse or dependence	24%	8%

The debate over drug treatment in prisons

Most people would agree that prisons are conceived, built, and operated for the purpose of punishment. However, when it is considered that almost all of the people in prisons will eventually return to their communities, many would also agree that society benefits by doing its best to ensure that these people do not go back to prison. Many programs exist that aim to reform or otherwise increase the probability that offenders will lead crime-free lives after release, but perhaps none is more important than drug treatment programs. Unfortunately, as stated earlier, the majority of prisoners do not receive treatment or receive only a limited program. Before being too critical of the correctional system, however, one should be aware that the history of prison drug treatment in the United States has been subject to opposing points of view about its purpose and benefits.

While people have used various treatments for inmates since prisons were first built, the first organized drug programs were the narcotics treatment programs run by the U.S. Public Health Service in the federal prisons in the 1930s. By the 1950s rehabilitation had become a major goal of U.S. prisons, and programs ranging from vocational training and education to intensive psychological counseling were widespread, as were all manner of drug treatment programs.

As the political storms of the 1960s and early 1970s settled on prisons, two views emerged, both of which served to curtail the use of drug treatment. Some on the political left charged that rehabilitation amounted to thought control and that the structure of treatment programs took sentencing decisions away from judges and placed it with correctional

Inmates at a state prison in Montana take part in a group therapy session at the facility's drug rehabilitation unit. These in-house programs are often followed by a stay at a halfway house after release to help prisoners reestablish connections with the community and maintain their drug-free status in a safe environment.

bureaucrats. Justice, these critics argued, called for punishment for crimes, not conformity to standards. By seeking to rehabilitate prisoners, U.S. prisons were being used to mold socially acceptable citizens, not to punish. One example used was the case of Martin Luther King Jr. Were Dr. King deemed in need of rehabilitation because he had defied the law in the Birmingham civil rights marches, he would have been placed in a program in order to rehabilitate him. Critics argued that teaching people not to use drugs was inappropriate: the government could legitimately punish people for doing this, but to change their behavior through programming was likened to Siberian work camps or Chinese reform prisons.

The other criticism was less philosophical and more operational. Many states used indeterminate sentencing during this era, in which offenders were sentenced to a minimum and maximum term by a judge, with the actual time to be served determined by correctional officials or a parole board. These administrators took into account factors like participation in prison treatment programs when making release decisions. Thus, critics argued, offenders were serving sentences based not upon their crimes but upon what they did in prison and whether prison officials approved of their activities.

At the same time that critics from the left were attacking prison drug treatment for being overly oppressive, critics from the right were attacking it for coddling prisoners. Prisons were for punishment, these critics argued, not for dealing with offenders' addiction problems. As former Georgia governor George Wallace said, "If a criminal knocks you over the head on your way home from work, he will be out of jail before you're out of the hospital [because] some psychologist will say he's not to blame, his father didn't take him to see the Pittsburgh Pirates when he was a little boy." These "law and order" critics of treatment were increasingly working to curtail the use of drug treatment programs, arguing that they wasted taxpayer money on frills for criminals.

Into this growing political storm came the now infamous Martinson report, or as it was officially titled, *The Effectiveness of Correctional Treatment: A Survey of Treatment Evaluation Studies*. Published in 1975, the 735-page report reviewed over 200 studies on correctional treatment conducted between 1945 and 1967. While at least half of the studies reviewed had some positive effects on both recidivism and drug use, Martinson and his colleagues used stringent criteria and as a result were skeptical about the overall effectiveness of treatment programs. Their lengthy and detailed report was simplified by policy makers to one sentence: "With few and isolated exceptions, the rehabilitative efforts that have been reported so far have had no appreciable effect on recidivism." This approach, coupled with the dissatisfaction of those on the left for entirely different reasons, created the perfect storm against prison drug treatment and largely blew it out of American prisons for the next twenty years.

In spite of all this, there were a number of practitioners and scholars who believed that prison drug treatment could be effective in reducing recidivism and postprison drug use, and that attempting to do so was a worthy endeavor. Although not at the same level as the earlier era, prison drug treatment continued to develop and, as with any scientific approach to a problem, the treatments got better and the outcomes more positive. Indeed, certain criminological research began to show that "criminality" (the propensity to commit crime) and drug use were symptoms of underlying complex behavioral disorders that could not be properly addressed through short-term outpatient treatment, vocational rehabilitation, or periods of imprisonment.

With the increasing crime rates and explosion in U.S. prison populations in the 1980s and 1990s, more and more people began to argue that drug treatment for prisoners was vital. Research by James Inciardi and Steven S. Martin at the University of Delaware showed that intensive, residential treatment in a therapeutic community program had significant effects in lowering recidivism and postrelease drug use among offenders who received treatment, compared with a group of offenders with similar backgrounds who did not receive treatment. These researchers also found that it was important to continue treatment through the reentry phase. That is, offenders who had in-prison residential treatment coupled with a stay in a halfway house that followed the same treatment regimen had better outcomes than those who had only the in-prison treatment.

Research in the late 1980s and 1990s continued to demonstrate that short-term outpatient programs were not effective. When one considers that addicts have mostly been addicted for years prior to arrest and that the underlying disorders that led them down these roads are deep rooted, it is no surprise that short-term programs are relatively ineffective.

It seems in some ways that treatment policies have come full circle. Drug treatment for prisoners was begun in the 1930s because it was thought that addicts, if cured of their addictions, could become functional members of society. As discussed above, the ensuing decades saw that notion attacked from all sides and eventually rejected. In 1994 the federal government authorized the RSAT (Residential Substance Abuse Treatment) program for state prisoners. The program provides grants to state departments of correction to implement drug treatment modeled on the research findings of the previous decade, which indicated that, to be effective, programs:

- should be 6 to 12 months in duration
- should be residential (offenders live in the program) in a separate unit of the prison, where residents would have no contact with other inmates
- develop inmates' cognitive, behavioral, social, vocational, and other skills to address underlying substance abuse issues
- require postrelease urinalysis testing and preferably a stay in a transitional treatment program followed by aftercare.

As of March 2001 there were more than 2,000 drug treatment programs operating in all U.S. states and territories, making drug treatment once again a major goal of U.S. corrections agencies.

D. J. O'CONNELL

SEE ALSO:
Continuum of Care • Crime and Drugs • Halfway Houses • Rehabilitation • Relapse • Therapeutic Communities • Treatment

Prohibition of Alcohol

The prohibition on the sale and consumption of alcohol in the early twentieth century was one of the most contentious additions to the U.S. Constitution. While it reduced deaths from alcohol, Prohibition increased crime and violence.

Attitudes toward alcohol have been ambivalent in the United States since the earliest European settlers arrived. Although the Puritans were considered highly moralistic and restrained, consumption of alcohol was widespread and a fairly frequent practice among the Puritans, who brought a considerable amount of beer, wine, and distilled spirits with them from England. While some Puritan clergy denounced heavy drinking and intoxication, drinking was considered a blessing and a daily necessity.

In eighteenth-century colonial America, alcohol consumption was estimated to be more than twice as high as contemporary patterns of use in other countries. Despite these higher levels, there was comparatively little concern about the harmful effects of alcohol at that time. Alcohol consumption actually increased substantially in the early nineteenth century, rising from an estimated 5.8 gallons of alcohol consumed annually per person aged 15 years and older in 1790, to 7.1 gallons per person in 1830. The use of distilled spirits (relative to beer and wine consumption) also increased significantly at this time. Alcohol was frequently used as a morning stimulant (long before caffeine became popular) at breakfast, and drinking alcohol was generally regarded as necessary for maintaining good health. Farmers would routinely take containers of alcohol with them into the fields, while employers often supplied their workers with alcohol at the workplace. Politicians routinely provided free liquor to voters, occasionally near polling booths on election days. Even young schoolchildren were reported to have drinks of whiskey at school.

One of the first prominent critics of American drinking habits was Benjamin Rush, a signatory of the Declaration of Independence and surgeon general of the Continental Army. Rush focused his criticism on heavy consumption of alcohol rather than occasional drinking. In 1784, Rush published *An Inquiry into the Effects of Ardent Spirits on the Human Mind and Body,* in which he stated that distilled spirits, or "hard liquor," was linked to serious health problems and addiction. Rush's work influenced religious leaders and those active in the temperance movement, with more than 200 local antiliquor organizations active by 1830. During the 1830s, in fact, alcohol consumption declined by more than 50 percent, from 7.1 gallons annually per person aged 15 years and older to 3.1 gallons per person. In the latter half of the nineteenth century, alcohol consumption was relatively stable at about 2 gallons per person each year.

Factors that led to Prohibition

Several factors contributed to the national prohibition of alcohol in the United States from 1920 to 1933. Prohibition reflected to some extent a moral and symbolic crusade based on the values and norms of those in the Women's Christian Temperance Union (and other antiliquor organizations) and conservative Protestant denominations. Some of these reform-minded people viewed the consumption of any alcohol as sinful and as the cause of many of the problems of the early twentieth century. Among the ranks of the reformers were merchants and those in the business class who viewed alcohol consumption as counterproductive to efforts to create a disciplined and efficient workforce.

Conflict theorists have hypothesized that Prohibition was merely a symbolic crusade to demonstrate the power of certain segments of society—conservatives, merchants, those living in rural areas, and Protestants, for example—to impose their values on other groups. Some conflict theorists do not believe that the prohibition of alcohol was intended to make workers more productive, but instead was a demonstration of which lifestyles would be regarded as respectable and legitimate.

The deaths and casualties resulting from the carnage of World War I (1914–1918) generated some utopian attempts to transform societies. The League of Nations, a predecessor to the United Nations, represented a utopian plan to alter the manner in which governments conducted inter-

Raids on producers of illegal alcohol, known as "moonshine," were often made public as a deterrent to others. Stills were allowed for personal use under the Volstead Act, but bootlegging on a commercial scale was regarded as a criminal activity.

national affairs and resolved disputes. The national prohibition of alcohol was in some ways also a utopian effort to alter and improve human behavior. Intoxication leads to a loss of control and restraint that can, in turn, lead to destructive and violent acts. Following World War I, any legislation designed to curb violence and destruction was likely to receive widespread support.

The Eighteenth Amendment and the Volstead Act

The National Prohibition Act—popularly known as the Volstead Act—was passed in 1919 by Congress to implement the general provisions of the Eighteenth Amendment. The constitutional amendment did not precisely define, for example, "intoxicating liquor"; the Volstead Act set the limit at 0.5 percent alcohol, or somewhat lower than most beer. Enforcement of the law was placed under the direction of a new Prohibition Bureau in the Treasury Department. Since mere possession of liquor was not forbidden by the law, searches of individual homes by Treasury Department agents were not permitted (unless there was proof that alcohol was being sold). Many individuals had stockpiled considerable amounts of liquor before Prohibition took effect, and production of alcohol for personal use (sometimes by "stills") also remained legal under the Volstead Act.

The effects of Prohibition

Rates of illness and deaths caused by alcohol consumption have been used as key indicators of the effectiveness of Prohibition. Hospital admissions at mental institutions for alcoholic dementia and alcoholic psychosis were reduced by about half following the Volstead Act. In 1910 the national death rate (per 100,000 people) due to cirrhosis of the liver was 13.9, and in 1915 the cirrhosis death rate was 12.5. In 1920 the rate declined to 7.1, and in 1930 it was 7.2. After Prohibition was repealed in 1933, the death rate from cirrhosis rose to 8.6 in 1940 and 9.2 in 1950.

Illicit purchases of liquor in the 1920s were significantly affected by large price increases; some estimate that the price of liquor increased by five or six times in the 1920s. Bootleggers made substantial profits as a result. Organized crime that focused on bootlegging was not the only form of criminal activity that increased during Prohibition. Homicide rates also increased significantly following implementation of the Volstead Act. In 1910 the national homicide rate was 5.9 per 100,000 people; it increased to 7.1 per 100,000 in 1920 and 8.6 per 100,000 in 1925. After the repeal of Prohibition, homicide rates (in contrast to cirrhosis death rates) fell significantly to 7.6 per 100,000 in 1935, 6.2 per 100,000 in 1940, and 5.3 per 100,000 in 1950.

Some researchers argue that statistical analyses of the effects of Prohibition have not been thorough. Prior research did not include control measures for factors such as changes in unemployment levels and age composition over time. Some simply conclude that Prohibition was a failure, without examining the data. Gary Jensen of Vanderbilt University hypothesizes that Prohibition significantly reduced alcohol consumption but increased homicide rates because of countervailing mechanisms. While Prohibition made it more difficult to obtain liquor, it also created competition and violent clashes over control of the new illegal market among bootleggers. Further, individuals who consumed alcohol did so in social contexts that were far more dangerous than at home or in formerly legal bars and taverns. Jack Gibbs, also of Vanderbilt University, points out that homicide is more likely to occur when individuals who are in a dispute do not have recourse to legal third-party social controls, such as the police and courts. Drinking at a speakeasy (an illegal drinking club) and then getting into an argument does not lend itself to calling the police to help resolve the dispute peacefully.

Restricting the measurement of prohibition to the period in which the Volstead Act was in effect may also be a misleading way to assess the effects of a legal ban on alcohol. Prohibition legislation in individual states preceded passage of the Volstead Act by several years, and cirrhosis death rates were in decline about a decade before passage of the federal law. Jensen points out that changes in death rates due to cirrhosis can be relatively quick. Although it may take many years for a person to develop cirrhosis, there are many people who are on the threshold of death from cirrhosis each year. A legal policy that restricts alcohol consumption can quickly reduce the death rate from cirrhosis by preventing many of those individuals at the near-fatal stages from crossing this threshold and then dying from cirrhosis. Long-term declines in cirrhosis deaths may also be expected as a consequence of Prohibition.

Controlling for factors such as unemployment rates, age composition, and immigration, Jensen finds that the number of states with a prohibitionist policy is a significant, negative correlate of alcohol consumption as measured by cirrhosis death rates. State-level prohibition was also a significant positive correlate of homicide rates, controlling for age composition, military conscription, and unemployment.

Repeal of Prohibition

In 1933 the Eighteenth Amendment became the only constitutional amendment ever to be repealed in the United States. One factor that led to the repeal of Prohibition was the declining power of the conservative, rural Protestants who had supported passage of the Volstead Act. A new middle class that was more highly educated, urban, Catholic, and non–Anglo Saxon was forming in the late 1920s and early 1930s, many of whom participated in recreational drinking and who rejected the idea of total abstinence. Even the elite business or merchant class endorsed repeal because they became disillusioned with the idea that Prohibition would make for a better and more efficient workforce—particularly in the wake of the great economic depression following the stock market crash in 1929.

Another major reason for repeal of the Eighteenth Amendment, or Prohibition, was the huge growth of organized crime profits from the illegal production and sale of alcohol, or bootlegging. Criminal gangs, which had previously been very small and localized organizations, developed incentives and the resources to coordinate and organize activities to sell alcohol illegally. The extent of organization and cooperation among criminal gangs is, however, easy to overestimate and romanticize. The business practices of bootleggers were not quite so rationally and fully developed as in large corporations. Gang warfare also was very common, with territory disputes involving notorious figures such as Al Capone, Dutch Schultz, and Lucky Luciano.

In nearly all states, by 1932, a majority of voters were in favor of repealing the Eighteenth Amendment. Fewer than 20 percent of voters in northern, urban states, such as New York and Pennsylvania, opposed repeal of Prohibition. In southern states, such as Alabama, Tennessee, and Mississippi, around 60 percent of voters favored repeal of Prohibition. In the national vote to repeal Prohibition, about three-fourths of the votes were cast in favor of repeal.

Since the early 1990s, alcohol use has declined significantly without resort to legal bans such as Prohibition. Legislation at the state level restricting drinking age and liquor outlets can reduce consumption without the accompanying negative impact on rates of violence created by Prohibition. The sweeping character of Prohibition and some of its negative legislative consequences can be avoided by more moderate efforts, including increased taxation of alcohol sales, control of drunk drivers, and treatment programs for alcoholics.

D. BROWNFIELD

SEE ALSO:
Drug Control Policy • Drug Laws • Legal Controls • Temperance Movements

Prohibition of Drugs

Prohibition of drug use is not a recent phenomenon—it has been going on for thousands of years. The arguments for controlling drug availability range from public health concerns to preventing more widespread use.

In 1854 James Johnson, professor of chemistry at the University of Durham in England, wrote about drugs, "from the most distant times…the craving for such indulgence…[is] little less universal than the desire for…consuming the necessary materials of our common food."

It is not only humans that seek to alter their moods through the use of drugs (including alcohol, tobacco, and caffeine). The African elephant will travel miles to seek out the fermenting fruit of a particular tree simply to get drunk. Cats love catnip; in the laboratory, monkeys will self-administer cocaine for as long as the researchers let them. It would seem that this desire for intoxication is innate for many animals as well as humans. At the same time, this desire can cause society immense problems—and the history of prohibition has been the history of the tension between what seems to be a basic human instinct and the need to control intoxication in society.

Concerns about intoxication go far back into ancient history. There are Egyptian hieroglyphs condemning those who fall down drunk in the street, and in Rome it was against the law to be drunk when in charge of a chariot. Women and slaves were forbidden to drink alcohol for fear that it would lead to sexual impurity in the former and loss of productivity in the latter. In general, the ancient world and tribal societies (both ancient and modern) have never had much of a problem with the substances that those societies successfully assimilated. For example, tribal societies in South America use very powerful hallucinogenic plants as part of their rituals and ceremonies. Because there are strict religious and social taboos about how and when these drugs are used, the tribe is able to contain any problems. By contrast, when Native Americans first encountered strong liquor from white traders, it caused serious problems within their communities.

From the sixteenth century onward, major changes in Western society made people much more receptive to the use and overuse of an increasing range of drugs. Life was becoming more urbanized, large numbers of people were crammed together, and drug-using behaviors were able to spread more quickly among societies that had been broken up and dislocated from their traditional rural existence. Scientific progress led to the processing of more powerful drugs through the distilling of whiskey and gin and the extraction of morphine and cocaine from opium and coca. More efficient ways of taking drugs were also developed, for example, the cigarette and the hypodermic syringe.

The World Health Organization estimated that in 2004 1.1 billion people smoked cigarettes, on average every person over 15 consumed 1 to 3 gallons of alcohol (5–10 liters) during the year, and that nearly 5 percent of the total world population has tried an illegal drug.

Reasons for prohibition

Why are some drugs illegal? Though the answer may seem obvious, it is more complex than might first appear. One answer, of course, is that drugs such as heroin, cocaine, or methamphetamine can be dangerous. Consequently, there is a public health imperative that demands that society makes some substances as hard to obtain as possible. Medical concerns raised by doctors about drugs go back to a time in the nineteenth century when drugs such as morphine, opium, and cocaine were perfectly legal ingredients for a wide range of medicines. As newer, safer drugs became available, the case for the legal supply of these and other drugs diminished and contributed to their final control under the law.

That, however, is not the whole story. Everybody knows how dangerous alcohol and tobacco can be, yet they remain legal. So too are a range of painkillers that can be lethal in overdose or least cause permanent damage to the liver. In fact, all drugs have the potential to be dangerous if misused. So there must be other factors in determining which drugs are legal and which are banned. One of the most influential is the degree to which society finds a particular drug acceptable or has managed to assimilate it into the culture. For example, alcohol can cause enormous damage not only to the individual but also to society through drunk driving and violence. Yet the attempt to control alcohol consumption in the United States through Prohibition (1919–1933) failed, mainly because the majority of people did not support it. By contrast, many Muslim countries, some of which have a long tradition of opium and marijuana smoking, ban alcohol. Certain types of drug use may also be tolerated among ethnic populations within a larger community. The importation and chewing of khat leaves by immigrant groups from some East African countries is permitted in the United Kingdom despite its amphetamine-like effects. As yet there are few concerns about khat because its use is largely confined to small populations, but any increase in problematic use among its native users or a spread in use to the wider community may eventually see khat placed on the schedule of controlled substances.

Although illegal drug use is prohibited in many parts of the world, efforts continue to prevent any relaxation of drug laws that might make drugs more freely available to a wider population.

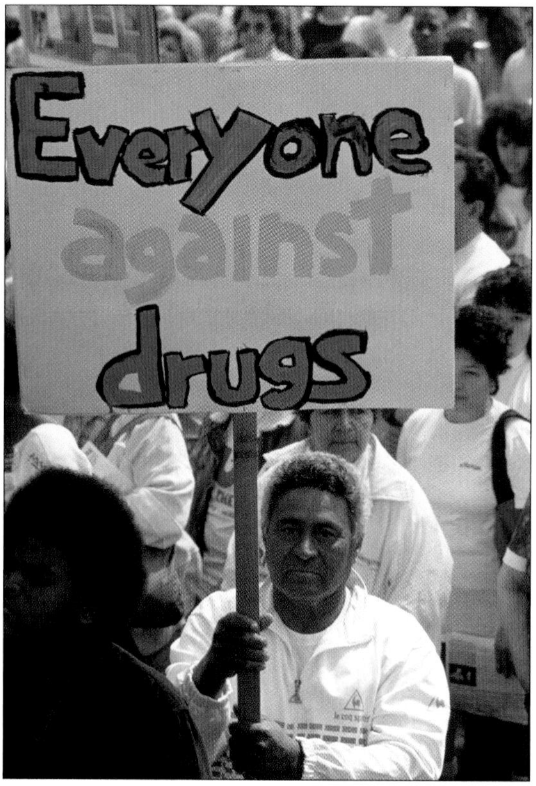

Commercial interests have long played a part in the decision to prohibit or legalize substances. The nineteenth century demand for patent medicines provided a buoyant market fueled by the easily available and highly addictive nature of many of its products. It was only when public concerns grew that the U.S. government decided to decommercialize drug distribution and put drug use in the hands of the medical profession, which it did by making drug sales subject to registration, taxation, and criminal penalties. Taxation has long been a method of controlling substance use. James I of England was vehemently against smoking but needed tobacco revenues for the financial good of the country. Both alcohol and tobacco sales continue to bring in substantial revenues to government treasuries all over the world. There is also the power of vested interests. The tobacco and alcohol industries have been very effective in maintaining their profits and position through their political influence. However, health concerns about passive smoking have created a growing backlash, leading to bans on smoking in public places in many parts of the world; these bans may yet have financial implications for the tobacco industry and the licensed premises that traditionally allowed smoking.

Religious and moral groups have also been able to influence policy. In the nineteenth century in Britain, but even more so in the United States, powerful middle-class temperance (anti-alcohol) and antidrug groups campaigned to have substances banned because they believed that intoxication of any sort was morally wrong and that it undermined progress in society by distracting people away from healthy pursuits and employment. This approach was not limited to capitalist economies—communist countries took a similarly dim view of drugs and alcohol as undermining the aims of the collective society.

Racism, too, has played its part in that the association of certain drugs with different ethnic groups in society has prompted selectively draconian responses. The backlash against the use of opium in the Chinese community in the United States during the latter part of the nineteenth century is one example.

ARGUMENTS AGAINST LEGALIZATION

Some of the main arguments for the maintenance of the laws against drugs are as follows:

- Drug use can cause significant harm to individuals, so the state has a duty to protect its citizens, even from themselves.
- Laws against drugs send out the message from government that intoxication can have harmful effects on society at large.
- To legalize drugs would make the drug situation far worse because those who are currently discouraged from drug use by the law would experiment, and those who are already using would probably use more.
- It is unrealistic to think that with so much money at stake, organized crime would cease if drugs were legalized. Criminals would find another way to be involved and make profits from selling drugs to undercut the legal price or overcome age restrictions. In any case, a drug such as marijuana can be grown anywhere, so there is every chance that the illicit market would thrive because the legal market would be heavily taxed.
- Those who want to legalize drugs have not answered some key questions. What drugs would be available? Who is going to have access to which drugs? Given how hard it is to regulate the markets for alcohol and tobacco —especially stopping young people from using—what controls can be effective against the use of a far wider range of drugs?
- People who use illegal drugs know the risks they are taking. People have to take responsibility for their own actions. Some of the reform options, such as decriminalization, would make matters worse. It would do nothing to undermine the illicit market while encouraging more widespread use.
- Legalizers say that legal and widely available alcohol and tobacco cause far more deaths and damage than drugs. How much more damage would there be if drugs such as heroin and cocaine could be obtained more easily? If alcohol and tobacco were currently illegal, it is unlikely they would now be made legal.
- There is no demand from the majority of the population for drugs to be legalized. Most people strongly oppose legalization. In some countries, experiments with decriminalizing certain drugs in some countries were rescinded once the consequences were felt by the wider community.

All of these factors and others came together between 1914 and 1939 to establish the national and international control system that is largely in place today. During that period, the production, manufacture, supply, and possession of the major plant-based drugs—opium, coca, and marijuana—and their derivatives were all severely controlled with stiff penalties. From the 1960s onward, as new drugs moved from legal or medical use to street drug, the law has intervened; LSD, amphetamines, barbiturates, and Ecstasy have been added to lists of controlled substances as their addictive or psychoactive properties have become perceived as a problem to society. Other than for established cultural uses, the majority of governments around the world prohibit recreational drug use and have a range of enforcement agencies in place to deal with illegal drugs and those who supply and possess them. There are also highly vocal and organized lobby groups, such as the Partnership for a Drug-Free America and Drug Watch International, that campaign against attempts to legalize or decriminalize drug use and support approaches aimed at prevention, education, law enforcement, and treatment.

H. SHAPIRO

SEE ALSO:
Drug Control Policy • Drug Laws • History of Drug Use • Legal Controls • Legalization Movement • Prohibition of Alcohol

Prostitution

There is a strong link between prostitution and drug use. While drug use usually precedes prostitution in adults, vulnerable teenagers may turn to drugs after they have entered the vice trade simply because the two environments overlap.

Prostitution is defined as the practice of indulging in promiscuous sexual relations, especially for money. Prostitution often involves young girls and teenagers as well as adult women. Historically females have been most often recognized as prostitutes; however, there have always been male prostitutes, and in the late twentieth century there has been a rise in the number of male prostitutes, including young boys and teenagers. Male prostitution receives less public attention in most countries and commonly involves homosexual activities, rather than heterosexual activities in which women initiate contact with male prostitutes.

Historical records demonstrate that prostitution has existed in various forms for thousands of years. There is a wide spectrum in which prostitution is practiced, including escort services, brothels (homes or businesses where clients visit), and streetwalkers (most common for young prostitutes and homeless substance abusers).

Research has demonstrated that there are at least three factors that contribute to entry into prostitution. These three factors are childhood sexual victimization, running away, and drug use. It appears that running away has a dramatic effect on entry into prostitution in early adolescence but little effect later in the course of life.

The outdoor street market carries the biggest risk for drug use among teenagers initiated into prostitution. Selling sex provides them with the money to buy drugs in an environment where both are condoned.

Drugs and prostitution

The connection between drug abuse and prostitution is strong, with the majority of prostitutes reporting use of alcohol and illegal drugs. When prostitutes entering treatment or the criminal justice system have been surveyed to determine the connection between prostitution and drug use, the majority have listed "money to get drugs" as one of the primary reasons they prostituted themselves. Among the most popular drugs reported by prostitutes are alcohol, cocaine, amphetamines, and heroin. The most frequently reported drug of abuse is crack cocaine.

The route into prostitution is linked to age and experience of using drugs. Those who turn to prostitution as adults frequently have a history of drug dependence, which they initially financed through legitimate sources or stealing. As dependence grows and there is more chance of criminal conviction or job loss, addicts, who often acquire prostitutes among their drug-using friends, may be introduced to prostitution as a source of income.

Among those under the age of 18, particularly vulnerable homeless or socially excluded children, prostitution usually precedes drug use. They are initiated by friends, sometimes predatory adults, as an adventurous way to make money that has less risk of getting caught than theft or burglary. The environmental overlap between the street sex and drug markets provides an opportunity to acquire drugs easily and there is little discouragement against using them.

Sexual and physical abuse

Research has demonstrated that the majority of young men and women who enter into prostitution have been physically or sexually abused. Childhood sexual victimization doubles the odds of entry into prostitution throughout the lives of women. Many of those who work as prostitutes are subjected to ongoing physical and sexual violence as well, which may in itself act as an incentive to use alcohol and drugs as a means of anesthetizing experience. Surveys of prostitutes show that many suffer from depression, post-traumatic stress disorder, and other psychological illnesses because of the nature of the work. Mental disorders are often linked to drug use as a way to self-medicate symptoms or feelings.

Some countries, including the United States, cite the sexual exploitation of children, including prostitution, as a major public policy, public health, and social welfare concern. Brazil is seeking to eliminate child prostitution, estimating that as many as 100,000 to 150,000 girls may be working as prostitutes. In Taiwan, juvenile prostitutes cited economic, emotional, and drug-related factors as their primary motivations for entering and remaining involved in prostitution.

The streets are thought to be the most dangerous setting for prostitutes because of an increased risk of violence, more difficult clientele, and more involvement with local law enforcement. In large cities young runaways are often recruited to enter into street prostitution following the promise of securing income, shelter, and drugs. Many cities in the United States have neighborhoods or specific streets that are known to be frequented by prostitutes and their clients. Often these are the same neighborhoods and streets where other criminal activity, including drugs, gangs, and violence, are prevalent.

Economic determinants

The majority of people who enter into prostitution cite economic factors as one of the primary contributors to their decision. This is particularly true with young prostitutes who have run away from home, report sexual or physical abuse, and are struggling to support themselves on the streets. In urban areas many of the women who enter prostitution cite economic factors as the major contributor both to their initial entry into prostitution and their difficulty leaving the lifestyle and finding other careers. These women are often marginalized by society already as a result of low levels of education, minority status, poverty, and drug abuse.

Health consequences

One of the primary public health concerns related to prostitution is the spread of sexually transmitted diseases (STDs), including HIV, which can lead to AIDS. Drug-injecting prostitutes are at particular risk of contracting HIV through sharing needles, although studies have shown that sexual transmission of HIV generally follows an infected male to female route. Unprotected sexual contact is one of the leading transmission routes for sexually transmitted diseases. When prostitutes and their clientele are surveyed, many report being unwilling to use condoms for a variety of reasons, including lack of sexual pleasure and lack of concern about the transmission of STDs. In the United States heterosexual women are one of the fastest growing groups of new STD infections, which are thought to be partially related to exposure by infected partners who have had illicit contact with prostitutes.

Links to organized crime

Organized crime is responsible for large prostitution rings that employ prostitutes from all walks of life and operate at the highest and lowest ends of the prostitution spectrum. International gangs involved in drug trafficking began to switch their efforts to the more lucrative and less risky smuggling of illegal immigrants during the 1990s. Many young women and children from poor countries are smuggled to service the vice trade, some of whom are introduced to drugs by pimps or brothel keepers to keep them dependent and compliant. At street level, local gangs may combine drug dealing with running prostitution rings and other forms of crime.

D. E. BIRON

SEE ALSO:
AIDS and HIV • Poverty and Drugs • Rape • Sex • Violence • Women and Drugs

Protective Factors

There are many influences that can work against the development of drug or alcohol abuse. These protective factors are generally positive mechanisms that involve family, social, and cultural activities.

A protective factor can be defined as an event, experience, or characteristic that helps to protect against or decrease the likelihood that an undesirable outcome (for example, drug or alcohol abuse or addiction) will occur. Typically, the term *protective factor* is applied to individuals who are already in a high-risk group (that is, they are at high risk for developing the undesirable outcome). For example, if a child is born into an area where alcohol and drugs are easily accessible, and he has peers who use alcohol and drugs, and he is suffering from depressive symptoms, then he is at risk for abusing substances. Protective factors would involve positive events, experiences, or characteristics that would help to protect him from abusing substances. Protective factors serve to buffer the impact of risk factors that exist for a person or groups of persons.

Just as a risk factor such as easy access to drugs or alcohol does not guarantee that the undesirable outcome (drug abuse) will occur, a protective factor does not guarantee that it will not occur. Protective factors do, however, decrease the likelihood or the chance that the undesirable outcome will occur. Some scientists have tended to view protective factors as the mere opposite of risk factors, but this way of thinking has not proved particularly helpful. For some individuals, a risk factor (for example, having an addicted parent) may also serve as a protective factor. The outcome will depend on a number of variables, including biology, physiology, social and community factors, cultural elements, and age. In the following sections, common types of protective factors for addiction and their benefits will be discussed.

Common types of protective factors

Over the past few decades, researchers have identified the majority of potential protective factors for addiction. Thus, researchers now know what events, experiences, or characteristics serve to help protect high-risk individuals or groups of individuals from addiction. Protective factors can be divided into two major groups: external factors associated with broad societal or community characteristics; and internal factors related to characteristics within the individual.

Family has been shown to be one of the strongest sources of external protection against adolescent substance abuse. Family-related protective factors include having a positive attachment to the family, positive family support, healthy family relationships, strong bonds among family members, a commitment to the family, good communication, and a belief in family values. Children and adolescents who feel close to their family members and who feel supported by them are at a lower risk for substance use. In addition, positive family relationship characteristics of trust, warmth, and involvement have been shown to serve as protective factors against substance use. These important family relationships can serve to discourage substance use initiation and help protect adolescents and adults from addiction.

Education is another significant external factor. Educational attachment and academic achievement have been shown to help protect against substance abuse. Thus, children and adolescents who earn good grades, function well in school, and are actively involved in school-related activities are less likely to abuse substances. This connection between educational achievement and reduced substance abuse may be the result of less free time, clearer goals, or closer and more supportive relationships between students and their teachers and coaches. Having after-school activities, such as supervised youth services, that run contrary to substance use is also very important and protective for children and adolescents.

Spirituality and religiosity have been identified as protective factors against alcohol and drug abuse, as well. Religious or spiritual affiliation, attendance, and belief have all been found to be inversely related to substance use. This may be, in part, attributed to social support, activities, a sense of belonging, and the meaning that many find in religion or spirituality.

Taking part in after-school activities, such as sports, often gives teenagers something to focus on in terms of setting goals, teamwork, and keeping busy. By filling their time positively, teenagers are less likely to be drawn to drugs.

In addition to the external factors just described, there are a number of internal characteristics that can help protect against substance abuse. Individuals who have good self-regulation are often more protected against substance abuse than those with poor self-regulation. A person who can set a future goal (for example, obtaining an educational degree), which can help regulate and direct daily behavior and activities, will be more protected against activities that run contrary to that goal (alcohol and drug use). Some research suggests that children who are shy may be more protected against substance abuse because they are less likely to have drug-using peers. Certain genetic and biological factors—a genetic risk for addiction or enzymes that regulate alcohol metabolism—may also serve as buffers against alcohol and drug abuse.

It is important to remember that none of these protective factors provide immunity from developing an addiction. For different individuals, certain protective factors will be more or less salient than others, depending on a number of variables, including genetic, age-related, psychological, and cultural factors. The overall combination of these risk and protective factors can help mental health professionals understand how to best intervene and who is at most risk for substance abuse.

Protective factors and treatment

Protective factors are critical in reducing risk for alcohol and drug abuse. Knowledge of protective factors can be used to help design optimal treatment interventions that are tailored to the needs of each individual. For example, teenagers who have several risk factors and no protective factors may need a higher level of intervention in order to help guide them away from substance abuse. Protective factors such as improved family communication skills or after-school activities may need to be put in place as part of a comprehensive intervention. In addition, protective factors that already exist for a particular individual can be emphasized and strengthened as part of the intervention process.

Addressing one protective factor can also have a positive effect on other protective factors. Promoting one may lead to improvements in another. For example, enhanced family relationships and bonding may lead to improvements in academic achievement because the parents are assisting the child with homework. Enhanced academic achievement may subsequently lead to more positive peer relationships, which will further serve to help protect the individual from substance abuse.

S. E. BACK

SEE ALSO:
Adolescents and Substance Abuse • Biopsychosocial Theory of Addiction • Intervention • Prevention • Risk Factors • Vulnerability

Prozac

Hailed as the "happiness pill," Prozac has been prescribed to millions of people worldwide. It undoubtedly alters mood but it has limited effectiveness in drug abuse treatment.

Pharmacological studies have provided powerful evidence that the imbalance of a natural brain chemical called serotonin (5-HT) is linked to depression. During the 1960s, scientists discovered that certain drugs that block the reentry of 5-HT into the nerve cell (5-HT reuptake), could improve depressive moods and behavior. Since then, much effort has been put into developing antidepressant drugs called selective serotonin reuptake inhibitors (SSRIs), which increase the availability and utilization of 5-HT in the brain. Among SSRIs, the drug fluoxetine, under the trade name Prozac, has become the most widely prescribed antidepressant. Prozac acts by blocking the reuptake of 5-HT, which in turn increases extracellular levels of 5-HT, thereby stimulating positive behavioral and physiological functions mediated by this neurotransmitter. Another effect that underlies the antidepressant action of Prozac is the suppression of 5-HT neuronal firing, which decreases 5-HT synthesis and turnover and leads to overall enhancement of serotonergic transmission.

Prozac has a long half-life of one to four days, and its active metabolite has a half-life of about one to two weeks. The antidepressant effect of Prozac increases with time and repeated doses, so it may take several weeks of treatment before symptoms lessen.

KEY FACTS

Classification
Unscheduled (United States, Canada, UK, and INCB)

Short-term effects
Quickly relieves depression

Long-term effects
Appetite loss, weight loss, nausea, anxiety, rashes, insomnia, loss of libido, and sexual dysfunction

Clinical indications for use of Prozac

Prozac is the first line of therapy for patients suffering from depressive illnesses. It is also effective in the treatment of depressive, methadone-maintained opioid addicts. Although Prozac appears to be moderately effective in the treatment of some depressed cocaine addicts, current evidence does not support its use in the treatment of cocaine addiction and dependence. Controlled clinical studies have demonstrated that Prozac reduces symptoms of obsessive-compulsive disorder, and it has also been successful in the treatment of panic and anxiety disorders, either alone or in combination with a benzodiazepine drug, alprazolam. Prozac significantly decreases binge-eating and purging activity in bulimia nervosa, but in the long-term treatment of obesity has been mainly unsuccessful. Prozac reduces alcohol consumption, and this may have an application for heavy drinkers.

Side effects of Prozac

In clinical trials, adverse effects commonly reported were complaints of the central nervous system, including insomnia, drowsiness, fatigue, sweating, and tremor, and gastrointestinal problems, such as nausea and diarrhea. Less common were allergic or toxic reactions such as rash, urticaria, and chills. A few patients experienced chest pain, hypertension, arrhythmia, and tachycardia; others reported bronchitis, rhinitis, and yawning. Urogenital problems were related to painful menstruation, sexual dysfunction, and urinary infections. Because of the long half-life of Prozac, active substances may be present for two months, even when no longer being taken, which could prolong the side effects.

A. VICENTIC

SEE ALSO:
Antidepressant Drugs • Compulsive Behaviors • Depression • Mental Disorders • Prescription Drugs • Psychotropic Drugs • Serotonin • SSRIs

Psilocybin and Psilocin

Certain species of mushrooms contain the psychoactive compounds psilocybin and psilocin. While considered less powerful than LSD, these mushrooms can produce uncomfortable feelings in anyone unprepared for their effects.

The plant kingdom is a rich source of psychoactive drugs; marijuana, cocaine, and opioids all have their origins in plants. Fungi are no exception, their effects giving rise to the name "magic mushrooms." Mushrooms belonging to the *Psilocybe* genus contain two hallucinogenic compounds, psilocybin and psilocin, chemically related to the neurotransmitter serotonin (5-HT) and to LSD. Although there are many species within the genus, *Psilocybe semilanceata* (the liberty cap) is the most widely available and the most reliable in terms of drug content. These compounds produce similar effects to LSD but have only about 1 percent of the activity of LSD. Psilocin is 50 percent more active than psilocybin. The *Amanita* genus of mushrooms, which includes *Amanita muscaria* (fly agaric), contains different psychoactive compounds.

The mushrooms of the *Psilocybe* genus can be eaten raw, cooked, or steeped with hot water to form an infusion. They can be dried or frozen for later use. Estimating a suitable dose is not easy. It depends on the size and freshness of the mushrooms and the subject's weight and stomach contents. Two to four mushrooms produce effects of relaxation and mild euphoria: 20 to 30 may be required for a full psychedelic experience, including euphoria, hallucinations, and overlap of sensory impressions ("seeing" colors and "hearing" sounds). The speed of onset of effects is determined by the method of consumption. Effects may begin within five minutes of an infusion, but are likely to be delayed 30 minutes or longer if the mushrooms are eaten. The desired psychoactive effects may be preceded by activation of the sympathetic nervous system, resulting in flushing, dry mouth, and increased heart rate. The psychedelic experience may last 4 to 8 hours but is much milder and less frenetic than with LSD. Bad trips are possible but less frequent than experiences with LSD. However, there is always a risk with mushrooms, particularly dried mushrooms of unknown origin, of poisoning and sudden death. Tolerance to the psychoactive effects develops rapidly (3 to 4 days of daily use), as does cross-tolerance to chemically similar drugs, such as LSD and dimethyltryptamine (DMT). There is no evidence of physical addiction, but psychological dependence may occur.

There is very little direct evidence on the mechanism of action of psilocybin and psilocin. The similarity of their effects to those of LSD is the most compelling evidence for a similar mechanism. Thus the ability of psilocybin and psilocin to mimic the actions of serotonin (5-HT) is generally accepted as the underlying mechanism. However, LSD's interaction with 5-HT receptors (and therefore by implication that of psilocybin and psilocin) is complex and incompletely understood. An agonist action at the subtype of receptors termed 5-HT_2 is the most generally accepted explanation of the hallucinogenic effects.

R. W. HORTON

SEE ALSO:
DMT • Hallucinogens • LSD • Tryptamines

KEY FACTS

Classification
Schedule I (USA), Schedule III (Canada), Class A (UK), Schedule I (INCB). Hallucinogen.

Street names
Boomers, magic mushrooms, musk, sherm, shrooms, Simple Simon

Short-term effects
Nausea, feeling cold, open-eye visuals, distortions of time, feelings of spiritual and emotional sensitivity. At high doses, users may become fearful and anxious over repressed memories. Closed-eye visuals and a feeling of "waking up" from everyday life are common.

Psychotropic Drugs

Chemicals that alter mental activity or behavior are known as psychotropic substances. A wide range of legal and illegal drugs fall into this category; they are used for medical and nonmedical purposes precisely for such effects.

Psychotropic drugs are chemical compounds that affect human behavior and mental state through their pharmacological action on the brain and central nervous system. This definition broadly includes all mood-altering drugs with hallucinogenic, stimulatory, or depressant effects. However, the term *psychotropic* is more frequently applied to prescription psychiatric medications such as Prozac.

There are around 150 psychotropic pharmaceuticals used in the treatment of anxiety, depression, and behavioral problems. Perhaps another 50 psychotropic drugs are illegally produced or diverted into illicit traffic from legitimate manufacture. Notable illegal psychotropics include the hallucinogens such as lysergic acid (LSD) and the widely used club drug Ecstasy (MDMA). Ecstasy has been shown to damage serotonin and dopamine-producing neural cells and, in rare but well-documented cases, to lead to a severe and fatal toxicity syndrome. Such drugs cannot be registered as safe and medically useful. Their undoubted popularity among some groups thus creates a major dilemma for scientists, drug policy makers, and law enforcement. The international legal framework for the control of these drugs was last updated in 1988 in the United Nations Convention Against Illicit Traffic in Narcotic Drugs and Psychotropic Substances.

Psychotropic drug treatment of mental illness

The most widespread use of psychotropic compounds is in the treatment of depression, for which more than 65 million prescriptions are written annually in the United States. The first major specifically psychotherapeutic drug was lithium, whose beneficial effects on bipolar (manic-depressive) patients were reported in 1949. In 1952 chlorpromazine was introduced for the treatment of schizophrenia, and Iproniazid was licensed in 1957 for the treatment of depression. Imipramine, the first of the tricyclic antidepressants, introduced around 1960, did not have the side effects of jaundice occasionally produced by Iproniazid and largely replaced this drug.

Analogs of Iproniazid and Imipramine were synthesized to improve their safety and activity; however, drugs with specific effects on neurotransmission that could pass strict clinical trials of safety and efficacy in alleviating depression proved difficult to identify. The breakthrough was the discovery that fluoxetine hydrochloride can block reuptake of the neurotransmitter serotonin. This compound, the first major specific serotonin reuptake inhibitor (SSRI), was marketed in 1987 as Prozac. It works because serotonin controls neural pathways affecting mood. Some depressed individuals have too little serotonin to enable fully effective communication to occur between neural cells. SSRIs prevent serotonin removal, thus enabling serotonin levels to rise and reestablish cellular communication without affecting other neurotransmission pathways. Over a period of weeks, Prozac raises serotonin to normal levels and has proved highly successful in relieving anxiety and depression.

Behavioral regulation with psychotropic drugs

Many of the tens of millions of current SSRI users do not fall into clinical definitions of severe depression but take the drug to relieve what may be mild and transient unhappiness, a situation that has given rise to ethical debate. More controversial still is the widespread prescription, particularly in the United States, of psychotropic stimulant drugs such as methylphenidate and its relatives, compounds related to amphetamines. These psychostimulants, the best known of which is Ritalin, are prescribed for the treatment of attention deficit disorders (ADD), usually in male children and adolescents.

D. E. ARNOT

SEE ALSO:
Antidepressant Drugs • Classification of Drugs • Controlled Substances • Hallucinogens • Narcotic Drugs • SSRIs

Public Health Programs

Public health agencies are responsible for identifying risks that may have a significant impact on the health of the community. Among these are risks associated with drug and alcohol use that can harm the wider population.

The public health system is a broad range of services that extend from the local community to the world as a whole. The majority of public health programs are led by governmental agencies. Their mission is to promote the integration of public health and health care policy, to strengthen partnerships with community-based organizations, and to collaborate with hospitals, service providers, governmental agencies, businesses, insurance, industry, and other health care entities.

Many local agencies are moving toward the view that public health is more than the delivery of health care and public health services. The spectrum of this broader public health view also includes strengthening the social, economic, cultural, and spiritual fabric of the community. Both governmental agencies and community-based organizations have begun to embrace the view that problem solving in health care will not occur in isolation but in concert with solving the social, economic, and other challenges that exist in the community. Each of the fifty states has an agency that is responsible for public health, as do cities and counties at the local level. At the national level, public health is the responsibility of the Department of Health and Human Services usually working through the National Institutes of Health (NIH) and the Centers for Disease Control (CDC). Under the NIH are agencies or institutes that address specific public health issues, such as the National Cancer Institute or the Substance Abuse and Mental Health Services Administration. The World Health Organization (WHO) provides the same services as local public health agencies but on an international basis. Developing countries depend on WHO to help them monitor health, provide treatment, identify emerging problems, and develop public health policy.

Drug use and prevention

Since the mid-1970s many public health departments have undertaken the task of educating communities about drug use because of the health risks and social costs. The prevention of drug use is a relatively new discipline. Prior to this century the primary drug use problem in the United States was alcohol, as it is today. In the nineteenth century drunkenness was considered a moral failing and a threat to society and the growth of the new country. Drug users at that time were primarily dependent on opiates and were either professionals, housewives, or Civil War veterans. They were not perceived as being as dangerous as the drunkard. Although addiction to morphine was undesirable, it was considered a vice, like tobacco smoking.

It has only been since the mid-1980s that public health programs have begun to sponsor education about and prevention of drug use. While most communities primarily use a criminal justice approach in dealing with drug use, public health programs have begun to view drug use prevention as important to healthy communities.

Responsibilities of public health departments

The services that public health agencies provide can be broad or narrow, depending on the needs of the regions that they serve. Most public health departments monitor the health status of the community, which involves keeping track of infectious diseases and hazards, including biohazards. Hospitals and physicians are required to report certain diseases to the Health Department, which may initiate an investigation into the problem. This helps identify the extent of the problem, available health services, and treatment required, after which risks can be identified and a suitable policy established. The community is informed about the risks and educated as to where to go for treatment and the types of treatments that are available.

The main purpose of public health agencies is to:

- Monitor health status to identify community health problems
- Diagnose and investigate health problems and health hazards in the community

DIFFICULTIES OF PUBLIC HEALTH PROGRAMS

While public health programs may place importance on warning the community about using drugs, little has been done to educate those who are already using drugs about ways for them to remain healthy. During the first ten years of the HIV epidemic, public health departments failed to prevent intravenous drug users (IDUs) from sharing needles. The fear that HIV could be spread to the noninjecting heterosexual community through sexual transmission finally convinced many communities to initiate HIV-prevention programs aimed at IDUs. However, by the time this was decided, many IDUs were already infected and had been transmitting the disease to others for a number of years.

A further problem existed. In many areas, laws against drug paraphernalia made the sale or use of syringes to inject an illicit substance illegal. In New York City these laws resulted in the creation of shooting galleries where needles were used repeatedly, causing HIV rates to soar, such that within a six-month period, prevalence rates in some groups shifted from relatively low rates to more than 40 percent. It was this increase that convinced public health officials to initiate a needle exchange program and to allow pharmacies to sell syringes. This gave IDUs the tools to protect themselves and their families. Slowly, the HIV rates began to decrease among IDUs, who still remain the greatest group at risk for contracting HIV.

While HIV rates have been contained among injecting drug users, the hepatitis C virus continues to be transmitted at high levels. Hepatitis is many times more infectious than HIV and results in prevalence rates of 95 percent or more. Thus, large numbers of individuals, including those that may have injected drugs once or twice, are likely to be infected with hepatitis B or C or both.

Public health programs, while providing sterile needles, have yet to develop comprehensive education and risk-reduction programs for IDUs. The major message has been to "just say no," which is not practical for individuals addicted to opiates or cocaine, who often have no access to treatment. There is no effective medication for cocaine use, and most users relapse to using drugs very quickly. The needle exchange and other HIV prevention programs have shown that when IDUs are given clean equipment they will protect themselves from health risks.

- Inform, educate, and empower people about health issues
- Mobilize community partnerships to identify and solve health problems
- Develop policies and plans that support individual and community health efforts
- Enforce laws and regulations that protect health and ensure safety
- Link people to needed personal health services and assure the provision of health care when otherwise unavailable
- Assure a competent public health and personal health care workforce
- Evaluate effectiveness, accessibility, and quality of personal and population-based health services
- Conduct research on new insights and innovative solutions to health problems.

It is the responsibility of the public health system to develop meaningful education programs for drug users. Such programs should include warnings about the dangers of multiple drug use and the risk of overdose. San Francisco, for example, has begun to distribute naloxone, the medication given for an opiate overdose, to intravenous drug users and other users of opiates. Other organizations have begun to publish educational materials about what to do when someone overdoses. Many lives could be saved if these simple measures were more widely known and put into practice.

J. S. WOODS

SEE ALSO:
Harm Reduction • Needle Exchange Programs • State Agencies • World Health Organization (WHO)

Race and Drugs

The type and extent of drug use varies between people of different races. Whites are the biggest consumers of all types of drugs, yet ethnic minorities suffer more from the effects of tobacco and alcohol and have problems accessing health services.

The nature and extent of drug use among different segments of the population have been explored for a number of years. Attempts to better understand the differences among ethnic minorities have spawned debate over the development of prevention and treatment programs to address diverse cultural issues facing persons with substance abuse problems. Treatment providers and policy analysts have yet to reach consensus, and little research suggests how best to meet the treatment needs of ethnic minorities. However, general information suggests substance abuse presents serious public health problems that exclude no racial or ethnic group in the United States. Alcohol is the most abused substance among all ethnic groups, with the exception of Asian Americans, for whom cigarette smoking is accruing devastating effects. While some minorities typically use less drugs than whites, tobacco and alcohol are major causes of morbidity and mortality among ethnic minorities.

Cultural views about drugs

When considering the problem of substance abuse, it is necessary to first realize that the way in which drugs are valued, judged, and used is socially constructed. Societies have, over the course of time and geography, differed in their ideas of what a drug is, how it should be used, under what circumstances, and whether people should face criminalization for misuse. In one culture, substance use may be seen as deviant; in another, it may be a condoned and respected activity. Throughout all societies, substances serve many uses on a continuum that includes spiritual or cultural ritual, medicinal use, recreational activity, and escape from the pain of mental illness, poverty, or marginalization. Majority values determine the appropriate use for substances, regardless of minority history, values, or ethnic identity. As a result, racial generalizations have become commonplace, often working to further push racial and ethnic minorities to the margins of American society.

No racial or ethnic minority has escaped the ravages of substance abuse, yet research suggests that Caucasians abuse all substances, including tobacco, alcohol, and illicit drugs, at greater rates than racial and ethnic minorities. Ethnic minority communities, however, suffer the effects of substance abuse in disproportionate rates that further exacerbate the problem of racial generalizations.

African American substance abuse has received considerable attention from the media, politicians, and the general public. Contrary to television and movie stereotypes, research suggests that African American youths have lower rates of substance abuse than Hispanics or whites. Societal misconceptions are further buoyed by media stories portraying African American men as drug-addicted thugs. The misconception that arises from the association between the African American community and the prevalence of drugs is largely geographical in nature. While many African Americans live in poverty-stricken urban areas where drug deals are a common occurrence, most residents there neither purchase nor use drugs. Such neighborhoods often provide a market for whites, who are the most common drug buyers. In addition, black males are more likely to be stopped, detained, and arraigned in disproportional rates for illegal drug possession than white males, regardless of the fact that approximately 80 percent of those arrested for drug possessions from 1985 to 1995 were Caucasian.

While the African American community receives perhaps the most widely labeled negative stereotypes, other minorities suffer from racial generalizations as well. Societal perceptions of Hispanic drug lords, drunken Native Americans, and the Asian American "model minority" continue to perpetuate myths that drive public perception and policies. These stereotypes result in further marginalization for Hispanic and Native Americans as well as the lack of research, prevention, and intervention to stem the public health crises resulting from excessive tobacco consumption in Asian American communities.

Social and environmental factors

There are multiple factors underlying substance and alcohol abuse for all groups. These factors have been the focus of researchers, who face great difficulty in determining what variables create fertile ground for substance abuse to take root. Some suggest that racial differences may be due to differential exposure to prevailing biopsychosocial risk factors related to social bonds, attachment to normative systems, learning experiences, peer association, family structure, and quality of parental interactions. In addition, ethnic minorities are often subject to the interacting effects of poverty, crime, and racism. This multitude of factors, combined with difficulties in sampling, hinders scientists' ability to make generalizations based upon samples of community members. Academic and governmental research has, however, produced valuable insights into ethnic substance use and patterns of abuse.

African Americans. Alcohol is the most abused substance among African Americans and has been found to have devastating effects resulting from co-occurring violence. Studies suggest that many perpetrators and victims of violence are under the influence of alcohol prior to fatal and nonfatal acts such as sexual assault and physical altercations. Deaths among African American and Hispanic males are, however, more likely due to gun violence resulting from drug trafficking.

African Americans tend to use fewer prescription drugs than whites, which may be the result of disparities in health care access. While African American and Hispanic women smoke less during pregnancy than white women, African American women are 10 times more likely to report illicit drug use than white females, particularly the use of crack cocaine. Prevalence rates of AIDS are 10 to 15 times higher in African American women than in white women. This trend emerged as a result of the crack epidemic of the 1980s, a dramatic demographic shift in which cocaine users were no longer predominantly wealthy whites but were largely younger, poor nonwhites. Crack cocaine has been associated with an increase in sexually transmitted disease, as crack users are often likely to trade sex for drugs. This drug has also been associated with further urban decay exemplified by poverty, crime, overcrowding, family dysfunction, destruction of social support networks,

Alcohol is a problem in Hispanic communities. Poverty and lack of access to services prevent many from getting treatment for substance abuse.

and the incarceration of a generation of African American community members.

Hispanic. The Hispanic population represents an extremely diverse population and, in sum, represents the United States' largest ethnic minority group. Despite their diversity, there are several commonalities. Hispanics are more likely to live in poverty then either African Americans or whites and are the least likely of all groups to have access to health care. While types of substance abuse differ widely across groups, alcohol dependence is the most prominent addiction among this ethnic group. Mexican Americans and Puerto Ricans report alcohol and opiate abuse, while cocaine is abused by more Hispanics of Cuban decent.

Native Americans. It is very difficult to assess the substance and alcohol use trends of Native Americans due to the extreme diversity among tribes' historical, cultural, and spiritual traditions, vast geographical differences, and measurement problems resulting from Native Americans being placed in a catch-all "other" category, eliminating the possibility of clearly understanding their particular use patterns. While it has been difficult to study this population as a whole, census data on economic indicators suggest that this ethnic group remains outside the economic mainstream, which results in continued marginalization and widespread poverty. Poverty and alienation have often been associated with substance abuse. Today, many Native American adults and youths have higher rates of tobacco, alcohol, and substance abuse than all other ethnic groups.

Substance abuse has significant effects on Native Americans and Alaskan Natives. Native American males die from vehicle crashes at nearly three times the rate of any other racial or ethnic group. The federal government reports that Native American men are twice as likely to commit suicide and seven times more likely to suffer from alcohol-related problems, such as cirrhosis of the liver. In addition, Alaskan Native males aged 15 to 24 have a suicide rate 14 times the national average, and fetal alcohol syndrome (FAS) occurs among Alaskan Native newborns at twice the national average. The rate of FAS is not surprising in that women in this group report high levels of binge drinking as well as abuse of other illicit substances, including marijuana, methamphetamine, and crack or cocaine.

Asian Americans. The Asian American population is ethnically and culturally diverse, comprising more than 30 different nationalities and ethnic groups with differing languages, cultures, and patterns of immigration. The vast majority of Southeast Asian immigrants entered the United States suffering from the consequences of war. Leaving behind family members and moving to a new environment has resulted in added stress in an acculturation process often marred by poverty, language barriers, and lack of social supports. This has given rise to co-occurring mental health and substance abuse problems.

Asian Americans and Pacific Islanders constitute one of the fastest growing ethnic groups in the country, yet little research has been done on substance use and abuse by this group. Some members of this culture place great social value on and encourage smoking among both adolescent and adult males. As a result, tobacco is having increasing health effects in many Asian groups, despite a lower level of cigarette use than that of other ethnic groups. In addition, rates of alcohol and opium use appear to be on the rise in these communities. Opium use has long been considered by some Southeast Asians to be at the center of ceremonial and recreational activities; however, upon migration, these individuals find that their cultural rituals are illegal. Research suggests that higher rates of opium addiction are found in immigrants from rural areas of Southeast Asia. Overall, Japanese Americans appear to have the highest rates of substance abuse among Asian immigrants. Some argue that this is a result of acculturation, since large numbers of Japanese Americans migrated to the United States prior to the arrival of other Asian American ethnic groups. Researchers believe that ethnic groups that maintain a balance between traditional practices and American ways of life tend to suffer less from the stress of a new environment, which can often lead to an increased dependence on substances.

Patterns of use among adolescents

African American and Hispanic youth remain the focus of most substance abuse research on adolescents due to the well-documented relationship between poverty, delinquency, substance abuse, and crime, as well as the relative size of these groups when compared with other ethnic minority groups in the United States.

Researchers have found these racial differences: African American adolescents are less likely to use illegal drugs than whites and have lower rates of substance abuse; Hispanics show intermediate rates; and whites have the highest rates. Large studies found that African American youths are less likely to initiate substance use than either white or Hispanic adolescents, with the exception of marijuana (Hispanic adolescents use marijuana at twice the rate). Hispanic youths are less likely to use alcohol or cigarettes than whites. When researchers controlled for socioeconomic status, no differences in the extent of drug use emerged.

When comparing only ethnic minorities, Hispanic youth report consuming more alcohol than African or Asian Americans. Native American and Alaskan Native youth report higher rates of binge drinking, cigarette use, and illicit drug use than any other group. They also appear to be experimenting with alcohol, inhalants, and marijuana at younger ages than other groups. Researchers have also found higher rates of co-occurring mental health problems in this group of adolescents. Inhalant use has been generally associated with Hispanic, African American, and Native American youth populations. However, white youths report greater use than either Hispanic or African American youths.

Smoking by young and adult males is encouraged in some Asian cultures and is increasingly showing negative health effects among this group.

While patterns of use among racial and ethnic minority adolescents have been established, most studies have primarily focused on African American youths. Negative peer influences, poor relationships with fathers, a lack of positive social values, poor attitudes toward police, positive attitudes toward fighting, poor school commitment, and perceived limited opportunities play a significant role in African American youths' delinquency and drug use.

Family structure and quality of parental interactions appear to be responsible for some racial and ethnic differences in adolescent drug use. While no differences in family structure were found to affect use rates among white and Hispanic adolescents, this has not been the case in some African American families. Some research suggests that the single-parent African American family, once maligned by the press and government policy makers, may actually provide greater protection from use than the two-parent family. Although deviance in mothers is highly predictive of deviance in the child, conversely, children whose mothers practice abstinence and who lack male adult drinkers as role models may be more likely to practice abstinence themselves. Neither adolescent alcohol experimentation nor consumption is supported in traditional African American cultures.

Differences between ethnic groups

Research suggests that genetics play a role in shaping alcoholism risk. While no specific gene has been linked to addiction vulnerability with certainty, one exception has been discovered. A genetic variation in the aldehyde dehydrogenase (ALDH2) gene found in certain East Asian and Jewish populations appears to dramatically affect the way in which they metabolize alcohol. Studies of Asian adults with this particular gene experience dramatically increased side effects of acute alcohol intake, including pulse-rate increases, skin flushing, and greater subjective feelings of being dizzy, drunk, or high. Chinese, Japanese, and Koreans have different prevalence rates of the ALDH2, alcohol use, and alcoholism. Preliminary research on Alaskan Natives, Indian Americans, and Mexican Americans suggests that they are not protected from the risk of alcoholism in the same way as Asians who possess the ALDH2 genotype. The relationship to risk for alcoholism in African Americans remains relatively unexplored.

Treatment of ethnic groups

Many different treatment theories and models vary regarding the necessity of cultural or ethnic matching of treatment providers and clients. The more important issue lies in the disparity of access to health care, institutional and community barriers, motivation to seek treatment, treatment adherence and retention, and motivation.

Most ethnic groups are diverse, heterogeneous, and culturally distinct. Treatment methods should mix universal interventions with culturally specific ones relying on traditional healing practices, language, customs, beliefs, and behaviors. Multiple barriers must be addressed, including adequate access to health care and insurance coverage, communication barriers, poorly trained staff lacking cultural competency, and continuity of care, as people with substance abuse must navigate through an extensive social service network in order to meet their physical, mental, substance abuse, financial, child care, transportation, and housing needs.

J. SCHROEDER

SEE ALSO:
Cultural Attitudes • Demographics of Substance Abuse • Hereditary and Genetic Factors

Rape

Rape and sexual assault are frequently aided by the use of alcohol or drugs. Sometimes sexual assault occurs with intoxication and sometimes with the purposeful assistance of "date-rape" drugs.

Young adults, particularly young women, are at high risk of experiencing sexual assault. *Sexual assault* is a term often used to refer to a range of forced sexual acts, including unwanted or forced sexual contact, verbally coerced intercourse, and attempted or completed rape. Rape is the most serious form of sexual assault and has been legally defined as involving penetration (vaginal, oral, or anal) due to use of force or threat of force, lack of consent, or inability to consent due to age, intoxication, or mental status. Although both men and women may experience sexual assault, existing data suggest that young women are the population at highest risk for experiencing rape. The U.S. Bureau of Justice Statistics reports that around 41 percent of all reported rapes are perpetrated against female victims aged 12 to 21. In national college samples, over half of women report experiencing some type of sexual assault since age 14, with about 15 percent reporting completed rape. Rape and sexual assault have been linked to long-term psychological problems such depression, post-traumatic stress disorder (PTSD), and alcohol abuse, as well as long-lasting effects on physical and reproductive health and increased use of health care services. In a small but significant number of cases, rape results in pregnancy, sexually transmitted infections (STI), and sometimes HIV infection.

Studies of college and young adult populations reveal that alcohol use has been associated with sexual assault. Over half of the cases of sexual assault involve drinking by the perpetrator, the victim, or both. Often the perpetrator and victim are drinking together prior to the assault. It is important to note, however, that although alcohol may increase a woman's vulnerability to sexual assault, the legal and moral responsibility for the assault lies with the perpetrator. Researchers have sought to understand the role of alcohol in sexual assault, with the goal of preventing further incidents. Because sexual assault is most commonly perpetrated against women by men, most of the research on alcohol and sexual aggression has targeted male-to-female sexual assault.

Characteristics of sexual assault incidents

Many women are concerned about stranger rape and take precautions to prevent its occurrence (for example, carrying mace, avoiding dark areas). However, the vast majority of rapes and other sexual assaults are perpetrated by someone known to the victim, such as a date, boyfriend, friend, or acquaintance. Assaultive incidents typically involve a single perpetrator who uses verbal coercion (for example, threats to end the relationship, making false promises) or physical force, such as pushing, pinning a woman with his weight, or holding her down, to obtain sex. Group or gang rapes occur less frequently but tend to be more violent and traumatic. Most assaults take place at the home of the victim or perpetrator. Many occur during a date or social event, and often follow consensual sexual activity, such as kissing. Alcohol-involved sexual assaults differ from noninvolved assaults in that they are more likely to occur after time spent at a bar or party (as opposed to a date), and the perpetrator tends to be someone less well-known to the victim, such as an acquaintance or casual date, rather than a boyfriend. Sexual assaults that occur when the victim is intoxicated are more likely to result in completed rapes than when the victim is sober, as alcohol impairs her ability to resist.

How alcohol contributes to sexual assault

The relationship between the perpetration of sexual assault and alcohol consumption is complex. There are several different pathways by which alcohol use by both perpetrators and victims contributes to sexual assault, including background and situational factors. Background factors are characteristics that are not part of the immediate situation, but which influence a person's behavior in that situation. Background characteristics include one's beliefs about drinking, aggression, and sex, previous experiences with sex or aggression, attitudes toward women and violence, and typical substance use. Situational factors are those specific to the drinking situation, including the context in which drinking takes place, and alcohol's effects on cognitive and motor processes.

Background factors

Research shows that men who are sexually aggressive differ from nonaggressive men in a variety of background factors. In general, sexually aggressive men tend to be heavier drinkers, are more likely to have been physically abused as children, and are more likely to have hostile, adversarial, or stereotypical views of women. Common stereotypes associated with sexual assault include the beliefs that women mean "yes" when they say "no," and that women who drink are sexually promiscuous. These men also tend to believe that alcohol increases sexual drive and aggression, and that intoxication excuses sexually aggressive behavior. There are no personality or attitudinal characteristics reliably associated with being a victim of sexual aggression. However, research shows that women who were sexually victimized as children are also likely to be revictimized during adolescence or adulthood. These women tend to be heavier drinkers and to have more sexual partners. One explanation for this association is that women who are sexually victimized as children are ambivalent about sex and use alcohol as a means of coping with negative feelings associated with sexual activity. Heavy drinking also has been associated with having multiple casual sexual partners, which increases the likelihood of encountering a sexually aggressive male.

Situational factors

Situational factors such as drinking context and cognitive and motor impairment often interact with background factors, resulting in the potential for sexual assault.

Contextual factors. Alcohol is often consumed at parties, bars, or in other social settings in which there is a potential for meeting prospective sexual partners. Drinking in such settings may raise a man's expectation that sexual activity will take place in that situation, particularly if he believes that alcohol increases sexual drive and that drinking women are sexually available. It is not uncommon for men and women who meet at bars or parties to engage in some consensual kissing or close dancing. Such activity

Alcohol is often used to make people feel relaxed, but its effects on cognitive processes can lead men and women into misreading each other's intentions.

may reinforce an intoxicated male's belief that sexual activity will ensue and may cause him to feel a sense of entitlement.

Cognitive impairment. Alcohol affects the ability to interpret and respond to environmental cues. These effects typically occur after three or more drinks but may begin after just one. Alcohol restricts an individual's capacity for attention, causing him or her to focus only on the most prominent, salient features of the situation and blocking out more subtle cues.

Often the most salient cues are those that are pleasant or motivating, and more subtle inhibiting cues are ignored. For example, an intoxicated man who meets a woman at a party and is attracted to her will focus on his feelings of attraction and sexual desire. He may fail to recognize cues that the woman is not sexually interested in him. As a result, he may continue to pursue her. Similarly, an intoxicated woman who is attracted to a man may focus on her desires to get to know him better and to establish a relationship. She may behave in a friendly manner to achieve this end, but may fail to recognize that he is misperceiving her behavior as sexual interest. She may also fail to recognize risk cues, such as the man attempting to move her to an isolated setting. Alcohol also impairs an individual's ability to respond appropriately to a situation. An aroused male may become frustrated at a woman's lack of reciprocation. If she persists in her refusals, he may resort to aggression to obtain sex. An intoxicated woman may fail to sufficiently express her objection to unwanted advances.Under the influence of alcohol or other drugs, she may find it difficult to exercise good judgment and protect herself. Nonetheless, it is wrong to place responsibility for a man's actions on a woman when drug-fueled encounters lead to sexual assault. Effective communication may reduce the risk of a sexual attack, but it will not necessarily prevent an attack.

Motor impairment. Alcohol impairs motor responses, making it difficult for a woman to ward off unwanted sexual advances or to fight off a sexually aggressive male. In the most extreme cases, intoxication can lead to incapacitation, thereby leaving a woman vulnerable to sexual assault while she is unconscious and unable to resist.

Drug-involved sexual assault

The role of drug use in sexual assault has not been studied as extensively as that of alcohol use. It is difficult to separate out the effects of drugs from those of alcohol. Drug-involved sexual assaults also usually involve alcohol use by the victim or the perpetrator. It is believed that many drugs have effects that are similar to those of alcohol, activating beliefs or expectancies related to drug use, aggression, and sex, and impairing cognitive and motor processes. Drugs also tend to be consumed in social contexts where there is a potential for sexual interaction, contributing to expectations that sex will occur.

One particular type of drug-involved sexual assault involves the use of date-rape drugs. Date-rape drugs are substances used to purposely incapacitate a victim, rendering her unconscious or unable to physically resist a sexual assault. Common date-rape drugs include GHB (gamma-hydroxybutyrate), ketamine, and Rohypnol. These substances come in a powder or pill form and are typically slipped into an unsuspecting person's drink, where they quickly dissolve. They are odorless and tasteless, making it difficult for the victim to detect them. The substances take effect quickly (usually 15 to 20 minutes), resulting in feelings of dizziness or nausea and eventually incapacitation. The perpetrator usually remains in close proximity, observing the victim, and sometimes offering to help when she begins feeling ill. He then escorts her to a more isolated setting where he sexually assaults her. The prevalence of rapes involving date-rape drugs is difficult to estimate. Most incidents are not reported. Often, the drug causes a loss of memory, so that the victim does not recall the details of what happened. She may not even be aware that she was drugged, particularly if she had been drinking prior to the incident. Involvement of date-rape drugs can be confirmed only through their presence in urine. If the woman does not seek testing quickly (within 12 to 72 hours), the drugs will not be detected. Lack of certainty of the details and shame or embarrassment often keep women from reporting such sexual assaults. Another difficulty in assessing the prevalence of assaults involving date-rape drugs is that women who are drinking heavily sometimes think that they were drugged, when in fact it was the large dose of alcohol that contributed to their incapacitation.

Substance-involved sexual assault is a serious, often underreported social problem. Reducing one's involvement in drinking and drug use can reduce the risk of substance-involved sexual assault.

J. A. LIVINGSTON, M. TESTA

SEE ALSO:
Club Drugs • Prostitution • Sex • Violence • Women and Drugs

Rave Culture

Rave is the most recent of the youth cultures that epitomize each generation. As with the 1960s counterculture movement, rave introduced a new type of music and a new range of drugs to a young audience.

To the young people participating in raves, rave culture represents freedom, a community outside the constraints of normal, adult life, a chance at transcendence, and, perhaps most important, a way to have fun. To more conservative elements in society, raves are dangerous, uncontrolled venues for illegal drug consumption and sexuality. Both views of rave contain some basis in truth.

Raves are all-night dance parties where the music is electronic; initially, the music style was techno, house, or garage. Although raves as organized events began in the United Kingdom, most of the music had its origins in the United States. House and garage music were first heard at the underground clubs the Warehouse in Chicago and Paradise Garage in New York, respectively. The rave phenomenon is thought to have begun on the Spanish island of Ibiza in the mid-1980s. Ibiza's reputation as a holiday paradise for young people keen on all-night clubbing and partying attracted DJs who popularized this type of new music. From there, rave was taken back to the United Kingdom, first in clubs and then in warehouses or farm buildings as its popularity increased. Early rave culture had all the makings of a youth movement: it was underground, often illegal, and musically it was a major departure from the pop and rock and roll to which many ravers' parents had listened. It also introduced a wider population to Ecstasy (MDMA), which became popular as a recreational drug in the United States during the 1980s before spreading to the United Kingdom. All of this followed the pattern set by rock and roll, which, although an American innovation, probably had its greatest exponents in British groups such as

The essence of a rave lies in the sensory overload of loud, fast-beat music and visual stimulation such as that produced by the glow stick pictured below. Drugs are not essential to the experience for many ravers.

the Beatles and the Rolling Stones. Of course, rave was not rock and roll and that was precisely the point; by the time rave was born, rock had become respectable and mainstream—rave was neither.

Drugs in rave culture

Like any countercultural movement, rave has attracted resistance from the mainstream of Western culture. As raves became more popular on both sides of the Atlantic, there were casualties, and drugs were visibly associated with a number of incidents. Despite the fact that a vocal segment of the rave culture claims to be drug and alcohol abstinent, raves have become associated with "club drugs," mainly stimulants (such as Ecstasy, amphetamines, and cocaine), the dissociative anesthetic ketamine, and the so-called date-rape drugs GHB (gamma-hydroxybutyrate) and Rohypnol. Figures collected by the Drug Abuse Warning Network of visits to emergency rooms show a rise from 253 incidents featuring Ecstasy in 1994 to 5,542 in 2001. Ketamine and GHB showed similar increases over the same period: ketamine rose from 19 to 679, and GHB from 56 to 3,340 reported mentions, although the figures have been declining for all three drugs since 2001. Psychedelic drugs such as LSD and psilocybin mushrooms are used by some members of the rave culture, often those who use them in other settings. *Club drugs* is essentially a term for the drugs used by the rave demographic; it does not describe any pharmacological or functional class of drugs, but rather the type of place where they are used. Ravers tend to be particular about where and how substances are used, generally restricting use to events or on weekends. They also frown on uncontrolled use and use of opiates, whose effects do not fit in with the feeling of shared experience that is a feature of raves. Alcohol is similarly excluded.

Rave culture includes childlike dress and accessories (pacifiers, candy, and so on) and a peaceful inclusive orientation (for example, the rave credo "PLUR" for peace, love, unity, and respect). It was this shared feeling of love and unity that made Ecstasy the drug of choice for ravers. Regarded as an empathogen, Ecstasy has the effect of lowering people's inhibitions and breaking down communication barriers. Its stimulant effect gives ravers the energy to dance all night and increases the heartbeat to around 120 beats per minute, an effect deliberately echoed in the rhythm of the music. While ravers are aware of the dangers of combining Ecstasy with alcohol, users often forget to drink enough water, and many casualties are the result of dehydration and heat exhaustion. There have also been deaths from drinking too much water and from taking other dangerous phenethylamines sold as Ecstasy, such as 4-MTA and PMA.

Although the relative risk of going to a rave compared with a bar or club has not been studied, it is quite probable that the danger level is similar. Bars and clubs are subject to fairly stringent regulation and, initially at least, raves existed essentially outside the law. Various Western countries, the United Kingdom being the first, enacted laws designed to control raves and to reduce the dangers with which they have been associated. In the United States, legislation has made rave promoters directly responsible for any negligence or criminal activity, including drug use, that occurs at their venues as an extension of "crack-house" laws passed during the U.S. crack cocaine epidemic. This application of the legislation was protested by many within and outside the subculture, who felt it placed undue burdens on the promoters. Web sites abound with recommendations on how to take Ecstasy safely, although there is no solid evidence that Ecstasy can be taken safely, and there are substantial indications that higher doses cause long-term neurotoxicity. First aid stations and chill-out rooms where people can cool down are not uncommon at larger events.

As with all drug trends, those associated with rave culture have changed since its inception. There is evidence that Ecstasy is being used more frequently and in higher doses. Methamphetamine use is also increasing, often in conjunction with Ecstasy, as is the use of hard drugs. Combining club drugs has also led to a rise in ravers reporting health problems from polydrug abuse and from risky sexual behaviors associated with Ecstasy use. While large-scale raves may have all but vanished, their associated drug use has crossed over into other walks of life.

R. G. HUNTER

SEE ALSO:
Club Drugs • Hippies and the Counterculture Movement • Music • Youth Culture

Recovery

Getting over an addiction problem can be a long and difficult process. Relapses are a common feature of the recovery process, and trying to maintain abstinence may require several attempts before the addict achieves stability.

In all problems, but especially in addiction problems, how we define and view the problem will dictate how we view the recovery process. For example, if we view alcoholism as an incurable disease, then recovery must entail abstinence. There are, however, a range of possible definitions of the recovery process.

Many perspectives on alcoholism suggest that, while controlled or reduced drinking may indeed be an option, the safer option is probably abstinence. Although the recovery goal (abstinence or moderation) is the choice of the individual, most therapists would recommend that anyone showing signs of physical dependence (for example, withdrawal) or cognitive damage (such as memory lapses) should abstain. Research has shown that physically dependent or cognitively damaged drinkers have difficulty exercising control over their consumption for any prolonged period. However, abstinence does not come without its own problems—since the vast majority of adults drink to some degree, someone who is abstinent can be regarded as unusual, which may lead to situations in which the alcoholic is offered alcohol and is tempted to drink. Obviously, although these same problems can arise concerning drugs, the fact that drugs are less accepted, and thus less common, in society suggests that temptation may be less of a problem for drug users.

Problems of abstinence

One assumption that underlies the proposal that abstinence is the only, or best, recovery goal is that there is no cure for alcoholism. That is, the alcoholic may stop drinking and may remain abstinent, but if he or she were to take another drink, then the alcoholism would be as severe as ever. Thus groups like Alcoholics Anonymous (AA) argue that there is no cure, only an arrestment of the disease. Evidence for this position can be seen in the fact that many alcoholics who, after a period of abstinence, consume any alcohol relapse to binge drinking. It has been argued that this type of relapse shows that the alcoholic has a different metabolism from social drinkers. However, two U.S. researchers (Marlatt and Gordon) have proposed a different interpretation of these observations. Instead of viewing relapse as a physical reaction, they argue that it is actually a two-stage psychological reaction, triggered by a perception of failure to adhere to an absolute state. They named the reaction the "abstinence violation effect," suggesting that the abstinent alcoholic who takes a drink (a lapse) perceives this act as proof of being unable to control his or her drinking either through moderation or abstinence. This apparent recognition of "failure" sparks a negative emotional state and a full-blown binge (a collapse). In this theory, no metabolic mechanism is required to explain relapse; a negative state of mind can explain relapse to alcohol, drugs, smoking, or food binges.

One of the main problems with abstinence is that, as with all absolute goals, it is difficult to both achieve and maintain; hence addiction has been called a relapsing disease. Indeed, it is rare that someone manages to successfully give up any addiction the first time. It is more usual for the alcoholic, addict, or smoker to undergo numerous attempts before he or she is successful. However, relapse need not always be negative. Relapse can be a learning process that reveals places or situations that should be avoided, for example, sitting in a bar every night drinking soda with familiar drinking companions. It can also strengthen resolve, since overconfidence is recognized and the difficulty of changing is actually appreciated. Many alcoholics and addicts feel that they can stop or change their consumption behavior whenever they want, but when they actually try they relapse because they have underestimated the magnitude of the task. Thus relapse can lead to more effort and a positive outcome. However, for some it can have the reverse effect, as continual relapse can lead to feelings of helplessness and hopelessness, which can severely inhibit recovery. This is a dangerous situation that therapists need to address by trying to increase the client's self-efficacy, or the belief that he or she can achieve and maintain sobriety. Research has shown that higher self-efficacy is predictive of a positive outcome in treatment of addiction. Moreover, it has also shown that this self-efficacy can influence other behaviors and activities. That is, having changed a major part of their lives, alcoholics often succeed in changing other aspects of their lives in a more positive way, for example, relationships, employment, and education.

Self-help groups

Self-help groups can help the individual to remain abstinent. Of course, the fact that there is a shared goal among the members is helpful, as is the example of others staying sober through problems and hardships. A 1996 study, Project MATCH, the largest study of alcohol treatment conducted to date, found that attendance at AA meetings after treatment helped individuals to remain abstinent. This was particularly true for people whose social circle mainly consisted of heavy drinkers who may encourage the recovering individual to drink. In this case AA provided an alternative social circle, an abstinent one. However, this shared view of the world can also lead to problems in recovery, as will be discussed later in this article.

Psychological changes

Recovery is not just about the absence of, or reduced consumption of, alcohol or other drugs. If recovery is to be successful, then consumption changes need to be accompanied by considerable psychological changes. AA and the other twelve-step groups recognize this and offer a program to accomplish these changes. While some may regard the program as pseudo-religion, the steps in fact make up an extremely practical recovery package for an addict, a package that does not differ too greatly from other more secular cognitive behavioral programs.

That AA apparently places considerable stress on confession and making amends could certainly be construed as being proof that the program is religious in nature. However, substance use is functional, that is, alcoholics and addicts drink or take drugs for a reason, though the reason may differ from individual to individual and may change over time. For many addicts, the reason they give for substance use is to cope with guilt for things they have done or not done. It would then seem that a very practical way to deal with the situation would be to bring commissions or omissions into the open and then to attempt to patch up differences with those people who have been harmed. This strategy attempts to deal with the guilt and helps the alcoholic or addict feel more acceptable and accepted. Moreover, it also teaches the addict a new broad strategy of dealing with problems, situations, and people; that is, to face and deal with the problems rather than run or hide from them. This lesson should produce a cognitive shift in the addict that should reduce the reliance on alcohol or drug use for coping and hence make relapse less likely.

Recovering alcoholics often feel that they have failed if they have a drink. Teaching them to understand that lapses are likely to happen during recovery can improve the chances of alcoholics achieving sobriety.

The twelfth step of AA ("Having had a spiritual awakening as the result of these steps, we tried to carry this message to others and to practice these principles in all our affairs") is designed both to perpetuate the organization and to produce another cognitive shift in the recovering alcoholic. This last step perpetuates the organization by producing a culture of helping that helps sustain meetings and keeps them open for newcomers. For the individual recovering alcoholic or addict, it again produces a shift of focus from selfish introspection to caring and accepting responsibility for others.

Social

For many alcoholics and addicts, recovery can be a time of mixed emotions. On the one hand, there is the joy and pride of having overcome a life-crippling problem. However, on the other hand, recovery can represent the end of a way of life and the loss of friendships that have been built up over years of drinking and drug taking. The sadness of these changes should not be underestimated; indeed, some researchers have referred to a period of grief, in which the old way of life is mourned before the new way of life is fully adopted. However, after this mourning period, the alcoholic or addict would normally be expected to have a lifestyle that is much improved. Indeed, if it were not one would not expect the "recovery" to be very long lasting. Even if it is stable, adopting to this new way of life may be difficult for both the addict and the family.

One regular criticism of AA, and other self-help groups, is that the alcoholic or addict is encouraged to spend too much time at meetings and working with other addicts. While time spent at meetings or other AA activity may be beneficial in terms of recovery and remaining abstinent, it may cause conflict with the family. It has been suggested that in order to recover from one addiction the addict needs to develop another more positive one, for example, AA and meetings. Nevertheless, the family may feel now that the addict is no longer intoxicated that they have a right to expect some respect and attention. The addict may feel that the family is placing too many demands and is inhibiting his or her recovery. Old resentments may start to boil over, and relationships that have survived the heavy substance use years can break up at the recovery stage.

Part of the reason for this problem may lie in the expectations of the family and in particular the partner. He or she may feel resentful at having waited for the addict to recover and for the return to a life that is familiar with a partner who is also familiar. However, the intervening period of substance use may have wrought quite fundamental changes in the addict that the partner has not shared. Hence the old partner may no longer exist. Indeed, the old life may have been part of the reason that the alcoholic or addict used substances, and a return could be undesirable as it could precipitate a relapse.

The final danger in recovery is that having accepted the need to make changes in his or her life, the addict starts to believe that the partner and family also need to make changes. Again, this can be a source of conflict as family members point out that the addict has the problem, not them. Some partners may interpret this conflict as betrayal or an attempt by the addict to shift the blame for his or her overindulgence, instead of accepting the damage that he or she did. AA and other step groups have family groups Al-Anon and Alateen for partners and children of alcoholics; however not every partner or child wants to join these groups. Indeed, for many family members, the heartfelt desire is to return to some semblance of normalcy with the alcoholic or addict not using substances. Their definitions of normalcy may not include meeting the partners of other alcoholics and addicts or taking part in soul searching.

Some have argued that *recovery* is an inappropriate term. Recovery has connotations of returning to a previous state; they argue that the cauldron of addiction and the process of recovery have forged a new person, better in many ways than if he or she had not been addicted. What is certainly true is that many people do recover from addiction and lead fruitful, happy lives. However, it takes time; some argue that it takes two years for recovery to be stable. The early stages of recovery can be traumatic as the alcoholic or addict moves from a destructive, but familiar, way of life to a more positive, but strange, new life.

J. MCMAHON

SEE ALSO:
Abstinence • Alcoholics Anonymous • Alcoholism Treatment • Dependence • Relapse • Self-esteem • Step Programs • Treatment • Withdrawal

Rehabilitation

Rehabilitation centers are places where addicts are prepared to return to society. During rehabilitation, participants are taught skills they will need to meet the challenges of recovery and ongoing abstinence from drugs.

Rehabilitation, or "rehab," refers to a specific type of treatment program that aims to restore the addicted individual to health through the use of therapy (or counseling) and education. Rehab centers are designed for individuals diagnosed with an alcohol or drug dependence, whose lives have been disrupted by their addictions. Addiction can harm physical, mental, and spiritual health, family and social relationships, school or work performance, and the ability to be a responsible member of society.

Since addiction is a biological, psychological, social, and spiritual disorder, rehabilitation aims to help the individual begin to address problems in these areas. At the most basic level, the goal of rehabilitation is to help the addicted person get sober from alcohol or other drugs, and to begin to develop skills that will help him or her stay sober after treatment. Rehab centers also help the person create a long-term plan to address these domains of recovery.

Short-term rehab programs

Short-term programs include inpatient hospital and residential programs in which the person lives at the facility between two and four weeks. Although the length of stay is based on clinical criteria, it is also determined by the patient's insurance. Some insurance companies pay for very brief stays (a week or less), while others pay for longer stays (three to four weeks).

These programs offer counseling or therapy, education, and Alcoholics Anonymous (AA) or Narcotics Anonymous (NA) meetings. Most programs are designed for people with any type or combination of substance addiction. Some are designed for specific populations, such as adolescents, women, those involved in the criminal justice system, or those with co-occurring psychiatric disorders. Programs for adolescents usually last longer than those for adults, as do programs for individuals with coexisting psychiatric disorders.

Rehab programs are staffed by certified addiction counselors, social workers, psychologists, nurses, doctors, clergy, dieticians, recreational therapists, and aides. Many employ recovering alcoholics or drug addicts, who use their life experiences in addition to their clinical skills to help patients. Some rehab programs offer services to family members as well.

The person may enter rehab after being detoxified from alcohol or drugs, or directly if detoxification is not needed. The goals of a rehabilitation program include helping the person:

- Overcome denial of the addiction and accept the need to change
- Become educated about addiction and recovery
- Understand the relationship between substance use and life problems
- Begin to learn skills needed to meet the challenges of recovery (for example, managing cravings or emotions, using a support system)
- Accept the need for ongoing involvement in recovery
- Develop a relapse prevention plan
- Involve the family or significant others in recovery.

Any individual with an addiction can benefit from a rehabilitation program, especially if outpatient treatment has been tried and has not worked. The decision as to which type of program is best for a particular individual is made with the help of an addiction treatment professional.

A rehab program is just a beginning step in recovery. An addicted person is not likely to continue to make changes or remain sober without following through with other professional treatment or AA and NA meetings upon finishing a rehabilitation course.

Some participate in rehab only once, while others go through several courses over many years. If a person returns to treatment it does not denote failure: with chronic disorders like addiction, some experience more episodes of illness and require more help than others.

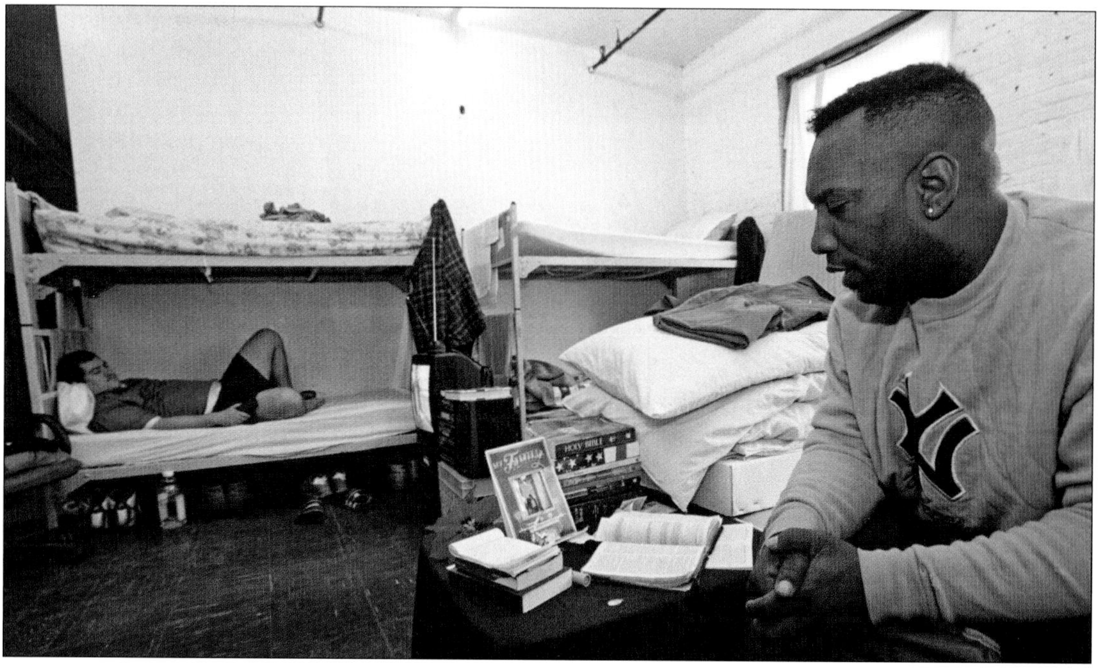

Life in a rehab center starts at six in the morning, when inmates shower and clean their shared rooms before starting a day of lectures, group therapy, and self-help sessions to overcome their addictions.

The rehab process

The size of a rehab center may vary from 20 to 100 or more beds. Most are for men and women, although some programs focus exclusively on one gender. Rehab patients usually room with each other to avoid isolation and to encourage sharing and mutual support.

One way to understand rehab is to review a typical day. After getting dressed, showered, cleaning up one's room, and having breakfast, the patient (or client) participates in a structured day with little free time. Many group therapy and education sessions are offered.

The treatment day begins with a community meeting in which rules and regulations and the schedule for the day are reviewed, new members in the center are introduced, and those leaving say good-bye and share their follow-up plans. A daily reading is reflected on and briefly discussed.

Several group treatments are held throughout the day. One type is a therapy group with 10 or fewer participants, which lasts one to two hours. The group members decide which personal concerns, problems, or recovery issues to discuss. Examples of issues discussed include: motivation struggles; effects of addiction on physical, mental, or spiritual health; the effects of addiction on family and social relationships; what patients will miss about getting high; fears of living sober; depression, anxiety, anger, boredom, shame and guilt; pressures to use alcohol or drugs; cravings; relapse; reactions to and experiences with support group meetings; and problems specific to an individual (for example, what it is like to be addicted and gay, a woman, an African American, and so on).

Education groups (sometimes called psycho-education or skills groups) include lectures by professional staff, discussions, and videos on a topic relevant to addiction or recovery. Examples of topics include the effects of alcohol or a specific drug, symptoms, causes and effects of addiction, the process of recovery, addiction and the family, the twelve steps of AA or NA, handling social pressures to use substances, managing emotions in recovery, developing sober relationships, identifying early signs of relapse, and spirituality. These groups last an hour or more, and may include the entire community rather than small groups. Recreational and social activities are offered so participants learn to reduce boredom and have fun without using alcohol or drugs.

Family groups may be held weekly, which involve family members attending sessions along with rehab patients. Individual sessions are held throughout the week with counselors or other professionals, such as a dietician or chaplain. These sessions focus on specific issues or problems of the patient, a review of the rehab experience, or planning for recovery after rehabilitation.

Recovery assignments are given in the form of readings, writing in a journal, completing a workbook task, or practicing a new behavior. These assignments aim to provide education, to help the person to relate material to his or her life, and to plan how to change and solve problems. For example, a patient beginning rehab may be asked to write a detailed personal history of substance use and addiction, then share this with his therapy group. A patient completing the rehab program may be asked to identify potential relapse warning signs and strategies to handle these, and then share this with his group. Alternatively, a patient who has difficulty asking others for help and support may be asked to reach out and initiate discussions on recovery with at least two other rehab patients.

Meetings of AA and NA are usually held several days each week onsite or in the community. Patients are encouraged to use the tools of AA or NA in their ongoing recovery (sponsor, twelve steps, slogans, and so on).

Long-term rehab programs

Some addicted people need longer-term treatment in residential settings where they have continued access to education and counseling, as well as vocational training or counseling. These individuals are not ready to return to their communities after a short-term rehab. Alternatively, they may not have the necessary financial, social, or family support to put their lives back together. They need more time and help in making personal and lifestyle changes and in developing skills necessary for long-term sobriety.

Halfway house (HWH) and therapeutic community (TC) programs were developed for such people. A stay at an HWH usually lasts several months or longer, while residence in a TC lasts months to a year or more. Therapeutic communities are generally more intensive in their treatment and more psychologically demanding than HWH programs.

The goals of HWH and TC programs are to continue developing recovery skills, to help the addicted person pursue educational or occupational goals, to form a network of sober people, and to prepare for independent living. TC programs further aim to get the addict to make personality changes, which is a difficult and long-term process. These programs focus more on psychological and interpersonal change, whereas HWH programs focus more on offering a supervised environment in which vocational goals can be pursued.

In fact, TCs are "habilitation" programs because they help residents develop skills that are lacking (for example, skills in developing and maintaining healthy relationships, solving problems, planning for the future). A unique feature of TCs is their focus on promoting values such as citizenship, honesty, love, charity, altruism, and responsibility to others.

Therapeutic communities were established for chronic drug addicts who have difficulty staying off drugs and functioning in society. They were originally designed to last two years and required a major commitment from the recovering addict. A number of modified TC programs have now been set up that last several months to one year or longer.

Similar to the case of the person who completes a rehabilitation program, the addict or person who completes an HWH or TC program should have follow-up in an outpatient clinic or self-help program. This provides the opportunity to continue with sobriety and change.

What happens after rehab?

All patients who attend rehabilitation programs are encouraged to continue their recovery and attend groups such as AA or NA. Many will also continue receiving professional services, such as individual or group therapy, in an outpatient program. Those who successfully access these services and attend AA or NA programs have the best outcomes.

D. C. DALEY

SEE ALSO:
Clinics • Continuum of Care • Halfway Houses • Recovery • Relapse • Therapeutic Communities • Treatment • Treatment Centers

Reinforcement

Reinforcement is a key stage in the process of addiction. If a person experiences a positive response to a drug-taking event, it is likely he or she will repeat it. A negative response, such as withdrawal, may also act as a reinforcing behavior.

Broadly, reinforcement theory attempts to explain the behavior of organisms by systematically analyzing the relationship (or *contingencies*) between the occurrence of a stimulus (a reinforcer) and changes in the subsequent probability of the behavior that preceded it. In the context of drug abuse and addiction, reinforcement describes the relationship between the behavior of drug seeking and drug taking and the consequences of that behavior, namely the biological and psychological effects of the drug.

Reinforcement learning was first systematically studied by the U.S. psychologist Edward L. Thorndike (1874–1949). Using a so-called puzzle box, Thorndike demonstrated that behaviors (for example, escaping from the puzzle box) that are followed by a pleasant consequence, for instance a food reward, have a higher probability of reoccurring in the future. It was the Harvard behaviorist B. F. Skinner (1904–1990), however, who most thoroughly studied and popularized the ideas of reinforcement learning, or what has become known as operant, or instrumental, conditioning. For his studies, Skinner developed a specialized test apparatus consisting of a chamber containing a lever (for rats) or a pecking key (for pigeons) that the animal could manipulate to obtain a food or water reinforcer. Much of the current research methodology and understanding of reinforcement learning comes from Skinner's meticulous work on how "behavior is shaped and maintained by its consequences."

Principles of reinforcement

Reinforcers that shape and maintain behavior fall into two general categories. First, positive reinforcers are stimuli that when presented increase the frequency of the behavior that precedes them. For instance, if a hungry rat receives a small amount of food reward after pressing a lever, the rat is more likely to press the same lever on future occasions to receive more food. Negative reinforcers, on the other hand, are stimuli that when removed increase the frequency of the behavior that precedes them. For instance, a rat will press a lever with increasing frequency if this prevents it from receiving a mild electric shock to the foot or some other aversive stimulus. Thus, although the psychological nature of positive and negative reinforcers are very different, their behavioral consequences are the same—they both increase the frequency of the behaviors on which they are contingent.

Two conditions produce the opposite effect—they decrease the frequency of behavior. First, when the presentation of aversive stimuli is made contingent on a behavior (that is, the behavior produces the stimulus), it typically suppresses the behavior. This is called punishment. Second, when previously reinforced behavior ceases to be reinforced, typically the behavior diminishes with repeated experiences with nonreinforcement. This is called extinction and, although it can be effective to suppress previously established (and undesirable) behavior, extinction is rarely permanent, and the behavior is readily recovered—a phenomenon called reinstatement.

Reinforcing stimuli such as food and water (positive) or electric shocks (negative) are called primary or unconditioned reinforcers because they are intrinsically able to reinforce behavior. Other stimuli, however, acquire their reinforcer qualities by having been associated with a primary reinforcer. In this case, a previously neutral stimulus becomes a conditioned, or secondary, reinforcer. In the context of addictive drugs, for instance, drug paraphernalia (for example, syringes or pipes) or environments (such as a crack house) that have been associated with drug taking may thus become secondary reinforcers that exacerbate drug taking or trigger relapse in recovering addicts.

Finally, an important variable in reinforcement learning is the schedule of reinforcement. Simple schedules of reinforcement can be classified into two categories. In the ratio schedule of reinforcement, the reinforcer is presented only when a certain number of responses have been performed. In the interval schedule of reinforcement, on the other hand, the number of responses is irrelevant and reinforcement is given after a certain amount of time has elapsed. Both ratio and interval schedules can also vary in whether the ratio or interval of reinforcement is regular (fixed) or is variable. In the laboratory, variations in the schedule of reinforcement have a profound and predictable impact on rates and patterns of reinforced behavior.

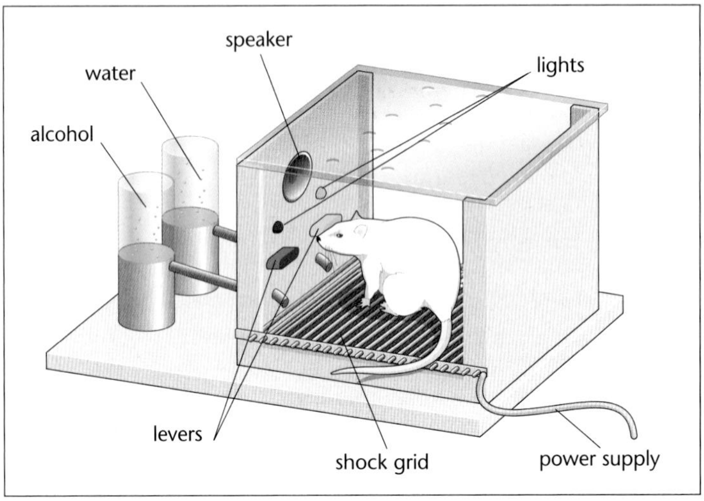

The Skinner box is used to test behavioral responses to cues such as lights or sounds. The animal learns to press the lever that will deliver food, water, or a drug. It can be further conditioned by the input of a negative stimulus such as a small electric shock to the feet.

Reinforcement models of addiction

There are two general reinforcement models of drug addiction. Traditionally, the action of drugs as negative reinforcers has been the central focus in addiction research. According to this view, drug use is maintained not because of the state that the drugs produce, but because the aversive symptoms associated with drug withdrawal are alleviated by taking the drug. Indeed, many addicts suffer from symptoms of physical and psychological distress upon cessation of drug intake. Additionally, drug-associated secondary reinforcers can trigger withdrawal-like states. Drugs may also be used to self-medicate preexisting aversive states such as anxiety or depression, explaining the comorbidity between these disease states and addiction.

More recent formulations have focused on the role of drugs as positive reinforcers. Thus, a positive reinforcement view of addiction suggests that drugs sustain self-administration because of the state they produce, not because they prevent or alleviate drug withdrawal. Most prominent among this category of explanations is the theory that the positive reinforcing effects of drugs are due to their pleasurable or euphoric effects. Thus, drugs are addicting because they produce a pleasurable feeling. Furthermore, drug-associated stimuli become secondary reinforcers, not because their absence can trigger withdrawal symptoms, but because they evoke druglike pleasurable effects that act to further motivate drug-seeking and taking behavior.

Although an increasing number of researchers have begun to question the usefulness of positive and negative reinforcement views as explanatory models of drug abuse and addiction, the principles and methodology of operant conditioning have been, and still are, widely applied to the study of drugs of abuse and addiction.

Methods of assessing drug reinforcement

A number of procedures have been developed to study drug reinforcement. Arguably the least complicated of these is the conditioned place preference test. This procedure involves several trials in which the animal is injected with the drug, paired with placement in a distinct environment containing various cues (for example, tactile, visual, or olfactory). The animal thus develops an association between the reinforcing effects of the drug and specific environmental cues. When tested in the drug-free state, approaches to and the amount of time spent in the compartment associated with the drug injection are used as indicators of drug reinforcement.

However, the most common technique for assessing drug reinforcement is the self-administration procedure using operant chambers. This technique allows direct measurement of the reinforcing effects of drugs of abuse and, with the development of intravenous catheter implantation techniques in different laboratory animals, it has become relatively easy and quick to evaluate the reinforcing effects of various drugs. Typically, in these studies a behavioral response such as lever pressing is followed by intravenous drug delivery using an infusion pump. The ability of the drug injection to directly reinforce behavior is determined by measuring operant lever-pressing rates and patterns.

Over the years, a large number of paradigms have been developed using drug self-administration procedures. For instance, drug discrimination procedures, in which animals can choose between one of two drug injections, can be used to assess differences in reinforcer efficacy. Also, animals can be tested for acquisition and maintenance of drug intake under different schedules of reinforcement. More recently, models have been developed to study the factors involved in regulation and escalation of drug intake. Drug self-administration procedures can also be used to assess the role of drug-associated stimuli in drug seeking and taking (that is, secondary reinforcement). By explicitly pairing cues (for example, discrete light or tone stimuli) with drug infusions during the drug-taking phase, the ability of the secondary reinforcers to maintain a response in the absence of drug reward (that is, under extinction conditions) can be measured. Finally, a number of laboratories interested in mechanisms underlying relapse have been studying the ability of drugs or drug-associated secondary reinforcers (or other stimuli) to reinstate extinguished lever pressing.

A number of procedures exist that indirectly measure the reinforcing effects of drugs. These methods are based on the notion that the reinforcing effects of drugs are dependent on neural substrates underlying other primary reinforcers, and thus should interact with these. In particular, addictive drugs appear to enhance or facilitate brain stimulation reward. This technique involves surgically implanting stimulating electrodes in brain regions where electrical stimulation is reinforcing (into dopaminergic neural circuits, as described below). Animals are trained to press levers to receive brief pulses of electrical stimulation to certain brain areas. Addictive drugs enhance the reinforcing impact of such electrical stimulation, providing a measure of the reinforcing effects of drugs.

The physiological basis of reinforcement

Using the above methods, investigators have been able to investigate the neural substrates underlying natural and drug reinforcement. The common currency for most rewarding and reinforcing stimuli appears to be activation of the mesotelencephalic dopamine system, comprised of neuronal pathways originating from the substantia nigra and ventral tegmental area—nuclei within the midbrain—that project to a forebrain area called the striatum, in particular to its ventral part containing the nucleus accumbens. Consistent with this idea, a large number of studies have shown that interfering with these dopamine systems decreases the motivational and reinforcing impact of stimuli. For instance, antagonist drugs, which selectively block the receptors for the dopamine neurotransmitter, or complete surgical destruction of the dopamine neurons using neurotoxins, impair operant lever-pressing for food, electrical brain stimulation, or intravenous drugs. These same manipulations also disrupt drug-produced conditioned-place preference. Furthermore, using a complicated form of the self-administration technique in which drugs are self-injected directly into the brain, rats will self-administer drugs into the appropriate portions of the dopamine system.

Based on these types of findings, it is now generally accepted that dopamine systems play a key role in the rewarding and reinforcing effects of various natural chemical and drug reinforcers. That is not to say that other brain areas are not involved in some way in these effects. There is mounting evidence, for instance, that a small region called the amygdala is critical for secondary reinforcement. Also, brain regions such as the prefrontal cortex, hippocampus, and subthalamic nucleus now appear to be involved. The emergent picture, therefore, is that the brain substrate underlying reward and reinforcement consists of a complex neural network involving interactions between various subcortical and cortical regions important for motivation, learning and memory, and decision-making processes.

H. CROMBAG

SEE ALSO:

Addiction • Addictive Behavior • Aversion • Conditioning • Dependence • Dopamine • Reward

Relapse

Giving up drugs or alcohol is not easy. Many addicts who have undergone treatment find that they are tempted back to their old ways. Teaching them to recognize and understand triggering factors can help avoid relapses.

Relapse to drug and alcohol use is most often associated with crime, arrest, and incarceration but can happen to any recovering addict. The return to drug use touches the very fabric of society and impacts children, parents, spouses, schools, employers, and perhaps every social structure and institution known today. As such, the cost is innumerable. Although there are a vast number of treatment services aimed at relapse preventive measures, the many and varied approaches to relapse prevention are based on one's definition of relapse and the factors that perpetuate relapse, prevent relapse, identify relapse risks, and define relapse-coping strategies. To further complicate matters, relapse education, prevention, risks, and strategies may vary from one treatment population and service provider to another. The variables involved in relapse are extensive, for example, age, delinquency, ethnicity, income, education, employment, gender, health, and so on.

Definition

There are various definitions applied to the term *relapse*. Several noted drug and alcohol treatment experts define relapse as a single drug-using event. Others define relapse as a psychological process that develops over a period of time and subsequently results in drug or alcohol use. Some professionals and recovering individuals also note that people cannot relapse if they have not sincerely begun to recover—physically, psychologically, and socially.

Although the term *relapse* varies with regard to application, the terms *lapse* and *relapse* are differentiated more clearly. In general, a lapse, or slip, is most often associated with a single drug- or alcohol-using incident, while a relapse, or setback, is most often associated with a return to a regular pattern of use. While the difference in terms may or may not seem significant, the interventions to restore abstinence contrast drastically. For example, a lapse that involves a single drug- or alcohol-using incident may actually have a greater psychological impact, rather than a physiological impact. Therefore, the planned intervention would most likely focus on guilt, shame, or remorse rather than physical withdrawal factors, or anxiety and depression caused by expected consequences from a pattern of drug or alcohol use and the resulting loss of employment, family breakups, criminal acts committed to purchase drugs, or wrongdoings committed while under the influence of drugs or alcohol.

Factors that lead to relapse

Renowned drug and alcohol treatment researchers George DeLeon and S. Swartz note that drug addiction is a chronically relapsing condition, and as such, in most cases relapse will occur despite treatment. Although contributing factors concerning relapse may vary between researchers, social workers, prison officials, and so on, most would agree that major relapse-contributing factors include: availability of drug and alcohol education specific to relapse triggers; post-acute withdrawal; biochemical factors; insufficient support systems; inadequate employment; people, places, and things; environmental issues; negative association; unresolved family issues; and transitional support. Failure to implement a comprehensive relapse prevention plan that includes these features may therefore contribute to a relapse.

All too often, treatment providers tailor their approach to relapse by their specific treatment philosophy or by way of the funding source's goals or concerns. Generally, a tailored or specific approach is appropriate when considering therapeutic interventions; however, the diverse components of relapse itself demand a comprehensive and broad-based approach. For example, a prison treatment program may focus on transitional concerns such as housing and employment, while a short-term residential program may choose to focus on the development of a twelve-step self-help support system. Others may choose to specifically focus on environmental and biochemical factors.

While consideration of each aforementioned relapse component is essential, professional addiction counselors must rely on credible client intake and assessment instruments to establish a treatment plan to support relapsed clients. While most professional counselors agree that a biopsychosocial or data-gathering questionnaire is paramount, the resulting information merely provides assistance to create a general client profile and subsequently establish a treatment strategy. In brief, there are no readily available instruments to measure a client's biochemical reaction once he or she is back in the community.

Unfortunately, addicted individuals do not understand the physiological sensation they may experience as a result of going back to their former drug-using environment. All too often, these individuals give way to old feelings and influences and resume their drug use. As such, it is best to educate the client as to what he or she can expect regarding all relapse-contributing experiences. A personalized strategy aimed at reducing relapse is usually best, yet at the same time a specific approach may inadvertently restrict a client's education.

Relapse prevention

As noted, one of the most effective ways to prevent relapse is to provide the client with a thorough knowledge of relapse-contributing factors. It is also essential to teach relapse prevention skills, preferably by way of an experiential method such as role playing. Role-playing and role-reversal techniques are a good way to develop relapse-prevention skills. For example, a client might identify his or her specific relapse triggers and stage a situation that has previously caused a relapse. Other members of the group might serve as characters that the client has contact with, such as family members, employers, drug-using associates, and so on.

It is also important to include or to establish a sober support system when role playing and to identify anticipated obstacles that might prohibit the individual from accessing these systems. Likewise, continuum-of-care arrangements should be clear regarding the objectives and services offered and the manner in which to ask for assistance.

Identifying risks

The identification of relapse risks can also be helped by educating individuals about relapse-contributing factors. Once the individual has been taught that temptation may arise in social, physiological, psychological, environmental, and familial circumstances, he or she can learn to avoid situations and emotional triggers that could lead to relapse. Generally speaking, most recovery-oriented support groups have adopted slogans that deliver a positive message and remind recovering individuals of presenting risks, such as "stay away from people, places and things," "if you always do what you always did you will always get what you always got," "pick up the telephone and call your sponsor before you pick up a drug," and so on. People who have gone through recovery have testified that recounting these thought-provoking phrases has actually helped them maintain their sobriety or prolong their abstinence. A client's previous relapsing experiences also provide a basis on which to assess a client's current risks.

Coping strategies

Terry Gorski, a well-respected drug and alcohol educator, is best known for his comprehensive educational approach to relapse prevention, which includes a specific focus on coping strategies. Most educators would agree that relapse prevention entails the ability to cope with or handle situations that might cause or perpetuate relapse. In brief, while knowledge is required to identify potential relapse-contributing factors, preplanned responses and a host of coping strategies and skills are required to maintain abstinence.

One such strategy may require that the recovering person engage in a deep-breathing exercise when confronted with an anxiety-producing situation that may include seeing large sums of money, a former drug-using associate, or drug paraphernalia. Another situation may require an exercise that uses self-talk and positive imagery to reduce the anxiety. Other circumstances may require that the relapse-prone individual develop patterned responses in an effort to curtail negative conversations. All in all, coping strategies are based on the individual's own knowledge of what might trigger a relapse.

R. A. BEARD, D. J. O'CONNELL

SEE ALSO:
Abstinence • Addictive Behavior • Counseling • Craving • Recovery • Treatment

Religion and Drugs

In the ancient world, drug use was common in religious rituals. In modern times, most religious faiths inspire followers to abstain from substance use. Participation in a religious group is thought to be a strong protective factor against drug use.

Many religions have acknowledged some relationship between psychoactive substances and spirituality. However, different religious groups have different norms and perspectives about drug or alcohol use, or both, as shown in their religious rituals.

Alcohol and marijuana

Alcohol and marijuana (*Cannabis sativa*) are the most often used substances in religion. Marijuana, also called hemp or cannabis, has other modern-day names such as pot or dope. Marijuana has been identified in religious rites and writings of early pantheists, Hindus, Buddhists, Zoroastrians, Essene Jews, Muslims, and African populations such as the Zulus. The use of marijuana was to enable humans to commune with their gods, to reach ecstasy in their communications with God, or to gain religious enlightenment. Substances that have similar effects include peyote and psilocybin mushrooms.

Carl Sagan postulated that hemp may have been the first plant cultivated by humans when they were primitive hunter-gatherers. For example, in the Kalahari region in southwest Africa, pygmies were hunter-gatherers until the time they started planting marijuana for religious purposes. Richard E. Schuyltes, Director of the Botanical Museum at Harvard University, noted that early humans experimented with all chewable plant materials and most certainly ate tops of marijuana plants. This produced a euphoric and ecstatic result that may "have introduced man to an other-worldly plane from which emerged religious beliefs, perhaps even the concept of deity. The plant became accepted as a special gift of the gods, a sacred medium for communion with the spiritual world and as such it has remained in some cultures to the present."

Marijuana is still used in India, where the primary religion is Hinduism. It is called ganja and is made into a drink called bhang. India also has a form of cannabis known as hashish, which is smoked or eaten. A text of Hinduism, the *Rig Veda* (1500 BCE) noted that marijuana was a gift from the gods, who "spilled a drop of nectar onto the earth. Where it touched the ground the hemp plant sprouted." Bhang is thought to foster a devotional act, emptying the mind of worldly distractions and filling it with thoughts of God. Marijuana is also used by Rastafarians and Ethiopian Coptic Christians, who regard it as a sacrament.

Western religions do not use drugs in rituals, but wine is used in religious services and in Christianity is said to represent or to be the blood of Christ. Substance abuse, however, is in fact considered a sin in many religions.

Some religions oppose the use of specific drugs or alcohol. Biblical scripture addresses alcohol use. Although there is no general condemnation of

Rastafarians regard smoking marijuana as a religious sacrament, but they shun the use of alcohol and tobacco.

alcohol in either Jewish or Christian scripture, there is clear condemnation of the excessive use of alcohol or drunkenness. Nonetheless, wine is used in the sacramental Christian observance known as communion. Most modern psychoactive drugs were not known at the time of biblical writings; however, some modern commentators apply the biblical condemnation of drunkenness to the use and abuse of drugs.

Almost every major religion has an opinion on drug use. Islam strictly prohibits any use of alcohol and most drugs, and trangression is punishable by imprisonment or death. In contrast, use of psychoactive substances is thought by some religions to create enlightenment or communion with God. For example, Native American and African religions used psychoactive substances such as peyote and ibogaine to experience a transcendent state that opened the mind to God and the spiritual realm.

Religion as a protective agent

Religious beliefs and spirituality are generally accepted as a deterrent to substance and alcohol abuse. Religious involvement is regarded as a protective factor against the use of drugs and in treating the problems of addiction. A study by Columbia University found that adults who do not attend a religious service are twice as likely to drink alcohol, three times more likely to smoke cigarettes, and eight times more likely to use marijuana than those who attend at least once a week. When religious people do use these substances, they are less likely to be heavy users or to suffer adverse consequences and impairment of major life functions. College students with religious backgrounds were found to drink less alcohol than their nonreligious peers, though health concerns and loss of control were cited as equally strong reasons as religious prohibition. Possible reasons for a relation between religion and reduced substance use or abuse, or both, include the notion that religious involvement takes up time, and this competes with substance use. Strong social contacts through religious institutions can reinforce moderation and even abstinence. Finally, a religious upbringing promotes values that may prevent a person from trying a substance, and having a religious peer group can reinforce this avoidance.

Some individuals use substances to self-medicate or to cope with difficulties in life. Religion may offer an alternative way to meet life's challenges.

Spirituality and adolescence

The most vulnerable time for addiction to take hold is during adolescence. The Columbia study found that teenagers who actively chose to pursue a spiritual life (rather than who were forced to follow the religion of their parents) were half as likely to develop addictions to alcohol or illicit drugs than those with no spiritual beliefs. This spirituality is not necessarily tied to an established religion but follows a need for meaning, communion, and transcendence. In some cases this need was met through a conversion experience or involvement in a more fundamentalist religious organization.

Help for addicts

Research studies have only begun to address the manner in which religion may help addicts recover. Alcoholics Anonymous (AA) is a leading organization that helps people recover from addiction to alcohol. Narcotics Anonymous (NA) is a similar group that helps people recover from addiction to drugs such as cocaine and heroin. One of the fundamental tenets of AA and its sister organizations is that a recovering person must relinquish his or her sense of control over addiction to a "higher power," which many would define as God. Other programs designed to treat addictions are run by Teen Challenge and the Salvation Army. Both of these programs are Christian in nature and include the acknowledgment of reliance on a higher power. Programs such as AA and NA have been remarkably effective in helping to treat alcohol and drug addictions. Various studies have shown that nearly half of recovering addicts in AA who are also receiving treatment manage to retain their sobriety for at least five years. Individuals who are successful at maintaining recovery show a greater spirituality and faith than those who continue to relapse.

J. L. JOHNSON

SEE ALSO:
Alcoholics Anonymous • Alcoholism Treatment • Ancient World • Cultural Attitudes • History of Drug Use • Temperance Movements

Research, Medical

Drug addiction is a complex problem that is known to have medical, chemical, and behavioral components. A great deal of research is underway to determine the biological bases that may lead to effective addiction treatments.

Drug addiction, defined as overwhelming and compulsive involvement with the use of a drug, involves complex interactions between biochemical processes, individual and group psychology, and social customs and mores. Scientists and physicians studying addiction are using the different research methods and approaches employed by molecular cell biology, neurobiology, and behavioral psychology. These research approaches share the view that there is a common, progressive aspect to the process of addiction. This model postulates that an individual uses a drug and obtains pleasure or reward that reinforces usage. This is referred to as the acute drug state. Continuing drug use leads in some cases to the development of tolerance, sensitization, and the dependence of the chronic drug state. Desire to exit from the addicted state and cessation of drug use leads to withdrawal symptoms during the short-term abstinence phase. However, it is widely recognized that persistent cravings can lead to stress-induced relapses from any established long-term abstinence state.

All psychoactive drugs "short-circuit" normal perception of the environment by acting directly on the brain to influence emotional state and behavior. Directly administered psychoactive drugs are clearly novel features of human evolutionary experience. In bypassing the adaptive information processing systems that have evolved over evolutionary time, drug taking can give the brain abnormal signals that it would not naturally receive. Thus psychoactive drug abuse would appear to be unlikely to help an individual maximize adaptation to the natural environment or enhance his or her "biological" fitness.

The heavy physical and psychological toll that drug addiction exerts on individual addicts lends general support to this somewhat crude evolutionary biological interpretation of addiction. Evolutionary insight can guide experimentation but is rarely useful in the practical treatment of addiction, and it is clear that psychoactive drugs can alleviate certain forms of mental illness and distress. Nor is it realistic to ignore the fact that psychoactive drugs such as caffeine and alcohol are widely used in human societies and are known to induce pleasures that are considered safe when used in moderation. Most current biomedical research on the causes and mechanisms of drug addiction is therefore not centered on the deep issues of human evolutionary biology but is concerned with trying to gain knowledge that can be used in the prevention and treatment of addiction.

The molecular and cellular basis of drug addiction

The molecular and cellular approach to understanding addiction seeks to discover the mechanisms that are involved in the interaction between the drug molecule and the brain cells. This approach also seeks to understand how persistent exposure to drugs causes adaptations that alter the function of the brain and to learn whether these alterations are temporary or permanent. The early stages in the process, that is, the acute drug state induced by opiates such as morphine and heroin, are probably the best understood in molecular detail.

On initial contact, all opiates stimulate the adenosine monophosphate pathway in neurons, a process commonly described as "up-regulation of the cyclic AMP (cAMP) pathway." The process is not simple, since acute opiate exposure also seems to down-regulate the cAMP pathway in some neurons, while chronic opiate exposure induces a compensating up-regulation of the cAMP pathway in other neurons. Up-regulation boosts the amount of other brain enzymes such as adenylyl cyclase and cAMP-dependent protein kinase A. Thus chronic up-regulation of the cAMP pathway actually opposes acute opiate down-regulation (inhibition) of the same pathway, and this seems to be the biochemical basis for drug tolerance. After removal of the opiate, the chronic drug-induced up-regulation of the cAMP pathway may explain why dependence, withdrawal, and craving for opiates occur.

These events are now known to occur in a single pathway deep within the brain, often referred to as the mesolimbic dopamine reward system of the locus coeruleus. This is the major center for noradrenergic nerve transmission in the brain. Stimulation of this pathway appears to be a common property of many and perhaps all highly addictive substances for humans, including opiates, cocaine, and alcohol. Up-regulation of the cAMP pathway in the locus coeruleus increases the rate of "firing" (neural transmission events) by these brain neurons. Increased locus coeruleus activity is also a characteristic feature of drug withdrawal symptoms.

The research findings of many groups indicate that addictive substance-induced up-regulation of the cAMP pathway is also occurring in other regions of the brain, such as the cerebral cortex and the hippocampus. Unnaturally high and persistent overstimulation may account for some of the more damaging and long-lasting effects of drug addiction. Interestingly, it has been proposed that such drug-induced alterations in the preexisting patterns of biochemical neurotransmission could be similar to the type of alterations in brain activity that have been proposed to account for other highly significant but

Discovering how drugs work in the brain requires the use of sophisticated technology such as this positron emission tomography scanner, which can be used to detect areas of the brain that become activated when different drugs are introduced into the body.

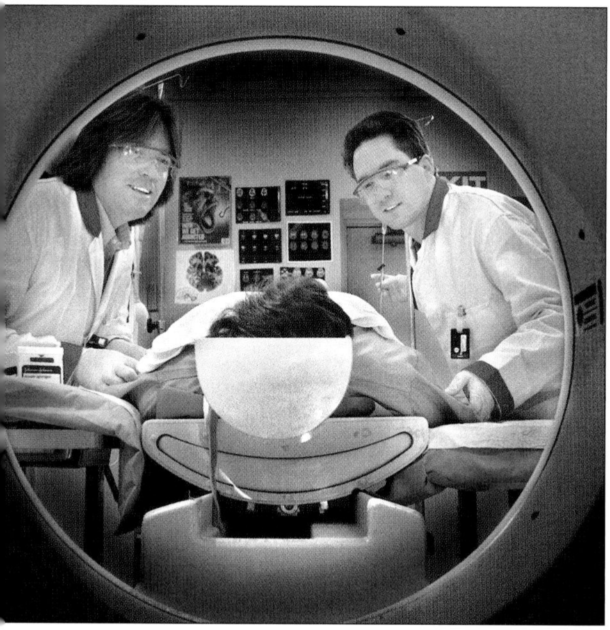

poorly understood properties of the human brain, such as long-term memory.

Memory and long-term adaptations in the brain are also proposed to involve stable changes in the patterns of gene expression in the brain. Gene expression is the biochemical term for the conversion of the DNA-encoded genetic information into enzymatic and structural proteins, via translation of messenger RNA, a short-lived copy of the DNA information. Changes in gene expression lead to changes in brain signaling (neurotransmission) and rerouting of connections between neurons. Long-term drug use can cause profound changes in brain metabolism, the number of receptors available for the drug of addiction, the patterns of gene expression, and the ways in which individuals respond to signals, or "cues," from the environment. The addicted brain thus becomes significantly altered by the persistent drug availability.

Research on drug addiction behavior

A key unanswered question about addiction stems from the observation that many people at some time self-administer a potentially addictive drug, but few people become addicts. How does use become addiction, and why are some individuals more susceptible than others? It is possible to carry out observational social research on this question, but scientifically testing theories of possible causes on humans is unethical as it would involve experimental administration of dangerously addictive drugs. Nonhuman animal models for drug addiction have been developed, and since the classic studies of Weeks in 1962, it has been known that rats will repeatedly perform certain actions that result in the intravenous delivery of potentially addictive substances. Most animals will self-administer nearly every drug that is abused by humans to the extent of redirecting their activity to drug use in preference to natural rewards such as food, water, and sex. The notable exception to mammalian drug preferences seems to be a nonhuman lack of interest in hallucinogens.

Research published in 2004 by Deroche-Gamonet, Belin, and Piazza at the Institute of Neuroscience in Bordeaux has exploited the rat model to gain more understanding of why certain individuals progress from occasional self-administration to the compulsive use that characterizes true addiction. They approached the problem by trying to define the diagnostic criteria that characterize human addiction and then testing to see whether rats, when allowed to self-administer intravenous cocaine, ever develop human-type addictive behaviors.

The first criterion of human-type addictive behavior was whether any rats ever continued to seek the drug even when it was unavailable. An experiment was designed to permit the measurement of this behavior by giving a green signal above a hole. When the green light is on, if the rat pokes its nose into the hole five times, intravenous cocaine is given through a tube inserted into a vein. This line is attached in such a way that the rat is able to move freely within the confines of the box. A red light above the hole indicates that the drug will not be fed into the rat, however many times it pokes the hole. Normal rats will learn to poke only when the green light is on. However, other rats can be selected who will continue to work for cocaine that they desire, but do not receive, when the red light is on.

The second human-type addictive behavior sought in this rat drug self-administration model was a very high motivation to get a drug, that is, a drug craving-type behavior. This criterion was measured by progressively increasing the frequency of nose poking (work) that has to be done to receive a dose of intravenous cocaine. At some point, around 30 to 50 nose pokes for most rats, the effort appears to exceed the benefit received by the rat and it ceases to work for the cocaine dose. However, a subset of rats will work significantly harder (up to 200 nose pokes) to obtain the cocaine dose.

The third human-type behavior sought was the continuing quest for a drug even when the drug was associated with a type of pain or punishment. This aspect of addiction behavior was approximated in the rat box by observing whether the rats would continue to work for intravenous cocaine, even when an additional blue light indicted that the cocaine delivery will be accompanied by an electric shock administered through a foot plate that the rat must step on. Again, while the great majority of the rats will learn that the blue light signals co-administration of the electric shock and cease to nose poke for cocaine, a few rats will continue to work for cocaine, despite the pain.

The novelty of these experiments is that the rats showed symptoms of addiction that were not initially present but developed over time in a minority of the rats. Only after at least one month of short self-administration experiences in the box, or after prolonged drug-access sessions, did some rats show signs of developing the more extreme behaviors that we associate with human addiction. Furthermore, although all rats would self-administer cocaine, 41 percent did not fulfill any of the three criteria of human-type addiction, 28 percent fulfilled only one criterion, and 14 percent showed two symptoms. Seventeen percent displayed all three symptoms of "human-type" cocaine addiction, a similar proportion to that actually occurring in humans. The experiment reveals that despite equal access and similar drug intake in all subjects, addiction behavior appeared in relatively few rats. This seems to imply that it is the combination of long exposure to the drug with some factor intrinsic to a minority of rats that leads to addiction rather than one of these factors acting alone. This research finding could have significant implications for how we view and treat human drug addiction.

It is surprising that the same drugs of abuse can induce addiction-type behavior across the animal kingdom. This striking observation seems to strongly support the hypothesis that these drugs are stimulating major neurological pathways that activate reward and pleasure sensations that have been conserved through mammalian evolution. It therefore seems likely that these novel and more realistic animal models of drug addiction can be of real value in future neurophysiological and neurobiochemical experiments designed to understand the molecular mechanisms of transition into drug addiction and the genetic basis for differences in susceptibility to drug addiction.

Is drug addiction a brain disease?

Illegal drug users and particularly addicts are viewed with ill-concealed horror and contempt by essentially all human societies. The most tolerant view is that the addict is a victim of a difficult upbringing or social situation. More common is the attitude that drug addicts are weak or bad and immoral people without the self-control to restrain their self-absorbed obsession. At its most extreme, there are

GENETIC TECHNIQUES

One of the biggest advances in addiction research has been in the field of genetics. Many scientists believe that some people are more susceptible to developing addictions than others and that certain behaviors and disorders may have a genetic basis. The decoding of the human genome and the development of new genetic tools has enabled scientists to investigate processes such as tolerance, sensitization, and dependence at the cellular and molecular level. One group has identified more than 400 different genes that are affected by long-term cocaine abuse. Research into alcohol and opiates is expected to find similar patterns. By identifying marker genes for addiction, researchers hope to develop therapeutic drugs that will prevent craving and relapse.

Genetic engineering has led to the development of animals that have had certain genes inactivated so that the role of these genes in addiction can be determined. These "knockout" techniques are used to test responses to a wide variety of drugs at the molecular, cellular, and behavioral level. By selecting a particular gene, such as one that is responsible for producing a neurotransmitter receptor or one that makes a protein that transmits signals within cells, scientists can determine what contribution a gene makes in modifying the body's response to a drug. For example, alcohol is known to increase levels of dopamine, the chemical that promotes pleasurable feelings in the brain's reward system. However, chronic use of alcohol depletes the number of D2 dopamine receptors, blunting the response. It is thought that alcoholics increase consumption to try to overcome this lack of reward. Transgenic rats that have had some of their D2 receptors knocked out show a preference for alcohol over water. By using gene therapy techniques, in which a virus is used to carry a replacement gene to target cells, the rats were able to produce more D2 receptor proteins and showed a marked drop in alcohol consumption. Such a treatment may one day be applicable to human alcoholics. Other scientists have developed "knockin" mice that show an increased sensitivity to nicotine that they hope will lead to better understanding of nicotine abuse and addiction.

many who feel that penal incarceration is the most appropriate form of treatment for drug addicts.

Essentially all who study drug addiction at present conclude that the available scientifically collected data support a view that addiction is an illness, caused by specific, drug-induced alterations to the brain. Long-term use of addictive drugs clearly causes detectable pathology. The major organ affected by the process of addiction is the brain, although there may be extensive damage at secondary sites, for example, cirrhosis of the liver following chronic alcohol addiction. In this sense, drug addiction is a brain disease, although obviously major social and historical factors ensure that it is not treated as an illness like any other. The most important new findings in addiction research are the increasing weight of scientific evidence for the special susceptibility of the mammalian brain to a few types of small drug molecules that appear to mimic the brain's highly evolved neural transmission pathways in particularly rewarding and potentially addictive ways.

Drug addiction thus appears to be a problem that is best addressed by a primarily scientific and medical approach, defining science as common sense used systematically to choose between alternative proposals and medicine, as science harnessed to healing the sick and distressed. It is possible that a more widespread adoption of this viewpoint, which excludes no therapeutic method proven to be effective, would at last pave the way for more humane attitudes and more effective public policies toward drug addicts.

D. E. ARNOT

SEE ALSO:
Causes of Addiction, Biological • National Institute on Alcohol Abuse and Addiction (NIAAA) • National Institute on Drug Abuse (NIDA)

Reserpine

Reserpine is derived from a plant used to treat high blood pressure. It works by reducing neurotransmitters such as dopamine and norepinephrine in nerve cells, which makes it an interesting drug for studying the natural causes of depression.

Reserpine is obtained from the dried roots of the snakeroot plant *(Rauwolfia serpentina),* a small evergreen climbing shrub native to the Indian subcontinent. Known in India as *sarpaganda,* the plant has been used for centuries as an antidote for snakebites, treatment of high blood pressure, fever, insomnia, and wounds. However, it was not until 1952 that an active chemical, reserpine, responsible for the effects of the plant, was isolated from *Rauwolfia.* Reserpine occurs as an odorless, white or pale yellow-colored crystalline powder that is sensitive to light and is insoluble in water.

The main clinical use of reserpine is to treat mild to moderate hypertension (high blood pressure). It acts by depleting the stores of signal-carrying transmitters such as catecholamines (dopamine and norepinephrine) and serotonin in many organs, including the heart and the brain. Catecholamines in general have a stimulatory effect on the heart and act to constrict blood vessels. By depleting catecholamine stores, reserpine prevents blood pressure from rising. The usual adult daily dose for hypertension treatment is up to 0.5 milligrams by mouth.

The effect of reserpine on transmitters in the brain causes central nervous system depression. Early use of reserpine exploited this to produce a tranquilizing effect and was used for the management of conditions such as schizophrenia and psychoses. Although reserpine is no longer used to treat these conditions, since newer and better antipsychotic drugs have been developed, it has often been called the original tranquilizer. Reserpine is often used as a tranquilizer in veterinary practices, especially to sedate show horses.

The side effects of reserpine are generally mild and infrequent. The commonly observed problems include drowsiness, dizziness, lethargy, increased dreaming, nightmares, abdominal cramps, and diarrhea. Reserpine is an unusual drug as it may take days to several weeks to reach its full effect and continues to have some sedative effects for weeks after treatment is discontinued. Its major side effect, however, is mental depression, which can lead to suicide. The fact that the drug is known to reduce concentrations of many of the brain's mood-enhancing chemicals makes it a useful tool for research into the causes of naturally occurring depression, which can be a trigger for drug abuse.

Although there are no documented reports of reserpine being abused as a psychedelic (producing visual hallucinations), the plant has traditionally been used by holy men in India to achieve detachment while meditating. The use of reserpine has dropped dramatically over the years because of the introduction of newer drugs. However, it is still the cheapest antihypertensive agent available. In the wake of mounting costs of treating hypertension, many have suggested that inexpensive older drugs such as reserpine should be given a second chance.

A. KAPUR, J. DERRY

KEY FACTS

Classification

Not scheduled in US, Canada, UK, or INCB.
Antihypertensive.

Short-term effects

Reduced blood pressure, diarrhea, dryness of mouth, loss of appetite, nausea, stuffy nose

Long-term effects

Some effects persist several weeks to months after drug withdrawal and might include mental depression severe enough to cause suicide, sedation, decreased sexual interest, and slow heartbeat.

SEE ALSO:
Depression • Mental Disorders • Norepinephrine • Suicide

Reward

The reward system of the brain evolved to provide a pleasurable sensation for maintaining vital functions such as eating, drinking, and sex. This system is also triggered by drugs and plays a key part in the process of addiction.

It is generally assumed that humans as well as other organisms engage in behaviors that have rewarding consequences. That is, if a specific behavior is followed by pleasurable feelings, the experience of these feelings will serve as positive reinforcement so that the behavior will be repeated in the future. This argument is often used to explain why drug addiction develops. In other words, individuals keep taking drugs because the drugs produce rewarding feelings, which are as pleasurable, and sometimes even more pleasurable, than the feelings produced by natural rewards, such as food, water, or sex. Although appealing because of its simplicity, this view blurs important differences between reward and reinforcement that are crucial to our understanding of the psychological and neurobiological processes involved in drug addiction.

Reinforcement

Reinforcing stimuli are events that follow responses and change the probability that these responses will occur in the future. This change occurs because reinforcing stimuli have the ability to enhance the formation of memories about the situations in which they are encountered, that is, the stimuli that precede a given response, the response itself, and the consequences of the response. Such memories increase the probability that, in the presence of certain stimuli, the response leading to reinforcement will be repeated in the future. It is important to note that this action of reinforcers is not dependent on their rewarding properties; it simply refers to their ability to enhance the storage of information in the brain. It is known from animal studies, for example, that electrical stimulation of certain brain regions following an experience can improve the memory of that experience, even though the stimulation lacks some of the intrinsic motivational properties. Also, some stimulatory drugs, such as strychnine and pentylenetetrazol, will enhance memory formation, but there is no evidence that either of them has rewarding properties. Amphetamine, on the other hand, is an example of a stimulatory drug that has memory-enhancing functions and is also rewarding. Animal studies, however, have indicated that the memory-enhancing and rewarding actions of amphetamine can be dissociated by injecting this drug directly into different brain regions, which is consistent with the notion that reinforcement and reward can be independently processed in the brain.

Reinforcing stimuli have another major function: they motivate behavior by conferring conditioned motivational properties on previously neutral stimuli. In other words, one effect of introducing a reinforcer into a learning situation is to confer motivational power to previously nonmotivating stimuli. This process appears to be dependent on the reinforcer's action on a circuitry composed of specific brain regions. Much of what is known about the biological mechanisms of reinforcement is based on studies showing that rats can be trained to press a lever for tiny electrical jolts to specific regions of the brain, a phenomenon known as intracranial self-stimulation (ICSS). On the basis of pharmacological, neuroanatomical, and electrophysiological studies, it has been determined that the mesocorticolimbic dopaminergic (DA) system is central to ICSS. Furthermore, rodents and nonhuman primates can be trained to self-administer intravenously a number of drugs that are typically abused by humans, such as amphetamine, cocaine, heroin, morphine, and marijuana. The mesocorticolimbic DA system is also central to drug self-administration.

The core of the reinforcement circuitry in the mammalian brain contains at least three neural elements: first, a descending pathway originating in the front of the medial forebrain bundle and projecting rearward to dopaminergic neurons in the ventral tegmental area; second, an ascending dopaminergic pathway originating in the ventral tegmental area, projecting upward and forward through the medial forebrain bundle onto neurons in the nucleus accumbens, prefrontal cortex, septum, amygdala, and hippocampus; and third, a descending

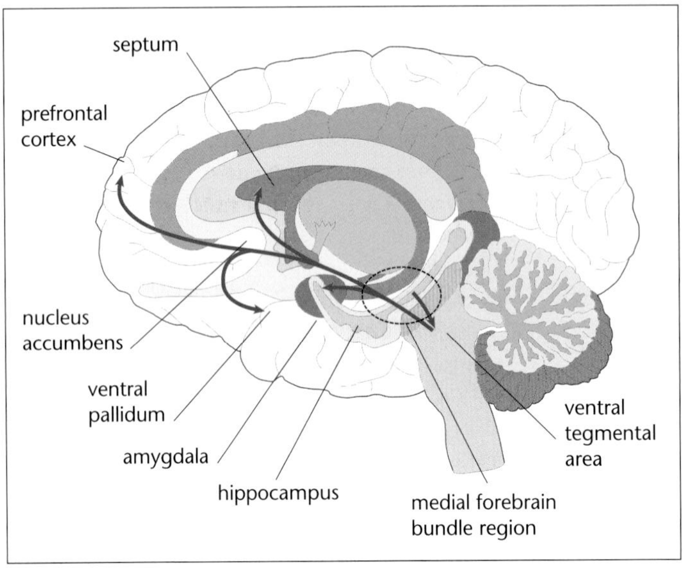

Dopamine pathways in the brain stimulate areas responsible for memory, motivation, and pleasure, which form the reward system.

pathway originating in the nucleus accumbens and projecting to the ventral pallidum. It appears that the dopaminergic fibers in this circuitry are crucial to the motivational properties of most reinforcing stimuli. In fact, both natural reinforcers and addictive drugs have the ability to enhance, although by different neurochemical mechanisms, dopaminergic activity in the nucleus accumbens. However, in contrast with the dopaminergic response to natural reinforcers, which habituates (becomes less responsive) with repeated exposure, drugs of abuse activate dopamine transmission without any loss of the rewarding effect. It has been hypothesized that this process abnormally strengthens stimulus-drug associations, thus resulting in the attribution of excessive motivational value to discrete stimuli or situations where drugs are available. Viewed this way, therefore, drug addiction is the expression of the excessive control over behavior acquired by drug-related stimuli as a result of abnormal associative learning following repeated stimulation of dopaminergic transmission in the nucleus accumbens.

Reward

Not only is reward different from reinforcement, but it also contains multiple psychological components involved in different aspects of drug addiction. These components are learning, affect or emotion, and motivation.

Learning is essential to the acquisition of information relating stimuli, responses, and their rewarding or aversive consequences. This knowledge is then used for predictions about expected rewards, for making anticipatory responses, for guidance by environmental cues, and for goal-directed actions. Some learning about rewarding stimuli is quite basic. This would be the case for reward prediction whereby a conditioned stimulus reliably predicts the occurrence of an unconditioned rewarding stimulus, leading an organism to exhibit preparatory responses before the presentation of the reward. Alternatively, specific instrumental responses to stimuli predicting rewarding outcomes may be strengthened by response-contingent reinforcement. Other learning about rewarding stimuli may be more complex. This would be the case when forming cognitive representations of situations that combine predictive and causal relationships between stimuli, responses, and rewarding outcomes, and which are ultimately used to guide explicit goal-directed behaviors.

The consumption of a reward also has affective components. In the context of drug addiction, however, it is important to note that the subjective emotional reaction to rewards may be dissociated from conscious awareness and from actual behavior. For example, experimental evidence has indicated that drug addicts will exhibit behavior reinforced by drugs such as stimulants and opiates, without being aware of doing so, and for drug doses that produce no discernable subjective effects. Also, it is fairly well-known that drug addicts typically complain about the reduction of pleasure associated with their drug use and express a strong desire to stop using, yet they keep self-administering compulsively. These and other observations have led psychologists to make a distinction between the affective and motivational consequences of rewarding stimuli.

The conscious pleasure associated with a reward has been equated to the subjective affective reaction it produces and has been termed *liking*. Examples of objective affective reactions of liking or "disliking" include a number of facial expressions displayed by mammals as a reaction to different tastes. Thus, sweet tastes typically produce tongue protrusions, while bitter tastes elicit gapes. It is interesting to note that dopaminergic activity in the mesocorticolimbic dopamine system is neither necessary nor sufficient to the experience of liking. Thus, a number of pharmacological manipulations that enhance or disrupt dopaminergic activity in this system have no effect on facial reactions to various tastes. This may explain why dopamine-receptor antagonists, at doses that do not produce gross motor and motivational impairments, generally have no effect on the feelings of pleasure associated with the use of amphetamine or the smoking of cigarettes in humans.

Motivational consequences

The motivational consequences of reward, on the other hand, have been termed *wanting*. Of course, rewards that are liked are usually also wanted, but nevertheless the two processes are dissociable. This motivational component of reward is termed the *incentive salience,* and it transforms the sensory information of a stimulus (sight, sound, smell, and so on) by giving it an attractive or desirable quality. The incentive value of rewards can be attributed to other stimuli, turning them into motivational magnets that elicit similar behaviors. For example, a crack-cocaine addict searching a table for unused crystals may have a response if he or she comes across spilled sugar or salt. Incentive salience, or wanting, unlike liking, is crucially dependent on dopamine activity in the mesocorticolimbic dopamine system.

Many of these learning and motivational processes are severely disturbed by chronic exposure to drugs of abuse. Furthermore, drug addiction is not a static phenomenon and, similar to other behavioral problems with biological determinants, there are different components that take part in the cycle as addiction takes hold. Within this cycle, reinforcement and reward processes change drastically. Positive reinforcement occurs when presentation of the drug increases the probability of a response to obtain the drug again. This typically occurs in the initial stages of addiction, when drugs have strong rewarding properties. With repeated use, however, negative reinforcement becomes more frequent as drugs are used to alleviate a drug-generated aversive state (drug withdrawal). At this point, use becomes a "coping strategy," and the rewarding effects of drugs become secondary to their ability to alleviate withdrawal. Crucial to the transition from positive to negative reinforcement is the disruption of an allostatic state.

Allostasis is defined as the process of achieving stability through change, and an allostatic state is defined as a state of chronic deviation of the regulatory system from its normal operating level. Chronic drug use is believed to directly alter brain systems involved in reward and reinforcement. It also activates neurochemical and hormonal responses aimed at compensating for these drug-induced alterations. Thus, from the drug addiction perspective, allostasis is the process of stabilizing reinforcement and reward functions by recruiting changes in the neural systems that process these functions. It is hypothesized that with chronic drug use these adaptive processes fail to return within the normal range, leading to further disruptions that make the allostatic state grow and induce additional drug use.

Such disturbances of the reinforcement and reward systems are believed to compromise the functioning of various neurotransmitter systems, including the dopamine and the natural opiate systems (endorphins and enkephalins), in specific components of the mesocorticolimbic system such as the nucleus accumbens, amygdala, and prefrontal cortex. Furthermore, brain and hormonal stress systems are also recruited, which induces abnormal activation of corticotrophin-releasing factor stress hormone and the norepinephrine neural systems. It is argued that the manifestation of this allostatic state as compulsive drug taking may be the result of activation of neural circuits in the cortico-striatal-thalamic system. These circuits are believed to be implicated in other repetitive or obsessive-compulsive behavioral disorders.

F. LERI

SEE ALSO:
Addiction • Causes of Addiction, Biological • Craving • Dependence • Reinforcement • Sensitization • Tolerance • Withdrawal

Risk Factors

The likelihood of becoming addicted to drugs is not the same for everybody. There are, however, a number of factors that have been identified as indicative of risk potential in children and adolescents.

The concept of risk factors first emerged through studies on public health, when researchers and scientists became interested in trying to learn more about what increases a person's risk for developing certain physical diseases. A risk factor can be defined as an event, experience, or characteristic that increases the likelihood that a particular outcome of interest (for example, cancer, obesity, or addiction) will occur.

A risk factor for addiction can be defined as an event, experience, or characteristic that precedes the onset of addiction and has been found to increase the likelihood that addiction will develop. Thus, in order to be a risk factor, the event or characteristic must temporally come before the addiction and must make it more likely that addiction will manifest. Note that a risk factor does not guarantee that the outcome of interest will occur, it only increases the chances of it occurring. For example, eating a high-fat diet has been shown to be a risk factor for obesity, but that does not mean that people who eat a high-fat diet will always become obese. The final outcome will depend on a number of other factors, such as how often they exercise, their metabolism, or genetic factors. Similarly, a risk factor does not necessarily cause the outcome of interest. It may only increase the likelihood that the outcome of interest will occur, for whatever reason. In the following sections, different types of risk factors for addiction and the role of intervention in reducing those risk factors will be discussed.

Types of risk factors

Researchers have identified a number of different types of risk factors for addiction. These can be subsumed under three broad risk factor categories: the person, the social situation, and the environment he or she inhabits.

Risk factors concerning the person include, for example, having positive beliefs about substance use, having expectations that the substance use will be beneficial in some way (for example, it will make him or her feel more confident or decrease feelings of anxiety), and lower perceived risk of negative consequences from using substances. In addition, certain types of behavioral characteristics and temperaments, such as a high degree of sensation seeking, impulsivity, aggression, and the inability to delay gratification have been found to be risk factors for substance use. Finally, having certain types of psychiatric disorders, such as major depression, bipolar disorder, antisocial personality disorder, and post-traumatic stress disorder, also increases the risk for addiction.

Risk factors involving the social situation include, for example, having close attachments with people who use drugs, social norms that facilitate drug use, having peers who use drugs, and a lack of social support. In addition, a lack of coping skills (not knowing how to resist offers from others to use drugs, not being able to be assertive and stand up for oneself, feeling excessively shy with peers) can increase the risk of using substances.

Environmental risk factors for addiction include having easy access to drugs, the price or cost of substances, being exposed to and having positive beliefs about media portrayal of substance use, lack of support from parents, relaxed laws and regulatory policies concerning alcohol and drugs, and low exposure to prevention programs.

Some of the risk factors mentioned above can be directly targeted in intervention programs. Other risk factors exist that are much harder to target directly—such as having a family history of substance use, being genetically predisposed to addiction, distressed family functioning, a history of stressful life experiences, and the biological mother's prenatal use of substances—which must be counteracted more indirectly through intervention programs.

It is important to remember that none of these risk factors in and of themselves indicates that a person will develop an addiction. Typically, a person's risk for addiction will depend on the types of risk factors, the particular combination of factors, and the overall number of factors that are affecting him or her.

Fighting, aggressive behavior, and constantly getting into trouble, together with personality disorders and a pro-drug peer group, are among some of the risk factors for developing an addiction.

Role of intervention in reducing risks

A great deal of research has been conducted on learning how to reduce risk factors for addiction. One of the main reasons that studying risk factors is so important is that risk factors are a prime target for intervening early in the process of addiction. First, a risk factor must be identified. Then, interventions can be developed to help treat or minimize the risk factor, which will in turn help reduce the likelihood that the outcome of interest (in this case, drug addiction) will occur. For example, scientists and nutritionists know that a diet high in fat is a risk factor for obesity, so programs have been developed to help people decrease their fat intake, which then decreases their risk for obesity. The same is true for addiction. Years of research have helped to identify risk factors for addiction. Then, programs have been developed to help address and treat these risk factors, which in turn helps to decrease the likelihood that addiction will develop.

One of the most powerful aspects of interventions designed to target risk factors is that they have the ability to help prevent addiction from developing in the first place. These interventions are very different from interventions that are designed to treat an addiction that has already developed. In many ways, it can be more effective to address risk factors for an addiction that has not yet developed than it is to treat an addiction that has already developed.

Another, related reason that intervention programs are so important in reducing risk is that they help to identify individuals who are particularly vulnerable to developing an addiction later in life. Not everyone has the same level of risk. Once individuals who are at a heightened level of risk or susceptibility are identified, steps can be taken to help reduce that risk with the overall goal of preventing the onset of addiction for that person, or for that group of people.

S. E. BACK

SEE ALSO:
Adolescents and Substance Abuse • Biopsychosocial Theory of Addiction • Intervention • Prevention • Protective Factors • Vulnerability

Ritalin

Many children diagnosed with attention deficit disorder are prescribed Ritalin to improve their concentration. However, Ritalin is a member of the amphetamine family, and therefore has potential for drug abuse.

Ritalin is the trade name for the drug methylphenidate used by the pharmaceutical manufacturer Novartis, and it has also become the common name for the drug. Methylphenidate is available from a number of other drug manufacturers as well, under a variety of names. Methylphenidate is a psychostimulant drug and, as such, belongs to the same pharmacological class as cocaine and amphetamine. Ritalin is most well-known as the treatment for attention deficit disorders (ADD), though it has also long been used in the treatment of narcolepsy and is sometimes used in the treatment of stroke.

Methylphenidate was first synthesized in 1944 and went on the market as a prescription drug in the mid-1950s. At the time it was recommended for the treatment of lethargy, narcolepsy, and depression. Since the mid-1960s, Ritalin has been the primary pharmacological treatment for ADD. In ADD, which is found most often in boys, though it is seen in girls and adults as well, patients are unable to concentrate, usually on schoolwork, and may become loud and disruptive in search of stimulation. Ritalin has been found to increase the ability of ADD patients to focus attention and to reduce the impulsivity and behavioral disruptions the disorder can produce. The exact mechanism by which Ritalin acts remains poorly understood. Like cocaine and amphetamine, Ritalin acts at the transporter proteins for the neurotransmitters dopamine and norepinephrine. There is some evidence that at therapeutic doses Ritalin principally effects norepinephrine, rather than dopamine. Dopamine is more strongly correlated with abuse potential, which may explain why methylphenidate is not as widely abused as cocaine or amphetamine. Therapeutically it is less likely to produce tolerance and toxic side effects than its relatives, and it is thus preferred for clinical uses.

Ritalin is not entirely benign, however. Concerns about its potential for abuse have been voiced since the early 1960s. The oral form used in prescriptions is not the preferred form for abusers; more often abusers will grind the pills into a powder and then either inject or snort it. All three routes have been reported clinically in abusers, and the latter two have been associated with a number of deaths. Ritalin is sometimes injected mixed with Talwin (pentazocine) or heroin as a speedball. Reports of abuse and toxicity have become more common as diagnosis of ADD has increased and the drug has become more available. During the period from 1985 to 1995, methylphenidate production in the United States increased nearly eightfold to more than 10 tons a year.

R. G. HUNTER

KEY FACTS

Classification

Schedule II (USA), Schedule III (Canada), Class B (UK), Schedule II (INCB). Stimulant.

Street names

R, Rit, Ts and Rits (with Talwin), Vitamin R, West Coast

Short-term effects

Like other psychostimulants, Ritalin can produce reduced appetite, agitation, increased activity, constricted pupils and verbosity. Anxiety and paranoia are common negative states associated with Ritalin abuse. In ADD patients, Ritalin has a paradoxical calming effect at therapeutic doses.

Long-term effects

Ritalin may increase the chances of seizures and cardiovascular events in predisposed individuals or in overdose situations. Withdrawal from Ritalin may produce major depressive episodes.

SEE ALSO:
Amphetamines • Attention Deficit Disorder • Cocaine • Norepinephrine

Rohypnol

Rohypnol is a brand name for flunitrazepam, a benzodiazepine drug similar to Valium. It is one of the so-called date-rape drugs, because some criminals use it to render their victims vulnerable to sexual assault or robbery.

Rohypnol (flunitrazepam) is a benzodiazepine, a class of drugs that also includes Valium (diazepam), Restoril (temazepam), and Xanax (alprazolam). These drugs reduce anxiety and can cause sedation by enhancing the action of GABA (gamma-aminobutyric acid), a neurotransmitter that calms brain activity. Sedative benzodiazepines also block memory formation during their period of action, which makes them useful for surgery.

Differences in potency, speed of onset, and duration of effect between individual benzodiazepines make them suitable for diverse applications. When Roche launched Rohypnol in 1975, its intended uses included insomnia treatment and the induction of anesthesia, since the drug takes effect within 30 minutes and has up to 10 times the sedative potency of diazepam. The effects of a dose of Rohypnol usually wear off within 10 hours.

Recreational use

Rohypnol soon became a street drug through the diversion of prescription supplies. In common with other benzodiazepines, it amplifies the effects of other central nervous system (CNS) depressants, such as alcohol and opiates. The high potency of Rohypnol increases the danger of death by accidental overdose for people who are accustomed to taking less potent benzodiazepines, such as temazepam. The combination of Rohypnol with alcohol can in some cases unleash violent and cold-blooded behavior by suppressing inhibitions and conscience.

Rohypnol counteracts the effects of CNS stimulants such as cocaine and amphetamines. Hence, some stimulant users take Rohypnol to reduce symptoms of anxiety produced by the stimulant or to bring the stimulant effect to an end and allow them to catch up on sleep.

Whether taken alone or with other drugs, the regular use of Rohypnol or any other benzodiazepine rapidly leads to increased tolerance and physiological dependence. Withdrawal symptoms are diverse and include irritability, restlessness, headaches, delirium, and hallucinations. Sudden withdrawal can cause seizures and heart failure several days after taking the last dose, and people who have become dependent on Rohypnol should reduce their intake gradually, with medical guidance and supervision.

In itself, the blister packaging of Rohypnol pills is no guarantee of legitimate manufacture or purity. The importation of Rohypnol to the United States has been banned since 1996, and supplies are of clandestine origin. Street names for Rohypnol pills include roofies, rope, ruffies, and Mexican Valium.

Drugged assaults

Rohypnol is odorless, neutral tasting, and colorless, and it dissolves easily in water. Hence, a person who intends to rape or rob can easily slip a sedative dose into the drink of an intended victim without detection. The drug also eliminates all memory of the crime, thereby protecting the criminal.

Roche has introduced a blue dye and sediment-forming material into Rohypnol pills in Europe, but illicitly manufactured doses have no such additives to assist detection. Partygoers should be vigilant of their drinks at all times and contact a responsible friend or staff member if sudden unexpected drunkenness indicates that a drink might have been contaminated.

M. CLOWES

SEE ALSO:

Benzodiazepines • Chloral Hydrate • Crime and Drugs • GHB • Rape • Tolerance • Valium

School and Drugs

Evidence suggests that students who attend schools where substances are used and sold are twice as likely to smoke, drink, or use illegal drugs as those who attend drug-free schools.

In the United States, adolescent drug use rates have stopped growing, but usage rates for 2004 still reflect a serious problem. Since 1972, alcohol and tobacco use has doubled, while marijuana use has tripled. Nearly half of all high school students had used illicit drugs by the time they finished high school. Of the 4.5 million people aged 12 and older who need drug treatment, 23 percent are teenagers. Heroin use remains alarmingly high. Illegal, prescription, and over-the-counter drugs are abused for recreation.

Scope of the problem

Malignant Neglect, a report by the Center on Addiction and Substance Abuse (2001), notes that in the United States, nearly 10 million high school students and almost 5 million middle school students attend schools where drugs are used and sold. For six consecutive years, these 12- to 17-year-olds have reported that drugs are the number one problem they face. The toll that substance abuse adds to the national education budget is estimated to be at least $41 billion per year. These expenses are hidden in the overall cost of class disruption, violence, special education and tutoring, teacher turnover, truancy, property damage, injury, and counseling. To an even greater degree, the costs to individual teens and their families are seen in skill deficits, lost opportunities, emotional turmoil, financial debt, crime, and for some, death.

Many adults look on adolescent experimentation with cigarettes, alcohol, and drugs as a benign rite of passage. Yet, a high proportion of students who experiment with alcohol and other drugs continue using them throughout their high school years. Research shows that people who make it through their teenage years without using drugs are much less likely to start using them when they are older. There are good physiological reasons to postpone use.

Scientists have discovered that the brain is not fully developed in early childhood, as was once believed, but is in fact still growing in adolescence. Introducing chemical changes in the brain through the use of alcohol, nicotine, and other drugs can have far more serious adverse effects on teenagers than on adults. Because their brains are still developing, teens who drink to excess may be destroying greater mental capacity than older drinkers. At a level of three drinks, younger drinkers demonstrate performance impairments 25 percent greater than older drinkers.

Media messages bombard children from an early age, promising that tobacco, alcohol, and other drugs can provide the things that most teenagers are searching for—popularity, escape, and feeling grown up. Typically, young people make choices about substance use between the ages of 10 and 12 and begin experimenting by the age of 13 or 14.

Because it is readily available, alcohol is the main drug of choice among teenagers. Nicotine use has increased and is the second most commonly abused substance among this age group. Marijuana ranks third, with heroin, cocaine, club drugs (such as Ecstasy), prescription drugs, and over-the-counter substances also popular. Household aerosols or inhalants are likely to be abused by younger children.

Why young people use drugs

Teenagers use drugs for a variety of internal and external reasons. There are two main internal reasons for adolescent drug use. The first reason that young people use drugs is simply to feel good or excited. Other reasons include feeling grown up, fitting in, belonging, taking risks, and satisfying curiosity.

The second reason that some young people use drugs is that they are doing so to feel better, or even normal. Students from this group are often stuck in difficult life situations such as poverty, abusive families, and families with untreated addiction or mental health problems.

Some studies indicate that as many as 10 million children and adolescents suffer from mental health problems, so that their ability to function is reduced, and they are at very high risk for addiction. These young people are not using drugs for recreation. Rather, they use drugs to medicate feelings and help

Life skills training programs are used in schools to prevent drug and alcohol use by developing self-esteem. The students are taught how to set goals and handle social situations and peer pressure.

them feel normal. This kind of drug use only masks deeper problems, often making them worse.

Both types of teenage drug users may be affected by the external environment at school. The school climate itself may encourage substance abuse. Learning and teaching occur best in school environments that are positive, orderly, and safe. Disruptive and violent behaviors decrease the effectiveness of teaching and learning for everyone. Students who attend schools where they feel afraid, or are teased, bullied, or harassed, may experience difficulty coping, and learning is compromised.

In an effort to be accepted as part of the school culture, some students yield to peer pressure and use substances to fit in with a group, thus avoiding the intimidation that can fester in a negative school climate. At times students use alcohol and other drugs simply to look "cool" and to imitate older students. Whatever the reason, drug use interferes with learning, friendships, and future planning.

Effects of drugs on students

The brain is the control center of the body and has different structures that handle different types of incoming information. When a teenager abuses drugs, all of these structures are affected. The areas specific to learning are those related to memory, language, math, and problem solving. Common warning signs include a drop in grades, shortened attention span, inability to remember tasks and assignments, failure to complete homework or class assignments, difficulty retaining new or recent information, decreased class participation, cheating, or not taking advantage of assistance offered.

Students who are harmfully involved with drugs begin to lose interest in things that once were important to them. Good grades, participation in sports, activities, and leadership opportunities no longer matter. Time and energy get focused on acquiring and using drugs. Denial and resistance dominate perception. Brain changes also slow memory, information processing, planning for long- and short-term assignments and projects.

The more a student uses alcohol, marijuana, and other illicit drugs, the lower grade point average is likely to be. Alcohol-dependent youths fare worse on language and attention tests than nondependent youths. Heavy and binge drinkers between the ages of 12 and 17 are significantly more likely than nondrinkers to say that their school work is poor and are more than four times more likely to say they cut classes or skip school. Academic concerns are often complicated by behavioral changes and disciplinary consequences. These "red flags" may indicate that substance abuse is at the root of these learning barriers, or that it may be contributing to another mental health issue such as depression.

Behavior changes

The limbic system is the place in the brain where emotions and impulses are generated. Because drug use affects so many places in the limbic system, a teenager's ability to control his or her impulses can be reduced. Also, because of the changes in certain neurotransmitters, a once happy and positive person can become negative and defensive subsequent to substance abuse. No one knows how long this process takes because it is dependent on the individual's genetic makeup and life stressors. For some, harmful consequences start shortly after use begins. For others, it takes longer.

Common behavioral warning signs include increased absences, lateness to school or class, stealing money or valuables, increased suspensions, verbally abusing peers and teachers, negative attitude, fighting, sudden outbursts of anger, denial of responsibility or blaming others, mixing with an older or younger social group, withdrawal, and lying.

What teachers can do

Teachers are a consistent influence in the life of a student, and supportive and caring relationships with teachers can be an important protective factor. Students who feel an attachment to their school use cigarettes, alcohol, and marijuana less often than students who do not feel as connected.

Adolescents are developing autonomy from parents and are engaged in the process of self-discovery. They need positive role models who can offer them both examples and new skills for looking at themselves and the world. When students encounter teachers who help connect them to the school and their peers in positive ways, students can experience a strong sense of empowerment.

Students who are empowered understand that they are in control of the decisions that they make. Teachers who provide practice in decision making, stress management, communication, and conflict resolution help young people see that there are positive and negative consequences associated with the choices they make. Every teacher can convey the message that, contrary to popular belief, drug use is not the norm for adolescents.

Not all substance abuse can be prevented, however. It is important that teachers know how to identify and work with students who experience learning barriers resulting from their use of drugs.

Suspecting drug abuse in students

When teachers take the time to develop a "strengths-based" approach, they can recognize changes that surface when students are harmfully involved with alcohol and drugs. Teachers are in the best position to detect small changes in students' academic performance, attendance, behavior, and health. In fact, a good teacher may address learning barriers that emerge in any of these four spheres without ever suspecting substance abuse as a root cause. The student who shows declines in any or all of these areas may be asking for help without ever uttering the words.

The first and best intervention when a teacher recognizes such changes is to talk with the student. Asking how the teacher can help, rather than telling the student how it will be done, is one way to open the discussion. Sticking with the facts is best, since objective and verifiable information is difficult to dispute, while subjective judgments about the student may generate resistance. Offering understanding of the pressures teenagers face in today's culture, while remaining firm, is key. Persistence and consistency in letting students know that no matter how bad the problem is, someone still believes in them, can be a tangible lifesaver.

However, students should not be rescued from the consequences of their drug use. An action plan can be developed, preferably one that involves parents. The plan is then given a run of several weeks to allow the student to improve. If the student is unable to keep appointments for extra help, turn in assignments on time, or show signs of progress, it may then be time to refer the student to the counselor or Student Assistance Program (SAP).

Once a referral to the SAP is made, the discussions that follow are confidential. The teacher may never know the outcome of the referral, unless the student

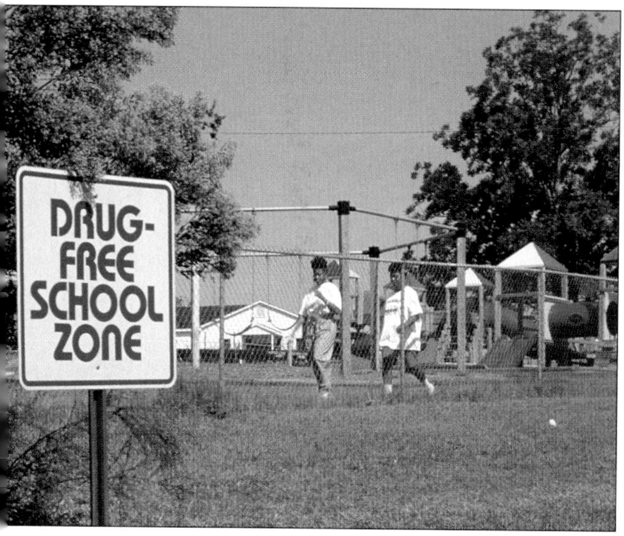

Some schools post signs around their boundaries to reinforce the message that drugs are not welcome on the premises and that use is forbidden.

chooses to discuss it. Students need to have a confidential and safe climate for working through issues such as depression, eating disorders, and substance abuse, without everyone knowing what the core issues are. The common ground where teachers, SAP, counseling, and parents meet continues to be in the area of developing strategies for helping the student succeed in school.

Intervention and treatment

Parents, teachers, and community members constantly debate how to stop drug abuse in schools, and there are no easy answers. Concerned adults who care about young people must ensure that intervention and treatment programs are available and fully funded so that substance-abusing teenagers have help and hope available.

It is easier and less expensive to stop use entirely, and thus prevent the development of addiction. This is not possible for all students, so safety nets, such as the SAP, can be helpful to students, their parents, teachers, schools, and the community at large.

Student Assistance Programs began as substance abuse intervention programs in the 1980s and were designed to help teachers identify danger signs and to help students and parents access treatment agencies. Today, SAPs work not only with alcohol and other drug problems, but help those students who suffer from the effects of violence and trauma, depression, eating disorders, self-injury, and other difficulties. In fact, SAPs can assist with any learning barrier.

The core of the program is usually a specially trained team of school personnel who work with referrals from concerned teachers, parents, administrators, and the students themselves. Students can and do self-refer to SAP. SAP screens the referral and then gathers information from everyone who works with the student to determine how best to help. Sometimes, an assessment with an agency that specializes in alcohol and drug problems or mental health issues is recommended. At other times, students are referred to in-school groups that help teenagers deal with a variety of issues from grief and loss to relationship troubles.

Several team members sit down with a student and his or her parents or guardians and talk about the facts. It is sometimes hard for teenagers and parents to face reality, while for others it can be a relief and an opportunity to get help. SAP teams help students during and after treatment with support groups, academic plans, and other strategies to get back on track.

The decision to get treatment for a young person is an important one, but the entire family, especially parents, suffers from the effects and needs treatment. In therapy, teenagers look at issues of motivation, build skills to resist drug use, replace drug-using activities with constructive and rewarding behaviors, and improve problem-solving skills. Behavioral therapy also facilitates interpersonal relationships and the teenager's ability to function in the home and at school.

Treatment and recovery is about helping the young person take back control of his or her life. Recovery from substance abuse is a process. As with other chronic illnesses, relapses can occur during or after successful treatment. Addicts may require longer treatment, and more than once, in order to finally achieve sobriety. Participation in self-help support programs during and following treatment often is helpful in maintaining abstinence.

S. TARASEVICH

SEE ALSO:
Adolescents and Substance Abuse • Education • Intervention • Peer Influence • Prevention

Secobarbital

Secobarbital is a barbiturate, one of a family of sedative drugs that can induce sleep and reduce anxiety. Although rarely used clinically, secobarbital is still used by addicts to reduce the excitatory effects of stimulants.

Secobarbital, also known by its trade name Seconal, is a sedative drug abused for its effects in reducing anxiety and producing relaxation and euphoria. Polydrug abusers use it as a "downer" to reduce the unpleasant side effects of repeated stimulant use. Conversely, secobarbital abusers will use stimulants to remain alert. Secobarbital is sometimes used for sleep induction prior to surgical anesthesia, as the antianxiety effect is very helpful in this setting. It is occasionally used by psychiatrists for its disinhibitory effect to help patients recover repressed memories after psychological damage.

KEY FACTS

Classification
Schedule II (USA), Schedule IV (Canada), Class B (UK), Schedule III (INCB). Sedative.

Street names
Barbs, F-40s, Mexican reds, pink ladies, red birds, red devils, secco, seggy

Short-term effects
Relaxation, euphoria, decreased inhibitions, coordination problems, sleepiness progressing to coma if taken with other depressants

Long-term effects
Insomnia, tremulousness, agitation, erratic behavior, paranoia, social isolation. Risk of fatal overdose.

Signs of abuse
Confused or drunken behavior, sleepiness, shallow breathing, unresponsiveness

Pharmacological effects

A typical adult oral dose of secobarbital for sleep induction is 100 to 200 milligrams, though abusers may take increasing amounts as tolerance develops. Secobarbital passes relatively quickly through the blood-brain barrier, though not as rapidly as pentobarbital. The drug is metabolized in the liver by the cytochrome P450 enzyme system and prolonged use induces the liver to synthesize more of these enzymes, leading to faster breakdown and contributing to tolerance. The half-life for elimination of the drug is 19 to 34 hours.

Barbiturates such as secobarbital work by enhancing the action of the inhibitory neurotransmitter gamma-aminobutyric acid (GABA) at its receptor on brain neurons. Secobarbital acts as a central nervous system depressant, slowing reflexes and reaction times, dulling the senses, and causing incoordination and slurring of speech before inducing sleep. Sedation occurs within 15 to 30 minutes after oral ingestion, more quickly for other methods of administration, and lasts 6 to 8 hours.

As with other barbiturates, breathing becomes depressed, hence, the risk of a dangerous overdose increases with prolonged use. Street addicts will sometimes dissolve the contents of the capsule in water and inject secobarbital intravenously, a particularly dangerous practice since an overdose can kill within minutes. Secobarbital is often taken together with other depressant drugs including the opiates and alcohol, a dangerous practice that can lead to coma and death. Barbiturate intoxication also impairs the memory, so users may forget that they have taken it and take additional doses. Tolerance develops quickly and contributes to the addictive potential. Dependence on the drug manifests initially as insomnia but can result in a severe withdrawal syndrome consisting of tremulousness, anxiety, delirium, hallucinations, and seizures.

L. J. GREENFIELD, JR.

SEE ALSO:
Amobarbital • Barbiturates • Gamma-aminobutyric Acid • Pentobarbital • Sedatives and Hypnotics

Sedatives and Hypnotics

Sedatives decrease excitement and produce a calming effect. Hypnotics induce sleep. Both effects are part of the same continuum that can lead to unconsciousness, anesthesia, and fatal depression of the respiratory system.

Probably the oldest sedative known is ethanol. Its effects are dose dependent and, as the dose is increased, the subject progresses through all of the stages identified above. Similar effects can be produced by bromide salts, which were introduced specifically as sedatives in the middle of the nineteenth century. Unfortunately, bromide salts produce significant liver and kidney toxicity. Subsequently, chloral hydrate, paraldehyde, urethane, and sulfonal were used for the same purpose before they were superseded by the barbiturates. Barbital appeared in 1903 and phenobarbital in 1912. The barbiturates were used widely for many years as both sedatives and hypnotics, despite the fact that many suffered fatal overdoses from their use. Indeed, one of the most difficult issues with the sedative drugs is their ability to augment the effects of other sedatives. Taking a barbiturate before bedtime would certainly facilitate a rapid induction of sleep, but taking a barbiturate with alcohol may mean that one does not wake up in the morning—the sad fate of both Marilyn Monroe and Jimi Hendrix.

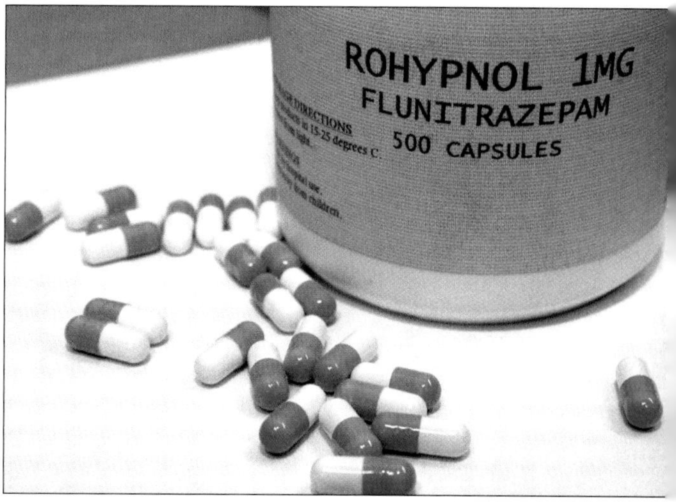

Benzodiazepines such as Rohypnol are much safer than barbiturates but can be used as date-rape drugs.

Safer sedatives

It was not until the introduction of the benzodiazepines in 1960 that efficacious and essentially safe sedative-hypnotic drugs became available to the clinician. As sedatives they proved to be extremely effective in the treatment of anxiety disorders. One such compound is diazepam, which is still widely prescribed today. The hypnotic effects of the benzodiazepines make them particularly suitable for the treatment of insomnia. Three commonly prescribed sleeping pills are zolpidem, zolpiclone, and zaleplon, which produce their sedative properties by binding to the same receptor sites in the brain. The effects of all of these drugs are exacerbated when taken with alcohol. However, the benzodiazepines have a singular advantage: when taken alone they display only part of the spectrum of activity of the older sedative agents. These drugs, even when taken at extremely high doses, rarely produce respiratory and cardiovascular depression. Despite their widespread use, there remain few, if any, documented fatalities from uncomplicated benzodiazepine overdose. The reason for the limited effects of the benzodiazepines is probably quite simple: that is, they have a particularly specific mechanism of action.

The benzodiazepines produce their overt effects by interaction with accessory recognition sites on a single family of receptors in the brain, the $GABA_A$ receptors. These are the receptors for gamma-aminobutyric acid (GABA), a simple amino acid that is responsible for essentially all of the inhibitory transmission within the brain. GABA interacts with two classes of receptors in the brain; the first one to be studied in any detail was the $GABA_A$ receptor, and the second, now commonly referred to as the $GABA_B$ receptor, plays no part in the action of the sedative-hypnotics. The clinically used benzodiazepines produce their effects by reducing the amount of GABA that is required to activate the $GABA_A$ receptor. The result is an increase in neuronal inhibition, leading to sedation and hypnosis. Many of the older sedatives appear to interact in a similar, though mechanistically distinct, manner with the $GABA_A$ receptor, but they are rather "dirty" drugs in the sense that they interact with several other proteins in the brain, which leads to the side effects that compromise their routine clinical use.

When the benzodiazepines were introduced into clinical medicine their advantages were immediately apparent: they were sedative and hypnotic but failed to cause fatalities in overdose. Clearly this was an enormous advantage; they quickly replaced the barbiturates and became the most widely prescribed medications in general practice. In 1983 some 28 million prescriptions for benzodiazepines were issued to a population of 54.8 million in the United Kingdom. They rapidly gained something close to notoriety in the popular press, and in 1985 an attempt was made to restrict what was seen as an overprescription of these agents. A limited list of benzodiazepines was made available for funding by the National Health Service. This approach proved effective and, although the worldwide sales of the benzodiazepine anxiolytics rose by 13 percent between 1981 and 1989, the figures in the United Kingdom fell by 58 percent. During this time, they were most often used to treat clinically debilitating anxiety disorders, allowing sufferers to once again lead productive lives. They remain the most effective pharmacological intervention for generalized anxiety disorder, which is thought to have a prevalence rate of around 10 percent of the population.

In the treatment of anxiety, there is essentially no evidence to suggest that people become tolerant to the benzodiazepines. There is also no evidence of dose escalation, which is a common indication of the development of tolerance. Everyone suffers from occasional anxiety; at times this can be beneficial because it provides motivation to achieve things such as a good grade in an examination or an improved sports performance. Most of us learn to live with a little anxiety. However, there is inevitably a proportion of the population who become dependent on prescribed drugs. Personality type certainly plays a part in defining individuals who become hooked on the benzodiazepines. Only about 20 percent of patients who have been taking benzodiazepines for a significant period of time will exhibit withdrawal symptoms upon cessation of treatment. These symptoms vary from mild, such as difficulty in sleeping for a few days, to more severe, in which the patient feels anxious and jittery once the drug has been withdrawn. Rarely, except after very high doses for prolonged periods, will the patient experience convulsions during withdrawal. Many of these withdrawal symptoms can be alleviated by slowly tapering the drug dose prior to stopping its use.

Drawbacks of sedatives

Since the 1960s, the benzodiazepines have been the drugs of choice for the treatment of the majority of the anxiety and sleep disorders. They are not without their problems but, for the vast majority of patients, they are a means of getting through a difficult time and returning them to a productive and effective way of life. However, the benzodiazepines have also been used as drugs of abuse. In the past, temazepam (Restoril) has been widely abused because it could be removed from gelatin capsules in a form that could be injected. Although changes in drug formulations have significantly reduced this problem, some drug abusers still use oral preparations of temazepam that have been acquired either through prescription or from illicit sources. There has also been an increasing use of some of these agents as so-called date-rape drugs. Rohypnol (flunitrazepam) has proved particularly troublesome in this regard, especially when combined with alcohol. Here an additional property of the benzodiazepines is being exploited: these drugs have pre-amnesic effects, meaning that the recipient is unable to recall what occurred immediately prior to the ingestion. This effect can be clinically useful, for example, when a benzodiazepine such as the short-acting midazolam is used as a pre-anesthetic.

Sedatives and hypnotics are valuable in therapeutic intervention. They improve the quality of life for many people who suffer from anxiety or sleep disorders. Like all drugs, they have their disadvantages. With appropriate medical advice, it is the responsibility of the individual to decide whether the putative gains outweigh any risks that may be involved.

I. L. MARTIN, S. M. J. DUNN

SEE ALSO:
Barbiturates • Benzodiazepines • Chloral Hydrate • Paraldehyde • Rohypnol

Seizures of Drugs

Evidence collected from seizures of drugs suggests that levels of production and smuggling into the United States are stable and declining. However, intercepting the the flow of illegal drugs is a constant struggle for enforcement agencies.

According to the United Nations Office on Drugs and Crime (UNODC), around 3 percent of the world's population, some 185 million people, abused drugs in the 12 months prior to June 2004. This statistic is regarded as reflective of success: the spread of drugs in the world is slowing down—apart, notably, from marijuana. Drug control efforts are increasingly limiting the harm caused by illicit drugs to a fraction of that caused by legal substances such as alcohol and tobacco. Between 2000 and 2002, UNODC figures show that deaths from drug abuse dropped by 20 percent. However, as global opinion still views these improved figures as unacceptable, particularly given the spread of HIV/AIDS among injecting drug users and the particular susceptibility of the young to drug experimentation, operations to seize and control drugs continue unabated.

According to the UN's *World Drug Report 2004*, the Americas rank top in terms of the amount of drugs successfully intercepted at 10.4 billion units or doses of drugs seized (12.1 doses per capita). Europe seized 7.4 billion doses, Asia 5.5 billion, Africa 2.4 billion, and Oceania 0.08 billion. Marijuana remains the most common drug seized, though the Americas have the world's highest rate of cocaine capture. Around 55 percent of all cocaine seizures took place in South America, with the United States second at 32 percent in 2002. Key to this success is the work undertaken by the various agencies tasked with finding and arresting drug dealers and their products.

Guarding the borders of the United States against the entry of drugs is an enormous job: each year, the U.S. Customs Service estimates that 60 million people enter the country on over 675,000 commercial and private flights. Another 6 million enter by sea and 370 million over land. Some 116 million vehicles enter via the land borders with Canada and Mexico. Over 90,000 merchant and passenger ships dock at U.S. ports, carrying more than 9 million shipping containers and 400 million tons of cargo. A further 157,000 smaller vessels visit the country's many coastal towns. In this mass of movement of goods and people, drug traffickers smuggle cocaine, heroin, marijuana, amphetamine, Ecstasy (MDMA), and methamphetamine.

Drug source countries

Drugs arrive in the United States from many different countries of origin. Cocaine mainly enters from Latin America, with Colombian drug traffickers commonly using the eastern Pacific Ocean as a trafficking route. An alternative route smuggles the cocaine to Jamaica and then to the Bahamas aboard fast motorboats and subsequently to the Florida coast in boats, pleasure craft, and fishing vessels.

Most of the marijuana found in the United States is smuggled in from Mexico, but a highly potent form is grown in Canada, and both types are smuggled in along the long land borders with these countries. Some marijuana originating from Southeast Asia is available on the West Coast, and some marijuana is grown domestically, mainly in California, Hawaii, Kentucky, and Tennessee. Much of the heroin destined for the U.S. market is also produced in South America and Mexico, with Southeast Asia and Afghanistan also main sources.

Clandestine "super labs" based in California and Mexico are the primary sources for the methamphetamine available in the United States, with increasing amounts also made by small independent "mom and pop" laboratories. The main access routes into the United States for Mexican methamphetamine have traditionally been via California, particularly San Ysidro. Most of the Ecstasy found in the United States is produced in Europe, particularly Belgium and the Netherlands, using Mexico as a transit zone, with a small amount produced domestically. A small amount of LSD is produced on the West Coast.

Seizure operations

Successes include the culmination of the U.S. Drug Enforcement Administration's (DEA) Operation Web Tryp. This operation, which ended in July 2004, investigated Internet Web sites that distribute dangerous designer drug analogs, mainly tryptamines and phenethylamines, under the pretense of selling "research chemicals." These are mainly shipped to the United States from China and India. The Web sites are known to have thousands of customers around the world, predominantly adolescents and young adults. One site alone is known to have conducted estimated sales of $20,000 per week. The operation resulted in 10 arrests and targeted five Web sites.

Another joint Mexico–U.S. DEA operation in 2004, Operation United Eagles, saw the arrest of two key lieutenants of the Arellano-Felix drug cartel and seven other principal members, effectively breaking it up. This criminal gang transported and distributed multi-ton quantities of cocaine and marijuana, as well as significant amounts of heroin and methamphetamine through Tijuana to San Diego, California.

Operation Streamline, another success, targeted the Colombia-based Ospina trafficking organization, which smuggled over 990 pounds (450 kg) of high grade heroin annually into Miami, Florida, for distribution to New York, Philadelphia, and Newark. The original targets, Orlando and Carlos Ospina, were arrested in Florida by the DEA in May 2003, and the search and arrest operation in January 2004 completely disrupted the organization.

As part of a further operation, 130 people were arrested in March 2004 as part of Operation Candy Box, a three-year, two-nation crackdown on a huge drug trafficking ring that manufactured large quantities of Ecstasy and marijuana in Canada and then shipped them to U.S. cities.

Operation Trifecta was initiated shortly after the December 2001 seizure of 20,500 pounds (9,290 kg) of cocaine from a fishing vessel off the Pacific coast of Mexico. In 2003 the joint Mexico–U.S. DEA operation resulted in the arrest of over 240 individuals and the seizure of significant quantities of drugs, including a cache full of 1,330 pounds (606 kg) of cocaine.

Longer-term operations include the Southwest Border Initiative (SWBI), which has been in operation since 1994. This initiative is a cooperative effort by federal law enforcement agencies to counter the significant threat posed by Mexico-based trafficking groups operating along the southwest border of the United States. Traffickers in this region smuggle multi-ton shipments of heroin, methamphetamine, cocaine, and marijuana.

The SWBI targets the communication systems of traffickers' command and control centers. The DEA, FBI, U.S. Customs Service, and U.S. Attorneys offices around the country work together to put in place wiretaps that identify all levels of the trafficking organizations. This surveillance allows the DEA to track the entire drug trafficking operation as it moves from the country of origin to the streets where the drugs are purchased. Specific successes include Operation Zorro II, Operation Reciprocity, and Operation Limelight. Together, these three operations resulted in the arrest of 156 individuals, the seizure of over 48,400 pounds (22,000 kg) of illegal drugs, and $35 million in cash.

A number of initiatives have been set up to track and seize shipments of drug precursors. For example, Operation Purple, launched in 1999, tracks shipments of more than 250 pounds (100 kg) of the key cocaine processing precursor potassium permanganate. The UN International Narcotics Control Board acts as central coordinator of the operation. Operation Topaz, modeled on Operation Purple, tracks acetic anhydride, a key precursor in heroin manufacture.

The Law Enforcement section of UNODC also assists countries in their drug law enforcement activities and is a key player in cross-border strategies. It also acts as a liaison with other international partners such as Interpol and the World Customs Organization. UNODC successes include work with Bolivia that saw, from 1993 to 1998, more than 20,000 antidrug operations that destroyed at least 13,500 maceration pits, 8,900 cocaine factories or laboratories, and 60 tonnes of cocaine—some 10 to 20 percent of the cocaine production in Bolivia.

L. STEDMAN

SEE ALSO:

Agriculture • Crime and Drugs • Drug Control Policy • Drug Enforcement Administration (DEA) • Drug Trafficking • Enforcement of Laws • Illicit Manufacturing • International Cooperation • International Drug Trade • International Narcotics Control Board (INCB) • Organized Crime • United Nations Office on Drugs and Crime (UNODC)

Self-esteem

Self-esteem is the concept of how we see ourselves and rate our standing in the world. Positive and negative estimates of self-esteem are regarded by many researchers as important factors in the development and maintenance of addiction.

Popular definitions of self-esteem generally involve our assessment of our own worth. Having a high self-esteem will result in having a pride in oneself and behaving like an upright and law-abiding citizen. Conversely, having a low self-esteem can result in any number of antisocial behaviors from crime and violence to teenage pregnancy and drug abuse. Clearly, low-self esteem is a debilitating and powerful force. In recognition of this position, most drug prevention education attempts to "inoculate" adolescents against low self-esteem to prevent drug use and abuse. The question remains, however: is there any truth in the above view or is it merely a myth? There are two main problems with this view of drug use: a definition of what self-esteem is, and beliefs about how this mechanism works.

The first problem with the above theory is that there is no clear consensus on a definition of self-esteem. It is seen variously as a generalized feeling about one's identity and place in the world, or as an assessment based on judgments of self in a number of areas of performance. To clarify, the first position, self-esteem as a generalized feeling, views self-esteem as being an emotional reaction that is generally more or less positive. It is based on a global view of the self that biases how we view specific aspects of ourselves, for example, intelligence or physical attractiveness. The second position suggests that self-esteem is actually made up of a cumulative judgment of all of these other aspects of ourselves. Thus, in this second view, one may have high self-esteem in some areas but not in others, whereas in the first view, self-esteem is either entirely high or entirely low. There is no clear consensus, and both views have strengths and weaknesses.

In the "common sense" view of drug use, low self-esteem leads to young people using drugs as a crutch to compensate for a poor view of themselves and, in turn, drug use prevents adolescents from building and maintaining self-esteem. Does the evidence support such a view? The answer to this question, unfortunately, is not simple. It would appear that studies of alcohol and drug abusers have shown that they have low self-esteem. This is certainly true of dependent drug users. So does this support the compensation, or common sense, view? Actually, it does not. It has been found that low self-esteem is a consequence of drug use, not a cause.

Spraying graffiti "tags" that are recognizable to their peers is one way that adolescents may try to establish an identity and self-esteem among a like-minded group.

The common sense view suggests that adolescents who have low self-esteem are attracted to drugs because drugs will make them feel good, or at least less bad, about themselves. Thus adolescents with high self-esteem will have no (or, at least, less) need or reason to take drugs. As an explanation, it is, at least superficially, highly plausible as it provides a mechanism, low self-esteem, that "causes" drug use and provides a prevention and treatment strategy that should be acceptable to all sections of the population, namely, improve the way adolescents view themselves and they will become model citizens.

The main problem is that the evidence points in the opposite direction. Rather than adolescents with low self-esteem using drugs as a crutch, it would appear to be the adolescents with high self-esteem who are using drugs. Research has shown that early use of cigarettes, alcohol, and drugs are all related to high levels of self-esteem. Initiation of early substance use appears to require a level of confidence and maturity that is not generally found in children who have low self-esteem. Confidence is required to mix with other more mature substance users in order to both acquire the substance and learn how to administer it. Contrary to the popular view of drug users as solitary figures cut off from society and their peers, almost all drug use is surrounded and governed by a rich and unique culture. For example, there are many types of marijuana and many ways to ingest it. The most common way is obviously smoking, but even with smoking there are conventions on how to roll the marijuana cigarettes or prepare pipes, for example, whether tobacco is used, what type, and how much. There are conventions concerning the method of smoking—how to inhale deeply and hold the smoke—and also about sharing. All rituals and customs need to be learned and observed if the adolescent is to fit into the group and also secure his or her supply.

Protection and maintenance

Although high self-esteem does not appear to have a protective effect against initiation of drug use and indeed appears to have the opposite effect, it does have a positive effect against the dilatory consequences of prolonged use. There is a link between low self-esteem and alcohol or drug use; the research suggests that addiction or dependence on a drug leads to low self-esteem. Part of the reason may be the feeling of not being in control of one's life but rather feeling as if a substance (or the need for a substance) is controlling one's decisions or behavior. These feelings of dependence on a substance can seriously erode the self-esteem that one possesses and these negative feelings can in turn lead to more drug use, as the person seeks comfort. Thus low self-esteem may have a role in maintaining drug use. Where high self-esteem does appear to have a protective effect is in regard to the erosion of self-esteem. Research shows that people who have the highest self-esteem at the beginning of drug taking tend to be more robust in respect to developing addiction, that is, they continue to have a good level of esteem and tend not to use drugs to obtain comfort. Alternatively, self-esteem appears to have a protective effect from the more extreme psychological and emotional problems often associated with addiction.

Self-efficacy

A concept related to self-esteem, self-efficacy has been found to be very important in the treatment of addiction problems. Self-efficacy is one's estimation of being able to perform a particular behavior or set of behaviors; for example, drug refusal self-efficacy would be the ability to refuse, or resist taking, a drug. Self-efficacy is usually measured under a variety of conditions; for example, feeling good, feeling bad, when encouraged by friends, at a party, and so on. People low in (drug refusal) self-efficacy under certain conditions—for example, when feeling low, would be at high risk of relapse when this condition is present. However, knowing the high risk situations allows the treatment to be tailored to address the deficit by giving the person strategies to deal with these situations. Having a strategy then increases self-efficacy, and, if the situation is successfully handled, further increases self-efficacy. Thus dealing with situations gets easier as success breeds success, which breeds self-efficacy. This success in self-efficacy in turn feeds back into self-esteem estimates, and the person feels more positive.

While popular opinion often cites low self-esteem among adolescents as a primary cause of drug use, the evidence does not support this view. Instead, addiction and dependency would appear to erode self-esteem. The resultant low self-esteem can maintain use, although a high initial self-esteem may provide some protection against this process. Thus high self-esteem does not appear to be a protective factor against initiation of substance use but instead protects against becoming addicted or the more severe consequences of addiction. Self-efficacy, however, is an important factor in recovery and treatment.

J. MCMAHON

SEE ALSO:
Adolescents and Substance Abuse • Dependence • Peer Influence • Prevention • Vulnerability

Sensitization

Some drugs lead to tolerance, a condition in which more of the drug is needed to produce the same response. However, the reverse of this process, sensitization, can also occur and may play a key role in maintaining drug use.

Much of our understanding of how addictive drugs affect behavior and the brain comes from studies in which laboratory animals are exposed to the drug only once. However, when given the opportunity, people and laboratory animals are likely to self-administer certain drugs repeatedly and sometimes compulsively. For that reason, it is important to understand how the effects of drugs change when they are administered repeatedly. It is well-known that repeated drug administration often results in a decrease in the responsiveness (or tolerance) to some of the drug's effects such that higher doses are needed to produce the same effect. The ability of morphine to suppress pain or of amphetamine to suppress food consumption decreases with repeated and prolonged exposure. The role of tolerance in the development of physical dependence and the role of physical dependence in withdrawal in sustained drug use has been a focus of research on addiction for many decades.

Less appreciated is the fact that not all drug effects involve tolerance and that other effects work in opposite ways. Thus, rather than showing a decrease, some drug effects show an increase with repeated exposure such that lower and lower doses are required to produce the same effect. This phenomenon is known as reverse tolerance, or sensitization. Since the 1990s the phenomenon of sensitization has received much attention among addiction researchers and many think that sensitization plays an important role in the development and maintenance of compulsive drug use and in the high rate of relapse observed in drug addicts even after extended periods of abstinence.

Behavioral sensitization

In a typical laboratory study examining sensitization, a constant dose of a drug is given repeatedly and the behavioral response to successive injections is measured. With this type of treatment procedure, there is a progressive enhancement in the ability of the drug to produce psychomotor activation as indicated by an increase in locomotor hyperactivity and stereotyped behaviors (typically repetitive head and limb movements). If different doses are then administered to generate a dose-effect curve, subjects who are already sensitized to the drug typically show a shift in the dose-effect function for psychomotor activation indicating that in sensitized subjects lower doses are required to produce a response comparable to that of drug-naive (placebo-treated) subjects.

Although sensitization has most thoroughly been studied and characterized using psychomotor stimulant drugs, for example, cocaine and amphetamine, there is substantial evidence that sensitization also occurs with repeated exposure to other abused or addictive drugs, including opiates (morphine and heroin), nicotine, alcohol, methylphenidate, Ecstasy (MDMA), and phencyclidine (PCP).

For practical and ethical reasons sensitization is most often studied in rats and mice. However, sensitization with psychomotor stimulant exposure has been shown in many species ranging from flatworms (planarians) and fruit flies (*Drosophila melanogaster*) to rabbits, cats, dogs, and nonhuman primates. Most important, there is now evidence of amphetamine-induced psychomotor sensitization in drug-naive human subjects. It appears, therefore, that sensitization is a common consequence of repeated exposure to drugs that have a high abuse potential in most species of animals, including humans.

Features of sensitization

Sensitization is a complex and rich phenomenon with many interesting features. First, and probably most striking, is how long sensitization persists after the drug treatments have ceased. In rats, for instance, behavioral sensitization to amphetamine's stimulant effects has been found as long as one year after the last drug exposure. Thus, it may well be that once sensitization is induced it will last for the life of the subject. Consistent with this notion, human amphetamine addicts have been found to be hypersensitive to the effects of amphetamine even after years of abstinence. Second, there is enormous individual variation in the susceptibility to sensitization, even in laboratory animals. Some subjects show rapid and robust sensitization even after a single injection of drug, whereas others sensitize very little or not at all. Third, when sensitization is produced by repeated exposure to one drug, a sensitized response is often seen to different drugs as well (cross-sensitization). Thus, preexposure to amphetamine often makes subjects hypersensitive to the effects of morphine. Cross-sensitization can also occur between drugs and nondrug stimuli, in particular, environmental stressors, such that drug preexposure makes subjects hypersensitive even to mild stressors, and vice versa.

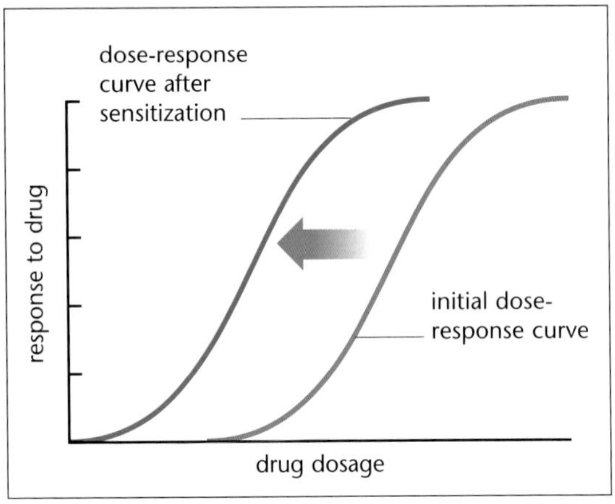

When a laboratory animal becomes sensitized to the effect of a drug, the dose-response curve shifts to the left, so that less of the drug is needed to produce the same effects.

Sensitization of motivational processes

Most studies showing that repeated administration of drugs of abuse produces sensitization involve some measure of the psychomotor activating effects. However, it is now known that not only do the psychomotor stimulant effects of drugs sensitize, but so do their motivational and rewarding effects. For example, prior exposure to a variety of addictive drugs increases the likelihood that animals will subsequently acquire a drug self-administration habit as well as increase the effort that animals are willing to exert to obtain the drug. Also, sensitized subjects are more likely to acquire a preference for places that become associated with drug administration.

However, the ability of sensitization to alter motivational processes is not confined to drug reinforcement and also applies to other aspects of motivation. For instance, animals sensitized to cocaine or amphetamine are more active in pushing levers when the response is reinforced by a stimulus previously associated with a natural reinforcer. Furthermore, the ability of stimuli that have been associated with natural rewards to influence goal-directed behavior is more effective in rats and mice previously exposed to amphetamine compared with control animals. These more general effects of drug sensitization suggest that drug-induced sensitization affects neurobiological reward processing in such a way that various aspects of reward learning become persistently altered; and compulsive drug seeking in addicts may be due to sensitization-related changes in the ability of stimuli to become associated with drug taking and seeking, thus reducing the likelihood that such stimuli will control behavior.

Factors that influence sensitization

Because sensitization affects motivational processes, and the possibility that these effects are critical for understanding addiction, much effort has been directed at identifying factors and circumstances that influence sensitization. Several factors have been identified, including gender-related, treatment-related, and environmental factors.

Gender-related factors. Female rats show more rapid and robust behavioral sensitization than male rats when repeatedly exposed to amphetamine or cocaine. This profound difference is not attributable to pharmacokinetic differences; it is more likely to result from complex interactions between the neurobiological actions of drugs and organizational (developmental) and activational effects of gonadal hormones (in particular, estrogen and testosterone). Sex differences in sensitization could explain differences in the pattern of addiction and relapse seen between male and female drug users.

Treatment-related factors. From laboratory studies we know that the pattern of drug exposure and the amount of time between drug exposures is an important factor in the susceptibility to sensitization. To produce robust sensitization, drug treatments must be given intermittently; and the more time between injections, the more robust the sensitization that is induced. Indeed, when drug injections are given close in time such that brain levels of the drug are chronically elevated, transient tolerance is more likely to occur.

Environmental factors. An important but poorly understood feature of sensitization is that its induction and expression are powerfully modulated by the circumstances surrounding drug administration. There are at least two ways in which environmental circumstances can influence sensitization. First, even when sensitization has been induced, in order for this hypersensitivity to be seen, the environmental circumstances at the time of testing must be similar to those during the drug preexposure phase. Thus, even small changes in the environmental context can profoundly influence whether sensitization is expressed or not. Second, the environmental circumstances can influence whether sensitization is actually induced. When amphetamine or cocaine are administered in the animal's living environment little psychomotor sensitization is often observed, even though these same doses will produce robust sensitization when given after the animal is placed in an unfamiliar or novel environment.

These examples of modulating factors demonstrate that sensitization is a complex phenomenon and not only the result of pharmacological factors. Similarly, we know that many people repeatedly try addictive drugs (for example, alcohol) but only a few actually develop a drug problem, suggesting that mere exposure to the drug is insufficient to explain addiction.

The neurobiology of sensitization

Since the mid-1990s substantial progress has been made in understanding the neurobiological basis of sensitization. Many cellular- and systems-level neuroadaptations have been reported in brain regions known to be important for drug-induced behavioral activation and reward. In particular, the neural system that involves dopamine projections from the midbrain to the nucleus accumbens, prefrontal cortex, and related neural circuitry, seem affected. For instance, sensitizing regimens of amphetamine or cocaine result in persistent increases in the subsequent ability of these drugs to increase concentrations of dopamine and glutamate in these regions—two neurotransmitter systems critically involved in psychomotor activation and reward. Also, sensitization has been associated with persistent structural changes in these regions as characterized by changes in the number and shape of neuronal dendritic processes. These findings are particularly interesting because dendrites are the primary sites of neurochemical information transfer between nerve cells, indicating that sensitization could involve a fundamental reorganization of the brain's neural circuits. Finally, many other cellular and molecular alterations have been reported as a consequence of sensitization. Whether any of these will turn out to be important or merely secondary to the above-mentioned alterations, remains to be seen.

Sensitization and addiction

In an influential review in 1993, Terry Robinson and Kent Berridge proposed the incentive-sensitization theory of addiction, the central tenet of which is that a state of hyperexcitability (sensitization) of the mesolimbic dopaminergic system might be the source of the cravings that drug addicts experience. They argued that potentially addictive drugs share the ability to produce long-lasting adaptations in neural systems that are normally involved in reward processes. As a result of these neuroadaptations, brain reward systems are rendered persistently hypersensitive ("sensitized") to drugs and drug-associated stimuli. Thus, the ability of drugs to produce sensitization-related changes in the brain's reward system may explain why the behavior of some drug users becomes increasingly directed at and controlled by drug and drug-related stimuli, even at the expense of other activities. Additionally, the persistence of sensitization may explain why addicts remain hypersensitive to the effects of drugs and are susceptible to relapse even after long periods of abstinence. It is because of this and because traditional positive and negative reinforcement accounts of addiction insufficiently explain addiction, that sensitization has increasingly become a central focus of drug researchers.

H. CROMBAG

SEE ALSO:
Causes of Addiction, Biological • Craving • Reinforcement • Reward • Tolerance • Withdrawal

Serotonin

Serotonin is one of the principal neurotransmitters implicated in the actions of psychoactive drugs. In its normal function it regulates sleep, mood, and body temperature through its action at various receptor sites in the body and brain.

Serotonin produces the psychoactive effects of psychedelic drugs such as LSD, as well as of entactogenic-empathogenic drugs such as Ecstasy. Serotonin also contributes to the unpleasant and sometimes life-threatening side effects of such drugs.

Insufficient serotonin activity is believed to be a cause of anxiety, depression, eating disorders, sleep problems, vulnerability to stress, and obsessive-compulsive behavior such as repeated unnecessary hand washing. Excessive serotonin activity causes serotonin syndrome—a variety of psychiatric and physiological disorders that can sometimes kill.

Formation and function

Serotonin forms from tryptophan—an amino acid derived from food—via 5-hydroxytryptophan (5-HTP). Both tryptophan and 5-HTP can cross the blood-brain barrier, whereas serotonin cannot. Hence, all serotonin in the brain forms there and cannot escape. Serotonin also forms in the gut, where it governs secretion into the gut and peristalsis, the wavelike contractions that propel material through the intestines. Serotonin also has roles in causing vomiting and the aggregation of blood platelets.

Serotonin in the brain accumulates in vesicles, or small vessels, near the transmitting ends of serotonergic neurons. When a nerve impulse arrives at the end of such a neuron, vesicles disgorge serotonin into the synapse, or junction, between the transmitting neuron and the receiving neuron.

The serotonin molecules can either stimulate or inhibit activity in the postsynaptic (receiving) neuron by attaching to receptor sites on its surface. Presynaptic receptors on the transmitting neuron restrict serotonin release when stimulated, and this helps prevent excessive serotonin release.

The attachment of serotonin to receptors is temporary, and dispersal of serotonin from the synapse prepares the receptors between bouts of neurotransmission. Transporter proteins in the

Two sets of serotonergic neurons emerge in opposite directions from the dorsal raphe. Those that descend toward the spinal column through the brain stem mediate pain signals. Those that ascend into the brain affect aspects of consciousness such as depression, aggression, compulsive behavior, and hallucinations.

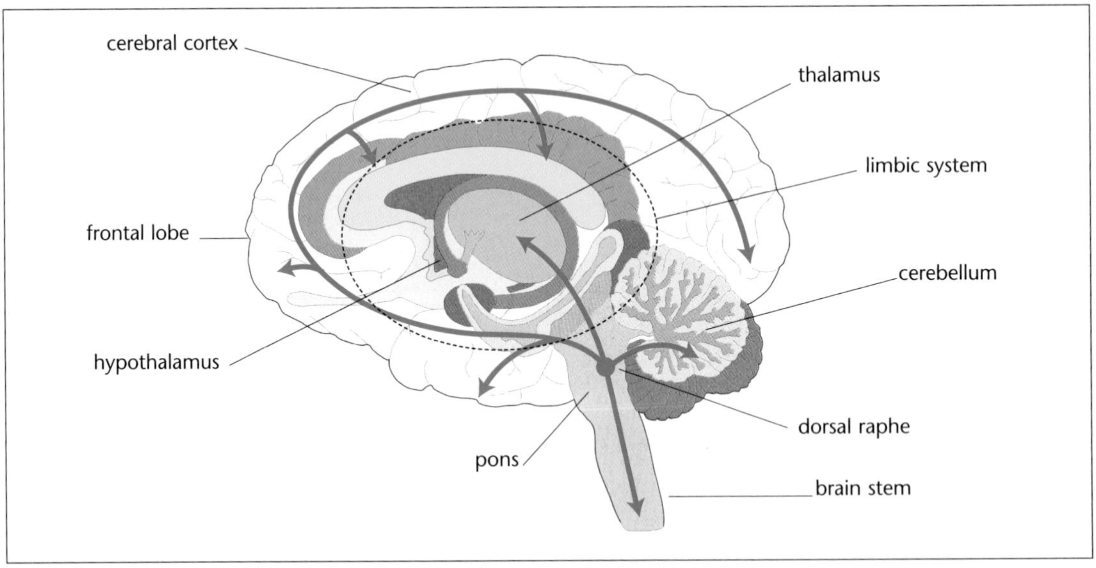

SEROTONIN SYNDROME

The normal Ecstasy trip typifies a mild case of serotonin syndrome. Its physical symptoms include overheating, sweating, shivering, jaw clenching, nausea and diarrhea, and increased heart rate and blood pressure. Psychiatric symptoms include confusion, euphoria, and hallucinations.

In more severe serotonin syndrome, extreme overheating can cause rhabdomyolysis—a breakdown of muscle tissues that releases toxic substances into the bloodstream. Those substances can cause kidney failure and other potentially fatal conditions. Serotonin syndrome also includes the formation of blood clots throughout the body, resulting in strokes and other circulatory problems.

Factors that increase serotonin levels include various types of antidepressants; stimulants such as amphetamine, cocaine, and Ecstasy; tryptophan-based food supplements; and electroconvulsive therapy. Any of these factors can be the sole cause of mild to moderate serotonin syndrome.

The risk of severe serotonin syndrome increases greatly by the combination of two factors that boost synaptic serotonin levels by different means. An example would be the combination of Ecstasy with a monoamine oxidase inhibitor (MAOI) antidepressant: Ecstasy triggers release of serotonin into synapses, while the MAOI impedes one of the means of removing serotonin from synapses.

A further risk arises from the length of action of MAOIs and many SSRIs, such as fluoxetine (Prozac). Users of amphetamines, cocaine, or Ecstasy can have severe serotonin reactions many weeks after finishing MAOI treatment because their MAO enzymes are still inhibited.

presynaptic neuron provide a reuptake mechanism that pumps serotonin back into the neuron, where some of it returns to vesicles for reuse. Some is destroyed by monoamine oxidase, an enzyme.

There are seven distinct types of serotonin receptors, and these are 5-HT_1 to 5-HT_7. (The abbreviation 5-HT refers to 5-hydroxytryptamine, an alternative name for serotonin.) These types include receptor subtypes identified by additional letters, such as 5-HT_{1D} and 5-HT_{5B}. Some of these receptors are on other neurons that transmit using serotonin; others are on dopaminergic neurons, where serotonin receptors regulate dopamine release.

Recreational drugs

Hallucinogenic tryptamines such as DMT have similar chemical structures to serotonin, so it is unsurprising that they produce their effects by interacting with serotonin receptors. Early studies suggested the hallucinogenic effect was due to drugs binding to 5-HT_{1A} receptors and impairing the filtering of sensory input by serotonergic neurons. In this model, disturbed perception occurs because the raw visual and auditory data overwhelms the brain. Subsequent studies have revealed that hallucinations are at least in part due to stimulation of 5-HT_2 receptors, but it is as yet uncertain whether 5-HT_{2A} or 5-HT_{2C} receptors are the main targets.

The hallucinations caused by LSD and some tryptamines and phenethylamines appear to occur by the same mechanism, despite significant differences in molecular structures. Evidence for a shared mechanism comes from reports of cross-tolerance—reduced sensitivity to a group of drugs through exposure to a single drug of that group.

The use of $5\text{-HT}_{2A/C}$ antagonist ketanserin diminishes the visual disturbances experienced with Ecstasy, which suggests they have a common origin to that of LSD trips. Ketanserin fails to reduce the stimulant and mood-lifting effects of Ecstasy, which suggests these effects occur through the action of Ecstasy at other receptors. These may be the same receptors as those stimulated by serotonin-boosting antidepressants, such as the selective serotonin reuptake inhibitors (SSRIs).

M. CLOWES

SEE ALSO:
Amphetamine Sulfate • Dopamine • Ephedrine • Epinephrine • Norepinephrine • Phenethylamines

Sex

Some people believe that alcohol and drugs can enhance sexual performance. While some substances may have an initial effect on the libido at low doses, heavy use or abuse of drugs generally has a negative effect on sexual desire.

It is difficult to make generalizations about substance abuse and sexual performance. Substance use and abuse interrelates with body size, food intake, amount of the substance, frequency and duration of use, psychological expectations about the effect, and the specific drug that is being used. Thus, use of substances interacts with the physiological mechanisms of the body, which in turn affects sexual performance. There is also a distinction to be made between psychological and physiological arousal. Many studies suggest that substances such as alcohol may increase psychological arousal but decrease physical arousal. Nevertheless, it is safe to say that substance abuse is likely to interfere with sexual performance and satisfaction, and may also interfere with the desire to have sex. Since alcohol is so often linked with sexual behavior, it will be considered separately from illegal substances such as marijuana, amphetamines, cocaine, and Ecstasy (MDMA).

Alcohol

The effects of alcohol on sexual desire and performance vary as a product of the amount of alcohol ingested. Small amounts of alcohol make the user feel less anxious and concerned. Thus, the alcohol reduces inhibitions (such as fear, guilt, or anxiety), and sexual excitement may be heightened. Further, a person may have the psychological expectation that a drink may enhance his or her own and others' sexuality. Because of this, individuals who drink tend to engage in sexual activities at a higher rate. Some research studies have shown that up to one-half of adolescents were using alcohol when they had their first experience with sexual intercourse. Other studies indicate that adolescents who report no use of alcohol were least likely to have had sexual intercourse.

Although the idea that alcohol serves as an aphrodisiac is largely viewed as a myth, young people may believe this myth and view alcohol as a way to facilitate sexual behavior. A major concern regarding alcohol as a disinhibiter and contributant to sexual activity is the relation between alcohol use and unsafe sexual practices. Alcohol may serve to disinhibit the psychological judgment processes that monitor and govern behavior. The decreased judgment that often accompanies alcohol use may result in unsafe and impulsive sexual practices, such as lack of condom use, acquaintance rape, or having sex with multiple partners. Unsafe sex practices may also result in sexually transmitted diseases, transmission of HIV, or unwanted pregnancies.

As greater amounts of alcohol are ingested, sexual desire, performance and satisfaction all decrease. Both males and females experience physiological changes that interfere with sexual performance. Since alcohol is a central nervous system depressant, the initial sense of disinhibition and relaxation typically degenerates into lack of coordination, slurred speech, and eventually a desire for sleep. With chronic use of alcohol, some of the physiological changes may be especially pronounced in alcoholics, who may cease sexual activity altogether.

Sexual dysfunction has been identified in both males and females as a result of heavy alcohol use. Males may experience difficulty in achieving an erection and orgasm. Females may report a lack of sexual interest and low frequency or lack of orgasm. Such sexual dysfunction may affect the partner of the heavy drinker as well. For example, a partner may experience a lack of interest in the heavy drinker for a variety of reasons. A heavy drinker who begins to value the alcohol over the intimacy associated with sexual activity will likely be unattractive to his or her partner. Studies have shown that male alcoholics and their wives report greater sexual dysfunction, including impotence, when compared with nonalcoholic couples.

A heavy drinker who becomes an alcoholic may experience physiological changes that impair sexual performance. For example, studies have shown that female alcoholics may experience infertility, menstrual disturbances, and changes in their secondary sexual characteristics (such as body and facial hair, bone density, and body form). Men may experience a decrease in serum testosterone levels, nerve damage, and disruption in the spinal nerves involved in erections. Clearly, chronic alcohol use affects the sexual physiology of the individual.

Programs to educate teenagers about safe sex aim to prevent risky sexual behaviors and unprotected sex that can result in the transmission of infectious diseases. Such programs also explore the realities, misconceptions, and dangers surrounding sex and the use of drugs and alcohol.

Other drugs

Similar to alcohol, marijuana also has a disinhibitory effect on sexual behavior. Sexual desire and activity that is normally inhibited has a greater chance of emerging when using marijuana. Thus, marijuana has a reputation as an aphrodisiac, and many users believe that it enhances their sexual experience. Since marijuana alters a person's perceptions, it is likely that psychological expectation (as opposed to actual physiological mechanisms) plays a large role in the individual's perception that marijuana enhances sexual experiences. As with alcohol, frequent and chronic use of marijuana has been related to male erectile dysfunction, disruption of normal sperm production, and lowered testosterone levels. For females, prolonged use can result in abnormal menstruation, pain with intercourse, and disruption of the menstrual cycle and egg production. Prolonged use of marijuana has also been associated with increased levels of apathy and lack of motivation, which can further impair an individual's ability for satisfactory sexual relations.

Amphetamines and cocaine are both considered aphrodisiacs. These substances produce a sense of well-being and physiological responses such as increased heart rate and blood pressure. Some researchers have pointed out that these physiological changes may be misinterpreted and labeled by the individual as sexual excitement, when in fact they are simply the product of the use of a central nervous system stimulant. Cocaine affects the brain's pleasure center; hence, it can intensify sexual fantasies and activities. Cocaine also produces greater sexual endurance, perhaps due to its effect as a stimulant.

Ecstasy (MDMA) is another substance that is often viewed as an aphrodisiac. Similar to stimulants, this substance may produce a general state of arousal or excitement that may be interpreted as sexual arousal. Further, this drug may be combined with Viagra, which will enhance sexual desire and performance. However, many users of Ecstasy experience a

PROTECTING YOURSELF FROM DATE RAPE

The disinhibiting and debilitating effects of drugs and alcohol can combine to leave an individual vulnerable in situations that others may seek to exploit. This is particularly true of social occasions such as parties or evenings out where alcohol and drugs are seen as part of the enjoyment of the event. However, certain nervous system depressants are used as a tool for rape and sexual assault. These substances include GHB, Rohypnol, and ketamine, and are usually administered through drinks, often in conjunction with alcoholic beverages. To protect yourself from becoming a victim:

- Never leave a drink unattended. It is better to buy another drink than to be a victim.
- Never accept a drink in a glass from a stranger, only directly from a server.
- When in a vulnerable position only accept drinks from a closed container such as a can or unopened bottle and open the container yourself. If the container looks as if it has been tampered with, just take it and put it down.
- Use a buddy system. Attend parties or bars with a group of friends and watch each other's drinks. Arrive as a group and leave together. If a friend shows symptoms of date-rape drug ingestion (for example, confusion, incoherence, vomiting, or passing out) seek medical attention immediately.
- Spread the word and be alert. Tell friends about the effects of date-rape drugs. If you see someone tampering with another person's drink, speak up. If you become a victim of drugged date rape yourself, notify the police immediately.

pronounced depression upon cessation of use. During this "down" period, sexual performance is impeded. As with all substances, use of Ecstasy can also contribute to unsafe sexual practices such as lack of condom use. Greater sexual risk taking has also been demonstrated in those who use marijuana, cocaine, or other illicit substances, and this is true of both males and females. Thus, there is a link between dangerous sexual practices and the use of illegal substances. Injecting drug users are at considerable risk of transmitting infectious blood-borne sexual diseases through the reuse or sharing of needles. Female teenagers are also at greater risk of contracting sexually transmitted diseases and HIV through unprotected sex, possibly because the cervix is too biologically immature to cope with fighting infection.

Many prescription drugs can also have a negative effect on the libido. Antidepressants, tranquilizers, and medications for high blood pressure can all reduce desire and impair sexual performance, as can some over-the-counter remedies for allergies and colds. Anabolic steroids, which are related to the male sex hormone testosterone, can have either a positive or negative effect on sexual desire in users. However, the sexual side effects of steroids may cause the testes to shrink and the breasts to enlarge in men, masculinization in women, and sterility in both sexes.

Sex and drugs

In general, much research evidence exists that alcohol and drug use may contribute to early and more frequent sexual activity and greater sexual risk-taking behaviors among adolescents. Sexual dysfunction (such as inability to achieve and maintain erections for males and inability to experience orgasm for females) may be associated with alcohol and substance use in adults. In alcoholics, these effects may be more profound and chronic in nature. Although alcohol and substance use may produce some psychological arousal as a result of disinhibition, the physical consequences of such use often ultimately include decreased arousal and other negative physical changes that affect the desire for sex.

J. L. JOHNSON

SEE ALSO:
AIDS and HIV • Aphrodisiac Drugs • Prostitution • Rape • Violence • Women and Drugs

Slang

Slang or jargon is defined as a language peculiar to a particular group. As with any other subculture, drug users have developed their own terminology to refer to drugs, how they are used, and the effects they produce.

The U.S. Office of National Drug Control Policy has a Web site with a link entitled "Street Terms: Drugs and the Drug Culture" that addresses drug-related slang and its use in the United States (www.whitehousedrugpolicy.gov). This is a good source for individuals wishing to learn more about slang, insofar as slang words continually evolve and change over time and such Web sites are frequently updated. Slang terms also differ in terms of ethnic, age-related, and geographical characteristics. Slang is used in youth and drug culture to give drug users a secret language that communicates while at the same time obfuscates these communications from law enforcement, family members such as parents, and nonusers. There is also slang associated with alcohol abuse; however, such terms are much less frequent, perhaps due to the fact that alcohol use is legal and there is little or no need for covert references. Since there is so much information on slang use within the drug culture that is beyond the scope of this article, only the most popular substances will be highlighted.

Marijuana

Hundreds of slang terms are associated with marijuana. Many of the terms relate to the geographical location where the marijuana was harvested. The location is important since it can affect the potency of the marijuana, which in turn affects the street price. A more potent type of marijuana requires less substance to produce the desired effect for the user. Thus, the more potent the marijuana, the more expensive it is, since the user's "stash" lasts longer. Blue sky blonde (Colombia), Culican (Mexico), dagga (South Africa), black gungi (India), Cam red (Cambodia), BC bud (British Columbia and other parts of Canada), kaff (Western Asian countries), and blue de hue (Vietnam) are but some of the terms used to describe marijuana grown and smuggled from various countries. "Domestic" refers to marijuana grown locally or in the United States. Of course, the users have no evidence that their purchase is actually from one of these countries, only the assurances of the drug dealer.

Some slang referring to marijuana is independent of the country of origin. African, Aunt Mary, baby, boom, chunky, reefer, dew, ding, Don Juan, grass, root, rasta weed, pot, hay, herb, hooch, joint, and weed are some of the more common terms generally applied to marijuana.

There is also slang referring to the process of using marijuana. A "bag" is the bag containing the marijuana, while "roasting," "toking up," or "torching up" refers to smoking marijuana. A "bong" or "toker" is one way of smoking it, while the standard way is to smoke a "joint" or "twist," which is a hand-rolled cigarette made of marijuana instead of tobacco. In the latter instance, a "roach clip" or a "zooie," which is a tweezer-like tool, holds the marijuana cigarette by the tip to afford the user the maximum chance to finish the entire cigarette. Marijuana is also smoked in a "pipe," or "bong," which is "packed" with the substance.

Marijuana is often combined or mixed with other substances and the unwitting user can experience serious and dangerous results. When marijuana is laced with PCP (loveboat, dust, lovelies, joy stick, leak, killer weed or KW, happy stick, donk, parsley, super grass, zoom), the user can have the unexpected experience of PCP ingestion, as opposed to marijuana ingestion. With marijuana, the user often describes a feeling of passivity, calmness, and euphoria. In contrast, PCP acts as a stimulant, often causing agitation, accelerated heart rate, and extreme restlessness. When the desired and expected effect is not produced, the user may experience confusion, concern, and even panic. More dangerously, the individual may experience heart racing and palpitations; the user may avoid seeking medical attention since he or she has ingested an illegal substance and may be fearful of being detected by law enforcement authorities.

Marijuana can also be sprayed with insecticide or mixed with other substances such as embalming fluid (formaldehyde). When marijuana is weak or lacking in potency, unscrupulous dealers may spray it with easily purchased insect killers which, when smoked, do produce neurological effects such as light-headedness, dizziness, heart rate increase, and other physical changes that may be attributable to getting high from the marijuana. Marijuana can also be mixed with other substances such as crack, heroin, or cocaine (primo, ozone, oolies, lace, and juice) to heighten the high. As with PCP, a user can experience unanticipated results from such combinations and may react with panic.

Stimulants

For amphetamines and the related substance of 3,4-methylenedioxymethamphetamine (MDMA or Ecstasy), there are over 150 slang terms referring to various names, use, and altered mental states. Common terms used to refer to amphetamines include B-bombs, black dex, bomb, bambita, bennie, benz, blacks or black beauties, jugs, oranges, peaches, ripper, road dope, splash, and sweets.

In addition to slang terms used to refer to amphetamines, there are terms used to describe the process and outcome of using these substances. For example, a person may be "amped" while "speeding" on amphetamines and "amped-out" when he or she "crashes" or becomes very fatigued after using for a period of time. A person may use an "L.A." (long-acting) type of amphetamine or use a type that is shorter acting.

Crack cocaine and powder cocaine also have slang terms, and many of them are interchangeable. Base, beam, big C, black rock, Carrie Nation, CDs, cola, coke, Connie, king, snow, and zip may all be used to describe crack and cocaine. Since the substance is typically in a powder form, it can be dissolved in water, smoked, or ingested as a powder. Thus, there are several terms used to describe the mode of ingestion. "Woolahs" are either tobacco or marijuana cigarettes laced with crack cocaine. A person may also inhale cocaine (toke, sporting, snorting, sniffing) or inject it (speedballing, shot). Another mode of ingestion is to mix the substance with water and sniff it up the nose as a nasal spray (liquid lady). Finally, cocaine can be "freebased" when it is "cooked" in a pipe over a flame prior to ingestion. The practice of looking for leftover crystals of crack and methamphetamine also gives rise to a number of terms—picking, chicken scratching, henpecking, ghostbusting, and base crazies.

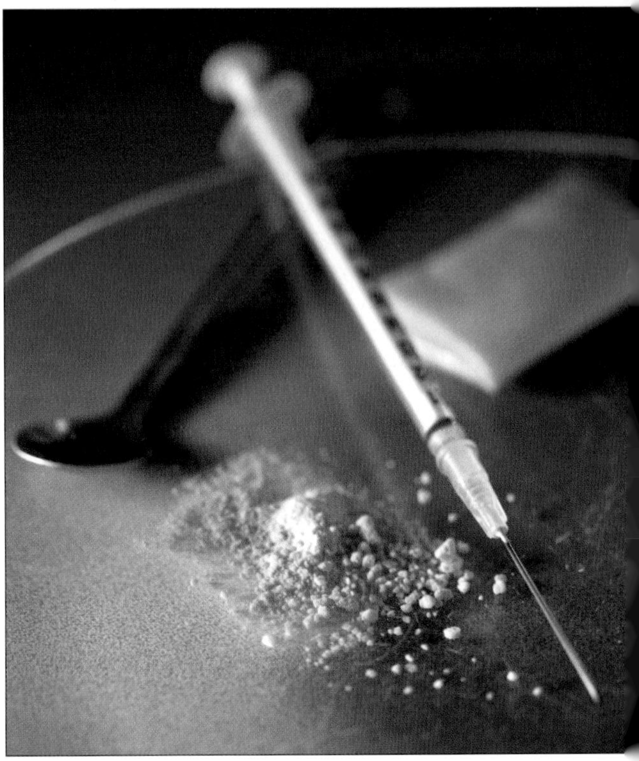

The terminology of heroin use includes words for the quantity of the drug (a wrap or bindle), a syringe (a glass or stick), and taking the drug intravenously (shooting up, a hit or fix, skin popping.)

Some slang terms refer to both amphetamine and crack cocaine—"jam" and "eye opener" are two examples—or a combination of powder cocaine and amphetamine (snow seals). "Chocolate" can refer to either marijuana, amphetamine, or opium, and "little bomb" can be heroin, amphetamines, or depressants. The similar sounding "chocolate ecstasy" is crack cocaine mixed with chocolate milk powder during production, and "coco rocks" is a type of dark brown crack made with chocolate pudding. The latter is not the same, however, as "chocolate rock," crack smoked with heroin.

Since some slang refers to several different substances, each with a different physical mechanism and associated behaviors, dangers are present for the user. For example, someone purchasing "chocolate" who thinks he will experience amphetamine-like results may actually be ingesting opium, which produces quite a different experience. Similarly, taking a "little bomb" that is actually heroin can produce overdosing, since different amounts of the substance are typically ingested depending upon the type of substance. A person who thinks he is taking an amphetamine may ingest a larger amount of the substance than one who thinks she is taking heroin. Thus, there is quite a bit of danger related to the fact that the same slang term may be used to refer to different drugs.

B-bombs, bibs, blue cases, care bears, debs, E, Ecstasy, green triangles, happy pill, hug drug, stars, pink panthers, supermans, and white dove are all words used to describe Ecstasy. "Raves" refer to large parties where users (candy ravers) meet and often dance to the point of exhaustion while under the influence of Ecstasy. A person who sells Ecstasy at bars and clubs that sponsor raves is known as a "hawker." A user may be described as a "peeper" and be "totally spent" when she experiences a hangover and state of extreme fatigue after prolonged use of Ecstasy. Ecstasy may also be combined with the sexual functioning enhancement drug Viagra (sextasy), PCP (pikachu), or mescaline (love trip).

Opioids

Narcotics such as heroin and opium have hundreds of slang terms associated with the substances and their use. To name just a few of the terms, heroin may be called witch hazel, horse, smack, tongs, thunder, sweet Jesus, skag, pure, Peg, muzzle, joy, golden girl, galloping horse, dogfood, dirt, chip, brain damage, and antifreeze. Opium is known as auntie, chandoo, dopium, and dream stick. There are also terms to refer to the combination of heroin and cocaine (dynamite, speedball, H & C). "Garbage" and "flea powder" refer to a low-quality heroin with a low potency, and injecting oneself or another is known as "giving wings." The lack of some of the more potent street opioids in rural areas has resulted in oxycodone being called "hillbilly heroin."

Hallucinogens

Users of hallucinogenics such as lysergic acid diethylamide (LSD), mescaline, and Psilocybe mushrooms also use slang to refer to the substance itself and the resulting effect. Acid, barrels, blotter, brown dots, coffee, dots, fields, orange barrels, Lucy in the sky with diamonds, rainbows, sugar cubes, and windowpane all refer to LSD. A person is "tripping" or "blowing his mind" when under the influence, and a frequent user may be called an "acid head." A "travel agent" is the provider of the LSD and "ground control" is a person who acts as a caretaker while others are tripping. Mescaline and Psilocybe mushrooms have relatively fewer slang terms associated with their use. Buttons, cactus, peyote, topi, sacred mushroom, and sherm all refer to mescaline and mushrooms.

As noted earlier, slang enables a secretive and covert form of communication designed to evade law enforcement and detection by family members. Thus, it is a critical endeavor for law enforcement officials and those in parental authority to remain aware of the meanings of slang as they attempt to combat use of these illicit substances. Additionally, there are dangers for the user, since slang terms may be used interchangeably to refer to different substances. For example, the descriptions "candy" and "bean" are both used for crack cocaine, depressants, and amphetamines—all substances with very different effects. Slang terms also frequently refer to combinations of various substances, and the user may be unaware of what he or she is ingesting. The "five way" is an extremely dangerous combination of heroin, cocaine, methamphetamine, Rohypnol, and alcohol. Finally, slang use is a product of the ethnicity, age, and geographical position of the user. Thus, slang changes with time as certain words are created and others no longer used. The generation that smoked "pot" in "reefers" or "spliffs" are now the parents of teenagers who prefer to use more up-to-date terms to differentiate themselves. Some terms have moved away from their specific drug-related meanings and have become more general. For example, "yen," "pad," and "hip" all had their origins in opium smoking but are now common parlance. Because of this, Web sites on the Internet will continue to be the most current source for slang words and their constantly changing meanings.

J. L. JOHNSON

SEE ALSO:
Drug Use Subcultures • Youth Culture

Smoking

Smoking tobacco releases nicotine into the bloodstream, from where it quickly passes to the brain. Nicotine is a highly addictive substance that causes feelings of alertness and well-being, prompting the urge to keep smoking.

Cigarette smoking is drug use. The cigarette is the vehicle for administering the drug; the drug is nicotine, a mood-altering chemical found in tobacco. Unlike other drugs of abuse, both the administration and the drug are legal, yet lethal. One in every five deaths in the United States can be attributed to tobacco use. This represents more deaths than are caused by alcohol use, illegal drug use, motor vehicle accidents, homicide, suicide, and AIDS combined.

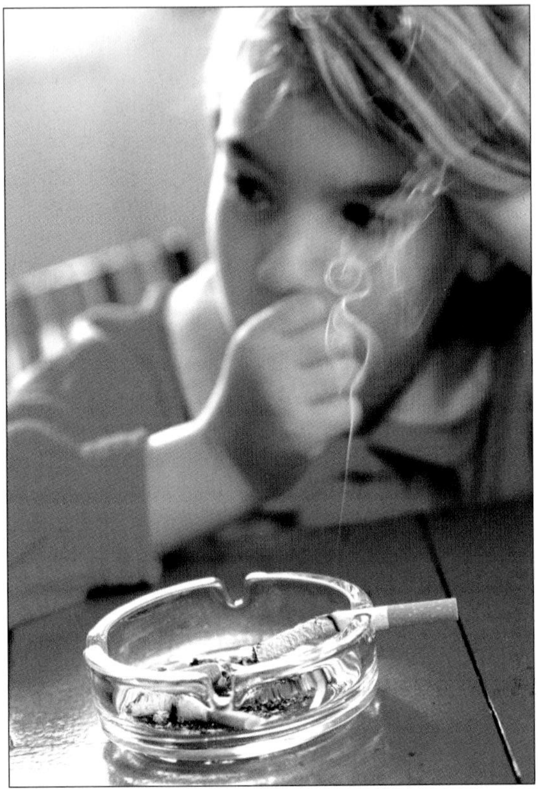
Secondhand smoke is a considerable hazard to nonsmokers. This smoke contains hundreds of dangerous chemicals that are normally removed by the cigarette filter before the smoke is inhaled.

How tobacco is taken into the body

When tobacco is burned, the chemicals in it form into two types of matter: particulate matter, also known as "tar," and vapor or gaseous compounds. As a cigarette is smoked, some of the particulates, including the nicotine, attach to the mucous membranes in the mouth and nose. The nicotine is immediately absorbed into the bloodstream. The rest of the smoke travels down the bronchial tubes. These are lined with little hairlike cells, called cilia, which are designed to catch dirt and dust particles to prevent them from going into the lungs. Many of the tar compounds are caught in the cilia, and may be coughed up and spat out later, but many more, including the nicotine, continue the journey into the lungs. Once in the lungs, the nicotine is absorbed by tiny air sacs called alveoli. These are responsible for the exchange of oxygen and carbon dioxide in the blood. The nicotine is absorbed into the bloodstream and reaches the brain within 10 seconds of being inhaled.

In the brain, the nicotine moves through the capillary walls and into the spaces between the neurons, normally occupied by chemical messengers known as neurotransmitters. These neurotransmitters are responsible for communication between nerve cells. Nicotine acts like a neurotransmitter by interacting with acetylcholine receptors. This stimulates the neurons into firing off multiple nerve impulses, increasing the electrical activity in the brain, which results in feelings of alertness. The nicotine also triggers the release of other neurotransmitters that are associated with feelings of pleasure and well-being, while it blocks or inhibits the release of an enzyme called monoamine oxidase B, or MAO-B. This enzyme is responsible for cleaning up the extra neurotransmitter substances between the nerve cells. When the MAO-B is blocked, the neurotransmitters continue to float around between the nerve cells, allowing them to continue firing off impulses. With repeated smoking, the brain adapts to this heightened activity but cannot maintain it without the nicotine. This process is what leads to addiction.

Typical quantities and potentiation

A cigarette manufactured in the United States contains 8 to 10 milligrams of nicotine and, under normal smoking conditions, a person's body absorbs 10 to 30 percent of it. However, cigarette manufacturers have found ways to increase the nicotine potency of the cigarettes, increasing the chances that the smoker will become addicted. One way is through the use of tobacco plants that have been genetically engineered to have a higher nicotine content. Another is through the use of chemical additives, such as ammonia compounds, which boost the body's absorption of the nicotine by changing its chemical composition. The addition of menthol to cigarettes may also contribute to the addiction process by reducing the irritation in the throat, leading to longer and deeper inhalation of the smoke into the lungs. Recent research also points to the possibility that menthol may increase the body's absorption of nicotine, affecting the release of neurotransmitters in the brain, making the cigarette more addictive.

Urges to smoke

Most smokers who try to quit find it difficult, not only because of the physical addiction to nicotine, but also because of the psychological addiction to the behaviors of smoking. Most smokers establish a pattern of behaviors that they associate with smoking, such as smoking after meals or while talking on the telephone. These smoking-related behaviors become associated with feelings of well-being and relaxation, making it more difficult to quit. These behaviors lead to urges to smoke, even when the brain does not need the nicotine.

Adolescents and smoking

Young people are likely to try smoking for the first time between the ages of 11 and 15 years, especially if they have friends, siblings, or other people in their immediate environment (such as home, school, work, or social activities) who smoke. Nearly one-third of young people who try cigarettes will become regular smokers by the time they are 18 years old. There tends to be a misperception that "everyone" smokes, making the person feel like he or she is left out of the group if he or she doesn't smoke. Cigarette advertisers know this and promote smoking as part of adventurous and glamorous adult activities. Research has shown that young people are more susceptible to the influence of cigarette ads than adults and that they associate smoking with popularity and relaxation and, consequently, are more likely to try smoking. Exposure to cigarette advertisements and other marketing techniques (promotional products, auto racing sponsorship, cigarette brands smoked in movies) exerts a greater influence to try smoking than does peer pressure. However, young smokers experience nicotine addiction and withdrawal when they try to quit, even if they have smoked only a short time. The likelihood of experiencing these negative effects (difficulty concentrating, irritability, cigarette cravings) increases with the length of time the person has been smoking and the amount smoked, making it harder to successfully quit. Only about one-fourth of teenage smokers are successful at quitting.

Gender and racial differences

Smoking among women was once a rare occurrence; however, the rate of smoking among females is now approaching that for males. National surveys in the United States indicate that smoking rates for females are highest among high school–aged girls (29.7 percent) and adult women who did not complete high school (30.9 percent).

The health consequences of smoking are also increasing among women. Until 1987 breast cancer was the leading cause of death from cancer among women. By 2004 it was lung cancer, and 90 percent of all lung cancer is caused by cigarette smoking. Women who smoke are also at greater risk of coronary heart disease, the number one killer of women. Smoking also negatively affects reproduction for women, causing problems with conception and fertility, increasing the risks of tubal pregnancies, miscarriages, and stillbirths. Smoking during pregnancy is also a known cause of premature birth and places the infant at increased risk of death from Sudden Infant Death Syndrome (SIDS). One of the reasons that many women start smoking is to control their weight; however, studies have shown that smoking is not associated with weight loss, although it does slow weight gain and decreases bone density, leading to increased risk of bone fractures. Another reason women start smoking is because they believe that smoking can help control negative moods, yet smokers are more likely to suffer from depression than nonsmokers.

Smoking is less prevalent among racial minorities, particularly African Americans, but the health risks are much greater for these groups. In 2001, 14.7 percent of African American high school students reported being current smokers, compared with 31.9 percent of Caucasian and 26.6 percent of Hispanic students. Among adults, the rates are much different, with 22.3 percent of African Americans reporting current smoking, compared with 24.0 percent of Caucasians and 16.7 percent of Hispanics. The three leading causes of death for African Americans—heart disease, cancer, and stroke—can all be attributed to smoking. Research has shown that African Americans metabolize nicotine at a slower rate than Caucasian and Hispanic people; it therefore stays in their bodies for longer periods of time, contributing to a higher rate of nicotine addiction and, ultimately, to more difficulty quitting. The quit success rate for African Americans is about 8 percent, compared with 14 percent for Caucasians and 16 percent for Hispanics. Three out of four African American smokers prefer menthol cigarettes, which also contributes to the addictive process. Finally, the tobacco industry spends a disproportionate amount of money advertising in African American communities and acting as corporate sponsors for many influential African American political, social, artistic, religious, and media organizations in the United States.

Passive smoking

The risks associated with smoking are not limited to the smoker. Environmental tobacco smoke (ETS), or secondhand smoke, is associated with about 38,000 deaths per year in the United States and contributes to over 1 million illnesses in children, including asthma, respiratory infections, and ear infections. ETS is a "Group A carcinogen" according to the U.S. Environmental Protection Agency, meaning that it is known to cause cancer in humans. The smoke that comes from the lit end of a cigarette (sidestream smoke) contains a greater concentration of cancer-causing chemicals than does the smoke that is inhaled through the filter end (mainstream smoke). These burning chemicals are readily absorbed through the mucous membranes of the nose and mouth.

The length of exposure is also a factor: while the smoker breathes in the mainstream smoke only while actively smoking, everyone living in a house with a smoker is constantly exposed to the polluted air. Children of smokers are particularly vulnerable because their lungs are still developing and they have

CHEMICAL

A cigarette is much more than tobacco and a filter wrapped in paper. A typical cigarette is a cocktail of chemicals. According to U.S. government figures, the six major cigarette manufacturers have listed nearly 600 ingredients that have been added to cigarette tobacco. The law requires only that the ingredients added to the tobacco are reported; therefore this list does not include chemicals and additives used in the paper or filter. The following is a description of what is really in a cigarette.

Paper

The white part of the paper is made up of cellulose that is bleached and dyed using unknown chemical agents. It is manufactured in two thicknesses, forming what are called "burn rings," which help determine how slowly the cigarette burns and how much smoke it produces while burning. The paper is treated with various chemicals, such as titanium, to keep the cigarette burning, to give the ash a more pleasant appearance, and to add aroma. The dyed paper covering the filter of the cigarette is called the tipping paper, which is coated with a substance to keep it from sticking to the smoker's lips. Add to this the glue that holds the paper together and the ink in which the brand name is printed. All of these substances are being inhaled by the smoker and those around him or her.

Filter

Filters were added to cigarettes in the 1950s in response to growing concerns about the health risks associated with smoking. The truth is that

CONTENTS OF A TYPICAL CIGARETTE

they do little to prevent the smoker from inhaling the particulates, or tar, or the vapor chemicals. In fact, how much tar and nicotine the smoker inhales is wholly dependent on the smoker. Even "light" and "ultra-light" cigarettes can deliver the maximum level of tar and nicotine depending on how the smoker holds the cigarette, how much of the filter is covered by the lips, or how frequently and how deeply the smoker draws on the cigarette.

The cigarette filter is made up of about 12,000 cellulose acetate fibers, a type of plastic used in photographic prints. These fibers are bonded together with a plastic glue called triacetin. Some filters also contain charcoal, which is supposed to reduce some of the toxic chemicals in the smoke. However, fiber fragments caused by the machine cutting of the filter to length, or charcoal dust in the charcoal filters, can come loose while a smoker is puffing on the cigarette, and the fibers or particles can be inhaled into the lungs with the smoke.

Most filters have a ring of tiny holes to allow fresh air in while the smoker is inhaling, thus reducing the amount of tar and nicotine inhaled with each puff. If the smoker covers these holes with his or her fingers or lips, they become useless in reducing tar and nicotine.

Tobacco

Cigarettes manufactured in the United States are made with a blend of bright, burley, and oriental tobaccos, but the majority of the tobacco used is not from the leaf of the tobacco plant but is a manufactured product called "reconstituted tobacco" in which the tobacco stems and ribs of the leaves are ground up with various chemicals and colorants, then dried in sheets, like paper. The paper is then shredded to make it smokable. Some manufacturers also use "expanded" tobacco, which is tobacco that is chemically bulked up to lower the cost of production.

Between 6 and 10 percent of the tobacco in a cigarette manufactured in the United States is a chemical additive. The manufacturers can add hundreds of ingredients to the tobacco to enhance the taste, moisture content, burnability, or pH of the cigarette. Although all of the additive ingredients listed are generally considered to be safe when used in food products that are eaten (ingredients such as menthol, brown sugar, caramel coloring, cocoa, corn syrup, licorice root, and glycerin), there is no indication that these are safe when burned and inhaled into the lungs. Indeed, glycerin, an ingredient added to keep the tobacco moist, becomes acrolein when burned, a known cancer-causing agent.

Burning tobacco produces as many as 400 to 500 individual gaseous compounds and at least 3,500 particulate compounds. The gaseous compounds have nitrogen, oxygen, and carbon dioxide as their major constituents, but also contain the following toxic or tumor-causing agents: carbon monoxide, benzene, formaldehyde, hydrogen cyanide, and others. In addition to tar and nicotine, the particulates in tobacco smoke include toxic substances such as seven known tobacco-specific nitrosamines, phenol, naphthalene, fluorenes, vinyl chloride, arsenic, and heavy metals such as nickel, chromium, cadmium, lead, and polonium-210.

a higher breathing rate. As a result, the concentration of nicotine in their blood is higher than that of adults who are exposed to ETS, making them more susceptible to smoking-related diseases.

There is no such thing as safe smoking. All cigarette smoking is dangerous to the smoker's health and to the health of everyone around the smoker. No one is immune to the negative health effects of smoking. The best way to avoid these health risks is to never start smoking.

M. D. REYNOLDS

SEE ALSO:
Gateway Drugs • Heart and Circulatory Diseases • Lung Diseases • Nicotine • Nicotine Replacements • Smoking Cessation • Tobacco

Smoking Cessation

Smoking tobacco is one of the most difficult addictions to overcome. There are a variety of methods to help people quit, but it may take a combination of nicotine replacement therapies and motivation techniques to achieve this aim.

Statistics show that every day in the United States more than 4,000 young people try their first cigarette, while another 2,000 become regular daily smokers. On this same day, nearly 1,100 people will die as a result of their smoking, and another 100 will die as a result of someone else's smoking. Meanwhile, 47,000 people will try to quit smoking, and maybe 2,800 will succeed.

There are many reasons people give for smoking—it relaxes them, it helps them to cope, and so on. These reasons narrow down to three: physical addiction, emotional connection, and behavioral habit. The three are intertwined to create a physical and psychological stranglehold on the smoker. Regular smokers are addicted to nicotine, a psychoactive drug that affects brain chemistry. The physical effect is a stimulation of nerve impulses, causing the smoker to feel more alert and better able to concentrate, an effect that cannot be sustained without continued smoking. Nicotine stimulates certain brain chemicals that create feelings of pleasure and well-being, leading to an emotional response to smoking. These "good feelings" become associated with certain behaviors of the smoker, such as smoking after meals or when talking on the telephone, which lead to the development of the habit. Successful smoking cessation strategies need to address all three aspects: the physical addiction, the emotional connection, and the behavioral habits.

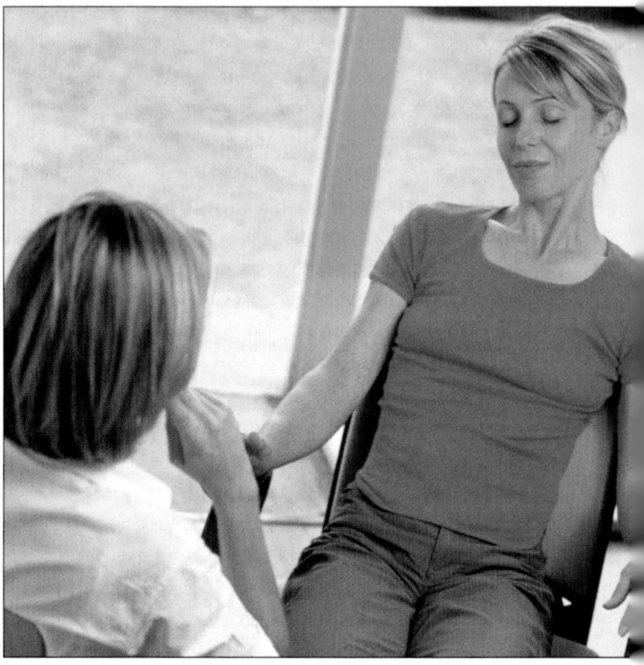

Hypnotherapy is sometimes used to help people give up smoking. Women often find behavioral approaches more successful because their body chemistry does not respond as well to nicotine replacement therapies as does that of men.

Withdrawal

When the smoker quits, he or she removes the nicotine from his or her brain and the result is withdrawal. Some common withdrawal symptoms are cravings, irritability, fatigue, inability to concentrate, insomnia, and hunger. All of these are temporary and will fade as the brain eliminates the nicotine. Some people will experience a cough, mucous buildup in the nose and throat, dizziness, and even tightness in the chest. These are all a result of the lungs clearing out the smoke and will disappear within days. Most withdrawal symptoms can be overcome by employing good health practices, such as engaging in some form of gentle exercise, drinking plenty of water, avoiding stressful situations, and relaxing. Eating low-calorie, healthy snacks such as fruits and avoiding caffeine also help overcome cravings and urges. Use of alcohol should be avoided while quitting, as it reduces the person's inhibitions and may also be psychologically associated with smoking.

Motivation

Although no one can make someone else quit, they can help motivate the smoker to want to quit. Motivation is the first step to successful smoking cessation. To help someone take that first step, it is helpful to remember the "three Rs." First, the smoker needs to know that quitting is *relevant* to him or her. That is, it has a direct and specific effect on his life and the lives of the people around him. The second R is that the smoker needs to be *reminded* of the risks associated with continued smoking, both for her and the people she loves. The third R is to point out the *rewards* of quitting, again being very specific as to what these are for the individual. Chances are that the smoker will not instantaneously want to quit when confronted with the three Rs, but it will reinforce the reasons for quitting.

Independent quitting

There are many strategies available to help an individual quit smoking. Some people prefer to do it on their own, a method often referred to as cold turkey—to one day put down the cigarettes and never smoke again. There are people who have done this and never smoked again. Then there are people such as the author Mark Twain, who said, "Quitting smoking is easy. I've done it a thousand times." It is hard to stay off cigarettes without help.

Most self-directed smoking cessation programs involve a standard format. The smoker who wants to quit smoking needs to prepare himself to quit by:

- Setting a quit date
- Getting rid of all smoking paraphernalia, such as cigarettes, cigarette cases, lighters, and ashtrays
- Garnering support from friends and family members
- Planning for situations that might lead to smoking relapse.

The research on self-directed programs shows that they are of limited effectiveness for long-term smoking cessation as the quit rate is only about 5 percent. The benefit is that these programs are inexpensive and can be widely distributed. They are best used as information sources for those considering quitting. More formal intervention is necessary to improve the chances for success.

Assisted quitting

Behavioral treatments are the most commonly practiced smoking-cessation methods. These programs generally address the habit of smoking and the emotional aspects of smoking. Brief person-to-person interventions with a physician or other health care provider have shown some success in helping smokers to quit. The U.S. Public Health Service has developed a set of guidelines for physicians to help their patients quit smoking. These guidelines recommend the use of the "five As" at each visit. The five As are:

- *Ask* patients about smoking
- *Advise* all smokers to quit
- *Assess* their willingness to make a quit attempt
- *Assist* those who want to quit, and
- *Arrange* follow-up visits for those trying to quit.

These two-to-three-minute interventions have a success rate of between 5 and 8 percent, depending on how often the smoker received this advice.

Problem-solving and skills-training methods have been developed to direct the smoker who is trying to quit to use behavioral strategies to avoid situations that might lead to smoking, to cope with urges to smoke, to replace smoking behaviors with positive healthy behaviors, and to deal with nicotine withdrawal symptoms. This training has been shown to increase the success rate by as much as 50 percent, meaning that if 5 percent of smokers quit without this training, 7.5 percent will quit with it. Behavioral interventions that teach the smoker to recognize the cues that lead him or her to want to smoke (talking on the telephone, finishing a meal, and so on) have not been found to improve the quit success rate.

Some research has been done to look at the use of offering financial rewards to people who are able to remain abstinent from smoking. In this type of program, the instructor collects a fee from the participants at the outset of the program. At each session, if the participant has not smoked, a portion of the fee is returned to him. This system of motivating the person to become a nonsmoker via rewards is very effective in the short term but does not significantly improve long-term cessation rates.

One behavioral strategy that has improved quit success rates is the use of a social-support network to encourage and aid the smoker in his or her cessation. The support may come from family members or friends who enroll in the cessation program with the smoker, or through the use of a group therapy model, in which the group serves as one another's source of support. Both have been effective at improving long-term cessation by 30 to 50 percent. Still, the quit success rate is less than 10 percent.

A behavioral treatment that gradually weans the smoker from nicotine by either having the smoker use low-nicotine-yield cigarettes, or special filters, or just smoking fewer and fewer cigarettes over time has met with some success. However, there are many problems with this method, and it is generally conducted in combination with other methods. These nicotine-fading combination methods have long-term success rates varying from 25 percent to 44 percent, much better than any other behavioral treatment methods alone, because they address the addiction to nicotine and not just the emotional and behavioral components of smoking.

Pharmacotherapies

As physicians and pharmacists learn more about the influence of brain chemistry on behavior, new medications are being developed to aid patients in overcoming addictions. One of the most widely used medications to aid smoking cessation is the drug to which the person is addicted, that is, nicotine. Nicotine replacement therapies (or NRT) are used to relieve nicotine withdrawal symptoms, hence addressing the addiction.

Zyban (bupropion) is an antidepressant medication that works by reducing nicotine withdrawal symptoms in smokers. It is a successful treatment for around 30 percent of smokers trying to quit.

NRT is available in several forms, and while most require a prescription from a physician, nicotine gum and the transdermal patch are also available over the counter. Nicotine gum was approved by the U.S. Food and Drug Administration (FDA) for use as a smoking cessation aid in 1984. Many studies have been conducted regarding the effectiveness of nicotine gum in helping individuals achieve long-term smoking cessation. The average quit success rate was 24 percent, and it was found to be most successful for people who are heavily addicted to nicotine. The nicotine patch became available in 1991. It delivers approximately 0.9 milligrams of nicotine per hour through the skin and should be used for a period of eight weeks. The long-term quit success rate is lower than the gum at 18 percent, and it cannot be used to curb sudden urges, unlike the gum.

The nicotine nasal spray offers a more immediate delivery of nicotine through the mucous membranes of the nose. One spray provides 0.5 milligrams of nicotine, with the recommended dose being 1 milligram (one spray in each nostril). The quit success rate with the nicotine nasal spray is 30.5 percent. The nicotine inhaler is a cigarette-shaped plastic tube that holds a cartridge containing 10 milligrams of nicotine and 1 milligram of menthol. It is recommended for use up to 12 weeks, then gradually decreasing use until cessation is complete. The smoker must puff on the tube 80 times to get the nicotine contained in one cigarette. Only a few studies have been done to measure its effectiveness; however, those show a quit success rate of 23 percent.

Two newer NRT methods are still being tested. One is the nicotine lozenge, which received FDA approval in 2002. Similar to nicotine gum, it delivers nicotine on an as-needed basis. The second new method is a nicotine tablet placed under the tongue that can last up to 20 minutes, delivering 2 milligrams of nicotine. It is recommended for people who are highly addicted to nicotine.

Bupropion SR (brand name Zyban) is an antidepressant medication that was approved by the FDA in 1997 for use as a smoking-cessation aid. Bupropion works by weakly inhibiting the reuptake of the neurotransmitters (chemical messengers) responsible for feelings of alertness and pleasure. It is available only by prescription, and the dose is 150 milligrams per day for three days, then increased to 300 milligrams a day for 12 weeks. The actual cigarette-quitting day takes place one to two weeks after starting the medication. Unlike nicotine, bupropion is not addictive but works to curb withdrawal symptoms. Bupropion is very effective at helping smokers quit, with a success rate of 30.5 percent.

No other medication has been approved by the FDA for smoking cessation. Nortriptyline, another antidepressant, has been tested. Like bupropion, the medication is started two to four weeks before the target quit date. Although the quit success rate is 30 percent, there are several negative side effects of the medication. Clonidine, a medication generally used for controlling high blood pressure, has also been tested as a smoking cessation aid. Patients start the medication several days before the quit day and continue for several weeks. Studies show the quit success rate to be 27 percent, but there are many unpleasant side effects, and many people do not complete the course of treatment.

Alternative therapies

When a person decides to quit smoking, he or she wants it to be immediate. The problem with addiction is that recovery is a long-term process. Many people invest in alternative methods with the hope that they can quit without really thinking about it. Hypnosis is one such method frequently promoted for smoking cessation. The hypnotherapist will use either a direct hypnotic suggestion to never want to smoke again, or suggestions that smoking will produce a negative reaction. There is also training in self-hypnosis to help smokers redirect their thoughts when the urge to smoke is greatest. Studies of the effectiveness of hypnosis for smoking cessation are inconclusive. Generally, it is most successful for people who are highly susceptible to hypnosis or when used in combination with other strategies.

Acupuncture is another alternative method for smoking cessation. The acupuncture does not create the desire for cessation but relieves the discomfort of withdrawal. The acupuncture needles are inserted into the outer ear. Some acupuncturists use clips or staples that the person wears for a period of time. Clinical studies of the method have found that it is no more effective than using nothing at all.

Aversive therapy is any method in which the therapist directs the smoker in behaviors that will make smoking unpleasurable, addressing the emotional component of smoking. One strategy is to have the smoker inhale deeply on a cigarette in rapid succession until the smoker becomes sick. Another requires him to smoke about twice as much as he normally would in a day, also resulting in making him sick. Another is to puff quickly without inhaling, resulting in breathlessness. All of these methods can have serious side effects (raising heart rates and blood pressure, raising carbon monoxide levels in the blood). Although they can produce quit rates as high as 40 percent when used in conjunction with other methods, the physical risks make them undesirable.

Relapse

Almost all smokers will lapse back to smoking at some point during their attempts to stop. The challenge is to prevent the lapse (having one puff or one cigarette) from becoming a relapse (back to the same rate of smoking as before the quit attempt). Most smoking cessation programs address the risks for relapse through helping the smoker identify high-risk situations for smoking and developing strategies for dealing with them. Risk factors for relapse include negative emotional states (depression, anger, boredom, weariness), being around smokers (especially family members who smoke), cravings, alcohol use, negative thoughts such as "I can't do this," and lack of alternative activities. Smokers who relapse generally return to their precessation level of smoking within a week and will often escalate the smoking to above the previous level.

The greatest successes at long-term cessation have been with combinations of behavioral and pharmacological treatments. However, no combination has been found to work for everyone. The smoker who is truly motivated to quit needs to find a combination of cessation methods that will address physical addiction, emotional connections, and the behavioral habits of smoking.

M. D. REYNOLDS

SEE ALSO:
Acupuncture • Addictive Behavior • Craving • Nicotine Replacements • Smoking

Social Acceptability

Perception of drug users has changed significantly over time. The view of addiction as a lack of self-control has largely been replaced, as research has shown that biological factors play a part.

Addiction is often perceived as being self-induced rather than the result of injury or an inborn problem beyond the individual's control. This perception has an effect on the individual in terms of feelings of self-worth and esteem and the social perception of addicted persons. Conditions that are perceived as the result of incidents beyond the individual's control, such as an accident, elicit a degree of compassion; stigmas that are seen as the direct result of a person's behavior are the target of social hostility and rejection.

Theories to explain compulsive addictive behavior can be placed in two categories. Addictive behavior is considered to be a character flaw, perceived as a weakness of will. These characteristics impute that psychosocial factors are the cause for the addiction. The second theory is derived from neuroscience and states that narcotic addiction, or the daily compulsive use of narcotics, has a metabolic origin. The belief about causality of addiction influences the formation of attitudes about addicts and the development of scientific theories.

Basis for stigmatization

Theories of addiction reflect the ideas of a particular era and form the underlying basis upon which addictive behavior is perceived and interpreted. Social biases (for example, class and race) that contribute to stigmatization of addicts are incorporated into these theoretical frameworks. However, socioeconomic class and race also influence the perception of addicted groups. Stereotypes based on these perceptions, especially in times of economic crisis, lay the foundation for the incorporation of related biases into theories of addiction and the type of legal statutes that are created to control addictive behaviors.

In the nineteenth century, opium was one of the most widely prescribed substances in the United States. Effective medications for diseases were rare, and physicians turned to those substances that were able to relieve pain and alleviate troublesome symptoms. Dependence on opiates (mainly laudanum) was not uncommon and affected many notable figures such as Benjamin Franklin and William Halsted, the father of modern surgery. Therefore, during the nineteenth century the major cause of addiction was through drugs prescribed by a physician to relieve discomfort and pain.

In the late nineteenth century physicians viewed addiction as a form of inebriety that was characterized by an underlying mental disturbance. The concept of inebriety merged two theories, known as degeneration and neurasthenia. Degeneration refers to worsening morbid conditions that are transmitted over generations within a family. Neurasthenia refers to an inherited inadequate nervous system that may make an individual prone to a variety of afflictions. Social factors may also play a part, and people in the upper classes trying to preserve their social status may "exhaust their nervous systems" and thus be prone to afflictions such as opiate addiction.

The concept of inebriation dominated the theoretical framework of addiction up to the early twentieth century. In Germany another theory was beginning to emerge that combined physiological and psychological theory. The psychological theory developed within the concept of the psychopathic personality, in which people were not mentally ill with delusion fantasies but acted without a moral sense. These two theories were further developed in the early twentieth century to help explain addictive behavior. In the nineteenth century African Americans had low rates of opiate addiction and it was hypothesized that they did not have the organized "delicate nervous systems" found among upper class whites to develop such conditions.

With the rise of industrialization and the waves of European immigration to northern cities in the 1890s, the addicted population was gradually transforming. Young male immigrants and the poor youth of native-born people in the slums and tenements began to smoke opium, snort heroin and cocaine, and inject morphine.

By the end of the first decade of the twentieth century, a distorted perception of the prevalence of opiate addiction in the United States was presented to the Senate by Hamilton Wright, the U.S. delegate to the Shanghai Commission (1909) and the Hague Opium Conference (1911), setting the stage for the passage of the Harrison Narcotics Act of 1914. This act was not originally intended as a prohibition law but instead as a measure to regulate the manufacture, distribution, and prescribing of opiates, coca, and their derivatives. An amendment in 1919 allowed physicians to prescribe narcotics for "legitimate medical purposes." The Narcotic Division within the Treasury Department took the position that addiction was not a disease and addicts were not legitimate patients; thus a physician who prescribed drugs to an addict was not legitimately prescribing. The immediate effect of the Harrison Act was the creation of a criminal underclass of narcotic addicts separated from legal and medical sources and forced into the black market to purchase needed drugs. The result was an almost immediate increase in drug-related street crime and the establishment of criminal networks for the distribution of drugs.

After World War II, the addict population was again transformed by two major population shifts. The middle class moved from the inner cities, which were centers of crime and drug abuse. They were replaced by poor Latinos and African Americans from southern rural communities. By the 1960s, poor black and Latino ghettos in the inner cities were epicenters of heroin addiction, which was reflected in public health and crime statistics. In the late 1950s and 1960s, injection of heroin became the major cause of death in New York City for young adults between the ages of 15 and 35. Hepatitis caused by injection of heroin with contaminated needles became a serious public health concern, and addict-related crime among nonwhite minorities and poor white ethnics became a major political issue.

Changing attitudes

Two major breakthroughs occurred in neuroscience research in the 1950s and 1960s. The first was the discovery by Olds and Milner of the brain reward system. This discovery changed the direction of neuroscience research into addiction. Psychological theories were challenged because of their circularity. For example, a drug addict uses drugs because of an "addictive personality." The discovery of the behavior reward system made possible the investigation of the neuropharmacologic properties of the drugs themselves and the common effects these drugs produce with humans and animals.

A second major breakthrough occurred at the United States Public Health Hospital in Lexington, Kentucky. Scientists such as Himmelsbach, Martin, and Jasinski investigated the physical aspects of addiction: tolerance, dependence, and abstinence in man and laboratory animals. For the first time, detailed records and measurements of the physiological changes that occurred during the different phases of addiction, withdrawal, and postaddiction were investigated.

In the 1960s there was another transformation. A new physiological theory was developed by Dole and Nyswander, who also developed methadone treatment. They hypothesized that addiction was a metabolic disease with neurological origins and conceptualized receptor cells, their location within the brain, and the description of a laboratory technique to locate these receptors when the technology became available. This laid the framework for the discovery of opiate receptors by Snyder and Pert at Johns Hopkins University.

Dole and Nyswander made perhaps a greater contribution by demonstrating that opiate addiction could be treated like any other chronic disease. They brought the treatment of addiction from the criminal justice system to the medical profession. This was an accomplishment in itself, considering the lack of understanding and resistance to the concept that a continuing opiate addiction had a strong underlying metabolic component. It must be realized that the work of Dole and Nyswander received sharp criticism from the start, which has continued. Like opiate addiction, methadone maintenance is widely misunderstood. While the differences between heroin addiction and methadone maintenance are profound, methadone patients still bear an invisible stigma derived from the perceived transfer of deviance associated with heroin addiction.

J. S. WOODS

SEE ALSO:

Class and Drug Use • Drug Use Subcultures • Harrison Narcotics Act • Media Attitudes toward Drugs

Social Services

Many people with addiction problems depend on welfare services for support. However, differences in funding and legislation can make it difficult for clients to gain access to the help they need.

When U.S. president Ronald Reagan told the story of a woman using government food stamps to purchase orange juice and spending the change to buy vodka as an attack on social welfare programs, he highlighted a major problem facing social services; namely, that many recipients are substance abusers. Social service programs in the United States grew out of the Great Depression, when millions of people were unemployed, homeless, and living near starvation. Prior to the 1930s, there was no safety net, or institutionalized government program to assist those who were destitute. During the Great Depression it became obvious that some form of assistance to the unemployed was needed, and the social welfare system was created. At that time, recipients were perceived as deserving the assistance they received. Subsequently, social services came to be seen as handouts, and recipients are often considered undeserving, especially if they are substance abusers. Indeed, as Ronald Reagan's story suggests, substance abusers sometimes use their government aid to further their addictions.

Though the question of whether substance abusers deserve social service assistance will not be debated here, the issue affects the way social service agencies approach substance abusers and is thus in the background of any discussion of the topic. The key questions for service providers include: how big a problem are substance abusers in terms of social services; how many of them are there and what special needs do they have; and which programs and policies are effective in dealing with these clients?

Numbers using services

Determining the number of substance users receiving social services is difficult because each state is responsible for its own social service delivery. As a consequence of different ways of defining substance use across states, differing systems, and confidentiality issues, there are no nationwide statistics kept on substance abusers receiving services. Funding cuts have made it more difficult to compile statistics, but studies conducted in the 1990s shed light on the issue. Data available from the National Household Survey of Drug Abuse show that people receiving social services are more likely to use drugs than those not receiving services. Twenty-two percent of those receiving services reported past year drug use in 1998, while 13 percent of those not receiving services reported past year use. Thus, when comparing social service clients to the general population, it seems clear that they are more likely to use drugs.

While comparing the general population statistics of those using drugs to those receiving services is important, it is more important to know the proportion of those receiving services who are dependent on or addicted to drugs. Again, these data are difficult to compile. It is also important to differentiate those who have a disorder that causes them to receive services from those whose use occurs at the same time they are receiving services for other reasons. The National Institute on Drug Abuse conducted a nationwide survey in 1992 and found that 3.3 percent of welfare recipients had a substance abuse disorder severe enough to cause them to be eligible for services, that is, they received assistance from the social service agencies because of their substance abuse. Two-thirds of these cases were alcohol related, while the other third were related to illicit drug use. More recent figures from the U.S. Department of Health and Human Services estimate that about 20 percent of people receiving services for other reasons also have substance abuse disorders. Substance abuse is higher among long-term recipients, suggesting that while it might not always cause them to be there, substance abuse can keep people in social services for longer periods of time.

The reason substance abusers receive services for longer periods of time is largely due to the myriad problems they tend to bring with them in addition to being dependent on drugs or alcohol. These range from little work experience, low education levels, transportation issues (especially in rural areas), having a criminal record, homelessness, child care and domestic violence issues (especially for women), health problems, and co-occurring mental health disorders.

Achieving independence

The overall goal of social services has always been to help clients achieve independence. The additional problems faced by substance abusing clients make this job even more difficult. Shrinking budgets and changes in social service practices that limit lifetime allowances for benefits make achieving independence both more difficult and more necessary for substance abusers. In the 1990s the federal government passed legislation limiting recipients of Temporary Assistance for Needy Families (TANF) to five years during the lifetime of any one individual. While it remains up to each state to decide how to meet that goal, in order to receive necessary federal assistance, states must comply. As a result of these issues, many states have formed partnerships with local substance abuse treatment programs in order to meet the goals of both systems.

According to the Welfare Information Network, substance abuse treatment shares the same goal as social services: independence. While social services seek independence through stable employment, treatment agencies seek independence from addiction for their clients. Obviously, substance abuse inhibits the ability to work, and stable employment is considered a key part of most recovery plans. Because these organizations were traditionally separate agencies, however, only recently have they begun working together and even then in spite of policies that serve to keep them apart.

In the 1990s Congress passed legislation that disqualified those convicted of a drug-related felony from receiving services for five years. Thus, those coming out of prison, most of whom have employment and housing issues—exactly the problems social services were created to address—were not allowed to access the services they needed. Other barriers were also placed in the way of providing services to substance abusers. Many states passed legislation that barred those known to be current drug users or practicing alcoholics from

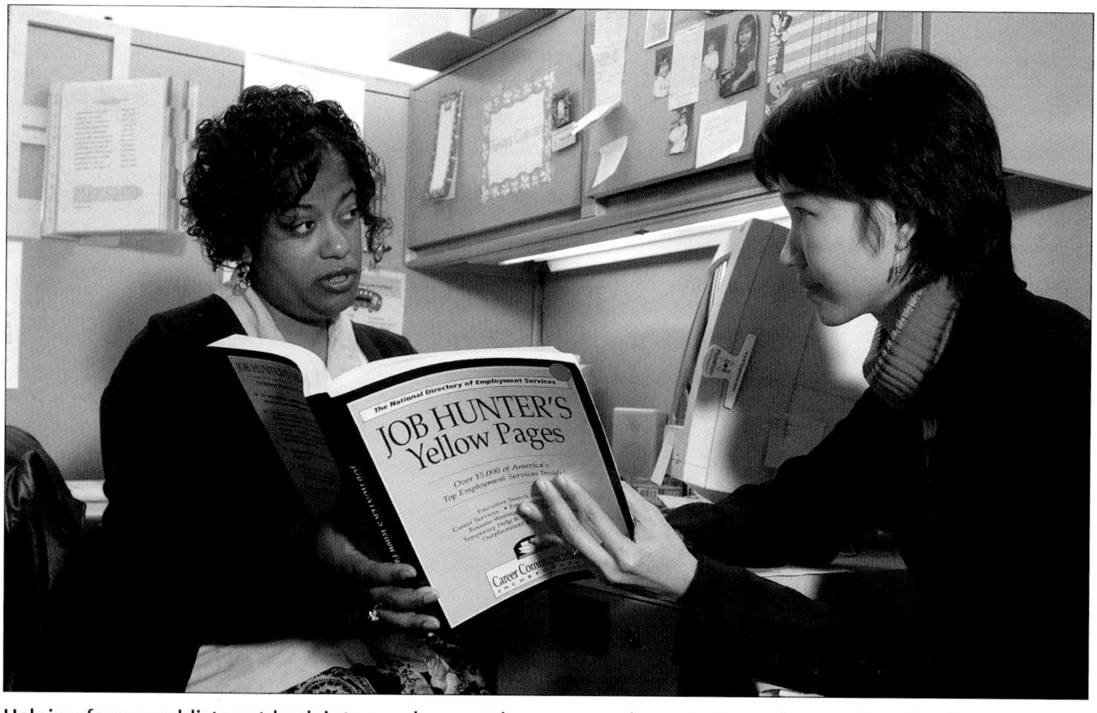

Helping former addicts get back into employment is seen as an important step by social service departments. A stable work environment can provide a sense of self-esteem and make people less dependent on benefits.

receiving services unless they were in treatment. The result was that clients quickly learned to lie about their circumstances. Clients would not inform their caseworkers of their legal problems and would hide their addictions from others. Doing so enabled clients to receive cash assistance and food stamps but, because their caseworkers were unaware of the underlying issues, clients were prevented from receiving the necessary assistance that would enable them to return to independence.

Linking services

Social service agencies have now begun attempting to link substance abuse treatment with services. Partly driven by new rules that limit clients to five years of services and that require them to be in either a work or training-related activity within two years, agencies have begun to address substance abuse. By using drug testing, creative financing, and innovative programs, social services have integrated substance abuse treatment and social services.

Many agencies have started to use urinalysis to test clients for drug use. This practice enables the agency to identify drug users, to monitor those in treatment, and to directly reduce drug use by sanction or threat of sanctioning those who test positive. It is too expensive to test all clients, but most agencies will test those they suspect of using, and then mandate treatment for those who test positive.

Social service agencies often mandate drug treatment for those discovered with substance abuse problems. Obviously, social service clients do not have the money to pay for their own treatment, so agencies use a number of ways to provide it. Because of changes in the law, it is difficult for social service agencies to directly fund treatment, so many states partner with their health departments, which receive federal grants to provide treatment. Teaming health departments with social services works for both agencies. Social services have clients in need but lack money, while health departments do not have such ready access to the affected population as do social service departments. Some states even have a full-time substance abuse counselor as part of their staff, often funded through the health department, which allows for direct referral of substance abusing clients and makes it much simpler to follow up on their progress.

While having on-site counselors is one innovative approach to substance using clients, numerous studies have shown that integrating social services, substance abuse treatment, and employment readiness programs increases the likelihood of a client achieving independence, both in terms of drug abuse and employment. A good example is the Casaworks for Families program, a national demonstration program being tested in New York by Columbia University, which draws on local, state, and federal funding to promote a milieu in which many services work together. Clients are assigned a case manager who coordinates 6 to 12 months of intensive drug or alcohol treatment, job training or educational services, as well as parenting skills, personal health issues, and a host of family services. An evaluation of the program found that after 12 months in the program, 75 percent of participants had quit using drugs and 40 percent were working, compared with 16 percent working at the start of the program. Only 13 percent were still receiving cash assistance. There is thus evidence that collaborative programs can assist clients with their substance abuse and employment issues.

A final way that social services and substance abuse are intertwined is through foster care of children whose parents are incarcerated. There were 24,000 children of prisoners in foster care in 1997. Foster care was much more likely to be the result of an incarcerated mother than an incarcerated father. Because of the established association between drugs and crime, it is reasonable to assume that social service programs like Casaworks would have the added benefit of keeping some people out of prisons and their children out of foster care.

The creative work of professionals in the social services system has been able to overcome both their clients' unwillingness to seek help and policies that grew from labeling substance abusers as undeserving; these initiatives are providing services that, instead of merely removing clients from welfare lists, enable them to leave voluntarily by becoming independent.

D. J. O'CONNELL, T. C. O'CONNELL

SEE ALSO:
Continuum of Care • Economic Costs of Addiction • Public Health Programs • State Agencies

Sports

The urge to gain a competitive advantage can drive many athletes to take substances that can improve their performance. Sports organizations are having to develop sophisticated techniques to detect the use of drugs.

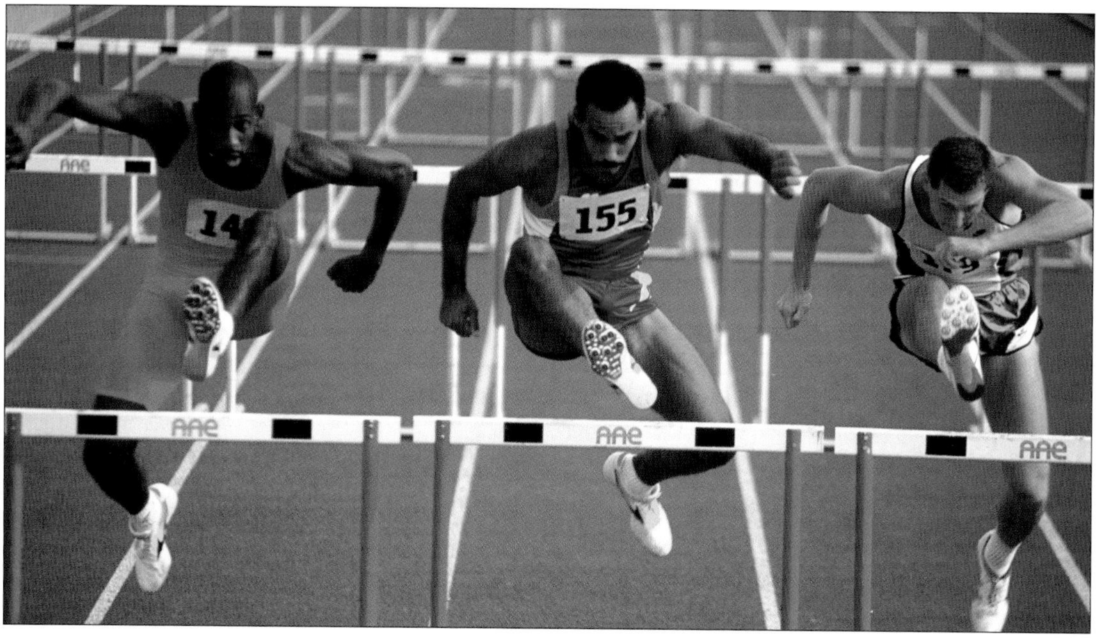

Most athletes train hard to be able to run or jump higher than their rivals. In doing so they must be careful not to take any food supplement or medicine that may be on the list of banned substances.

The use of substances to gain a competitive edge in sports has been of interest since ancient times. Olympic athletes in ancient Greece reportedly experimented with opium, mushrooms, and herbal potions to improve their athletic performance. Ancient Aztec runners consumed extracts from cactus plants as stimulants to reduce fatigue in long-distance events. In the 1800s, when the stimulants amphetamine, ephedrine, and strychnine became available, American and European athletes began using them. In the 1940s the male hormone testosterone and similar compounds were produced and subsequently used by athletes to increase muscle growth and strength. The term *doping* (derived from the Dutch word *doop* for a type of viscous opium juice) is typically used to denote the use of performance-enhancing drugs in sports.

The use of drugs by athletes in the modern era has become a prominent problem and concern. The use and risk of stimulants became prominently exposed after a cyclist died during competition in the 1960 Olympic Games in Rome, a death that was associated with the use of amphetamine. Similarly, a cyclist in the 1967 Tour de France collapsed and died during the race, also attributed to the use of amphetamine. Anabolic-androgenic steroids became popular with strength athletes in the 1960s and 1970s and continue to be the most abused class of drugs in the modern Olympics.

Why athletes take drugs

Serious, competitive athletes desire to maximize their performance, not only from extensive training, but also from proper nutrition, adequate sleep, using the best equipment, and other rational means. This often includes the use of nutritional dietary supplements, such as vitamins and minerals. However, the desire, pressure, and incentives to succeed and win at any and all costs entices some athletes to resort to illicit means, including the use of performance-enhancing drugs. Wealth, prestige, and fame often accompany athletic success in society, where winners are regarded as heroes. Some athletes may feel that their only chance of winning or making it to the next level is by gaining an unfair advantage. Further, some athletes may feel compelled to use banned drugs because they believe that their competitors are using them.

Competitive athletes generally train with teams, partners, or groups. Hence, the pressure to keep up and improve is greater. If some members of the group use drugs to improve their performance, they may encourage the other members to do so as well. If the athlete is successful—whether or not the success can be attributed to drugs—the other athletes may feel that taking the same drugs will produce the same success. Some athletes have even been unscrupulously doped by their country, without their consent or knowledge, in order to produce winners in international competitions.

Effects of drugs on performance

An ergogenic drug is one that increases work output, and for athletes it is one that improves their performance. The following drug classes are commonly used by athletes as ergogenic aids: stimulants, narcotics, anabolic-androgenic steroids, diuretics, and peptide hormones. Although there are numerous other drugs, dietary supplements, and other products that are promoted to enhance athletic performance, scientific evidence to support many of these claims is notably lacking.

Stimulants include such drugs as amphetamine, methamphetamine, cocaine, ephedrine, and caffeine. Amphetamine and related compounds stimulate the brain and the heart. They can potentially improve athletic performance by increasing alertness, strength, endurance, and they can reduce fatigue. These drugs can also cause euphoria (a feeling of well-being), and they can increase confidence and aggression. Some athletes take drugs or dietary supplements that contain these substances to assist with weight loss.

The side effects of these stimulants can be serious, particularly at high doses or when different stimulants are taken together. Such effects include insomnia, restlessness, nervousness, irritability, rapid and pounding heart rate, abnormal heart rhythms, thermogenesis (increased heat production by the body), stroke, seizures, and death.

Narcotics are drugs that stem from opium or similar compounds. These agents are used in sports primarily to relieve pain or to increase the pain threshold. Other effects of narcotics include euphoria and an increase in the athletes' perceptions of their abilities (sometimes to the point of feeling invincible). Side effects of narcotics include nausea, vomiting, constipation, sedation, altered judgment, and mood changes. Long-term use can result in physical and psychological addiction, and overdoses can result in respiratory depression and death.

Anabolic-androgenic steroids are compounds that are similar in chemical structure and actions to the male sex hormone testosterone. These compounds are considered anabolic because they promote the growth of muscles and bones. They are also classified as androgenic because they have masculinizing effects too, similar to testosterone and other androgens. When combined with intense physical training and high-protein diets, these drugs can help increase muscle size and strength. Abusers of these agents often take more than one particular anabolic-androgenic steroid at the same time, a practice that is called stacking. In an attempt to minimize side effects, some abusers take anabolic-androgenic steroids for a specific period of time (usually 6 to 12 weeks), and then stop for a period of time. This process is referred to as cycling. Further, some abusers take higher and higher doses during the cycle, and then they taper the dose back down in increments, a method known as pyramiding.

Anabolic-androgenic steroids have complex effects in many organs and tissues. In addition, their presence in the body alters the regulation and secretion of other natural hormones because the brain and sex glands work in conjunction to determine the right balance of testosterone and other hormones to produce. In males, for example, since the body senses these compounds to be androgens, the brain signals the cells in the testes to pause from producing testosterone.

In males, side effects of anabolic-androgenic steroids include a decrease in the size of the testicles, enlargement of the prostate gland, a decline in the production of sperm, infertility, impotence, and changes in sex drive. Further, since these drugs are partially converted to estrogenic compounds (the female hormone), they can cause enlargement of the breasts in males. This is potentially irreversible and may require surgical treatment. In females, anabolic-androgenic steroids have a masculinizing effect, which includes the growth of facial hair, deepening of the voice, and baldness. Other effects in females include enlargement of the clitoris, menstrual irregularities, and changes in sex drive. Additional side effects of anabolic-androgenic steroids in both males and females include high blood pressure, acne, male-pattern baldness, fluid retention, elevated blood cholesterol, myocardial infarction (heart attack), strokes, and cancer. Changes in personality can occur, including aggression and hostility. In adolescents, these drugs may cause the bones to cease growing sooner than normal, which can result in a shortened growth span. Finally, these drugs may lead to addiction and dependence, especially when taken in high doses. Withdrawal can result in depression and suicidal thoughts.

IN THE GENES

For those desperate to improve their performance, new techniques developed for medical research could be used to enhance athletic achievement. Gene therapy, which is seen as a possible cure for cancer or multiple sclerosis, could also be used to boost the gene that produces natural erythropoietin in the blood. Existing tests can spot synthetic versions of erythropoietin but may not be able to detect genetically boosted natural production. There can be drawbacks. Too much erythropoietin can elevate blood pressure and result in a heart attack or stroke. Altering genes could aggravate such dangers, especially as the technique is still experimental. Antidoping agencies are trying to stay one step ahead by searching for tiny changes that occur when the body is exposed to certain genes, in the hope that these may then be detected in blood samples.

Diuretics are often referred to as water pills. These medications enhance water and salt excretion through the kidney and increase the production of urine. Thus, some athletes use diuretics to improperly "make weight" for sports that have weight classifications, such as wrestling, boxing, and weightlifting. Diuretics also have been used to dilute the urine of athletes who are using banned substances, with the hope that they can cheat or fool a drug test. Since urine drug tests require a minimum concentration to reliably and accurately detect a drug, diluting the urine can reduce the concentration of a drug below the detection threshold. However, since diuretics are often banned by sports agencies, the detection of a diuretic will result in a positive drug test. Side effects of diuretics include dehydration, mineral imbalance, cramps, weakness, and nausea.

Peptide hormones include naturally occurring hormones consisting of various amino acids. Some of these hormones have positive ergogenic effects, and their synthesis has made them available for abuse. Athletes have used human growth hormone, hoping to increase muscle size and strength, and they often combine this with the use of anabolic-androgenic steroids. Erythropoietin is a hormone that stimulates the production of red blood cells, which carry oxygen to muscles and other organs in the body. The use of synthetic erythropoietin provides a competitive advantage for endurance athletes, since their blood has a higher oxygen-carrying capacity. Other hormones have been used by athletes even though any ergogenic effects have not been scientifically proven. These highly active compounds can also produce undesirable or adverse effects. For example, adverse effects from the use of human growth hormone include depression, antisocial behavior, abnormalities in blood sugar and fats, heart disease, and a disorder known as acromegaly. Problems associated with the abuse of erythropoietin include high blood pressure, iron deficiency, convulsions, myocardial infarction, and stroke.

It is not the intent of the sports-governing bodies to deny athletes the use of medications needed to treat medical conditions. These organizations supply lists of banned and permitted drugs under their purview, and for some banned or restricted drugs there is a mechanism for the athlete and his or her physician to petition for a medical exception.

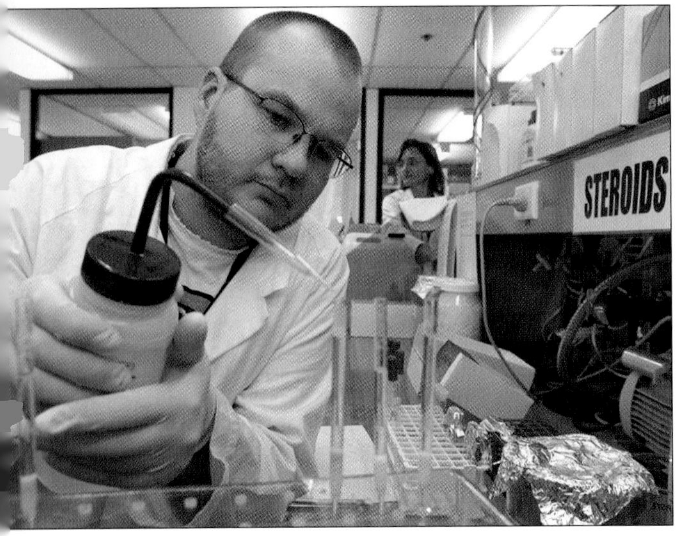

Staff at the 2000 Sydney Olympic drug-testing unit made routine analyses for a number of banned drugs. Random testing is the only way to ensure that cheating is stamped out in competitive sports.

Incidence of drug use in sports

The incidence of drug use in sports varies according to the sport and the level of competition. According to various studies and surveys, 4 to 11 percent of high school males and 0.5 to 2.5 percent of high school females have used anabolic-androgenic steroids. The use of these agents in college sports has ranged from approximately 1 percent to a high of 20 percent; the lower incidence was observed in more recent years after the institution of drug education and testing policies. During a recent survey of college athletes, the use of stimulants (amphetamines and ephedrine) was approximately 7 percent. Although rumors, claims, and anecdotal reports suggest that the use of anabolic-androgenic steroids and stimulants is prevalent in some professional sports (for example, football and baseball), the true incidence is not known. In one study, as many as 55 percent of elite weight lifters had admitted to the use of anabolic-androgenic steroids. In a review of the modern (1896–2002) summer and winter Olympic Games, there were 29 documented cases of the use of anabolic-androgenic steroids, 22 cases of stimulant use, and 7 cases of the use of diuretics. However, wide-scale drug testing at the Olympics was only instituted in 1972, and only since 1984 has it been technologically possible to rapidly and accurately test urine samples for a wide array of banned substances. Moreover, athletes are fully aware that drug testing will be conducted at Olympic events and are able to discontinue the use of drugs prior to testing. Some Olympic officials estimate the incidence of doping to be about 10 percent, while some athletes, coaches, and trainers believe the prevalence is much higher.

Drug testing of athletes

Drug testing (doping control) is one of the methods employed to deter the use of banned substances in sports. Drug testing aims to protect the health and safety of athletes and their competitors, and to maintain the dignity and integrity of sports by ensuring fair and equitable competition. Ideally, it also assures athletes that their competitors are not allowed to cheat, so they too will not feel compelled to break the rules.

Drug testing is routinely conducted on urine specimens; however, testing for the use of erythropoietin has consisted of both blood and urine tests. Urine specimens are used because the collection of samples is noninvasive, and because drugs and their metabolites are concentrated in the urine, which renders it easier to detect them. Testing is generally conducted just after a competition is completed. However, drugs such as anabolic-androgenic steroids are used during training and may not be detectable during competition if the athlete stops using the drugs long enough to allow them to clear from his or her system. Therefore, out-of-competition testing for these drugs is conducted at random times during the year and with short notice to the athlete.

Athletes who test positive for banned substances are subject to sanctions imposed by their specific sports-governing organization. Penalties generally include disqualification, and a number of Olympic athletes have had their medals stripped and records erased due to positive drug tests. Further, athletes who test positive for banned substances are usually banned from future competition for a specific amount of time.

P. J. AMBROSE

SEE ALSO:
Anabolic Steroids • Drug Testing • Erythropoietin • Human Growth Hormone

SSRIs

Selective serotonin reuptake inhibitors (SSRIs) are first-choice drugs for the treatment of depression, social phobia, obsessive-compulsive behavior, and eating problems. They produce fewer side effects than older antidepressants.

Depression is an alarmingly common condition that blights the lives of its sufferers by dulling their capacity for hope and pleasure in life. In 2003 a study by the U.S. National Institute of Mental Health revealed that 16 percent of U.S. citizens require treatment for depression at some stage in their lives, and at any time there are 13 to 14 million U.S. citizens suffering from the condition.

SSRIs are now the drugs in most frequent use for the treatment of depression, and they can help 60 to 80 percent of patients feel better within two to six weeks. Several SSRIs have come into use since the 1987 launch of fluoxetine (Prozac); the top sellers in 2003 were paroxetine (Paxil) and sertraline (Zoloft).

Accumulated experience with SSRIs has revealed their usefulness in the treatment of bulimia, general anxiety disorder (GAD), and obsessive-compulsive disorder (OCD), as well as major depressive disorder (MDD), the original target for the drugs. Growing confidence in the safety of SSRIs led to their being prescribed "off label," meaning for conditions and age groups beyond the original scope of the drugs. That trend is now reversing, however, and regulatory bodies such as the U.S. Food and Drug Administration (FDA) are requiring or recommending more restricted use of SSRIs, particularly for adolescents.

Before Prozac

Since the 1950s, antidepressant medications have targeted neurotransmission by norepinephrine and serotonin, since these systems are usually underactive in the brains of depressed people. Two older classes of antidepressants use different means to increase the persistence of these neurotransmitters in synapses (the junctions between neurons) so as to reinforce neurotransmission. The tricyclic antidepressants (TCAs) inhibit the reuptake mechanisms that return neurotransmitters to the neurons that secrete them; monoamine oxidase inhibitors (MAOIs) block the enzymes that render neurotransmitters inactive.

Both TCAs and MAOIs are effective treatments for depression, giving improvements in around two in three patients, compared with one in three patients treated with inactive placebo tablets. A major problem with these types of drugs is that they can be fatal in overdose. They also have side effects that can discourage patients from taking the drug.

Many of the side effects of TCAs and MAOIs stem from the fact that they produce overactivity of other neurotransmitters apart from those implicated in depression. In particular, they cause undue increases in the activities of acetylcholine, histamine, and epinephrine; the resulting side effects include dry mouth, blurred vision, altered heart function, constipation, and urinary retention.

Benefits of selectivity

SSRIs resemble TCAs in that they inhibit neurotransmitter reuptake and have similar success rates in lifting depression. The important difference is that SSRIs act only on serotonin reuptake, so there is less scope for adverse effects due to overactivity of other neurotransmitters. The selectivity for serotonin also vastly reduces the risk of death by overdose.

SNRIs (serotonin-norepinephrine reuptake inhibitors) such as venlafaxine (Effexor) selectively inhibit reuptake of both neurotransmitters. They can be helpful for patients who fail to respond to SSRIs, especially if lethargy is a symptom.

Adverse effects and withdrawal

Some side effects are caused by serotonin itself. They are usually mild, and they include excessive sweating, nausea, and headaches. Disruption of male sexual function can occur and is more problematic, since it makes patients more likely to abandon treatment.

Greater problems are likely to occur if SSRI treatment overlaps with MAOI treatment, since the combined actions of these drugs can cause dangerously high levels of serotonin. The result is serotonin syndrome—a collection of unpleasant symptoms that can sometimes be fatal. For this reason, courses of MAOIs and SSRIs must be separated by at least two

THE MARKET FOR PROZAC AND OTHER SSRIs

Prozac (fluoxetine) had annual sales of $2.7 billion when the patent that guaranteed exclusive sales rights to Eli Lilly expired in August 2001. The expiration allowed other companies to make and sell fluoxetine and sell it cheaper.

By 2003, Lilly's sales of Prozac had fallen to $0.2 billion, while Par Pharmaceutical sold $0.4 billion of generic fluoxetine. These sales are a fraction of the sales of Zoloft (sertraline; $2.8 billion) and Paxil/Paxil CR (paroxetine; $2.2 billion)—both SSRIs that have exclusive patents until 2005. Together with SNRIs, the SSRIs are the highest-value group of U.S. prescription drugs.

The fall in the market for fluoxetine is not just a result of lower prices. Drug companies focus on marketing drugs that have current licenses and are therefore more profitable. Prescriptions of such drugs then increase at the expense of those for cheaper generic drugs in the same class.

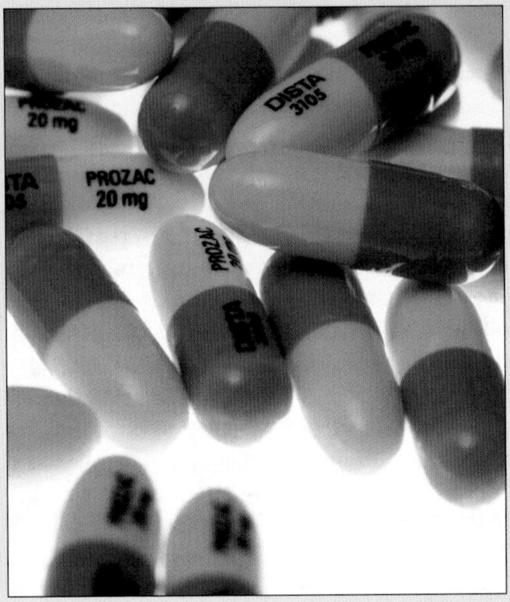

weeks for the drug to clear from the system and, in the case of MAOIs, for monoamine oxidase activity to return to normal.

Withdrawal from SSRIs can be problematic, as the brain has to adapt to falling levels of serotonin. Slow dose reduction over a period of weeks or months can keep symptoms such as dizziness, disturbing dreams, and fatigue to a minimum. There is also less likelihood of falling back into depression if the drug is withdrawn gradually rather than suddenly.

Abuse potential

The fact that sudden SSRI withdrawal can cause adverse reactions does not equate to SSRIs being addictive in the sense of a recreational drug. There is no evidence for SSRIs provoking drug-seeking behavior in humans or animals, and a drug user seeking a high from SSRIs is likely to be disappointed when the physical side effects of SSRIs set in without there being a noticeable high. Combinations of Ecstasy with SSRIs are also ineffective, since SSRIs block the mechanism by which Ecstasy and its analogs produce their effects. There have been some cases where SSRIs have caused flashbacks in individuals who had taken LSD in the past, but the mechanism of this effect is unknown.

Caution for adolescents

There have been cases where patients have become agitated and attempted suicide within a few days of starting on SSRIs. In the main, these patients have been adolescents suffering from depression, and there is much debate about whether the depression or the drug is to blame. In December 2003 the U.K. Committee on Safety of Medicines issued an urgent statement advising doctors against prescribing six of the main SSRIs and SNRIs—Prozac excluded—for depression in patients under 18 years of age. This statement followed a review of clinical trials in which only fluoxetine proved effective against depression without increasing the risk of suicide or self-harm.

M. CLOWES

SEE ALSO:
Antidepressant Drugs • Homicide • MAOs and MAOIs • Norepinephrine • Serotonin • Suicide

State Agencies

Providing treatment for drug addiction in the United States usually falls to the responsibility of individual states. Funding for programs is a joint venture between the federal government, the state, and counties or cities within the state.

Since the mid-1970s, growing attention has focused on providing drug treatment services through state networks because of regional organizational differences and the size of the United States. State agencies have a greater knowledge of the needs of their citizens in their respective areas. States and state agencies also coordinate services and funding from several sources, including the National Institutes of Health, Department of Health and Human Services, Centers for Disease Control, Substance Abuse and Mental Health Services Administration, National Institute on Drug Abuse, and National Institute on Alcohol Abuse and Alcoholism. Federal funding supports the majority of governmental funding, with the state and county or city providing a portion. This can often mean that state officials are involved in policy and decisions regarding federal money.

In every state there are a variety of programs that are involved in drug prevention and treatment. This provision has arisen since the 1970s as the use of drugs increased and drug abuse began to be recognized as a problem. Certainly the use of drugs was not new and, depending on the era, various groups have been affected by drug use, with the largest number of addicted Americans peaking at the beginning of the twenty-first century. The main difference from earlier eras is that until the 1960s drug use was prominent among older rather than younger age groups.

All states have one primary agency that is responsible for ensuring that citizens of the state have access to treatment, educating communities about drug use, and policy making. For the majority of states the agency responsible for drug-use issues is part of a larger agency, such as the state department of health. In larger states, or in states with a larger drug problem, drug use often has a separate agency (*see* table on p. 809). A state's view of drug use is often reflected by the agency that has oversight. It demonstrates the confusion that frequently arises about whether drug use is classified as a medical condition. Some states may place an agency with the Department of Health or Public Health, while at the same time regarding drug use as a social and rehabilitative problem.

Federal oversight agencies

The primary federal agency involved with drug use and mental health is the Substance Abuse and Mental Health Services Administration (SAMHSA), which is an agency of the Department of Health and Human Services (HHS). SAMHSA was established in 1992 by an act of Congress, Public Law 102-321. Created to focus more attention on improving the lives of individuals with mental health and substance use disorders, SAMHSA is separate and distinct from the National Institutes of Health (NIH) or the National Institute on Drug Abuse (NIDA) or any other agency within the HHS.

SAMHSA interacts with the states, national and local community- and faith-based organizations, and public and private sector providers. SAMHSA's primary mission is to ensure that people with a mental health or addictive disorder and those individuals at risk have the opportunity for a fulfilling life that includes a job, a home, and meaningful relationships with family and friends.

As the substance abuse and mental health systems of services evolve, SAMHSA conducts research and then translates these findings into best practice with the goal of facilitating science-based knowledge to community-based services. State programs are supported through the block grant program, and discretionary grants are offered to implement programs and practices. It should be noted that in addition to the 50 states, various territories such as Guam, Puerto Rico, and the Virgin Islands receive funding, as does the United Indian Health Services, which oversees funding for Native American nations.

SAMHSA has three centers that carry out its mission and interact with state agencies, community-based programs, research centers, and nonprofit and private organizations. The Office of Applied Studies collects, analyzes, and disseminates national data on

Provisions made by states to combat addiction vary widely. Some may provide 24-hour hotline advice; others may only have limited funds for treatment.

practices and issues related to substance use and mental health disorders. The Center for Mental Health Services (CMHS) works to improve the quality of community-based services and make them more accessible. The Center for Substance Abuse Treatment (CSAT) promotes the availability and quality of community-based substance abuse treatment services.

What do state programs do?

Each of the 50 states and the various territories have some agency that is responsible for coordinating the various prevention and treatment efforts that are undertaken in the state. In general, it can be said that the greater the state's drug problem, the larger the agency. Nearly all state agencies have an educational or prevention branch that travels to schools and community-based programs and gives presentations. These programs are more effective than criminal justice agencies because the people providing the education are trained professionals who know not only about the criminal aspect of drug use but about treatment and the social issues that are often associated with drug use.

A second large part of most state programs is providing treatment, which includes outpatient counseling, residential, and medication-assisted treatment (such as methadone and buprenorphine). State agencies license programs and provide oversight to ensure that citizens are not being harmed. Many state agencies are also involved in the funding of these programs. Every year the federal government through SAMHSA carries out a needs assessment for each state and then provides funding. Usually the federal money does not cover all the treatment costs, and typically it is broken down to 50 percent federal money, 25 percent state money, and 25 percent local money. In some states, public medical assistance pays for drug treatment; in others, citizens are expected to pay for drug treatment themselves. This can be costly to individual citizens when one considers that drug addiction is considered a chronic relapsing medical condition.

Each state agency is designated by SAMHSA to be the state methadone authority (SMA) and have oversight and licensing of all programs in the state. This is a recent development, following the change in the federal methadone regulations and the change in oversight from the Food and Drug Administration (FDA) to SAMHSA. The SMA provides state oversight and technical assistance to methadone programs in the state and is involved in policy making and state regulation.

Many state agencies are involved in the training of professionals who work in the field and in the credentialing of persons who work in programs, such as counselors. Each state issues its own credentials, such as "certified substance abuse counselor." Professionals must maintain their credentials or they will not be allowed to work in a state-licensed program.

While each state agency's mission may sound similar, the ways in which their goals are implemented are as varied as the 50 states. Some state agencies are very small, having only a few employees, while other state agencies have offices throughout the state, a research division, a media and public relations division, and provide direct advocacy to citizens through an advocacy center, to name but a few spheres of activity. Some departments in the agency may address specific issues within the state, such as homelessness, a cocaine epidemic, an HIV epidemic, neighborhood youth programs, and so on. Some state agencies even have a local weekly cable program to educate their citizens about drug issues in the state.

STATE AGENCIES RUNNING DRUG PROGRAMS OR THAT HAVE OVERSIGHT

Department of Health

Arkansas
Hawaii
Nevada
New Mexico
Pennsylvania
Tennessee

Department of Public Health

Iowa
Massachusetts
Montana

Department of Mental Health, Mental Retardation, or Developmental Disabilities

Alabama
Georgia
Kentucky
Mississippi
North Carolina
Rhode Island
Virginia

Mental Health and Addiction Services or Behavioral Health

Connecticut
Idaho
Indiana
Oklahoma
Utah
West Virginia
Wyoming

Health or Human Services

Alaska (Social Services)
Colorado
Delaware (Social Services)
Minnesota
Nebraska
New Hampshire
New Jersey
North Dakota
South Dakota
Vermont
Washington (Social Services)

Community Health

Michigan

Social and Rehabilitative Services

Kansas

Children and Family Services

Florida

Separate Agency

Arizona
California
District of Columbia
Illinois
Louisiana
Maine
Maryland
Missouri
New York
Ohio
Oregon
South Carolina
Texas
Wisconsin

Source: *Monitoring the Future Study,* 2001

Core issues for states

Each of the 50 states has core issues that have been developed with SAMHSA to take its goals from vision to practice. These priorities are linked to principles that help ensure that state programs will meet the highest standards, driven by a strategy to improve accountability, capacity, and effectiveness:

- Promoting accountability; SAMHSA tracks national trends and establishes measurement and reporting systems to monitor services.
- Enhancing capacity; by assessing resources, supporting systems of community-based care, and improving service financing and organization, SAMHSA promotes a strong, well-educated workforce and improves the nation's capacity for treatment and prevention services.
- Assuring effectiveness; at the federal level SAMHSA works to continually improve services by identifying and promoting evidence-based approaches to care and by providing technical assistance and workforce skills training.

J. S. WOODS

SEE ALSO:
Economic Costs of Addiction • Public Health Programs • Treatment • Treatment, Cost of

Step Programs

Many addiction recovery programs are based on a self-help system known as a step program. The concept was first developed for Alcoholics Anonymous, but its principles have found application in helping treat other addictions.

The last two decades of the twentieth century witnessed an explosion in the growth of self-help groups for all types of problems. One prominent researcher estimated that in the state of California alone there were 275 different self-help groups, including groups for addiction such as Alcoholics Anonymous and Gamblers Anonymous, and groups for mental health problems such as depression and agoraphobia. The growth of these groups accompanied an increased interest in alternative, or complementary, medicine.

The interest in self-help (or, more correctly, mutual help) groups was a reflection of a growing discontent with conventional medicine and the over-weaning reliance on medication as the answer to all problems. When celebrities openly began discussing their addiction problems and proclaiming their allegiance and gratitude to self-help groups, in particular Alcoholics Anonymous (AA), it became more acceptable to discuss addiction, leading some cynics to suggest that addiction was becoming a fashion accessory. Regardless of the hyperbole attached to the latest celebrity's revelations about his or her battle with drugs or alcohol, the publicity has had some benefits. To a large extent it demystified and destigmatized addiction problems and made people aware of a readily available source of help, the self-help group.

Origins

Step programs have been described as the instruction manual for addressing various behavioral problems, most famously alcoholism. This manual, or program, consists of a number of tasks, or steps, that need to be followed to recover from the problem. In its current and most recognizable form, the program consists of twelve steps (*see* box, p. 812), mainly because subsequent groups adopted the program as it was exemplified by AA. However, even in AA the program has not always consisted of twelve steps, as the organization's history reveals.

The man generally credited with the authorship of the twelve-step program is Bill Wilson, an American stockbroker and alcoholic. In his writings he describes his constant struggles and failures with alcohol until, in 1934, a friend took him along to a meeting of the Oxford Group, an evangelical Christian society. It was there that he found some basis for his personal sobriety and later made plans for what was to become AA. He found that the Oxford Group practiced a program based on a few simple principles: acceptance of powerlessness, honesty with self and others, making restitution, and seeking guidance through prayer and meditation. Bill found that by practicing these principles he no longer craved alcohol and began trying to spread the message to other alcoholics. The message, a modified six-step version of the Oxford Group's principles, was not particularly well received, and in 1939 Bill, with some help from other sober alcoholics, wrote the book *Alcoholics Anonymous* (the so-called Big Book). In this book he expanded on the six steps, and the program as practiced today was born. A 1941 newspaper article by Jack Alexander publicized the program, and the membership of AA eventually grew from around 100 to the worldwide fellowship of around two million that it is today. The apparent success of AA led to other self-help groups being organized along the same lines and adopting, with minor modifications, the twelve-step program. The earliest of these was Al-Anon, the group for the families of alcoholics, then Alateen, for the children of alcohol abusers. Similar groups for other addiction problems began to emerge, for example, Narcotics Anonymous and Gamblers Anonymous, and the spread has continued.

Key concepts

The key concepts of the groups continue to be the principles that Bill Wilson learned from the Oxford Group back in 1934. They include admission of helplessness, honesty, reparation, working with others, and prayer and meditation. These are principles that are often lost in a life of addiction, which is often characterized by dishonesty and selfishness. Supporters of the program argue that someone who adopts these principles and makes radical changes in his or her life can undergo a powerful transformation, and there are many personal stories to support this case.

While many people exhort the program as a transformer of lives, it is not difficult to find other reasons that AA and other step programs might work. The first reason is fellowship—all or most of the people attending these groups will be in a similar situation, hence the mutual support and practical advice will be both helpful and motivating. Second, AA meetings tend to be attended by members who have been sober for varying lengths of time, and the example of long-term sober members can be motivating. Third, there are the sayings of AA, which, although they have become rather clichéd, are both profound and powerful. Take, for example, the saying "one day at a time." Any counselor attempting to help someone with problems knows the value of breaking the problem into manageable pieces. This approach is precisely what is being advocated by this saying; that is, do what can be done today. Thus, twelve-step groups may work on multiple levels.

The program

It is usually suggested that when someone embarks on the twelve-step program he or she acquire a sponsor who will assist the person through recovery. The sponsor is normally someone who has been a successful member of the group for a long time and has also successfully completed the program. In AA (and groups tackling substance use) the goal is abstinence, although this can be a barrier for those who would like to be able to control their drinking. However, AA argues that this is an impossible goal, since alcoholics suffer from a disease that dictates that they can never control their drinking, a position not shared by all commentators on alcoholism. For some other addiction problems, regarding this predisposing condition as a disease is more theoretically problematic and is often glossed over, if not ignored. Much of the program, especially the early steps, consists of talking and attitude change. However, later steps entail actual behaviors, for example, making direct amends and carrying the message to others. Some AA members argue that one never completes the program and that it is an

Step programs rely on an experienced sponsor to help the recovering addict through difficult times.

ongoing process. Others argue that although one never finishes the program, steps 10 to 12 are used as a maintenance program.

Advantages and disadvantages

There are many advantages to twelve-step groups. First, they are free. A collection is taken, but this is a voluntary contribution, and there are no fees for membership or attendance. Meetings are plentiful; AA can be found in most towns and cities in the United States and in almost every country in the world. The same principles, if not practices, apply in all meetings; visitors are generally reassured by the familiar format. There is an emphasis on helping others to help oneself, so there tends to be a great deal of help available to newcomers and returning members.

There are two major disadvantages for some people with twelve-step groups—their religious nature and the creation of what can become a substitute addiction. As discussed above, twelve-step programs can trace their origin to the Oxford Group. It was from there that the concepts of confession (being truthful with self and others), surrender (to a higher power), penance (making amends), and prayer and meditation were derived. For AA detractors, and there are many, the historical and contemporary religious overtones are too strong for them to accept AA as a treatment program for themselves or others.

THE TWELVE STEPS OF ALCOHOLICS ANONYMOUS	
Step 1	We admitted we were powerless over alcohol—that our lives had become unmanageable.
Step 2	Came to believe that a Power greater than ourselves could restore us to sanity.
Step 3	Made a decision to turn our will and our lives over to the care of God as we understood Him.
Step 4	Made a searching and fearless moral inventory of ourselves.
Step 5	Admitted to God, to ourselves, and to another human being the exact nature of our wrongs.
Step 6	Were entirely ready to have God remove all these defects of character.
Step 7	Humbly asked Him to remove our shortcomings.
Step 8	Made a list of all persons we had harmed, and became willing to make amends to them all.
Step 9	Made direct amends to such people when possible, except wherever to do so would injure them or others.
Step 10	Continued to take personal inventory and when we were wrong promptly admitted it.
Step 11	Sought through prayer and meditation to improve our conscious contact with God as we understood Him, praying only for knowledge of His will for us and the power to carry that out.
Step 12	Having had a spiritual awakening as the result of these steps, we tried to carry this message to alcoholics and to practice these principles in all our affairs.

Source: Alcoholics Anonymous (1976).

AA and other twelve-step programs have long argued that they are not religious, that instead the program is a spiritual one. They further argue that all references to God are nondenominational; however, the vast majority of members are Christian. There is no doubt in this more secular age that the apparent religious nature of AA and the twelve-step program is viewed by many as a barrier.

The second disadvantage is that many who join step groups can substitute attendance at these groups for their obsessions for substances or other behaviors. The aim of joining such groups is to change one's behavior, and these groups state that behavior change must come from a change from within. However, these changes are not always palatable to the family. For example, the recovering alcoholic may spend almost all of his or her time at meetings or helping newcomers. Or the individual may demand that, now that he or she has changed, the family must change as well. This type of new behavior can lead to relationship difficulties at a time when the family had thought that its problems were about to diminish.

Outcomes

It is difficult to state how successful AA or twelve-step programs are compared with other treatment regimes. It is true that there are millions of people around the world who would attest that they would not be sober today if AA did not exist. However, in terms of proof, this kind of evidence counts for very little. It has been difficult to conduct scientific research into AA because the anonymous nature of its organization means that there are no records of its members. Therefore it is difficult to know how many people attend AA meetings and never become sober or fail to complete the course. A 1996 study into recovering alcoholics, Project MATCH, tested three different types of treatment: cognitive behaviour therapy (CBT), motivational enhancement therapy (MET), and twelve-step facilitation (TSF). This study found that there was no difference in outcome between any of the treatments. However, it further found that attending AA following treatment, regardless of what treatment had been given, was associated with remaining abstinent. Although it should be stressed that TSF was not actually a twelve-step group but consisted of encouragement to join and a guided tour of the first five steps, nevertheless the study is hailed as the first evidence for the efficacy of AA.

J. McMAHON

SEE ALSO:
Alcoholics Anonymous • Gamblers Anonymous • Narcotics Anonymous • Recovery • Support Groups

Stress

Stress is a common occurrence in life. Sometimes it can be a positive influence, but it can have negative consequences if people begin to use addictive substances as a means of coping with stressful demands.

Stress is most concisely defined as the response to physical or psychological demands upon the body. More specifically, a state of stress involves various external and internal challenges to the body and brain, usually termed stressors. Stressors come in various forms. For example, a form of physical stress may be working a 12-hour shift or not getting enough sleep for an extended period of time. Psychological stress may be represented by academic deadlines, time commitments, or conflicts with family or friends. Not all forms of stress are negative. Positive events that are also stressful include graduating from school, starting a new career, and getting married.

Stressors cause many physiological changes in bodily function. Stress can activate the sympathetic nervous system, which is part of the body's "fight or flight" system. Activation of the sympathetic nervous system results in an increased heart rate, constriction of blood vessels, tense muscles, and dry mouth. Therefore, a body that is under chronic stress may be more prone to cardiovascular problems, ulcers, and suppression of the immune system. Emotional centers in the brain can also become active during stress, making concentration difficult. Another primary effect of stress on the body is the activation of the hypothalamic-pituitary-adrenal axis, otherwise known as the HPA or "stress axis" (*see* diagram).

Activation of the HPA axis begins with release of corticotropin-releasing hormone (CRH) from the hypothalamus into the portal system of the pituitary gland. CRH induces the release of adrenocorticotropic hormone (ACTH) from the anterior pituitary into the blood circulating throughout the body. Finally, ACTH enhances the release of cortisol into the blood from the adrenal glands, located just above the kidneys. Cortisol is often referred to as a stress hormone. The daily production of cortisol can rise markedly during severe stress to regulate the physiological effects of stressors. Chronic activation of the HPA axis and elevated levels of cortisol can be dangerous to human health. For instance, students are more likely to get sick during or after final exam periods, since they endure a prolonged period of stress. Sustained stress and subsequent overactivation of the HPA axis can lead to critical long-term health complications, such as a weakened immune system, psychological disorders, and cancer.

Some people are more vulnerable to the biological and psychological effects of stress as a result of an inherited overactive neurobiological system. The combination of genetics and environment plays a pivotal role in the coping mechanisms and behavioral responses to stressors. A common model used to explain the relationship between genes and environment is the diathesis stress model. In this model, individuals inherit tendencies to express certain traits or behaviors that may be activated under conditions of stress. In this definition, the diathesis is genetic vulnerability and the stress is environmental exposure to general life events. For

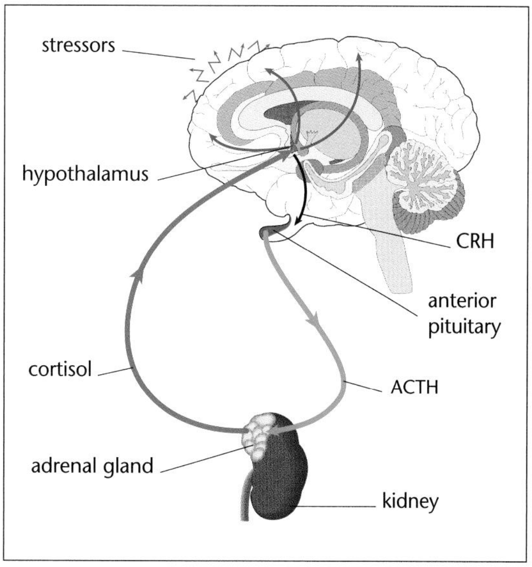

Once activated by external or internal stressors, the hypothalamus in the brain directs the pituitary gland to release the hormone ACTH into the bloodstream. ACTH induces the adrenal gland to release cortisol, a so-called stress hormone.

example, if two men are fired from their job one man may immediately search the Internet for new job leads, while the other man may develop a deep depression. Genetic vulnerability does not mean that an individual will definitely develop a disorder associated with a stressful situation—he or she is merely more prone to the psychological and biological effects of stress.

The most common behavioral responses to stress are maladaptive. These responses to stressors are often unconscious reactions at the onset of stress. However, conscious efforts to alleviate stress in a constructive manner, such as exercise, can be advantageous to a person's health. Examples of maladaptive responses include preoccupation, edginess, tension, negative affect, sleep disturbances, eating disturbances, and withdrawal from social situations. Conscious decisions to deal with stressful events can also be maladaptive and potentially harmful to one's health. For instance, after a hard day at work some people may go out for a few alcoholic drinks, or smoke cigarettes. This may initially be a way to cope with stress, but because of the addictive and rewarding properties of drugs of abuse, this coping mechanism can develop into an addiction and substance dependence.

Stress and drug abuse

As suggested above, stressful life events are a primary factor leading to drug abuse and dependence. Some scientists split the continuum of drug abuse into three stages: initial acquisition, maintenance, and relapse. Stress may contribute to all three of these levels.

Initially, drug abuse is often a coping mechanism for people during stressful situations. While alcohol and nicotine are the two legal drugs of abuse most often sought to cope with stress, illegal drugs such as marijuana, cocaine, and heroin are often used as a form of self-medication to alleviate stress. However, the acute effects of these drugs provide only minimal relief from stress. Therefore, individuals may continue abusing drugs in order to cope with or ignore their stress. However, drugs of abuse become physically addictive, and the individuals soon find themselves depending upon the drugs to ameliorate stressful events. This leads to the second phase in drug abuse: maintenance.

Maintenance refers to the stage in which a person continues abusing drugs after the initial acquisition period. At this point, various factors influence an individual's conscious or unconscious use of drugs. Stress may still be a contributing factor, but other determinants, such as physical addiction and dependence, have a greater influence over the continued abuse of drugs.

Once an individual becomes physically dependent upon drugs, abstaining from this behavior may prove to be very difficult, even after years of being drug free. The propensity for relapse is a very serious issue in the treatment of addiction. Stressful situations drastically increase the likelihood of drug-seeking behavior being resumed. For example, if a former alcoholic is faced with an acutely traumatic event, such as the death of a spouse, he or she may resort to dealing with this stress by having an alcoholic drink. This one seemingly insignificant exposure to alcohol may lead to a full relapse into drug abuse by triggering a state of craving. Likewise, a student who has recently recovered from cocaine addiction may want to return to college. Reexposure to academic stress, commitments, and the same social arenas significantly increases the probability of relapse.

Biologically, residual changes in the central nervous system following a period of drug addiction and subsequent abstinence may contribute to the vulnerability of relapse. Specifically, the HPA axis releases the stress hormone cortisol into the bloodstream during stressful situations. Increases in circulating cortisol are believed to contribute to the reinstatement of drug-seeking behaviors. Animal models of relapse have shown that exposure to stressful events, for example, an electric shock, increases the levels of corticosterone (cortisol in rodents). As a result, the animals begin to self-administer drugs. Blocking this increase by pharmacological manipulation reduces the likelihood of drug-seeking behavior and self-administration. Therefore, cortisol-blocking agents, such as CRH-antagonists, are being studied in human clinical trials as novel drugs to treat drug addiction and the propensity for relapse.

K. PHILPOT

SEE ALSO:
Causes of Addiction, Biological • Hormonal Effects • Relapse

Suicide

Drug and alcohol use are often implicated in attempts at suicide. This can either be a direct link, in which drugs are used to cause death, or indirect, when attempts to self-medicate other symptoms result in overdose.

Although the risk factors for suicide are widely accepted as extremely complex and often interlinked, it is a fact that in the United States alcohol and illicit drugs are involved in around 50 percent of suicide attempts. In 2000 suicide was the eleventh leading cause of death in the United States, accounting for 1.2 percent of all deaths, and the second leading cause of death among 15- to 24-year-olds. Some 25 percent of successful suicides are drug abusers or alcoholics, and substance abuse is seen as the main factor behind the increased risk of suicide among people under the age of 30. The suicide rate among alcoholics was found to be 18 times that of non-dependents in a key 1980s U.S. Epidemiological Catchment Area study.

The most vulnerable members of the population are the young and the elderly. Adolescents are particularly prone to depression and suicide, as the research suggests—28 percent of high school students were found to have experienced severe depression—but nonabusers were also found to have the lowest levels of depression and suicidal thoughts. The 2002 report of the National Household Survey on Drug Abuse, which periodically asks youths aged 12 to 17 if they have thought seriously about killing themselves, or have tried to kill themselves during the past year, found that almost three million young people were potential victims. Those using any illicit substance other than marijuana were nearly three times as likely to be at risk than abstainers.

Psychological factors either deriving from or predating alcohol and substance abuse also have to be taken into account, as do other factors such as age, sex, ethnicity, and social situation. For instance, alcoholics who commit suicide tend to be older, are more likely to be male, have a mood disorder, partner relationship difficulties, and other personal problems. In all cases, such risk factors may act cumulatively to significantly increase the chances of suicide.

An important study published in the American Journal of Psychiatry confirmed that family, childhood, personality, psychiatric, and physical risk factors contribute to suicidal behavior in cocaine-dependent patients. Polydrug abuse—the parallel use of other substances—was a very significant factor. Forty-nine of the 84 patients who had attempted suicide had a history of alcohol dependence (58.3 percent, compared with 34.6 percent among the group that had never attempted suicide), and 16 of the patients had a history of opiate dependence (19 percent, against 9.2 percent in the group that had not tried suicide). In all, 39 percent of the cocaine-dependent patients had made suicide attempts. The American Foundation for Suicide Prevention found that in one year 20 percent of victims under the age of 60 used cocaine just before committing suicide.

The fact that alcohol and drug-related behavior can lead to incarceration exacerbates the problem: a U.S. national study of jail suicides (1981) and a further update in 1986 showed that 30 percent of arrests for nonviolent crimes were alcohol- or drug-related. It also revealed that 50 percent of suicides died within 24 hours of incarceration, highlighting the possible role of withdrawal symptoms in suicide attempts, with isolation as an aggravating factor.

Co-occurring disorders

Mental health can be an important factor, and research from the United States has shown important links between bipolar disorder, substance abuse, and suicide. Studies have also made a strong, specific link between a particular type of bipolar disorder, substance abuse, and an increased risk of suicide. Psychological and social stressors were seen as extremely important additional risk factors. A study undertaken by the International Consortium for Research on Bipolar Disorders showed that substance abuse increased the risk of suicide by a factor of 2.2 among a group of severely ill people diagnosed with bipolar or nonbipolar major affective disorder. Studies have also shown that antisocial personality disorder and drug abuse, which often occur in genetically predisposed males who become alcoholics early in life, is also linked to suicide attempts.

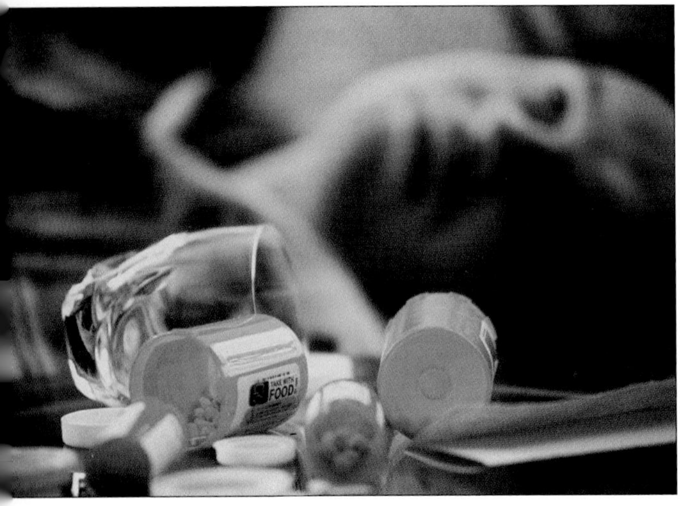

Prescription drugs are frequently used for intentional and accidental suicides, often combined with alcohol.

Alcohol and other substances

Most studies consistently support the view that substance abuse is strongly associated with a risk of suicide, particularly in young people. The substances most often implicated in suicide are alcohol, stimulants, and opiates. Recent studies disagree on whether there is a link, albeit weak, with extreme cannabis use. Use of cocaine, methamphetamine, and other stimulants is associated with high rates of completed suicide and suicide attempts. Opiates are also strongly linked with suicide—in an analysis of nine studies involving around 7,500 subjects, suicide among heroin addicts was found to be some 14 times more common than in nonusers. It is likely the statistics are clouded by other factors: drug abusers, particularly heroin addicts, often adopt high-risk behaviors that are likely to lead to death. Such fatalities may not be listed as suicides.

Alcohol may also play a part in suicides among nonalcoholics: heavy drinking during young adulthood was linked in a Swedish study of military conscripts to suicide in middle adulthood. Alcoholism increases the risk of death from many other sources, such as liver disease, accidents, and pancreatitis, but suicide remains the main cause of death. The 1980s San Diego Suicide Study, for instance, found that over 50 percent of 274 consecutive suicides had links to either alcoholism or substance abuse, although other contemporary studies into drug abuse–linked suicides showed that 5 percent were substance abusers, compared with up to 35 percent who were alcoholics.

This high level of coincidence is probably due to the strong link between alcoholism and major depression, which is 50 percent more common in alcoholics than nonalcoholics. Evidence from treatment programs suggests that alcoholics and drug abusers may drink to reduce feelings of depression, but that the initial state of well-being is replaced within hours by anxiety, depression, and increased suicidal thoughts. No cause-and-effect relationship between alcoholism or drug abuse and suicide has been established, but it may be that such substances reduce inhibitions and affect judgment to the extent that any suicidal thoughts are more likely to be acted on. Certainly, a report to Congress in the 1990s suggested that alcohol is linked to impulsive rather than preplanned suicide.

It is not only illicit drugs that have been linked with suicide: the antidepressant Paxil, known in Europe as Seroxat, was withdrawn as a prescription drug for young adults in European Union member countries after surveys linked its use among this particular group with a possible increased risk of suicide. The European regulatory agency covering such drugs, the European Agency for the Evaluation of Medicinal Products (EMEA), issued an advisory to member states suggesting that it be prescribed "with caution" to anyone under 30. The drug is a member of a group of drugs known as SSRIs, or selective serotonin reuptake inhibitors. The U.S. Food and Drug Administration has also warned that for this age-group, taking the drug could increase suicidal impulses.

Withdrawal from the use of steroids—taken by athletes and bodybuilders to enhance performance—has also been linked to an increased risk of suicide. Depression is known to be one of the major risks when ending use of these drugs. Researchers note feelings among former users of "paranoid jealousy, extreme irritability, delusions, and impaired judgment stemming from feelings of invincibility." Left untreated, depressive symptoms can last up to a year.

L. STEDMAN

SEE ALSO:
Depression • Mental Disorders • Overdose

Support Groups

After detoxification or treatment, many addicts face the difficult problem of maintaining abstinence from substance use. Support groups often provide a way for former addicts to help themselves stay away from drugs and alcohol.

Support groups for substance abuse have a long history. The first, Alcoholics Anonymous (AA), began in 1935 in Vermont as a self-help movement for alcoholics. In 1939 the basic text used today (entitled *Alcoholics Anonymous*) was published. This text contained the twelve steps to recovery and case histories easily recognized in today's AA support groups. Groups such as AA have helped millions of individuals attain and maintain their sobriety.

Many groups have modeled themselves after AA, including Narcotics Anonymous (NA), founded in 1947, and Gambler's Anonymous (GA), founded in 1957. There are also support groups for family members of someone who is chemically dependent (for example, Al-Anon, Alateen). These groups are found in most small and medium-sized towns, and there are often multiple groups in major cities. The Internet also houses these groups in the form of online chat rooms and twelve-step programs modeled after AA, and there exist multiple Web sites for group resources. The goal of all of these groups is for group members to help and support each other to achieve and maintain sobriety through abstinence.

Aims of support groups

Physicians, clinical psychologists, social workers, and counselors tend to agree that involvement in a support group is critical to successful recovery and maintenance of sobriety. Thus, support groups are typically recommended as aftercare and follow-up to detoxification or inpatient hospitalization and rehabilitation. Many individuals attend a substance abuse support group while they are in psychotherapy targeted at rehabilitation. Support group involvement thus serves as an important adjunct for more formal mental health treatment. Some individuals attend meetings every day or even twice a day, while others may opt for once a week or even once monthly.

Support groups are often anonymous, and members use only first names to protect their privacy. They are also open-ended, and group composition changes as members come and go. Typically, a support group will meet for 60 to 90 minutes, and the agenda for discussion is set by the group members. Attendance is often free of charge, especially for AA groups. Some recovering alcoholics and addicts attend support groups for years after detoxification in order to maintain their sobriety.

In general, support groups are different from groups emphasizing counseling or psychotherapy. They aim to support sustained changes over time rather than initiating personality changes, symptom reduction, or interpersonal change. For example, a substance abuser who is in a support group may seek the social support and experience with others to maintain sobriety. A therapy group often has the quite different goal of personality change or amelioration of symptoms such as depression, anxiety, bereavement issues, marital distress, or chronic illnesses. Further, many support groups are associated with self-help movements and are not led by licensed mental health professionals. The principle here is that the recovering person is the most suitable person to assist others in recovery, and that trained mental health professionals are less able to understand and cope with addictions if they have not been through the experience themselves.

Filling the gap

One major feature of a support group is that it is designed to help the person with the lifelong process of drug or alcohol rehabilitation. Thus, each support group may have a variety of goals that affect nearly every aspect of life. Goals may include, but are not limited to, education about chemical dependency and alternatives to using, recovery and relapse prevention, and school- or work-related issues.

Group members may discuss alternatives to using a substance, such as identification of other pleasurable activities that can be substituted for drug taking. This issue is important, since many addicts experience a sense of loss and a void when they stop using the substance. Substance abuse is time consuming, and when ceased, there is a need for replacement activities. For example, an alcoholic who spent three or four hours nightly in a bar will need to develop other activities to occupy those hours. Otherwise, the alcoholic may go to the bar out of habit or lack of other things to do, which increases the probability of relapse. This can be a difficult task, especially if such individuals have been abusing substances for a prolonged period of time. Group members can provide their personal insights about how to develop alternative activities while simultaneously acknowledging the difficulties in doing so.

Other goals for a substance abuse support group may include discussions about successes and difficulties associated with recovery, communication with other individuals experiencing similar problems, and decreasing feelings of isolation. It is believed that support group involvement helps the individual better understand his or her own addiction through listening to and empathizing with similar individuals. Further, feelings of shame and guilt associated with the substance abuse can be discussed with others who understand and can provide words of encouragement. Some discussions may be more confrontational than others, particularly when a group member seeks excuses for relapse or behaves in self-defeating ways. It is important for support group members to trust each other, despite varying opinions and confrontation, inasmuch as the overall goal remains that of helping each other stay sober.

Maintaining abstinence

As the group members form a bond with each other, an important function of a support group is to establish new relationships and have peer pressure to maintain sobriety. Many times the addiction results in estrangement from family and friends as the abuser comes to value the substance use over relationships, often damaging them irretrievably in the process. Further, it is common to avoid individuals formerly associated with the substance abuse, leaving a void in the person's circle of friends and acquaintances. Because of the estrangement and the need to avoid active users, there is a need to reconnect with nonusing individuals and form positive bonds. Group members can be honest with each other regarding their cravings for the substance and temptations to start using again, and this honesty is typically experienced as emotionally positive. They can also reinforce each other's attempts to avoid the substance and help focus on positive aspects of sobriety. Providing help to another group member is gratifying and results in positive affect. Typically, the better a person begins to feel about himself or herself and others, the less the risk for relapse.

In terms of peer pressure to maintain sobriety, knowledge that other group members care about the individual's sobriety and would be disappointed if he or she used again can serve as an important deterrent to relapse. This knowledge can help the person avoid triggers or tempting situations. In fact, if the sobriety is recently gained, support group members may form a "buddy system" in which a member has a sponsor who can be telephoned when the individual is feeling tempted to use a substance. The sponsor may dissuade the member over the phone or meet in person to help him or her avoid obtaining the substance.

In terms of recovery and relapse, support group members may discuss issues and hazards associated with holidays or other triggers. They may discuss the need to avoid acquaintances and environments associated with the substance use or certain emotional states (such as sadness) that may increase their risk for relapse. However, a support group does not typically address the reduction of the sadness, but rather focuses on the link between this emotion, the risk of relapse, and how to avoid it. Along similar lines, the group may discuss how job stress contributes to relapse risk, as opposed to trying to ameliorate the source of the job stress.

Substance abuse support groups are likely to remain an important aspect of the recovery process in the future. Most professionals agree that they are effective in treatment and relapse prevention. Further, they have many positive advantages in addition to the major goal of abstinence. Support groups are readily available in almost any location and they welcome new members, making them generally a positive experience and a critical resource for recovering substance abusers.

J. L. JOHNSON

SEE ALSO:
Alcoholics Anonymous • Gamblers Anonymous • Narcotics Anonymous • Step Programs • Treatment

Temperance Movements

History has had a changing view of the benefits and demerits of alcohol. Initial campaigns against the evils of distilled spirits led to movements that advocated a total ban on all forms of alcohol and eventually resulted in Prohibition.

Temperance means moderation or restraint. Temperance in relation to alcohol, then, means moderation or restraint in the consumption of alcohol. Temperance movements are social movements that attempt to convince others, either through morality or law, to restrain from or at least moderate their alcohol consumption. These movements have a long history and are in some ways still alive today.

Although the first movement would not arrive for two centuries, the idea of moderation in alcohol consumption was evident in the earliest American colonies. In 1619 the colony of Virginia enacted a law against drunkenness that also required drunkards to be "reproved by ministers." Political temperance movements, however, began in Ireland and England in the 1700s as campaigns against distilled spirits such as whiskey and rum. These movements and others in northern Europe in the early 1800s only focused on distilled drinks and never progressed to the prohibition of all alcoholic beverages. That path was followed only in the United States.

Morality and alcohol

Historians generally divide the U.S. temperance movement into three phases: from the turn of the nineteenth century to the Civil War; post–Civil War until Prohibition; and from the early 1980s through the present. While this division is overly simplistic, the breakdown does allow for ease of conceptual presentation.

The first phase traces its origin to Benjamin Rush, one of the signatories of the Declaration of Independence. In 1785 Rush published a paper titled *Inquiry into the Effects of Ardent Spirits upon the Human Body and Mind.* In it he argued that ardent or distilled spirits corrupted individuals and caused many social ills. He devised a scale, which he called his Moral and Physical Thermometer, which was a classic example of the temperance movements' view of spirits. It also showed that Rush believed that alcohol itself was not evil. The thermometer began with water and milk, which he associated with health, serenity, happiness, and temperance. Moving down the thermometer, one crossed the line into intemperance, which is associated with vice, disease, and punishment, ending eventually in suicide, death by disease, or from the gallows. Beer and wine were above the intemperance line, and only spirits were below, a distinction still in use.

Rush's paper had little effect at first. In fact, alcohol consumption continued to climb in the United States, peaking in the 1830s at about three times the modern day intake rate. Indeed, in the early 1800s, most Americans believed that distilled alcohol was good for you, that it warded off disease and gave strength. Rush and others like him continued their campaigns however, and the first temperance organization was formed in Saratoga, New York, in 1808, followed by many others. The first statewide organization, the Massachusetts Society for the Suppression of Intemperance, was formed in 1812. The formation of the American Society for the Promotion of Temperance, better known as the American Temperance Society, in Boston on February 13, 1826, gave the movement its first national organization. By the 1830s there were more than 8,000 local temperance societies in the United States. These early movements continued to grow in popularity through organized church efforts, pamphleteering, and lectures, attracting a wide range of supporters, from employers and church leaders to women who feared the effects of spirits on their husbands.

Taking the pledge

The shift from spirits only to all forms of alcohol being viewed as dangerous can be traced to the Connecticut minister Lyman Beecher, who published a small book in 1826 titled *Six Sermons on the Nature, Occasions, Signs, Evils and Remedy of Intemperance.* Beecher argued eloquently about how alcohol affected the country on many levels: individual health, social status, labor, self-interest, husbands, wives, children, and indeed the entire nation. His main shift from earlier advocates such as

Carrie Nation was one of the most ardent temperance campaigners of her day. She joined the movement after her first husband died from alcoholism. When her words failed to convince saloon owners of the perils of alcohol, she took to smashing their premises with a hatchet. She was arrested more than 30 times and imprisoned on a number of occasions.

Rush was his pronounced insistence that all alcohol was bad. If alcohol was a poison, he argued, one could not realistically prescribe restraint or moderation, because less poison was still poison and would eventually lead to ruin. Advances in printing technology as well as the already organized temperance organizations around the country ensured that Beecher's book would be read by hundreds of thousands of people. Eventually his message would prevail, and the American Temperance Society would in 1836 change its definition of temperance from moderation to complete abstinence from all alcoholic beverages.

As the movement grew, it became popular to "take the pledge," that is, to pledge not to drink any alcohol, anywhere, under any circumstances. Father Theobald Mathew of Ireland toured the United States from 1849 to 1851, administering the pledge of total abstinence to some 600,000 persons in 25 states. Local temperance societies and church groups received pledges from thousands of others during the same era. The movement reached its peak in the 1850s, when first Maine and then nine other states—all in the Northeast and Midwest—passed laws against the sale of alcohol. Some of these laws were vetoed by governors; others, such those of Delaware, were declared unconstitutional by the courts. It can only be speculated whether this cresting wave of temperance would have progressed to national prohibition, because the first phase of the temperance movement ended when the Civil War began. We do know, however, that alcohol consumption in 1855 had fallen by about two-thirds since its peak in the 1830s.

Women join the battle

Temperance sentiments continued through the Civil War, but the war made the continuation of organized movement difficult. Once the war and its immediate aftermath subsided, however, advocates began to organize with new vigor. Reformers in the North felt that the antislavery movement had achieved its goal: the end of slavery. They now set their sights on a host of social ills, including intemperance. The base of the movement shifted to Ohio, and the leaders became women. In numerous states, women's groups began visiting local saloons and holding "pray-ins," in which they would pray for and beseech the saloon owners to stop serving their husbands alcohol. In Ohio, women began suing saloon owners under the state's Adair law, which allowed wives of alcoholics to sue saloon owners for damages resulting from their husbands' alcoholism. On December 24, 1873, a group of about 70 women led by Eliza "Mother" Thompson began praying and singing in front of drugstores and taverns in Hillsboro, Ohio. Unlike their predecessors, however, these women kept their protest going, day after day, through June of the following year. News of what became known as the Woman's Crusade spread, and soon other groups were practicing the same tactics. At a convention in Cleveland in December 1874, several groups merged to form the Woman's Christian Temperance Union (WCTU).

The WCTU focused primarily on alcohol but also began to champion a host of causes, from suffrage to Native American rights. As the movement gained national attention, the Prohibition Party was formed in 1880. Beginning in 1880, a second wave of state-level prohibition laws passed. Only six states outlawed alcohol altogether at this point, but numerous others began allowing "local option," in which a town or county could outlaw alcohol if it so chose. Bowing to pressure from temperance activists, South Carolina sought to dispense distilled liquor through state-owned dispensaries. While corruption quickly killed the South Carolina model, states such as Pennsylvania still practice this "state store" method of selling distilled liquor.

Progress was being made in the late 1800s, but divisions in the movement began over whether temperance organizations should focus exclusively on alcohol, or whether they should become agents for broader social change. This split brought about the end of the Prohibition Party, as leaders shifted their attention toward the most common alcohol outlet, the saloon. The result was the Anti-Saloon League (ASL), which formed in Washington, D.C. in 1895. The ASL's initial focus was on spreading the local option to ban saloons and the sale of liquor, but as it grew in popularity, the movement—as the earlier temperance movement had done—advocated an outright nationwide ban on alcohol. Uninterrupted by war, this movement eventually succeeded in a ban on the sale of alcohol in 1919, with ratification of the Eighteenth Amendment to the U.S. Constitution. The law took effect in 1920, reflecting the long-standing bans in most states, but was repealed in 1933. Prohibition may be considered the result of both these early movements. Generations of families had taken the "pledge" as a result of the first movement. The second movement started in the 1870s, so by the time Prohibition took effect 50 years later, much of the current generation had been thoroughly exposed to the temperance message.

Temperance today

The modern temperance movement began in the late 1970s. When the voting age was lowered from 21 to 18 in 1971, many states began to lower the drinking age as well. People who fight and die in war and vote, it was argued, ought to be allowed to drink a beer. The modern movement is not focused on banning alcohol or saloons, but on restraining drunk drivers. As driving fatalities related to alcohol began to rise in the 1970s, people became angered that those responsible were rarely and lightly punished. In 1978 a movement began in the eastern United States called RID (Remove Intoxicated Drivers). In 1979 Mothers Against Drunk Drivers (MADD) was formed, followed two years later by Students Against Driving Drunk (SADD).

These organizations have had a great impact on drinking and driving laws in the United States, increasing penalties and lowering the amount of alcohol required to be considered drunk. They also lobbied the government to raise the drinking age, and beginning in the mid-1980s, the federal government began withholding highway maintenance dollars from states who did not raise their drinking age to 21. The move was successful, and all states currently require people to be 21 years old to purchase or consume alcohol. While MADD and RID focused exclusively on legal issues, SADD is more focused on providing options for students to avoid drunk driving. They advocate a contract between parents and students in which transportation is provided for a student who has been drinking, and an agreed-upon cooling off period is required before parents question or punish the student.

Temperance is thus a reoccurring theme throughout U.S. history, predating the country and continuing to the present. While it has only fully succeeded once, during Prohibition, temperance movements have had an undeniable impact on the American use of alcohol.

D. J. O'CONNELL

SEE ALSO:
Alcoholism • Legal Controls • Mothers Against Drunk Driving (MADD) • National Institute on Alcohol Abuse and Alcoholism (NIAAA) • Prohibition of Alcohol

Terrorism

Much has been made of a link between drugs and terrorism. While there is evidence that some terrorists are funded by drug trafficking, eliminating one problem will not necessarily eliminate the other.

The phenomenon of terrorism is not new. The first recorded act of terrorism took place between 66 and 73 CE in Palestine, when a small religious sect called the Sicarii targeted Jews who were prepared to negotiate with the Romans. In the nineteenth century anarchists used terror tactics in an attempt to overthrow the Russian czars. In more modern times, terrorism is an immensely complex issue involving many different groups across the world.

In general, terrorists are groups of people who have become disillusioned with peaceful means to achieve political aims. They attempt to attract attention to their cause by creating a climate of fear through random acts of violence such as suicide bombings, kidnapping, assassinations, and more recently the use of chemical or biological weapons. However, the term *terrorist* is very subjective; to their respective followers or opponents they may be regarded as freedom fighters, patriots, rebels, resistance fighters, or guerrillas.

Terrorism now has an international face. Groups no longer operate in isolation as they trade technology and intelligence with each other. Terrorists from one group might also be involved in the training of others; for example, members of the Irish Republican Army were captured with Colombian rebels in the jungle.

With the end of the cold war and the fall of communism in the West, an important source of funding for terrorism dried up. Drug trafficking provided a lucrative cash alternative—not only for those groups previously receiving communist funding, but also for those groups located in and around the main trafficking routes. This ushered in so-called narcoterrorism, in which criminal gangs with no political agenda forged alliances with terrorist and guerrilla groups to maintain supply routes through rebel areas and to gain protection against government forces. A prime example is the association between the cocaine cartels in Colombia and various left-wing rebels in South America. Other groups with links to the drug trade include the Kurdistan Workers Party (PKK) of Turkey and paramilitary groups in Northern Ireland. Ironically, some of this narcoterrorism has been supported directly or indirectly by the West when the fighting has been directed against communism. For example, the U.S.–trained Afghan mujahideen fighters who fought the Russians in the late 1970s paid the West for arms with money earned from the opium trade.

Funding of terrorism

The links between drugs and violence are long established. The word *hashish* has its origins in a murderous eleventh-century Persian sect called the Hashshashins that used the drug; the word *assassin* also derives from this group. Similarly, the link between drugs and terrorism is not new—many of the organized crime groups that launder money from drugs also launder money from illegal arms sales, often to insurgent or anarchist groups in countries where conflict prevails. Some terrorist groups may also be involved in all aspects of the drug trade, from cultivation and processing to trafficking and distribution on the streets.

Even where the drug trade is legal, profits can be significant. It is thought that part of Osama bin Laden's war chest for terrorism was originally funded by his family's involvement in the cultivation of khat, a plant found in East Africa and in the Middle East, whose leaves are chewed for their stimulant effect. There have been allegations that al-Qaeda received drug money from the Taliban in Afghanistan, but money for this terrorist network appears to come mainly from private donations and possibly from governments sympathetic to its cause.

Wars on two fronts

Since the events of September 11, 2001, the "war on terrorism" and the "war on drugs" have become increasingly intertwined, which has had repercussions for the drive to stamp out the drug trade. Regarding Colombia, the United States has changed its attitude toward a number of drug-linked guerrilla

Eradication of drug crops often requires military intervention in areas where rebel forces act as protectors of farmers and drug cartel operations.

groups, designating them as terrorists. As a result, funding has been switched from operations against drug trafficking to counter-terrorism measures. Even if these terrorist groups were eliminated, it would not stop the Colombian drug trade—the cartels would simply find another way to protect their product. In addition, extraditing guerilla leaders to the United States on drug trafficking charges threatens to damage the fragile politics of Colombia and thus jeopardizes a solution to the drug problem.

The attempts to destroy al-Qaeda's terrorist stronghold in Afghanistan have also had a negative effect on the supply of opium and heroin to the West. Prior to September 11, the Taliban acceded to international pressure to reduce the country's considerable opium crop. Following the 1999 record crop of 4,600 tons (4,140 tonnes), the Taliban reduced production in 2001 to 185 tons (165 tonnes), most of which came from areas controlled by the rival Northern Alliance forces. Nevertheless, elimination of the opium fields was used as a supporting argument by the international coalition that invaded Afghanistan to root out the Taliban and al-Qaeda. That this aim backfired spectacularly on the coalition was evidenced by the resumption after the war of poppy growing at even greater levels, culminating in a record area under cultivation in 2004. Opium is now the biggest contributor to Afghanistan's shattered economy, which could destabilize attempts to establish political order and has led the United Nations to express fears that the country could become a "narco-state." Efforts have been stepped up to implement a strict counter-narcotics policy that will combine eradication with compensation and alternative development strategies. A secure system for prosecution of drug smugglers will also be instigated to prevent the organization of cartels.

Critics of the George W. Bush administration's policy on terrorism argue that, despite the seeming link between the two, the war on terrorism and the war on drugs are incompatible and that fighting terrorism will require an escalation in the war against drugs. This has already led to conflicts within the administration over resources. After September 11, many agents working in the Drug Enforcement Administration and the U.S. Coast Guard were diverted to antiterrorism duties. This led to complaints by the DEA chief, Asa Hutchinson, that concentrating on terrorism was enabling South American dealers to exploit less monitored routes into the United States via the Caribbean. While increased border security measures to prevent further terrorist attacks initially led to an increase in drug seizures, there is little evidence to suggest that the market has been significantly disrupted in the longer term.

Some commentators have warned that the war on terror has lessons to learn from the war on drugs. Opponents of the war on drugs point to the fact that despite spending by the United States of some $40 billion annually, prohibition of drugs has not succeeded in reducing demand or the effects of addiction. The arrest and death of the Colombian drug baron Pablo Escobar led to an escalation in violence but no interruption of the drug supply. Focusing attention on an individual or group of people also risks elevating the target to martyrdom or alienating a whole culture or social group, which may have greater repercussions than the original threat.

H. SHAPIRO

SEE ALSO:
Drug Trafficking • International Cooperation • International Drug Trade

Therapeutic Communities

Therapeutic communities are residential treatment programs that operate on a self-help basis. Peer influence, behavioral change, and acquisition of social skills are key components of this sometimes controversial method of treatment.

Therapeutic communities as drug treatment systems have long been a source of debate. Most often the term *therapeutic community*, or TC, has been associated with drug treatment programs that employ confrontation as a primary means of treatment. Another controversial aspect of TCs is their greater use of clients—referred to as community members—and recovering addicts as change agents, rather than professional personnel. Although the TC treatment process seems to lead to successful outcomes, the methodology is considered by many to be undefined. Despite the ongoing controversial issues and ambiguous features, TCs have been used as a credible means of substance abuse treatment since the mid-1960s, especially within criminal justice systems.

Therapeutic community defined

The first TC, Synanon, was founded in Santa Monica, California, in 1958 by Charles Dederich, a recovering alcoholic. As such, TCs continue to be fundamentally grounded in the Alcoholics Anonymous twelve-step, self-help philosophy. According to George DeLeon, director of the Center for Therapeutic Community Research, Synanon did not consider itself a treatment agency, but a "learning community." Correspondingly, present day TCs consider every experience or event within the TC environment as an opportunity to provide insight into the community member's attitude and behavior and as an opportunity for learning. In effect, the environment becomes the teacher, and the treatment setting or community a learning community.

Many researchers have sought to define what constitutes a TC. They generally agree that the basic model is an organized and structured community in which the staff and members interact to reinforce positive behaviors and social skills that will enable the recovering substance user to live a drug-free life when back in society. In particular, the community members' interactions within the specifically defined treatment system serve as the primary means of treatment. In this regard, TCs differ in their approach to treatment from traditional drug and alcohol treatment programs. While traditional programs use professional personnel as teachers or catalysts for facilitating insight and change in the client, the TC uses the community and the treatment personnel—who often include recovering substance users—collectively as change agents. The community and the all-encompassing experiences within the TC environment become the teacher. Although TCs use professional personnel as well, all staff members are regarded as sources for help within the therapeutic environment.

Use of a therapeutic community

Most individuals admitted to TCs have extensive histories of substance abuse. A 2002 research report by the National Institute on Drug Abuse (NIDA) notes that these individuals frequently have other severe problems, including multiple drug addictions, involvement with the criminal justice system, lack of positive support, mental health problems, antisocial disorders, and so on. In brief, these individuals' overall social and personal responsibilities have been hindered by their substance abuse. For them, recovery involves rehabilitation or relearning appropriate social skills. Some TC participants or community members may have never acquired an appropriate level of social functioning. Their participation in a TC may be their first experience with living in a disciplined or organized environment of any kind. For these individuals, the recovery process entails habilitation or learning acceptable social skills for the very first time.

One NIDA research study conducted between 1991 and 1993 showed that of the 2,315 admissions to residential TC programs, 80 percent met the diagnostic criteria outlined in the American Psychiatric Association's *Diagnostic and Statistical Manual of Mental Disorders* for cocaine dependence, while 45 percent met the diagnostic criteria for alcohol dependence. The NIDA study also reported that two-thirds of the admissions had involvement with the criminal justice system and that approximately one-third had been referred from the criminal justice system for treatment. Other statistics from this report indicate that one-third were women, approximately one-half were African American, and 60 percent had prior substance abuse treatment.

Therapeutic communities are used in numerous settings and for a diverse range of treatment populations. Overall, the TC approach can be modified to correspond with the targeted treatment population, for example, dual diagnosed populations, women, women and their children, juveniles, and men. TCs are also used in a host of settings, including detention centers, jails, prisons, and halfway houses. TCs can be structured as long term, usually consisting of a 12- to 24-month residential stay, and short-term or modified programs, usually consisting of a 3- to 6-month residential stay that may or may not include a continuum of care arrangement.

Life in a therapeutic community instills discipline and social skills, such as doing chores and attending group therapy sessions, as part of a structured day.

Key concepts

The primary concepts concerning TCs are based on self-help, reciprocal and mutual help, peer influence, community as method, and shared responsibility with respect to maintaining a therapeutic environment. Researchers and practitioners insist that the TC environment be conducive for change and, as such, must be physically and psychologically safe for its participants.

Prison-based TCs in particular need to remain isolated from the general population to accomplish this task. Positive social principles, such as honesty, industriousness, and a genuine commitment to the welfare of others, are strongly promoted and encouraged. Additional essential principles concerning the development and maintenance of a therapeutic environment require the use of appropriate confrontation techniques, behavioral limits, role modeling, learning through crisis, consistency, internalization of healthy values, open communication, social learning through social interaction, and consistent graduated sanctions, to name a few. The key concepts, although somewhat varied among substance abuse researchers and clinical practitioners, remain firm in that the treatment structure must function as a peer-driven system and that the community itself serve as teacher and primary change agent.

Programmatic functions

It is a well-established fact that there are a number of programs that promote themselves as TCs and yet fail to employ the most basic TC components and programmatic elements. In an attempt to be identified as a TC, many programs have adopted the descriptions "third generation" and "modified" TCs. All too often, the deficient outcomes and internal problems related to these treatment structures are passed on as another TC failure. Worse yet, the indiscriminate implementation of such structures contributes to the existing misunderstandings regarding TCs.

The programmatic components used within TC structures (*see* box p. 826) are systematically designed to bring about positive changes for treatment participants. Therefore, it is essential that management and clinical personnel understand the mechanisms associated with each component and their contribution to the environment and to individual community members as well. A lack of understanding of the basic theory of each activity promotes misuse of therapeutic concepts, perpetuates haphazard strategies, and often fails to provide an opportunity for individual growth. Knowledge

ELEMENTS OF A TC

In an attempt to clarify the components of a therapeutic community (TC), NIDA has adopted George DeLeon's "basic TC model," which identifies 14 components usually found in a typical TC. The following components are adaptable to various treatment settings:

- community separateness
- community environment
- community activities
- staff roles and functions
- peers as role models
- structured days
- work as therapy and education
- phase format
- TC concepts
- peer encounter groups
- awareness training
- emotional growth training
- planned duration of treatment
- continuity of care.

of TC structure, culture, philosophy, essential components, and associated mechanisms is therefore important for staff members.

Advantages and disadvantages

One of the advantages of criminal justice–managed TCs is the ability to support coerced treatment. Numerous studies have suggested that coerced clients do as well as voluntary clients. Steve Martin and James Inciardi of the University of Delaware Center for Drug and Alcohol Studies (CDAS) report that the one consistent finding among substance abuse researchers is that the longer a client stays in treatment, the better the outcome in terms of reductions in drug use and criminality.

Another advantage of operating TCs within correctional facilities is that there is also a drop in incidents concerning violence, drug use, and overall rule violations. The 2002 Sentencing Trends and Correctional Treatment in Delaware annual report notes that the costs associated with operating TCs are offset by reductions in disciplinary actions, reductions in security and correctional counselor staffing, and lowered maintenance costs. The report states that there was an annual cost reduction of approximately $400,000.

The major disadvantage of TCs seems to be the lack of understanding regarding the methodology itself. While there is a general understanding as to the basic components and therapeutic elements, the process itself remains somewhat ambiguous. Developing a suitable framework for future TCs requires further study and a proper evaluation of existing TC theory and practice. Lack of expertise, inexperienced personnel, inability to select participants, lack of mental health professionals, staff burnout, and pressure to adhere to state licensure standards are other potential disadvantages to the efficient functioning of TCs.

Program outcomes

TCs have been evaluated from several different methods of research. Substance abuse research into drug abstinence is usually based on self-report or an examination of probation or parole records. However, the CDAS research projects use self-report and urine samples to determine project participants' abstinence. Ongoing studies show that the reductions in relapse and recidivism for TC graduates continue for a period of five years after release from prison.

A Delaware Department of Correction (DOC) comparison project shows that participants in the prison-based and halfway house continuum of care arrangement did better than the participants in the DOC-managed non-TC treatment program or the solely prison-based program regarding percent arrested for any felony within a 24-month period.

All in all, extensive research in North America, Norway, the United Kingdom, and a host of other countries strongly suggests that TC participants experience positive outcomes overall regarding drug and alcohol use, depression, employment retention, criminal behavior, rearrest, and recidivism.

R. A. BEARD

SEE ALSO:
Continuum of Care • Halfway Houses • Prison Drug Use and Treatment • Rehabilitation • Treatment

Tobacco

Tobacco, the main source of the addictive chemical nicotine, is a major crop in many parts of the world. It is estimated that one-sixth of the global population smokes tobacco, which is a significant factor in the health of millions of people.

For a drug whose use causes such a wide range of potentially fatal diseases, tobacco has an innocuous pedigree. The tobacco plant *Nicotiana tabacum* is a member of the Solanaceae family, the same group as the potato, tomato, chili pepper, and deadly nightshade, and is native to North and South America. European civilization first encountered the plant in November 1492, when the explorer Christopher Columbus was given dried tobacco leaves by Native Americans.

History

The tobacco plant has a long and complex history of use. Native Americans appear to have used the tobacco plant some 1,500 years ago, smoking it in pipes for medicinal and ceremonial purposes. The Mayans of South America wrapped the dried leaves in corn husks or palm leaves to form crude cigarettes, and the Aztecs are known to have both smoked tobacco and used it as snuff. Tobacco was also chewed, eaten, rubbed onto the body, and drunk as an infusion during this period.

However, details of the plant's history during this period are unclear. Some authors claim that tribes were smoking tobacco as long ago as 6000 BCE, and there have been various arguments about whether it was used purely for ceremonial purposes or on a casual basis, as well as which tribes did or did not smoke.

Tobacco's spread across the Atlantic began with Spanish sailors who became avid cigar smokers. The Portuguese were instrumental in spreading tobacco

When tobacco leaves have been harvested, they are hung onto racks for drying. The racks are then placed in barns away from sunlight, where they cure in the air or with the assistance of heat. Curing produces the familiar yellow and brown colors and brings out the aromas of the tobacco.

use to the rest of Europe, being the first to cultivate the plant outside the Americas. By 1558, snuff (dried and ground tobacco) was on sale in Lisbon's markets.

It was the French who gave the plant its botanical name, *Nicotiana,* after the French ambassador to Portugal, Jean Nicot de Villemain, sent specimens of the plant back to Paris in 1559. By 1620, snuff had become highly fashionable in the French court.

Tobacco traveled to Italy again through Portugal, after the Papal Nuncio at Lisbon sent specimens to Pope Pius IV. The plant then spread to the rest of Italy and into Germany, Hungary, and (aided considerably by the traveling soldiers of the Thirty Years' War, 1618–1648) into northern and central Europe.

Historians have concluded that tobacco probably came to England in 1565 directly from the New World. Records show that John Rolfe began cultivating tobacco commercially in Virginia as early as 1612, subsequently shipping it to England. The early English settlements were in Virginia, where the Native Americans smoked pipes. The English preference was for pipe smoking, whereas Portuguese-influenced tobacco users tended to take it as snuff. Walter Raleigh claimed to have been the first to have brought tobacco to England, along with its cousin, the potato. The English spread tobacco to Holland and those parts of Europe not reached by the Portuguese and Italians.

By the end of the sixteenth century, tobacco had reached Turkey, probably brought by the Portuguese. The Turks planted tobacco in Macedonia and spread its use east to Persia and central Asia. The well-traveled Portuguese were again instrumental in bringing tobacco to India, and it was in fact from India that the cigar was introduced to England.

The Portuguese also took tobacco to Japan, in the 1570s, from where it spread to Korea, where it is still the country's main agricultural export. China had various routes of entry: from Korea and from Portuguese Macao and Spanish settlements in the Philippines. Tobacco spread from India and China to the remainder of Eurasia. Western Africa was introduced to tobacco as early as 1607 by the Portuguese, with the Dutch taking the habit, and the plant's cultivation, to the south of the continent in 1652.

HOW CIGARETTES AND CIGARS ARE MADE

Manufacturing cigarettes is a fast and highly automated process. Cigarette-making machines produce between 8,000 and 12,000 cigarettes a minute. Spools of cigarette paper up to 6,000 yards long are rolled out and a mixture of shredded tobacco and processed tobacco pulp is released from a hopper onto the center of the unrolled paper. The wrapper is then closed over the tobacco, making one long cigarette known as a rod.

Machines slice the rod into shorter lengths, insert filters, and then cut the shorter lengths into single, filter-tipped cigarettes. Next, the cigarettes are sorted into groups according to the size of pack they are intended for, wrapped in foil to preserve their aroma, and placed into cartons.

A premium or super-premium cigar is handmade and is built up from three parts—filler, binder, and wrapper. The filler is the interior of the cigar. "Long filler" means the cigar's interior consists of full tobacco leaves, which require skillful rolling to ensure that the cigar burns evenly. "Short filler" consists of loose clippings of tobacco leaves left from long filler cigar production. The binder consists of several layers of leaves that the cigar maker will wrap around the filler, forming it into a cylindrical shape. The final component, the wrapper—a smooth, high-quality tobacco leaf—is then rolled around the outside of the binder.

Machine-made cigars use homogenized tobacco leaf (HTL) as a binder. This is made from tobacco stems and fiber, mixed with water and cellulose, forming a paste that is spread on a drying belt and emerges in rolls, similar to cigarette paper. The cigars are then made in a process very similar to that used for cigarettes. A few premium machine-made cigars use tobacco leaves rather than HTL as a binder.

Tobacco types and uses

There are a number of different types of tobaccos and methods of curing the plant; choices depend on its intended use. The three main types grown in the United States are Virginia, burley, and oriental tobaccos. Virginia tobacco is widely grown for its mild and sweet flavor and is most popular for pipe and flake tobacco mixtures. Burleys have little natural sugar and are dryer and more aromatic than Virginia tobaccos. They are usually air cured and burn more slowly at a cooler temperature. Oriental tobaccos come from Turkey and the Balkan regions. These tend to be dry and have a sour aroma and are popular in the cigarettes smoked in Arabic countries. Curing, by which moisture is removed from the leaves, is either a natural process, where leaves are left to hang in open barns or spread out in the sun, or is heat assisted. Of these, flue- or fire-cured tobaccos are used for snuff and chewing tobacco. Dark air-cured tobaccos are used for chewing tobacco, and flue-cured Virginia tobaccos are used for cigarette and smoking mixtures. Air-cured cigar tobaccos are used for cigar wrappers and fillers. Air-cured burley tobacco is used for cigarette, pipe, and chewing tobacco. Most oriental tobaccos are sun cured.

Manufactured cigarettes are the main form of tobacco used around the world. They are made from shredded tobacco leaves, processed with hundreds of different chemicals and encased in a paper cylinder. In 1939 Brown & Williamson introduced the tobacco industry's first cork-tipped filter cigarette. Filter-tipped cigarettes jumped from under 1 percent of the market in 1950 to 87 percent by 1975.

Lower tar and nicotine cigarettes were introduced from the mid-1970s to the early 1980s, with manufacturers producing a variety of "light" and "ultra-light" cigarettes. Smokeless tobacco contains nicotine, which is absorbed into the blood through the oral mucosa and the gastrointestinal tract and has been shown to have similar health effects to normal tobacco.

Reynolds Tobacco began producing two purportedly safer cigarettes, the Premier in 1988 and the Eclipse in 1996. Both of these produce smoke by heating rather than burning tobacco, thus reducing the effects of tar and nicotine. Flavorings, mainly menthol, are also added to cigarettes to increase their appeal.

Tobacco products exist in many other guises: the next most popular form after cigarettes, the cigar, comes in various shapes and sizes and consists of air-cured, fermented tobacco in a tobacco-leaf wrapper. Varieties include the cigarette-sized cigarillo, coronas, and cheroots. Pipe smoking involves placing a small amount of tobacco in a pipe bowl and inhaling through the stem. A variant of this, the water pipe, or hookah, in which tobacco is burned in a bowl and then passed through a container of water before inhalation, is popular in western Asia, North Africa, the Mediterranean, and parts of Asia.

Bidis, popular throughout Southeast Asia, are small, cigarette-like smokes made from a tiny amount of tobacco, wrapped by hand in a temburni leaf and tied with string. *Kreteks*, widely smoked in Indonesia, are clove-flavored cigarettes that contain a range of flavorings and eugenol, an anesthetic, which allows the smoke to be inhaled more deeply. Sticks of sun-cured tobacco known as *brus* are wrapped in cigarette paper and smoked.

Chewing tobacco, known as plug, loose leaf, or quid, is most popular in Southeast Asia. In this region pan masala, or betel quid, consists of tobacco, areca nuts, and slaked lime wrapped in a betel leaf. This type of tobacco product can also contain a variety of flavorings and sweetening agents.

Moist snuff is often packaged in small paper or cloth packets, or is wadded and placed in the mouth between cheek and gum. Dry snuff is inhaled, usually through the nose but also orally.

Production and consumption

The manufacture of tobacco started modestly enough. Records show that in 1616, Virginia sent just 2,300 pounds (1,050 kg) to London. Two years later, Virginia was sending more than 20,000 pounds (9,100 kg), and by 1620, 40,000 pounds (18,200 kg) were being exported.

Cigarette smoking enjoyed a similar exponential increase. In 1865, less than 20 million cigarettes were produced in the United States. By 1880, this figure had risen to 500 million; five years later, 1 billion cigarettes were being made. Another five years later, the number had doubled to 2 billion. By 1895, 4 billion cigarettes were being produced annually.

Overall global consumption of tobacco is still rising steadily. In some countries, consumption is leveling off or decreasing, but worldwide the number of smokers continues to rise and is expected to reach 1.3 billion by 2010. Five and a half trillion cigarettes are produced every year. Asia and Australia are the biggest consumers, smoking 2.7 trillion cigarettes annually, followed by North and South America (745 billion), Eastern Europe and Russia (631 billion), and Western Europe (606 billion), with a further 818 billion smoked in countries not included in this list.

Tobacco is now grown in more than 125 countries, over a wide variety of soils and climates on nearly 10 million acres (over 4 million ha) of land, a third of this in China alone. More than 1 percent of all agricultural land around the world is devoted to tobacco growing. The global tobacco crop is worth $20 billion, a small fraction of the total profits from selling tobacco-related products. Brazil, China, Turkey, India, and the United States produce two-thirds of the world's tobacco. Growing the crop alone has caused serious environmental problems with 45 percent of the deforestation in the Republic of Korea attributed to tobacco plantations.

Health effects

For much of its history, it was believed that tobacco gave, rather than took, health. Native Americans believed it could be used to cure toothache, frostbite, burns, venereal ulcers, and tumors. European and Chinese doctors believed it healed wounds, sores, and broken bones and cured bubonic plague, breast cancer, goiter, and malaria.

Medical research since the mid-1950s has proved something very different. Smokers have a considerably greater risk of dying from many different cancers, notably lung cancer. The list of other directly linked illnesses is long: emphysema, heart disease and strokes, macular degeneration and cataracts, peripheral vascular disease, stomach and duodenal ulcers, infertility and impotence, osteoporosis, early menopause, and diabetes. Chewing tobacco has been shown to cause cancer of the tongue, lip, and mouth.

Studies show that the relative risk of dying from lung cancer is estimated as 14.9 times higher in smokers compared to nonsmokers, 12.7 times higher for chronic obstructive pulmonary disease, 1.6 times higher for ischaemic heart disease, 1.3 times higher for cerebral thrombosis, 1.4 times higher for cerebral hemorrhage, and 4.1 times higher for aortic aneurysm. The risk rises with the number of cigarettes smoked and years spent smoking.

Research in the United Kingdom has shown that about 20 percent of deaths from coronary heart disease (CHD) in men and 17 percent of deaths from CHD in women are due to smoking. Smoking has also been linked to low birth weight in babies. There is also an increased risk of spontaneous miscarriage, premature or stillborn births, birth defects, and possible long-term physical and mental side effects. If a pregnant woman smokes, she also increases the number of nicotine receptors in the fetal brain, making the child more likely to eventually start smoking.

Regulation of tobacco

Although smoking even in moderation is recognized as harmful, its use is not prohibited except in limited circumstances: the state of California, the city of New York, and Ireland, for instance, have banned smoking in public places. Generally, there are few restrictions around the world on the purchase of tobacco by adults.

Partly, this is an accident of history. The addictive nature of nicotine ensured tobacco's spread around the world following its introduction to Europe in the fifteenth century. Until firm medical proof of harm began to surface, tobacco smoking was seen as promoting steady nerves (cartons were given to soldiers during wars) and, through movies, as a glamorous pastime.

A picture has slowly emerged since the mid-1930s of the true nature of tobacco and the harm that smoking causes, beginning with an early U.S. study in the 1930s linking smoking to lung cancer and a Reader's Digest article, *Cancer by the Carton*, in the 1950s. However, it was not until 1995 that the U.S. Food and Drug Administration (FDA) declared nicotine a drug. This opened the door for federal legislation regulating the sale and marketing of tobacco products. A law had already passed in the United States in 1985 prohibiting the sale of tobacco to minors. In 1993 Vermont's Clean Indoor Air Law became the first statewide statute to completely ban smoking.

Statistics show that tobacco kills half of all lifetime users—more deaths than AIDS, drugs, road

The highest-quality cigars are made individually by skilled workers in factories in Cuba. Cigar rolling is considered an art that takes many years to perfect. The skill lies in wrapping loose tobacco in a binding leaf so that it does not fall out. The fastest workers can produce around 400 cigars in a day.

accidents, and homicides combined. One of the most significant factors is the young age of first-time smokers. World Health Organization statistics show that more than 30 percent of smokers sample their first cigarette before the age of 10; evidence suggests that tobacco is attractive to minors due to shrewd marketing (smoking is depicted as "cool") and peer pressure. The younger a person is when he or she begins to smoke, the more likely it is that he or she will contract smoking-related diseases.

The tobacco industry has acknowledged that it targets young people. In 1987 U.S. tobacco product manufacturer Liggett Group issued a statement saying: "We at Liggett know and acknowledge that, as the Surgeon General and respected medical researchers have found, cigarette smoking causes health problems, including lung cancer, heart and vascular disease, and emphysema. Liggett acknowledges that the tobacco industry markets to 'youth,' which means those under 18 years of age, and not just those 18 to 24 years of age."

The projected health cost for the world is enormous. In China, which has the world's largest population at 1.3 billion, government statistics predict that by 2025 the number of people dying from smoking-related illnesses will reach 2 million a year. The World Health Organization estimates that 1.1 billion people smoke, about one-sixth of the global population, and projects that 10 million people a year will die from smoking between 2025 and 2030.

Why not just ban smoking? Attempts have been made. In 1901, there were only two U.S. states—Louisiana and Wyoming—that had not passed laws restricting the sale and public smoking of cigarettes. Some states prohibited both, but the antismoking lobby was unable to obtain a federal prohibition, so the suppression did not last. While the number of cigarettes produced fell to 2 billion in 1901, it was back up to nearly 8 billion by 1910. By 1928 the number of cigarettes produced annually in the United States had reached 100 billion.

The reason that no modern government has simply banned tobacco purchase or consumption is largely due to the tax benefits from the sale of tobacco, along with the sheer difficulty of enforcing a wholesale ban and vociferous opposition from the influential tobacco lobby. Between 1987 and 1988, the U.K. government alone raised the equivalent of $3.5 billion in excise duty and sales tax from the sale of tobacco products—equivalent to one-fifth of the country's defense budget. World Health Organization figures suggest that smoking-related diseases cost the U.K. economy $2.1 billion. The cost to the U.S. economy is reckoned to be significantly greater at $76 billion.

L. STEDMAN

SEE ALSO:
Advertising • Agriculture • Antismoking Laws • Nicotine • Plant-Based Drugs • Smoking

Tolerance

When a drug is taken for the first time, it can upset the mechanisms that the body uses to maintain its functional equilibrium. Over time, the body gradually adapts to the drug's presence. This process is called tolerance.

Tolerance can be defined as a decreasing responsiveness to a drug over time. In other words, a person who develops tolerance to a drug requires higher doses of a drug to achieve the same effect. For example, a person prescribed the opiate drug morphine for pain relief must slowly increase the dosage over time in order to maintain the pain relief. Tolerance can happen during an initial exposure to a drug, but more generally it is considered to happen over multiple drug doses. Like many phenomena involving the brain, the process and function of tolerance are not well understood. However, one general explanation of tolerance is that a drug alters the preset levels, or homeostatic "set points" of a variety of systems in the body. The function of these homeostatic set points is to keep the various systems of the body running at an optimal level. If a drug alters a body system in one direction, the body alters the system in the opposite direction in response, in an attempt to maintain the homeostatic set point. These actions of the body to oppose the effect of the drug lead to tolerance to the drug, requiring that more of the drug would have to be taken to overcome the effects on the body and cause the same net effect. The function of tolerance is to maintain biological homeostatic set points in order to keep the body running at optimal levels.

An analogy of tolerance and withdrawal involves being in love. In terms of mood, a person cannot always be manic or depressed but instead lives his or her life in a normal, "average" mood. The body is designed to achieve this balance so it can function normally. However, when someone begins a new relationship and falls in love with another person, he or she feels a euphoria, or giddiness—the presence of the other person produces a "high." Since that other person pushes one's mood out of the normal homeostatic set point, the body responds by acting on its physiological systems to oppose the effect of that other person, pushing the mood down to a normal level. Indeed, over time, that initial excitement fades until one feels more normal in the relationship and in the presence of that other person. This effect on mood is akin to drug tolerance. The body develops a tolerance to the euphoric effect of the other person in an attempt to maintain a functional, homeostatic set point. Now imagine what happens if the influence of the other person is suddenly taken away, for instance in a breakup of the relationship. The balancing, negative influence of the body's actions is unopposed by the positive effect of the other person, causing the overall mood to go in the other direction, and one feels sad or depressed. This is an example of withdrawal. The presence of the other person is taken away and one feels negative effects from having the actions of the relationship on the body taken away. Over time, however, the negative effect of the body on itself fades away in order to maintain the homeostatic set point and return the mood to its normal state of being.

Developing tolerance

Some types of tolerance take place rapidly within the first or first few exposures to the drug. This type of tolerance is called acute, or initial, tolerance. Acute tolerance is most often caused by the depletion of a substance in the body that is required to cause a drug effect. It does not even need to be a direct effect of the drug at its receptor, but an indirect effect, which then causes acute tolerance. For example, several drugs cause effects not by direct interaction with receptors in the body but instead by acting at other cellular sites to release substances that are stored in the body. These substances are inactive in their stored form, but once released by certain drugs they can activate their own receptors, causing a cascade of effects resulting in actions attributed to the drug. If these drugs are taken frequently enough to cause these substances in cells to be released faster than they can be replenished by the body, then they will be depleted. As the stored quantity of the physiological substances is reduced, the net effect caused by a certain dose of the drug is also reduced, resulting in acute tolerance. An example of acute

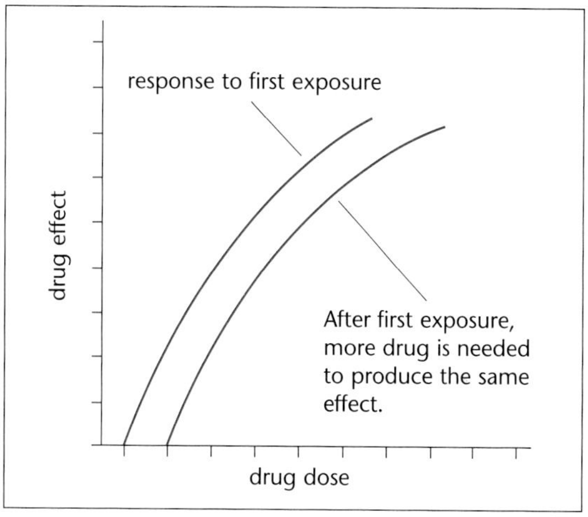

The effect of increasing tolerance requires larger doses to be administered to gain the same effect.

tolerance is the effect of morphine on flushing of the face, neck, and upper throat. Morphine causes the release of histamine, which is stored in various cells of the body, which results in this flushing. If small doses of morphine are given over long periods of time, this effect never diminishes. However, if large doses of morphine are given over a short time, this flushing effect rapidly diminishes because the stored histamine is depleted.

In contrast to acute or initial tolerance, a more slowly developing tolerance called acquired tolerance usually develops only over the course of many exposures to a drug. Acquired tolerance to a drug can take place in two different ways: either the concentration of the drug changes, or a decreased reactivity at a site of action in the body (usually through a decreased number of drug receptors) occurs. The first case of tolerance is called drug disposition tolerance, while the second is called cellular, or pharmacodynamic, tolerance. In drug disposition tolerance, a drug decreases its own absorption or rate of transfer across a barrier. For example, ingesting alcohol (ethanol) or barbiturates increases the activity of metabolic enzymes that degrade those drugs. However, disposition tolerance is minor compared with cellular tolerance (a decreased response of receptors). Cellular tolerance accounts for most of the tolerance seen for drugs that act on the brain to produce changes in mood and behavior. The manner in which cellular tolerance takes place is not very well understood; however, it generally appears that there is some change or decrease in the activity of target cells in the brain that render them less sensitive to those drugs.

A good example of cellular tolerance to a drug is shown by ethanol. Even though ethanol increases the activity of enzymes that metabolize ethanol, this drug disposition tolerance is small compared with cellular tolerance induced by ethanol. This tolerance can be illustrated by an experiment in which a large amount of ethanol is given to two separate groups of rats. One group has become tolerant to ethanol through daily injections, while the other group has never been given ethanol before. The dose of ethanol is so large that both groups of rats rapidly become unconscious. However, the rats who have become tolerant to ethanol quickly wake up. The other group stays asleep for a much longer period of time, even though they have similar levels of ethanol in their bodies. These rats do not wake up until the level of ethanol in their bodies is much lower than that of the other group when they awoke. In the case of ethanol, it appears that cellular tolerance is caused by a reduction in the number of cellular targets to ethanol, particularly a receptor called the GABA receptor.

It appears that the development of tolerance may occur by several different mechanisms, and sometimes more than one form of tolerance may take place at the same time. As mentioned above, tolerance to ethanol can occur by both drug disposition tolerance (by altering the activity of metabolizing enzymes) and also by cellular tolerance (by changing the reactivity of brain cells). The same situation is true for morphine. Additionally, the amount of tolerance that takes place also varies from drug to drug. People can become so tolerant to morphine that a tolerant person can take a dose of morphine that is several times higher than the lethal dose for a nontolerant person. By contrast, although a person who has developed tolerance to ethanol will show fewer impairing effects from a moderate dose of ethanol than a nontolerant person, both individuals will be impaired almost equally by high, near-lethal doses of ethanol.

Another interesting point about tolerance is the phenomenon of cross-tolerance. If tolerance develops to a particular drug, that person will also have some tolerance to other similar drugs belonging to the same class, even though he or she has never been exposed to those other drugs. For example, a person who develops tolerance to morphine will also be tolerant to heroin, methadone, and other narcotics, but not to caffeine, alcohol, or other drugs in different classes. The cross-tolerance will disappear when administration of the drug that caused the cross-tolerance is stopped.

Relationship between tolerance and dependence

Drug dependence is a condition in which the drug user has a compelling desire to continue taking a drug to either experience its effects or to avoid the discomfort of the drug's absence. Drug dependence has two distinct independent components: physical and psychological dependence. Physical dependence refers to an altered or adaptive physiological state of the body in response to the long-term exposure to a drug. The effects of becoming physically dependent on a drug only become clear when the drug is abruptly discontinued or when an antagonist of the drug is given (an antagonist will block the actions of the drug on the body). Either one of these actions will result in a withdrawal syndrome, which is characterized by intense negative effects on the body. The severity of the withdrawal syndrome depends on the drug and the amount of dependence that has been induced. For example, withdrawal from barbiturates, narcotics such as morphine, and alcohol is very severe. In fact, withdrawal from alcohol and barbiturates can be lethal. These effects of withdrawal are so severe that a person who is dependent on these drugs will keep taking these drugs to avoid the withdrawal effects—a striking example of physical dependence. However, no physical dependence occurs with LSD, and no or only very slight physical dependence with marijuana; hence these drugs cause no withdrawal syndrome.

In contrast to physical dependence, all of the drugs of abuse, including LSD and marijuana, can cause mild to strong psychological dependence. Psychological dependence is characterized by an emotional or mental urge to keep taking a drug because the user feels the drug is necessary to maintain a sense of optimal well-being. The amount of psychological dependence depends on the personality of the user and the specific drug. This is a complex interaction and can lead to a compulsion to keep taking the drug. This compulsion is a big problem in drug abuse because it means the person has lost control over the drug, and the drug has taken control over the person. Some drugs such as marijuana cause no physical dependence, so psychological dependence is the only dependence factor involved in their abuse.

Many drugs that can cause dependence also cause tolerance, although these phenomena are different and may occur independently of each other. For example, tolerance occurs to nitrates such as nitroglycerin, which is taken for heart problems, but no dependence occurs with this drug. However, psychological dependence on drugs may occur even without any tolerance. In addition, some drugs may induce tolerance and psychological dependence without any physical dependence, as is the case for the hallucinogen LSD. However, drugs that cause physical dependence almost always induce some tolerance.

Environmental cues

An interesting facet of tolerance involves the effect of environmental cues on tolerance. Indeed, the setting in which the drug is taken has a large effect on the degree of tolerance achieved. If a drug capable of inducing tolerance is routinely taken in a specific setting, then exposure to that setting alone will cause a response in the body in the opposite direction as that of the drug. This effect of environmental cues on the body's response can be seen by comparing the effect of a drug in its usual setting against a new setting in which the drug is not normally taken. For example, a person in a retirement home is always given morphine for pain relief in a certain treatment room. For a change, one day that person is taken outside and given the same routine dose of morphine. In the absence of the environmental cues contained in the treatment room to oppose the effects of morphine, it is entirely possible that person could overdose from the treatment simply because of the unfamiliar environmental setting.

J. JAWORSKI

SEE ALSO:
Causes of Addiction, Biological • Craving • Dependence • Sensitization • Withdrawal

Toxicity

The majority of drugs, whether therapeutic or illicit, have a threshold point at which they become poisonous, or toxic, to the body. Toxic effects may manifest themselves as adverse reactions and, in the most severe cases, death.

The single biggest problem in developing therapeutic drugs is the occurrence of side effects, or adverse drug responses that are the undesirable manifestation of a degree of drug toxicity. When the toxicity cannot be removed by chemical modification of the drug, variation of the dose, or method of administration, and it clearly outweighs the therapeutic benefit of the drug, the development project must be abandoned. The economic loss to the drug developer can be very heavy, and the unpredictability of the appearance of drug toxicity, even late in the clinical development process, constitutes a major challenge to the pharmaceutical industry.

The evaluation of drug toxicity

After more than a century of experience with drug toxicity problems, the pharmaceutical industry and its regulators follow a well-established protocol to detect and evaluate the problem. If a drug is to be licensed for sale in the world's largest market, the United States, a developer must submit a detailed body of pharmacologic and toxicologic information derived from preclinical studies in animals to the U.S. Food and Drug Administration (FDA). Equivalent bodies exist in Europe and Japan.

The developer or sponsor's objective is to obtain approval for investigational new drug (IND) studies in humans. The FDA must be satisfied that the levels of acute, subchronic, and chronic toxicity of the drug in experimental animals are such as to indicate that there is an acceptable, that is, very low, level of risk in allowing testing of the new drug in human beings. Among the assumptions underlying this process are that the effects of different drug doses in animal models will be generally similar to those in humans and that the high-dose administration experiments in animals will permit detection of potentially rare toxicity events in humans.

Extensive testing in animals and humans is required before any new drug can be prescribed. This testing helps eliminate any potential health risks and minimize side effects in patients.

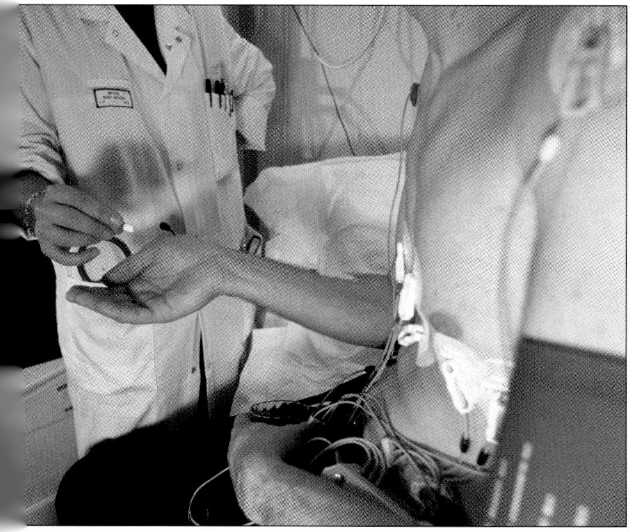

Detection of toxicity in animal models

The preclinical trial data submitted with the IND application must include studies on acute toxicity that determine the actual lethal drug dose. This is measured as the LD_{50}—the dose required to kill 50 percent of the experimental laboratory animals—and the LD_{90}—the drug dose that will kill 90 percent of the animals. These data must be obtained using at least three animal species, including one nonrodent species. Acute toxicity must be determined using at least two routes of drug administration, normally oral and intravenous or intramuscular injection.

Subchronic toxic effects of an investigational drug are measured using three drug doses, ranging from the expected normal therapeutic dose to levels high enough to produce toxicity. The duration of these tests is normally 90 days, with daily drug administration, if possible, via the route that will be used in any human study. At least two animal species must be used; laboratory testing of blood and urine to monitor drug and drug metabolite levels as well as physical examination of the animals are carried on continuously. After the end of the study, the animals are sacrificed and a full pathological examination of all animals is carried out to ascertain whether organs show signs of toxicity-induced damage.

Chronic toxicology testing in animals involves administering the new drug for the entire lifetime of the species. This can involve testing for up to two years in the case of laboratory rats and mice and longer for nonrodents such as rabbits. Three dose levels are used, ranging from nontoxic low doses to high doses that are expected to show some toxicity. Physical and laboratory tests on the animals are carried out continuously, and particular attention is paid to microscopic examination of tissue sections from periodically sacrificed animals. This examination is intended to detect potential tissue damage and induction of cancers. The effects of chronic drug administration on the reproductive organs and cycles of rats and rabbits are also studied.

Testing in cell cultures and nonanimal systems

So-called in vitro (Latin, meaning "in glass") toxicity studies can provide faster and cheaper data on toxicity and do not involve animal testing (in vivo studies). However, in vitro toxicity studies are not accepted as substitutes for animal testing, only as supplemental data. A very widely used test is the Ames bioassay for testing the capacity of a drug to cause mutations in bacteria. Bacterial mutagens are often, but not always, human carcinogens. Research has also exploited the large-scale study of proteins, or proteomics, particularly when the search for possible drug toxicity has moved into the human clinical testing stage and biological markers, such as urine proteins, can be compared between subjects.

Human clinical trials

If the animal testing data indicate that a new drug is sufficiently safe, then approval may be granted to initiate Phase I of the human clinical testing process. The clinical trial protocol detailing the conditions and personnel involved in the study must be approved by both a hospital Institutional Review Board (IRB) and by the FDA, which will then issue an IND exemption permit.

Phase I studies are primarily intended to test the safety of the drug and establish at what level of dose signs of toxicity first appear in humans. This involves giving the new drug to between 20 and 80 healthy male volunteers aged between 18 and 45. These volunteers must give their informed consent to the study protocol before they can participate in a clinical trial. The first step in the trial is administration of a single dose of the drug, followed by monitoring of all recipients for any sign of adverse reactions or toxic side effects. If no adverse reactions occur, the dose of the drug will be progressively increased to a predetermined level, or until evidence of toxicity is found. During this process the patient's absorption, metabolism, and urinary secretion of the drug will be closely monitored.

If satisfactory initial evidence that the new drug is safe is obtained, a Phase II clinical trial protocol will be submitted to the IRB, and a larger group of trial volunteers will be recruited. The objective of the Phase II clinical trial is to obtain the first set of data on the effectiveness of the drug in treating or preventing a specific disease or disorder, in addition to expanding the data set available on possible toxic side effects of the drug. Patient volunteers should, if possible, have no health problems other than the condition being treated. The study will randomize the treatment group, "blinding" the medical personnel administering the drugs from the knowledge of which patient is receiving the new drug and which patient is receiving the older, or prototype drug. If no prototype drug exists, a harmless, unrelated substance may be given as a placebo.

Phase II trials are the most crucial test of a new drug because they will verify if it is useful in treating its target disease or disorder, determine the best treatment dose (the optimal dose-response range) and assay the effects of long-term administration of the drug to affected and thus, in some degree, unhealthy human beings. The data from the Phase II trial will determine whether a new drug seems worth the expense and effort of proceeding to new and yet more extensive testing in larger human trial groups. Successful Phase I and II trials indicating that a drug is useful and without unacceptable toxicity will usually lead to Phase III expanded trials that will continue until the drug is licensed for sale. Phase III trials will involve thousands of patients and are intended to obtain further evidence that the drug is safe and effective. When the sponsor feels that sufficient trial data has been collected, a full New Drug Application will be filed with the FDA.

Most new drugs will not pass this rigorous testing process, and this is no doubt as it should be. However, unexpected clinical utility has also been discovered during clinical testing. Most famously, Sildenafil was originally intended to be a therapy for angina, but its effectiveness for treating erectile dysfunction was noted in clinical trials. This led to its ultimate, profitable reemergence as Viagra.

Drug toxicity management in clinical practice

It is frequently the case that a drug has known problems of toxicity, yet it remains the most effective treatment available for a serious condition. An example of this is the widely used immunosuppressive drug cyclosporin A, employed to prevent rejection of skin grafts and organ transplants. Cyclosporin A is now known to cause kidney toxicity in nearly 40 percent of those treated. This toxicity is associated with increased secretion of calcium, resulting in calcification of kidney tubules that can lead to fatal kidney failure. Yet we do not have a better immunosuppressant than cyclosporin A, and many patients, particularly children with leukemia, will die without a bone marrow graft. Thus toxicity must be closely monitored and managed as well as possible by dose modulation, while research continues to produce safer drugs or, alternatively, drugs that can alleviate the toxicity of other essential but problematic drugs.

Unexpected toxicity problems

Many common adverse events derived from toxic drug side effects cannot be detected in animal models. These include depression, headaches, gastrointestinal problems such as heartburn, and hearing problems such as tinnitus (ringing). Often such problems may be quite real, but occur only in a very small proportion of the human population. The preclinical and clinical testing process is relatively insensitive and is unlikely to detect adverse effects that occur in less than 1 in 1,000 of those who receive the drug. Thus there is a Phase IV clinical testing process, conducted after a new drug is approved and starts to become generally used. Such studies are termed ongoing studies in large populations.

Even after a drug has been on the market for some time, toxicity problems in a relatively small population may be severe enough to cause the withdrawal of a drug from sale. An example that came to light in 2004 was the discovery of an increased risk of heart attack and stroke events in those using Vioxx, an arthritis pain reliever. Despite the fact that the drug had been sold since 1999 and was used by more than two million people, this low-incidence toxicity effect was sufficiently serious to cause its manufacturer, Merck, to withdraw the product from the market.

D. E. ARNOT

ABUSE LIABILITY

The side effects produced by therapeutic drugs, while considered unwanted by drug developers, are often the reason that the drug is deliberately used for recreational purposes. For example, the euphoria produced by opiate painkillers is rarely felt by those experiencing physical pain but is immediately triggered by those using them for nonmedical purposes. New drugs that have an effect on the central nervous system undergo further tests to determine whether they have any potential or liability for abuse. Initial tests on animals are not always indicative, as some animals may not develop dependence toward a particular drug. Human trials are therefore necessary.

There are advantages to testing on humans: the subjective effects of many drugs are not always apparent from assessments of animal behavior. Humans can tell researchers what they are feeling or whether there is an unexpected reaction. Most of the volunteers used for these studies are experienced drug users who can assess whether the new drug has a greater or lesser potential for abuse than the one they know. Light social drinkers are also recruited to test combinations of alcohol with medications such as sleeping tablets or diet pills.

SEE ALSO:
Adverse Reactions • Controlled Substances • Food and Drug Administration (FDA) • Metabolism • Pharmacokinetics • Pharmacology

Trauma and Addiction

Trauma and addiction are closely linked; trauma may be the result of addiction, or addiction may follow severe trauma. Although recovery can take a long time, with perserverance and support, it is possible.

In its simplest meaning, trauma is any event that causes distress and has lasting effects upon a person. There are two broad categories of traumatic events: mental trauma and physical trauma.

Mental trauma refers to the damage that can result from a frightening or emotionally trying situation, such as sexual abuse or the death of a loved one. Victims of mental trauma often experience severe psychological, emotional, and social problems. Physical trauma is any serious injury or shock to the body, sustained through accident or violence. Physical trauma can be life threatening and is a major cause of death among teens and young adults.

Trauma has a complicated relationship with addiction. In fact, doctors often cite trauma as both a cause and result of substance abuse and other addictions. For example, a person who undergoes an emotionally traumatic event might be more likely to develop an addictive disorder than someone who does not experience such trauma. In such a case, trauma is a precipitating factor in the development of addiction. Victims of mental trauma sometimes turn to substance abuse, compulsive gambling, or other behavioral addictions, such as compulsive sex or eating, to help cope with feelings of anger or despair. In other cases, trauma is the result of substance abuse. Because substance users can suffer from a lack of judgment, a person with a substance abuse disorder, such as heroin addiction, is more likely to sustain a serious physical traumatic injury than someone who does not use drugs. As a result, the majority of all traumatic injuries treated in emergency rooms involves alcohol or drugs.

Mental trauma and addiction

While the most effective and highly recommended treatment for mental trauma is often counseling under the guidance of a certified professional, such as a psychologist, victims of mental trauma sometimes try to find ways to escape the reality of their situation. One of the ways that victims of mental trauma attempt to cope with their feelings of hopelessness and despair is to turn to alcohol and drugs. While mood-altering substances can provide a temporary diversion to emotional stress, substance abuse can compound psychological problems. For example, suppression of mental trauma through alcohol or drug use interferes with a person's ability to progressively work through his or her problems. Because they are unable to adequately cope with their trauma while struggling with addiction, mental trauma victims are more vulnerable to addiction relapse upon recovery.

Post-traumatic stress disorder

Rates of addiction in individuals who have suffered mental trauma are notably higher than in the general population. This is especially true among people who suffer from post-traumatic stress disorder, or PTSD. The U.S.–based National Center for Post-Traumatic Stress Disorder defines PTSD as a psychiatric condition that can occur in people who experience severe mental trauma through life-threatening events such as military combat, natural disasters, terrorism, severe accidents, or personal violence, such as rape. People who suffer from PTSD often have trouble coping with their trauma and vividly relive their experiences through nightmares and flashbacks. PTSD can be a debilitating condition, affecting many aspects of a victim's daily life. Scientific studies have shown that individuals with PTSD are more likely to have multiple psychiatric disorders and more severe problems with addiction, increased hospital time, and higher potential for relapse. One possible explanation for the high rate of addiction among the PTSD-diagnosed population is the negative emotional states that are characteristic of PTSD. After severe trauma, individuals with PTSD can experience panic attacks and episodes of emotional distress. Thus, individuals with PTSD often self-medicate with alcohol and drugs to alleviate such feelings, and may develop substance use disorders. These negative emotions have also been shown to increase alcohol and drug cravings in

The majority of accidents that cause traumatic injuries involve alcohol or drug use.

PTSD-diagnosed individuals with a history of substance use. Victims of mental trauma are not only vulnerable to substance-based addiction but also to a variety of behavioral addictions. Because many victims experience mental trauma at a young age, behavioral and emotional development can be interrupted, and emotional needs can be left unmet. In such cases, a person who develops a behavioral addiction might not be suppressing angry feelings, but instead might be trying to meet his or her needs in a way that is familiar. For example, sexual abuse can cause shame and confusion in children, which can then lead to unhealthy sexual development during adolescence. A person in this situation might experience many failed relationships and low self-esteem and ultimately might develop a sex addiction. Because the traumatic event suppresses his or her ability to support healthy and loving relationships, such a person then attempts to meet healthy needs in an unhealthy manner. Addiction can result when a mentally traumatic event robs a person of the skills to maintain a healthy lifestyle.

Physical trauma and addiction

The main risk factor for physical trauma is impairment by drugs and alcohol. Substance abusers experience increased risk for traumatic injury, including auto accidents, falls, burns, and drowning. Substance users are also at a greater risk of sustaining violent injuries, such as stabbings and gunshot wounds, due to accidents and drug-related violence. Also, people who experience trauma while under the influence of substances are often unable or unwilling to cooperate with emergency personnel. This can make injury diagnosis and treatment difficult for emergency physicians and trauma surgeons.

Scientific research has shown that people who continue to use alcohol and drugs after surviving physical trauma are more likely to experience additional traumatic injuries. At the same time, the reality of sustaining a traumatic injury can frighten a patient into recognizing the severity of the situation, and thus provide the motivation to seek treatment. For this reason, emergency and trauma physicians are in a unique position to intervene in the cycle of addiction and trauma. A patient who is admitted to a hospital with a traumatic injury often experiences a window of opportunity when he or she is more likely to talk and learn about addictive behaviors. At this time, physicians and hospital staff can inform patients about the available treatment options and can arrange for patients to enroll in counseling or treatment programs. If a physician recognizes symptoms of substance abuse in a patient, discussing and encouraging treatment could prevent the patient from experiencing future injuries.

There are barriers, however, that can prevent physical trauma victims from receiving treatment for substance abuse problems. For example, many emergency doctors and trauma surgeons focus solely on repairing injuries and do not believe that it is their responsibility to screen trauma patients for alcohol or drug use. Such doctors might take alcohol or drug intoxication into consideration in assessing the proper course of treatment for the patient's traumatic injury but would not use this information to identify patients with addiction problems. In addition, in the United States, the Uniform Accident and Sickness Policy Provision Law (UPPL) allows health insurance companies to deny coverage for any injury sustained while the victim was under the influence of alcohol or drugs. Any patient who receives a traumatic injury could be held responsible for large medical bills if tests prove he or she had alcohol or drugs in the bloodstream at the time of the accident. A patient faced with such a situation often cannot pay, thus creating a liability for the hospital. To avoid this situation, many trauma doctors do not screen their patients for drugs or alcohol, and so guarantee that insurance companies will cover costs. In this way, many patients who would benefit from alcohol or drug intervention fail to receive treatment and often return to the emergency room with additional potentially preventable traumatic injuries.

Treatment and recovery

Left untreated, addiction, whether substance-based or behavioral, can destroy the health and relationships of victims and their families. Treatment allows individuals to recover from addiction and return to a healthy lifestyle. While there are many steps involved in recovery, one factor is essential for the successful treatment of addictive disorders: the individual must be ready and willing to recover. The first step of admitting and accepting his or her problem is often the most difficult stage of recovery for a person struggling with addiction. For a victim of mental trauma struggling with addiction, recovery is often contingent upon psychotherapy for the underlying psychological problems associated with the traumatic event. However, because such therapy can be long and emotionally painful, simultaneous recovery from substance abuse can seem impossible. Similarly, a person who sustains repeated traumatic injuries attributable to substance abuse might not be ready to accept change. Repeated visits to the emergency room with addiction-related trauma could indicate severe substance dependence and resistance to advice and education offered by doctors and addiction specialists. Such a person might be at risk for a variety of other comorbid, or simultaneous, psychological problems, such as depression, that could also complicate recovery.

Treatment options

Once ready to recover, there are several treatment options for trauma victims struggling with addiction. Because addictions can plague individuals for decades, identification of an individual's problems and professional treatment are the options that offer the most long-term hope. Mental health professionals, such as psychologists, can help individuals manage emotional problems and prepare them for a program of recovery from addiction. Addiction recovery programs are diverse and can consist of inpatient care at hospitals or regulated care facilities, one-on-one outpatient therapy with a specialist or psychologist, or self-help sessions through organizations such as Alcoholics Anonymous (AA) or Narcotics Anonymous. The therapy selected depends on a patient's preferences. Inpatient therapy may focus on a patient's medical and biological needs, such as chemical detoxification or pharmacological treatment with drugs to reduce cravings. These programs can be demanding and require patients to leave their families for extended periods. Conversely, self-help programs require a patient to share feelings with large groups—a concept that makes some people uncomfortable.

Trauma victims can work within these options, and psychologists might use specialized diagnostic instruments to create customized treatment strategies for patients with both mental disorders and substance abuse disorders. There are support groups, such as Dual Recovery Anonymous (DRA), for people with both a chemical dependency and an emotional or psychiatric illness, which can help victims cope with addiction and mental health problems by sharing their feelings with others in a similar situation. Or, patients can explore their feelings in family therapy groups. Patients might have to explore several options before deciding on the path to recovery. Successful recovery depends on the realization that it requires patience, dedication, and perseverance. No treatment strategy is guaranteed to work for every patient, but with support, it is possible to break free from the cycle of trauma and addiction.

A. N. DONATO

SEE ALSO:
Clinics • Disability and Drugs • Driving While Impaired • Medical Care • Recovery • Treatment

Treatment

Treating an addiction is not a straightforward process. The circumstances and problems surrounding the addiction are unique to the person and must be assessed for each individual. With the right program, addiction can be overcome.

Substance use disorders (SUDs) are experienced by more than 16 percent of adults in the United States. SUDs include abuse or dependence on alcohol, cannabis, cocaine and other stimulants, opiates, sedative-hypnotics, hallucinogens, inhalants, or the "club" drugs. Alcohol abuse and dependence are the most common of the SUDs. Many people with these disorders use multiple substances.

SUDs are associated with many problems for the affected individual. For example, more than 30 diseases are associated with alcohol problems. Intravenous drug use is associated with higher rates of HIV infections and transmission. SUDs cause or worsen numerous medical, psychological, family, social, legal, occupational, academic, economic, and spiritual problems. An untreated SUD can end in death or other negative consequences, such as losing a job or family, incarceration, or a severe medical or psychiatric disorder.

Substance use disorders also have many negative effects on the family and its members, including children. Family breakups and divorce are higher in families in which a parent has an SUD. Children who have one or both parents with an SUD are at increased risk for substance abuse, psychiatric disorders (anxiety, depression, or combined disorders), behavioral problems (for example, aggression or oppositional behaviors), and academic problems. These disorders cost society hundreds of billions of dollars each year as a result of lost productivity at work and the costs of medical, criminal justice, social and treatment services.

Treatment helps individuals restore their health and overcome or reduce other problems. Treatment also helps families overcome the emotional burden caused by SUDs.

Obtaining treatment

Most people with SUDs never receive treatment. While some are able to stop using on their own or with the help of mutual support groups such as Alcoholics Anonymous (AA) or Narcotics Anonymous (NA), others require professional treatment to help them stop using substances and make changes in themselves and their lifestyle.

The person with an SUD may enter treatment voluntarily or involuntarily as a result of:

- Realizing that substance use is a problem and help is needed.
- Taking the advice of a religious, health care or social service professional, attorney, teacher, coach, employee assistance counselor, boss, colleague, friend, loved one, or other concerned person. This advice may be actively sought by the person. Or, it may be offered by the significant other out of concern for the person with the SUD.
- Giving in to pressure from an intervention in which loved ones meet with the person with the SUD and share observations of substance use and impaired behaviors, as well as how they have been affected. A professional may or may not be present to guide this process.
- Agreeing to a legal mandate by the court related to a charge or conviction in which substance use was a factor. An attorney may be instrumental in persuading a client to get help with an SUD.
- Treatment can be effective even if not entered voluntarily. In fact, there are some advantages to having a legal mandate or pressure from an employer to seek help. Often, the person will initially seek treatment because of such pressure but will eventually come to realize a serious problem exists. Those who stick with treatment as a result of a mandate may eventually develop a desire to change as motivation shifts from external to internal.

Determining appropriate treatment

Treatment services recommended depend on the unique problems and needs of the individual with the SUD. The American Society on Addiction

Medicine (ASAM) recommends that treatment decisions be based on a comprehensive assessment of six dimensions of functioning. This assessment determines the severity of the SUD and related medical or psychiatric disorders and other significant problems, which in turn determines the level of care needed.

The assessment is conducted by a physician, nurse, psychologist, social worker, or counselor trained in addiction medicine who gathers information from interviews with the affected person, her family, significant others, a physical examination, and laboratory studies (for example, liver function levels, urinalysis, and blood-alcohol tests). The six dimensions that make up the assessment include:

- *Intoxication and withdrawal potential.* This potential determines if medically supervised detoxification is needed before engaging in rehabilitation or counseling.
- *Biomedical conditions and complications.* These conditions determine if treatment is needed in a medically supervised setting.
- *Emotional conditions or complications.* This element determines if treatment of a co-existing psychiatric disorder is required. If so, the person may be referred to a dual diagnosis treatment program.
- *Readiness to change.* Motivation or readiness to change has an impact on whether or not treatment recommendations are followed.
- *Recovery environment and social support.* The availability of supportive family, friends, or community groups plays a role in making treatment recommendations. Some environments are more (or less) conducive to recovery than others.
- *Relapse potential.* Prior attempts at treatment and recovery and history of relapses impact treatment decisions.

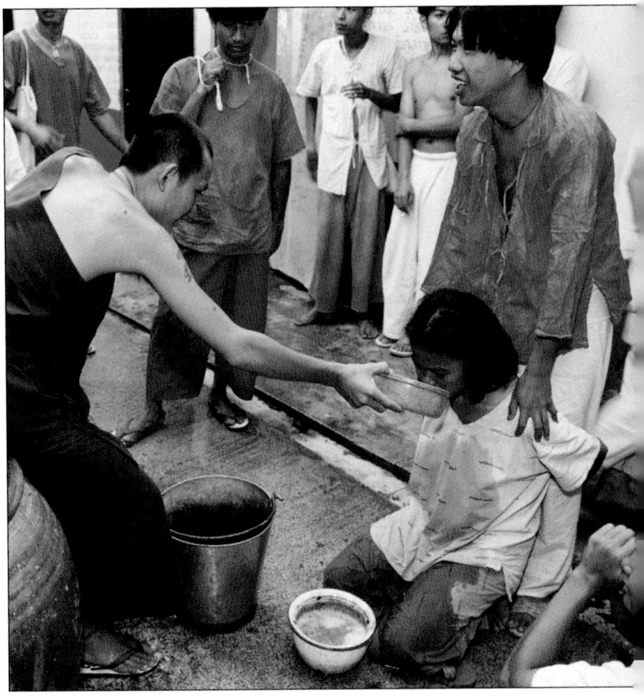

The treatment of addicts at the Thamkrabok monastery in Thailand may seem harsh by Western standards, but the method has saved many from continuing addiction. Five days of purging to rid the body of toxins are followed by several weeks of meditation and community involvement to build up the patient's willpower and resistance to returning to old patterns and lifestyles.

Continuum of care

Treatment requires a continuum of services that can meet the needs of people with different types and severity of SUDs. This continuum includes professional services specific for SUDs, services for other types of problems (for example, medical, vocational, educational, housing, economic, legal), and mutual support groups such as Alcoholics Anonymous or Narcotics Anonymous.

ASAM recommends that treatment be matched to the problems of the individual with the SUD based on the assessment. Treatment settings from the least to most intensive include the following:

Outpatient counseling (OPT). Individual, group, or family counseling may be offered. Frequency of sessions depends on the needs and problems of the individual with the SUD and the concerns of the family. Individual counseling involves talking one-on-one with an addiction counselor, usually up to an hour at a time. Group counseling involves meeting with one or two counselors with a group of six to ten other individuals who also have SUDs, usually for one to two hours per session. Goals of outpatient treatment include: determining if an SUD exists and what to do about it; stopping substance use; making personal changes to support abstinence; learning to spot early signs of relapse; and dealing with problems contributing to or resulting from the SUD. Some attend only a few sessions, while others attend many sessions over several months or longer. Group counseling sessions are usually held weekly, while individual and family sessions may initially be held weekly, then reduced to less frequent sessions.

Intensive outpatient (IOP) or partial hospital (PH) programs. These programs have the same goals as outpatient counseling and are used with more severe types of SUDs. Individual, family, and group counseling may be offered as part of IOP or PH programs. IOP is less intensive than PH, and may involve the person attending a program 3 to 5 days per week, for up to 10 weekly hours of education and counseling. A PH program involves attending sessions 4 to 7 days per week, up to 20 weekly hours or more per week. Both IOP and PH each may last 2 to 6 weeks.

Ambulatory detoxification. Some clinics offer supervised detoxification in addition to OPT, IOP, or PH services. This service involves meeting with a nurse or doctor who monitors withdrawal symptoms and vital signs and provides counseling and education. Medications are used to help the person safely withdraw from alcohol or other addictive drugs. This service usually lasts just a few days. A major goal is to get the person being detoxified to remain in treatment. If withdrawal symptoms significantly worsen, the person may be referred to an inpatient detoxification unit in a hospital or rehabilitation program.

Residential rehabilitation programs. A primary rehabilitation program lasts up to three or four weeks; a halfway house program (HWH) lasts several months or longer; and a therapeutic community (TC) lasts several months to more than a year. All of these programs aim to provide education, support, and counseling to help the person with the SUD learn ways to stay sober and solve problems without relapsing to substance use. Many of these programs use addiction counselors who have personal experiences with addiction and recovery. Some, such as TCs that specialize in helping individuals with criminal histories, may also have counselors who are ex-prisoners.

A primary rehabilitation program provides a structured treatment day in which the person attends many treatments. These include recovery education groups, therapy groups, individual counseling, leisure or recreational counseling, and mutual support groups such as AA or NA. Clients are often given reading, writing, or workbook assignments to help them personalize the material covered during the treatment day. For example, a client may be asked to write an extensive personal history of alcohol and drug use (types, amounts, and frequency of substances used, as well as effects on oneself and others), and then share this with a counseling group. Peers then share their opinions on the seriousness of this person's SUD. A client nearing program completion may be assigned an interactive workbook task in which he or she develops a follow-up plan with the names, addresses, and telephone numbers of specific resources he or she will use to help stay sober (professional and self-help programs). This client may also be asked to list potential relapse warning signs and risk factors and what can be done to manage these without using alcohol or drugs.

While in an HWH, the client may get involved in vocational counseling and training or focus on academic issues (for example, getting a GED or finishing college). The HWH provides support and treatment to help the client pursue these other goals.

A TC program is generally more psychologically intense than other rehab programs. It is often used for those individuals whose lifestyle evolved around addiction and who have had problems with the law in addition to their addiction. Many residents of a TC have poor academic, occupational, and social skills and need help acquiring these skills, which are needed for success in life.

A TC aims to help the resident become part of a community in which people help each other by confronting and changing negative, unhealthy, and addictive behaviors, and acquiring more prosocial behaviors. In addition to teaching ways to manage recovery from addiction, a TC aims to teach values such as citizenship, honesty, love, charity, altruism, and responsibility to self, family, and others. This type of program is considered more "habilitation" than "rehabilitation" because many residents of a TC never learned some of the requisite skills needed to function responsibly and effectively in society.

BEHAVIORAL TREATMENTS

- Cognitive-behavioral therapy focuses on helping the client change beliefs and learn behaviors that are incompatible with substance use.
- Community reinforcement approach involves receipt of rewards or reinforcements for sobriety, along with personal and family counseling.
- Cue exposure teaches the person to control reactions to stimuli that trigger desires to use substances.
- In group drug counseling, several addicted individuals work together to learn about addiction and how to manage the day-to-day challenges of sobriety, for example, cravings and social pressures to use, or how to deal with upsetting emotions.
- Individual drug counseling helps the person learn to manage addiction through the use of twelve-step programs, building a recovery support system, and managing relapse warning signs and risk factors.
- MATRIX model (for methamphetamine and cocaine) provides a comprehensive program to manage addiction and reduce relapse risk.
- Motivational enhancement therapy helps the person develop motivation to change.
- Relapse prevention helps the person learn to identify and manage early signs of relapse and high risk factors.
- Social skills training (also called coping skills training) helps the person learn to manage relationship conflicts or internal conflicts (cravings, negative emotional states, thoughts of using substances).
- Family therapy and social network therapy engages members of the addicted person's family or social network, both to help the addicted person and to help themselves.
- Twelve-step facilitation therapy helps the person recover through involvement in AA or NA and the use of a sponsor, the twelve-steps, and other tools of AA.

Medical detoxification. This process occurs in a medically managed unit of a hospital or a medically monitored unit of an addiction rehabilitation program. The main difference between the two is that the former is for individuals with more severe withdrawal syndromes or those with significant medical or psychiatric problems in addition to an active addiction. Detoxification usually lasts 2 to 5 days and involves monitoring withdrawal symptoms, taking medications if symptoms warrant this, and participating in educational or counseling services.

While some individuals use only one type of service, others use multiple services, either during the course of their current episode or as a result of relapses following periods of sobriety. For many people, addiction is a chronic and lifelong disorder. Like chronic medical or psychiatric disorders, their addiction may require multiple episodes of treatment over time. Periods of recovery may be followed by recurrent episodes of use.

Behavioral therapies

There are many effective behavioral or psychosocial therapies and programs, medications, and combined approaches available to treat people with SUDs. Typical behavioral or psychosocial treatments are shown in the box at left. These approaches may be used in any of the levels of care described earlier. Although the theory behind each treatment model and the clinical techniques vary, all aim to help the affected person manage the SUD and make personal and lifestyle changes.

Medications

Medications help addicted people safely and comfortably withdraw from substances such as alcohol, opiates, or sedatives. Medicines used depend on the drugs to which the person is addicted.

Medicines may be used to take the place of the addictive drug. Methadone maintenance (MM) helps heroin addicts transfer their addiction from street drugs to methadone, which is administered and monitored in a licensed clinic. Nicotine replacement therapy in the form of gum, patches, or nasal spray helps some people stop smoking.

Antagonist or mixed replacement (agonist/antagonist) medications are used for some opiate addicts. Naltrexone "antagonizes" the effects of heroin, so the addict does not get high if he or she ingests heroin while using it. Buprenorphine has both replacement and antagonist effects. It can be used to help the addict withdraw from heroin or other opiate drugs. Buprenorphine also helps the addict in maintenance therapy. Medications may be used to reduce craving among alcoholics and those addicted to smoking. Naltrexone reduces the alcoholic's craving, and buproprion reduces the smoker's craving.

Disulfiram (Antabuse) serves as aversive therapy for alcoholics. If the alcoholic consumes alcohol with disulfiram in her system (which stays in the system up to 7 to 14 days after the last dose), she becomes nauseous. This aversive reaction is a motivator for some alcoholics not to drink. The idea is to "buy the alcoholic time" so that she does not drink when craving alcohol. If she perseveres until disulfiram is out of her system, her craving to drink may subside.

Medications that eliminate or reduce psychiatric symptoms may lower the desire to drink or use drugs. Medications that improve mood or help organize thinking can indirectly support the client's resistance to use substances.

One of the practical problems some addicts face is the pressure from others in recovery to not use any drug, including a medication. Some misguided people perceive medications as the same as addictive substances and do not see their potential benefits.

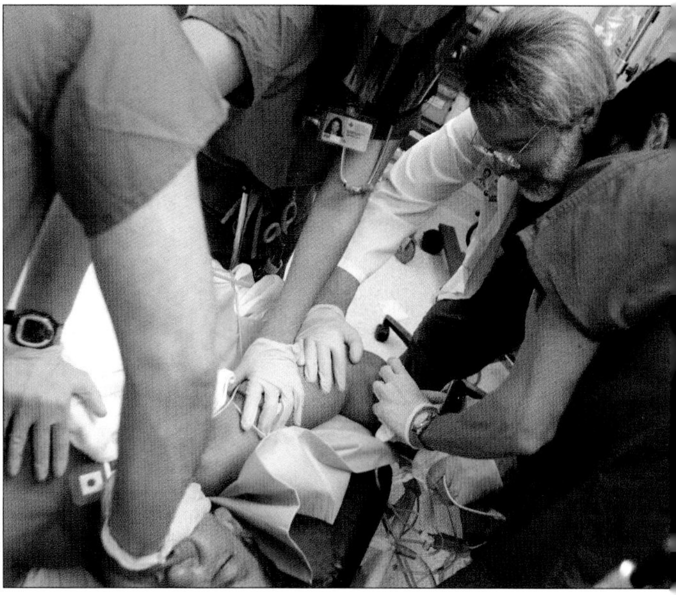

Treating drug addiction sometimes begins when an addict is rushed to an emergency room following an overdose. However, addicts often lack the resources to complete a proper treatment program.

Other services

To address other problems common among those with SUDs, a variety of services are needed. These include vocational assessment and training, case management, housing, and social services. Case managers help clients with SUDs with problems related to housing, transportation, applying for benefits, and accessing medical, psychiatric, or addiction services.

Principles of effective treatment

The National Institute on Drug Abuse (NIDA) has published principles of treatment that serve as an important guide to providing care for those with SUDs. Because no single treatment fits all individuals, NIDA recommends that a variety of levels of care and treatment approaches are provided. Treatment must be readily available and easily accessible, or the person may find reasons not to get the help he needs. It is also important that all the client's needs are assessed. Many with SUDs have medical, psychiatric, and psychosocial problems that require help. Treatment does not have to be voluntary to be effective. Clients mandated to treatment by the court or an employer often benefit from it. Although motivation is external at first, it may later shift to internal as the person realizes an addiction exists and develops motivation to change.

Once the client is part of a program, the treatment plan may need to be modified based on the changing needs and problems of the client. Treatment is an active process, and the focus can change over time according to the needs and problems of the person with the SUD. Adequate time in treatment is a prerequisite for the client to benefit. Less than three months in treatment is seldom effective, and outcome is often associated with time in treatment. The highest risk period of dropout and relapse is the first 30 days in treatment. Any co-occurring mental disorders should be treated in an integrated manner. The treatment plan needs to address both the substance and the psychiatric disorders, as an untreated psychiatric disorder can contribute to relapse.

Most treatment programs start with detoxification, which prepares clients for ongoing treatment. Once the client is clean, it may be helpful to monitor any further drug use during treatment, as external checking motivates some clients to stay sober. Urinalysis reports help identify recent use and provide the caregiver with information that can be used in counseling sessions. Treatment programs should also test for HIV/AIDS, hepatitis, and other infectious diseases. Counseling can then focus on helping the client to reduce behaviors that increase the risk of diseases, for example, using dirty needles, cotton, or rinsing water for IV users, unprotected sex, and sex with multiple partners.

Recovery can be a long-term process requiring multiple episodes of treatment. Addicted clients are no different from those with mental disorders in that some are sicker, have more difficulty with recovery, and need more professional services than others. Even after they finish professional treatment, many remain involved in recovery by attending mutual support groups such as AA or NA.

Special populations
Some programs are designed to help unique populations based on demographic or clinical characteristics. An entire program or a track within a program may address a single population, for example, pregnant women, clients in the criminal justice system, clients with co-occurring psychiatric disorders, African Americans, Native Americans, women, adolescents, the elderly, gays and lesbians, or multiple relapsers.

Self-help groups
Many people with SUDs recover primarily with the help of mutual support programs such as AA or NA. Others use both professional treatment and support groups. Professionals routinely teach their clients about these programs and facilitate their attendance. Many treatment programs offer on-site AA and NA meetings. AA and NA are fellowships of people who share their experiences, strength, and hope to help one another recover from addiction. Members help each other by providing education, support, and mentoring. Established members sponsor newcomers by helping them learn about the twelve steps and twelve traditions.

Treatment effectiveness
There is much scientific evidence that treatment for SUDs is effective. Positive treatment outcomes and examples from studies include:

- *Reducing or stopping substance use.* One major study found that at one-year follow-up, alcoholics reduced the percentage of drinking days per month from 80 percent to 20 percent, and reduced the average number of drinks per drinking day from 17 to 3.
- *Reducing or stopping high-risk behaviors that increase the risk of infectious diseases.* Many studies show greater reductions of HIV rates among treated clients compared with those who do not receive treatment.
- *Improved physical, mental, or spiritual health.* Treated individuals use fewer medical services after treatment and report a more positive mood than untreated individuals.
- *Improved family relationships.* Treatment helps families function more effectively and reduces their emotional burden. Mothers often reunite with their children after they get involved in treatment.
- *Increased ability to hold a job and fulfill responsibilities.* Opiate addicts on methadone maintenance show increases in rates of employment as a result of treatment.

Conclusions
SUDs are associated with many problems and increased rates of mortality. However, many effective behavioral treatments and medications exist to help individuals with SUDs and their families. A variety of professional services and mutual support programs are available to address this serious health care problem. It is clear from outcome studies that there are substantial benefits to treatment.

D. C. DALEY

SEE ALSO:
Addiction • Alcoholism Treatment • Clinics • Counseling • Detoxification • Diagnosing Substance Abuse • Family Therapy • Heroin Addiction Treatment • Intervention • Medical Care • Recovery • Rehabilitation • Relapse • Step Programs • Support Groups • Treatment Centers

Treatment, Cost of

Treating alcohol and substance abuse both publicly and privately can cost a great deal of money. Not treating it can be even more expensive in terms of lost productivity and earnings, crime, and health care costs.

The cost of treating alcohol and drug addiction is enormous. Costs vary substantially between types of settings and types of treatment. Existing data collected by the Substance Abuse and Mental Health Services Administration (SAMHSA) is presented in the table below to demonstrate basic treatment costs. Outpatient treatment is much less expensive to provide than inpatient treatment, but because the number of clients is increased the total cost per year is very similar. Research has not demonstrated significant treatment gains by providing inpatient treatment, which has lead to an increased use of outpatient treatment as a cost effective means of providing treatment.

The high cost of providing alcohol and drug treatment often comes under attack, especially when state and federal budgets need to be cut. Legislators are quick to look at the money spent on alcohol and drug services and often make decisions based on negative stereotypes and biases about substance users.

However, research has shown that there are direct public benefits from paying for alcohol and drug treatment. These benefits come in a variety of forms, including cost savings in the economy, recovery of lost wages, increases in taxpayer spendable income, decreases in criminal justice spending, and less taxpayer expense for health care and emergency services. For example, the number of patients undergoing treatment and who were involved in accidents decreased from 14 to 1 percent, patients' children who missed school dropped from 5 to 1 percent, and the number of spouses who missed work went down from 10 to 1 percent.

These cost-savings benefits are often neglected during policy debates related to funding for substance abuse treatment even though the total cost of treatment in the United States is nearly $20 billion annually. It is important to understand that although treating alcohol and drug use, abuse, and dependence has a high cost, not treating it costs even more. Simple comparisons of treatment costs versus possible savings yield valuable data.

Crime-related cost savings

The reduction in criminal activity following substance abuse treatment is difficult to measure and therefore difficult to report with certainty; however, research has shown that the majority of persons arrested and convicted of crimes are people with alcohol and drug use, abuse, or dependence histories. In 1996 the total costs of crime (property losses, justice costs, and so on) averaged $47,971 per patient in the year prior to treatment; that figure dropped to an average of $28,657 in the year following treatment. The significant reduction of $19,314 was more than the cost of treatment: $2,828 for methadone maintenance, $8,920 for residential treatment, and $2,908 for outpatient treatment.

COSTS OF TREATING SUBSTANCE USE DISORDERS IN THE UNITED STATES

Type of treatment	Average cost per day	Average length of treatment (days)	Average cost per admission	Estimated annual costs
Inpatient	$76.13	45	$3,840.00	$2,736,348,408
Outpatient	$11.24	144	$1,433.00	$3,083,179,207

Source: ADSS (Alcohol and Drug Services Survey) Cost Study, 2004. Figures given are based on estimates of 1997 costs extrapolated to 2002.

Mortality rates and preventable illness

The number of people killed each year as a direct result of alcohol or drug use is huge. Figures from the Centers for Disease Control estimate that 75,766 people died from alcohol-related (AR) causes in 2001. Of these, 34,800 were from chronic AR diseases; the remainder were from accidental and nonmedical causes such as suicide and homicide. All AR deaths are considered preventable. The number of deaths from other drugs was estimated as 17,000 in 2000. Of the emergency admissions to hospitals in 2002, more than 670,000 were for drug-related matters, of which one-third involved alcohol.

ESTIMATED ECONOMIC COSTS OF ALCOHOL ABUSE IN THE UNITED STATES, 1998

	$ millions
Treating alcohol use disorders	7,466
Medical consequences	18,872
Lost productivity due to alcohol-related illness	87,622
Lost earnings due to premature deaths	36,499
Motor vehicle crashes	15,744
Crime (including loss of productivity)	16,413
Social welfare administration	484
Total	**183,099**

Source: 10th Special Report to Congress on Alcohol and Health, June 2000

Economic costs

Researchers have found that drug treatment improves the employment and earning potential of alcohol and drug abusers. Statistics show that only 31 percent of alcohol and drug abusers were employed at the start of treatment; almost 45 percent were employed after treatment. Similar increases have been found in the number of patients seeking work (from 9 to 13 percent) following treatment. Most important, employed patients earned more after treatment, which translates into increased tax revenues and increases economic spending, which benefits all.

Health-related cost savings

It is difficult to measure cost savings in the health care arena. Researchers have demonstrated, however, that alcohol and drug treatment reduces emergency room visits, primary care visits, mental health visits, incidence of sexually transmitted diseases, and health care costs related to accidents, suicide attempts, and other alcohol- and drug-related behavior.

Sources of funding

Paying for alcohol and drug treatment has always been difficult. Private health care companies have become increasingly reluctant to pay the costs for inpatient treatment and may limit the number of days spent in outpatient treatment. Taxpayers, when asked about programs they would like to see their tax dollars fund, rarely endorse alcohol and drug treatments as an option. Government agencies that fund alcohol and drug treatment are not able to meet the need for resources and frequently experience budget and program cuts. These cuts reduce the number of treatment beds available and make seeking and receiving treatment more difficult.

During the early 1990s there began to be a sharp decline in availability of private alcohol and drug treatment. The sharpest decline has been in inpatient services, but private outpatient services have declined as well. At one time it was customary for a person with insurance to spend 14 to 28 days in the hospital when receiving treatment for alcohol or drug use. Hospital stays are now very rare and the number of local hospitals with inpatient recovery units has decreased dramatically. When insurance companies paid for 14- to 28-day stays in a hospital or private treatment setting, these units could be found in most private and public hospitals and some hospitals were founded with the express purpose of providing alcohol and drug treatment.

Since these changes in the health care market, nonprofit, grant-funded treatment programs that historically provided treatment to uninsured or underinsured patients have increased in an attempt to fill the void left by private and public hospital settings and are now the primary source of inpatient treatment services for all persons seeking treatment. This places a majority of the burden of financing these services on federal, state, and local governments.

D. E. BIRON

SEE ALSO:
Economic Costs of Addiction • Medical Care
Mortality Rates • Treatment

Treatment Centers

Addiction treatment has a number of different components that vary with the needs of the client. By adapting established methods and adopting new techniques, centers can provide specialized treatment for a wide range of clients.

In the 1950s, the American Medical Association (AMA), the national professional organization for physicians in the United States, first recognized alcohol and drug addiction as a disease. Since that time, alcohol and drug dependence has received increasing attention, and treatment efforts have steadily improved. In this article, the most common types of services and programs offered to treat alcohol and drug addiction will be reviewed. In addition, several well-known and historically important treatment centers will be discussed in detail.

Provision of services

Treatment centers can vary widely in their approach to treatment and in the services they deliver. Types of centers include hospitals, private clinics, halfway houses, therapeutic communities, and prisons. Treatment is generally provided as a residential or outpatient service for a set period of time. Several basic treatment services are typically provided, including assessment, detoxification, medication management, and individual and group psychotherapy. Before 1990 alcoholics and drug addicts were treated in separate programs, but since the two programs were merged, the majority of substance abuse programs treat both types of addicts.

Most treatment programs for substance abuse in the United States are funded federally, usually through state grants, local or county agencies, or directly by the government. Just over a third of the costs are provided by private sector sources. Federal funding comes from the substance abuse block grant, which was $2.5 billion in 2004. Despite this level of funding it is estimated that a large number of people needing treatment are unable to access services. Difficulties arise primarily from a lack of treatment places, which creates waiting lists; facilities being sited outside affected communities; a reluctance to fund lengthy inpatient treatments; eligibility for Medicaid; and the limited availability of specialist services for certain populations. The general policy toward abstinence as a goal has also restricted the availability of harm reduction and methadone maintenance programs in some states. There are also issues with federally funded treatment over the lack of choice of the type of treatment offered, integration with other services (such as welfare and housing), provision of aftercare, and how states target their funding. In contrast, people with private health insurance generally have around 90 percent of their treatment fees paid and have a wider range of treatment providers to select from than those requiring government-funded assistance. However, the relapsing nature of addiction means that even insured addicts may face restrictions on how many times they can access treatment.

Elements of a treatment center

Treatment centers are set up according to the needs of their target community. Most provide a core outpatient and day care program with provision for or access to residential treatments. The majority of clients seeking treatment for drug or alcohol problems receive services on an outpatient basis (that is, they present for meetings or appointments at the clinic but do not reside there). Inpatient services are provided for clients suffering from severe psychiatric or medical conditions. Inpatient treatment allows the client to receive continuous care in a safe environment. It is, of course, significantly more expensive than outpatient treatment and is generally brief (for example, several days to weeks). Other functional components can include aftercare, community outreach, helplines or advice centers, and research programs.

The staffing of centers reflects the services offered. These usually include medical and psychiatric physicians and nurses, counselors and psychotherapists, social and family liaison workers, occupational therapists, and support staff. Halfway houses and therapeutic communities also employ recovered addicts as staff members.

When a person is first admitted to a treatment center, a comprehensive assessment is performed.

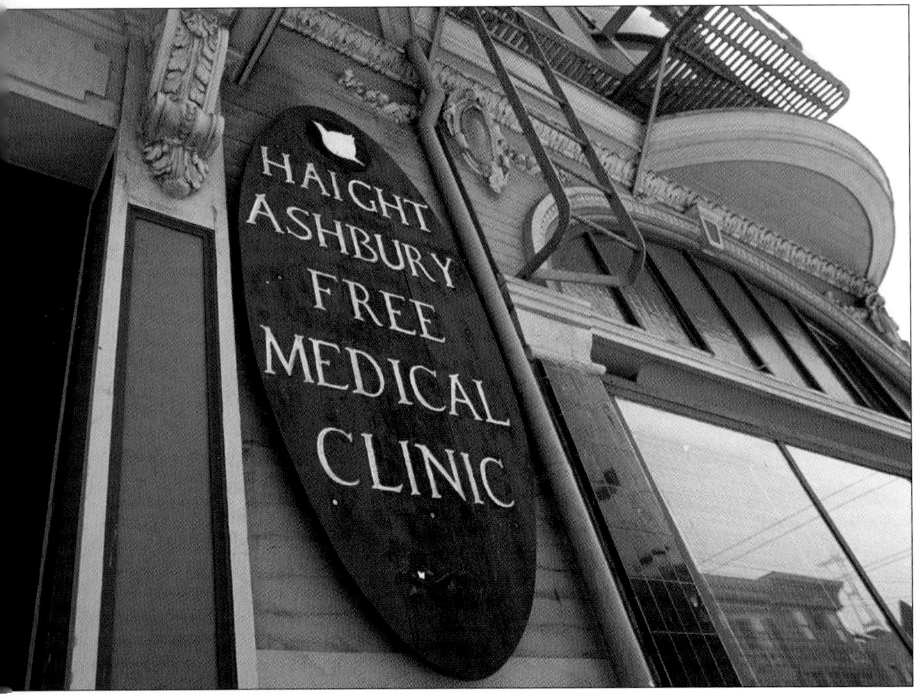

The Haight Ashbury clinic was set up in 1967 to provide free medical care to drug users in a nonjudgmental environment. Its innovative approach to drug treatment became a training ground for health workers studying addiction.

This can sometimes require several visits to accomplish, and may include, for example, a urine drug-screen test, breathalyzer test, clinical interview, and physical examination.

Using all the information gathered during the assessment phase, initial decisions are made about the type of therapeutic services that will be the most helpful to the client. An individualized treatment plan is then developed for each client. The treatment plan is determined with the input of a number of different individuals, such as the clinician who performed the initial assessment, the medical director of the clinic, the client and his or her family members, and other treatment providers. The finalized treatment plan is discussed with the client to ensure that the client understands the plan, agrees with the plan, and feels that he or she will be able to comply with the specific details. The treatment plan is then reviewed periodically to ensure that the plan is being implemented correctly, to consider whether the plan is serving the client's needs and is resulting in improvements and treatment gains, and to decide whether the treatment plan needs to be modified to benefit the client.

Medication management

Following assessment and treatment plan development, therapeutic services are implemented. In addition to assessment services, most treatment centers offer medication management and psychotherapy. Generally, the medical director of the clinic oversees the pharmacological treatment (that is, medication treatment) of clients to ensure that they receive appropriate medications and are carefully monitored for side effects. In alcohol and drug abuse centers, medications such as Antabuse, naltrexone, or methadone are sometimes provided, when appropriate, to help decrease cravings for alcohol or drugs, discourage clients from using, and to help reduce the effects of withdrawal from drugs.

The majority of clients (76 percent of men and 65 percent of women) who enter drug and alcohol community treatment centers also have co-occurring psychiatric conditions that require medical and psychological treatment. Some of the most common co-occurring disorders are anxiety disorders (phobias, post-traumatic stress disorder) and mood disorders (major depressive disorder). Thus, medications may also be prescribed to address both the substance use disorder and any other co-occurring psychiatric conditions.

Individual and group therapy

Group therapy is the most common type of treatment offered for alcohol and drug dependence. Depending on the type of treatment center, a number of different types of groups may be offered. For example, some centers offer groups for women only, for men only, for adolescents, for men with domestic violence charges, for health care professionals who are addicted to substances, for Spanish-speaking clients, or for family members of persons addicted to substances. Groups are often held on a weekly basis in outpatient settings and on a daily basis in inpatient settings.

There are a number of important advantages to group therapy. It is economical, costs the client less, and may be just as helpful as individual therapy for some clients. In addition, group therapy offers clients the opportunity to hear how other individuals in similar situations are coping with drug and alcohol problems, and to receive support from their peers. Finally, group therapy can help motivate clients, help battle against the social stigma of addiction, and remind clients with alcohol and drug problems that they are not alone.

Individual psychotherapy, which may be offered in addition to or in lieu of group therapy, also has several advantages. A key advantage is that it provides a more private, confidential setting, which can seem safer and less threatening to some clients. Some clients do not feel comfortable in group settings, particularly in the early stages of treatment. Thus, it can be helpful to start a client in individual therapy when he or she first enters treatment, and then work up to joining group therapy. Finally, individual therapy also has the advantage of being able to address and concentrate on one person's issues rather than many persons', as is the case in group therapy, and it provides a more individualized pace.

Examples of treatment centers

The Betty Ford Center. The Betty Ford Center (BFC) was cofounded by former first lady Betty Ford, wife of former U.S. president Gerald Ford. Prior to establishing the BFC, Betty Ford completed her own treatment for alcohol addiction. It was during her treatment that she realized the need for more specialized addiction services. Ford and ambassador Leonard Firestone cofounded the nonprofit BFC in California. BFC treats men and women, and offers inpatient services, residential day treatment, and outpatient treatment.

In the inpatient treatment program, clients live in one of the halls on the BFC campus. Ongoing medical and psychological problems associated with early recovery and abstinence are targeted in the inpatient treatment program. In the residential day treatment program, clients live in housing that is off-campus, but they have assigned roommates and participate in daily activities at BFC. Typically, meetings and groups also take place on the weekends. In the outpatient treatment program, clients participate in daily meetings but live and work outside the center.

When clients first enter treatment at BFC, they receive detoxification, if necessary, and undergo further assessment, which is used to develop their individualized treatment plans. BFC offers several specialized programs addressing, for example, spirituality, children and family issues, and professional education. Treatment at BFC is based on the twelve-step philosophy, which is also the basis of Alcoholics Anonymous, a national, peer-led, outpatient organization. The twelve-step philosophy views spirituality as a basis for recovery from addiction. To this end, the BFC has a spiritual care program designed to assess and incorporate each individual's spiritual path into the treatment plan. Each client's spiritual concerns (for example, the meaning and purpose of his or her life) are identified and addressed during treatment.

The BFC emphasizes that numerous individuals are affected when a person is dependent on alcohol or drugs. They offer a four-day children's program for children aged 7 to 12 who have a family member with alcohol or drug dependence. During the program, children are taught about alcohol and drug dependency and they learn a variety of coping skills such as problem-solving skills and self-care activities. Parents are invited to participate during the latter part of the program. The BFC also offers a five-day family program to help support and educate adult family members.

Once a client has completed the primary treatment at BFC, plans for continuing or aftercare treatment are made. This need reflects the long-term treatment that is often necessary to fully recover from alcohol and drug addiction. Aftercare at BFC may include, for example, scheduled telephone contacts or local weekend retreats. The weekend retreats are held several times a year and involve workshops, lectures, and small-group activities.

Finally, a professional education training program is offered for treatment care providers. This program is designed to help treatment providers increase

Betty Ford set up her clinic after her own battle against addiction. A particular focus there is specialized programs for women, who often have different treatment needs than men.

awareness and understanding of alcohol and drug addiction and treatment skills.

Hazelden. Hazelden was established in Minnesota in the late 1940s by Austin Ripley. Ripley initially sought to establish a center for priests with alcohol problems, but this idea was expanded to include a broader client base. Since it first opened, Hazelden has expanded geographically, and additional treatment centers are now located in Florida, New York, and Illinois. Similar to the BFC, Hazelden was founded on the twelve-step philosophy. It has since incorporated other, multidisciplinary treatment approaches (spirituality, meditation, family) but maintains a twelve-step philosophy foundation.

Treatment at Hazelden begins with a diagnostic assessment and evaluation. For a comprehensive evaluation, individuals may come to Hazelden and stay for several days, during which time they complete a number of assessments (called a "battery" of assessments). Hazelden, like most treatment centers, promotes a goal of abstinence from all substances. They approach treatment in a holistic way, addressing issues related to the mind, body, and spirit. To accomplish this task, they have staff members with medical and counseling backgrounds, as well as those with expertise in fitness, spiritual care, and recreation.

Hazelden offers treatment for family members through its Hazelden Center for Youth and Families. A four-day parent program is designed to help support and educate parents and caregivers who have children or who are taking care of a young adult with an addiction. The program helps parents understand addiction, the effects of alcohol and drugs on the child's development, and new techniques for parenting children with addiction problems.

Finally, Hazelden offers a number of other specialty programs including, for example, a center for women's recovery and a meditation center. In addition, Hazelden has a research center, which monitors new advances in treatment outcome research so that these can be incorporated into the services being offered.

Haight Ashbury Free Clinics. The Haight Ashbury Free Clinics (HAFC) were founded in California in 1967 by David Smith. An initial goal of the HAFC was to provide free health care services to the drug-using counterculture community of San Francisco. Today, HAFC offers a number of programs designed to help treat addiction and associated problems. For example, the Oshun Center was developed by the HAFC in 1999. It is a 24-hour, 7-day-a-week drop-in center for women and their families. The services provided by the Oshun Center target substance abuse and relationship problems, such as domestic violence or childhood trauma, that often co-occur with substance abuse. Group and individual therapy are provided, as well as family counseling, crisis intervention, and advocacy.

A culturally specific treatment program developed by the HAFC is the Western Addiction Recovery House, a 20-bed treatment program specifically for African American men. Services provided there include assessment, substance abuse education and counseling, parenting classes, and job skills training.

S. E. BACK

SEE ALSO:
Clinics • Counseling • Drop-in Centers • Family Therapy • Halfway Houses • Medical Care • State Agencies • Therapeutic Communities • Treatment • Treatment, Cost of

Tryptamines

The tryptamines are a group of compounds that includes hallucinogens as well as the neurotransmitter serotonin and the hormone melatonin. Many tryptamines occur naturally in plants and animals; others are synthetic substances.

The tryptamine structure is present in a number of known psychoactive substances, such as DMT, LSD, and the psychoactive constituents of various "magic" mushrooms and other fungi, plants, and animals. As a group, the tryptamines have much in common with another class of compounds that includes some hallucinogens, namely the phenethylamines.

Availability to the brain

The first similarity between the tryptamines and the phenethylamines is that neither parent compound has detectable psychoactive effects if swallowed or otherwise absorbed into the bloodstream. Both tryptamine and phenethylamine have unmodified amino ($-NH_2$) groups that are good targets for monoamine oxidases. Hence, these enzymes rapidly convert unmodified tryptamine into inactive compounds as the start of its elimination from the body. Furthermore, the same amino groups are significantly polar, and this property prevents tryptamine from passing through the nonpolar membrane material of the blood-brain barrier.

These "magic" Psilocybe mushrooms contain psilocin and psilocybin—both tryptamines that cause hallucinations and emotional disturbances as well as muscle relaxation and pupil dilation. The toxic and psychoactive components in mushrooms are extremely variable, and the effects from their use can be unpredictable.

Psychedelic tryptamine derivatives tend to have alkyl groups such as methyl ($-CH_3$) or ethyl ($-C_2H_5$) in place of one or both hydrogen atoms of the amino group. Such groups hinder the action of monoamine oxidase, so the compounds persist in the body for longer. Alkylation also reduces the polarity of the amino group and makes it easier for such compounds to cross the blood-brain barrier, a prerequisite for any kind of psychoactivity.

Nature uses polarity to keep serotonin inside the brain. Serotonin (5-hydroxytryptamine, or 5-HT) is more polar than tryptamine because of its hydroxy ($-OH$) group. Hence, serotonin that forms in the brain is unable to escape through the blood-brain barrier. Conversely, this effect explains why it would be futile to attempt to boost serotonin in the brain by taking serotonin food supplements or injections.

Psychoactivity and receptors

Once a tryptamine gets inside the brain, its profile of psychoactive effects depends on how it interacts with receptors there. Most of the psychoactive effects of tryptamines stem mainly from interactions with serotonin receptors. In a few cases, interaction with norepinephrine receptors causes stimulation.

The implication of serotonin receptors in the effects of tryptamines is no surprise, since serotonin itself is a tryptamine. Other members of this group of compounds have more or less similar shapes and charge distributions to those of serotonin. These are the key factors in determining how well a molecule fits a receptor and whether the molecule activates it.

The interaction with serotonin receptors can be agonistic, in which case the tryptamine binds to the receptor and activates it in the same way as serotonin does. Alternatively, antagonistic tryptamines bind to serotonin receptors but fail to activate them and also prevent serotonin from activating them as long as the tryptamine occupies the receptor site.

CHEMICAL ANALOGY TO PHENETHYLAMINE

A brief look at the tryptamine molecule reveals its similarity to phenethylamine. Knowledge of the structure also helps explain names of tryptamines.

The first point of similarity is that both tryptamine and phenethylamine consist of an amino group (–NH_2) linked by a two-carbon chain to a ring structure. The twin-ringed indole structure in tryptamine also resembles the phenyl ring by its aromatic bonding. Such bonding makes the rings flat and puts diffuse clouds of negative charge on either side of the plane of the rings.

As is the case for phenethylamine, there are various sites where nature and laboratory processes can introduce chemical groups to substitute for hydrogen atoms in tryptamine. The principal sites are labeled at right. Alkyl (hydrocarbon) groups such as methyl (–CH_3) can also replace one or two hydrogen atoms on the nitrogen at the end of the ethylamine chain. Hence, *N*,α–dimethyltryptamine has one methyl group attached to the ethylamine nitrogen and a second on the α carbon. Similarly, 5-hydroxytryptamine (serotonin) has –OH at the 5 position of the indole structure.

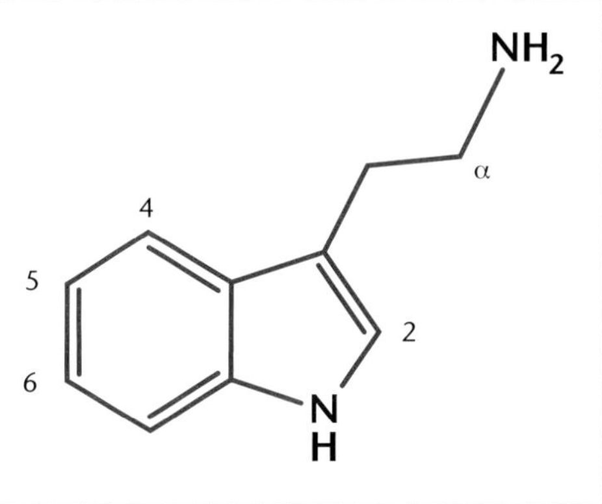

The nature of the psychoactivity of any given tryptamine depends on its balance of agonistic or antagonistic effects at different subtypes of serotonin receptors. Some tryptamines can therefore cause hallucinations, while other drugs that alter the serotonin system are not hallucinogens, such as various types of antidepressant drugs.

Studies of LSD (lysergic acid diethylamide) suggest that this and other psychoactive tryptamines might produce their hallucinogenic effects by interactions with 5-HT_2 receptors—most likely by activation of 5-HT_{2A} and 5-HT_{2C} subtypes. Stimulation of 5-HT_2 receptors has also been linked to anxiety and might provide the mechanism that can cause nightmarish bad trips on certain occasions.

Hallucinations can occur in various sensory modes, notably those of sight, sound, and touch. These hallucinations are often distortions of what is actually seen or heard, although visual hallucinations can sometimes be increased by closing the eyes to shut out visual input. The curious effect of synesthesia occurs when one form of sensory input creates a hallucination in a different sense. For example, visual hallucinations may occur when listening to music. The intensity of hallucinations depends on the type of tryptamine, the dose, and the individual.

DMT and related compounds

As previously explained, alkyl groups on the amino group of tryptamine produce compounds that are less easily destroyed by monoamine oxidase (MAO) and that pass into the brain more readily than is the case for tryptamine itself. The simplest of these compounds is *N,N*-dimethyltryptamine, or DMT.

DMT occurs in numerous plant sources and is present in *cohoba,* a traditional Amazonian snuff. The two methyl groups fail to give full protection against MAOs, and it is usually smoked to ensure fast delivery to the brain so the psychoactive effect can take place. Hallucinations can be strong when DMT is taken this way, but the experience is brief. MAOs destroy DMT at a sufficient rate to terminate the trip within 30 minutes to one hour, although the DMT user often feels the trip has lasted much longer.

An alternative means of taking DMT is in ayahuasca, a traditional brew used in South American shamanic rituals. In this case, DMT-bearing plants are mixed with others that contain natural MAO inhibitors, or MAOIs. The combined infusions produce longer-lasting hallucinations, as the MAOI protects the DMT from destruction. The same principal applies to pharmahuasca, a mixture of synthetic DMT and a pharmaceutical MAOI.

Bufotenine is simply DMT with a hydroxy (–OH) group at the 5 position of the tryptamine system. It is present in various frog venoms, but the polar hydroxy group limits its psychoactivity by hindering its entry to the brain. Test subjects injected with bufotenine often reported hot flashes, which are consistent with stimulation of serotonin receptors around the body. This is no surprise, since bufotenine is a dimethylated version of serotonin.

Bufo alvarius frogs produce 5-methoxy-DMT in their venom, which can be milked from the frog and dried before smoking. The methoxy (–OCH_3) group is much less polar than hydroxy, so this compound gets into the brain more easily than bufotenine and is a much more potent hallucinogen.

Psilocin and psilocybin are the main hallucinogens in species of "magic" mushrooms, such as *Psilocybe cubensis.* Psilocin is 4-hydroxy-DMT, and psilocybin is the phosphate ester of the same compound. Human experiments with the pure compounds reveal them to be equally potent, which suggests that the human body might convert psilocybin into psilocin. These compounds seem less prone to destruction by MAOs, since they are effective even when eaten and their effects typically last for 3 to 6 hours—much longer than DMT, for example. It is probably their greater persistence in the body that allows them to be psychoactive despite their polarity.

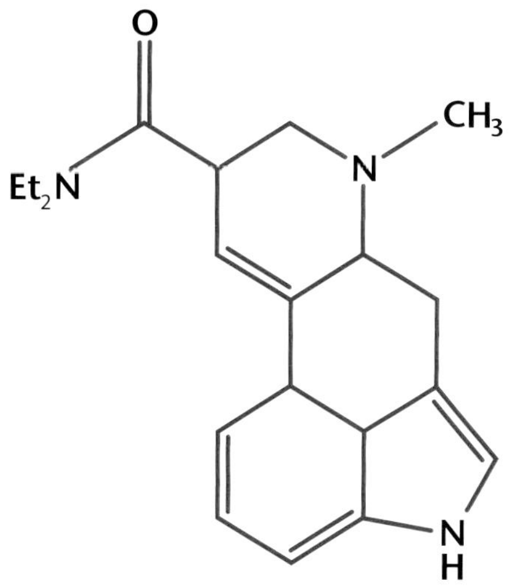

Lysergic acid diethylamine (LSD) has the amino group of tryptamine bound up in a complex four-ringed molecular structure.

Other tryptamines

Chemical synthesis allows scientists to produce a multitude of tryptamines that have never been found in nature, in addition to many that have. One chemist who has explored the possibilities of producing new psychoactive tryptamines is Alexander Shulgin. He reported the results in *Tihkal (Tryptamines I Have Known and Loved): The Continuation,* the sequel to *Pihkal,* a similar book about the synthesis and testing of phenethylamines.

Two synthetic tryptamines that have come to the attention of drug enforcement agencies in recent years are Foxy Methoxy and AMT. The chemical name of Foxy Methoxy is 5-methoxy-*N,N*-diisopropyltryptamine. The position of the methoxy group makes it a relative of the hallucinogen in *Bufo alvarius* venom, but the replacement of methyl groups with isopropyl (–$CH(CH_3)_2$) provides more protection against MAOs, so the hallucinogenic effects are stronger and last for longer than for 5-methoxy-DMT.

AMT is alpha-methyltryptamine, the tryptamine analog of amphetamine (alpha-methylphenethylamine). As with amphetamine, the methyl group at the alpha position makes this compound an analog of norepinephrine, and this gives AMT a stimulant effect in addition to its hallucinogenic effect, a combination similar to that of Ecstasy.

More distant relatives of tryptamine include lysergic acid derivatives and harmines. The former group includes the potently hallucinogenic LSD, and the latter are natural MAOIs that are often used to potentiate tryptamines and phenethylamines.

M. CLOWES

SEE ALSO:
Bufotenine • DMT • Harmine and Harmaline • LSD • MAOs and MAOIs • Phenethylamines • Psilocybin and Psilocin • Serotonin

United Nations Office on Drugs and Crime (UNODC)

At an international level, policies to combat the drug trade are handled through a directorate at the United Nations. The UNODC works with governments to reduce production, trafficking, and financial gains from drugs.

The United Nations Office on Drugs and Crime (UNODC) was established in 1997 and consists of the Drug Program and the Crime Program. Based in Vienna, UNODC relies mostly on voluntary contributions from governments for its funding and carries out its operations through 22 field offices and two liaison offices in Brussels and New York.

The Drug Program evolved from the United Nations International Drug Control Program, which was established in 1991. The aims of the Drug Program are to educate the world about the problems associated with drugs and to strengthen international action against drug production, trafficking, and drug-related crime. These aims are achieved through a variety of means such as crop monitoring, alternative development assistance, rehabilitation programs, and detection of money laundering and organized crime. In addition, UNODC's Global Assessment Program (GAP), launched in 1998, provides an authoritative source for statistics on worldwide drug use.

Programs and policies

Alternative development assistance recognizes the complex circumstances surrounding the cultivation of drug crops. Many farmers in poor countries rely on drug crops for their livelihood. Drug crops may form a substantial source of income, but farmers are vulnerable to having their crops eradicated by law enforcement officers, as well as being vulnerable to exploitation by drug cartels. The Drug Program assists communities in finding alternative means of income, such as the growing of coffee and cacao rather than coca.

The Illicit Crop Monitoring Programme (ICMP) focuses on six countries: Peru, Bolivia, Colombia, Myanmar, Laos, and Afghanistan. A variety of techniques are employed to carry out this monitoring, including analysis of satellite imagery and ground level assessments.

The Global Program Against Money Laundering (GPML) attempts to prevent organized crime from disguising their illegal profits. With changes in financial markets, such as deregulation and market integration, and the increasing speed with which financial transactions occur, monitoring laundered money has become more difficult. The GPML uses several strategies to assist in the detection of laundered money, including offering training workshops, technical assistance to developing countries, and research programs.

The Crime Program was established in 1997 and is the United Nations office responsible for crime prevention, criminal law reform, and criminal justice. Its various programs include the Global Program Against Trafficking in Human Beings and the Global Program Against Transnational Organized Crime. In recent years UNODC has recognized the importance of an integrated approach to tackling drug and crime issues. Drugs and crime are known to be interrelated, so departments within the UNODC that may once have operated separately now work closely together to enhance the effectiveness of their policies. The experience acquired by the crime program, for example, in preventing the trafficking in human beings or arms may be related to the experience of the drug program in the trafficking of drugs. Both are dealing with the illegal movement and sale of "commodities." Other issues that UNODC now emphasizes are the importance of creating drug and crime programs that recognize the need for sustainable methods of development and the importance of finding an effective balance between preventing drug abuse and enforcing laws against drugs.

P. G. THOMPSON

SEE ALSO:
Illicit Manufacturing • International Cooperation • International Drug Trade

Valium

Valium is a tranquilizing drug often used by stimulant abusers to overcome the excitatory effects of amphetamines and cocaine. Valium itself has dependence potential and can produce unpleasant withdrawal symptoms.

Valium is the trade name for diazepam. It is the most widely prescribed and thus the most well-known member of a family of drugs called benzodiazepines. At the height of its clinical use (mid-1960s through to the mid-1980s), Valium was a household word, but the name is less well recognized today because the patent is long expired and Valium has been largely replaced with generic versions of diazepam.

Diazepam is used clinically to reduce the symptoms associated with a range of anxiety disorders without producing overt sedation. Typical doses of diazepam are 6 to 30 milligrams daily in divided doses taken by mouth. With increasing dosage, sedation and sleep induction become apparent, hence its use to treat insomnia. Diazepam is also used to treat the convulsions associated with alcohol withdrawal in dependent subjects.

The sedative and hypnotic effects of diazepam and other benzodiazepines have led to their illicit use to "come down" from abuse of central nervous system stimulants, such as amphetamines and cocaine. The availability of benzodiazepines in liquid form (including syrups and capsules) has been restricted to minimize illicit intravenous use.

Although all benzodiazepines produce similar effects, they differ in their duration of action. Diazepam is classified as long acting, which means that its effects will be apparent for at least eight hours after a normal single oral dose. Common adverse effects of diazepam are slowing of reaction time, impairment of concentration, and reduced performance in carrying out skilled tasks. Subjects taking diazepam are routinely advised against driving motor vehicles or operating machinery, because the drug's adverse effects may result in hazards to themselves or others. The occasional use of diazepam to promote sleep will also result in impaired function the following day. Diazepam can also depress respiration, which may become significant in those with breathing disorders, such as bronchitis or asthma.

The most important drug interaction of diazepam is its additive effect with other drugs that suppress activity of the central nervous system. The interaction with alcohol is particularly important. Small amounts of alcohol in combination with diazepam produce sedative effects that are greater than the sum of the individual effects and can be fatal.

Tolerance and dependence have long been recognized as a problem when benzodiazepines are taken in large doses for long periods of time. Diazepam, with its long half-life and moderate potency, has a moderate dependence potential. Drug withdrawal in dependent individuals results in a distinct withdrawal syndrome, the symptoms of which are clearly distinct from preexisting medical conditions. Withdrawal symptoms may take up to two weeks to develop and may persist for up to six months.

R. W. HORTON

KEY FACTS

Classification

Schedule IV (USA), Schedule IV (Canada), Class C (UK), Schedule IV (INCB). Sedative and anxiolytic.

Street names

Downers, tranks, V

Short-term effects

Relaxation, intoxication, mild drowsiness, slurred speech, confusion, lack of coordination

Long-term effects

Physical and psychological dependence, confusion in elderly patients. Withdrawal symptoms include tremor, cramps, vomiting, insomnia, and sweating.

SEE ALSO:
Benzodiazepines • Librium • Rohypnol • Sedatives and Hypnotics • Tolerance • Withdrawal

Vicodin

Vicodin is a pain reliever used as an analgesic and cough suppressant. Vicodin tablets are composed of hydrocodone, an opioid analgesic, and acetaminophen, a nonopioid analgesic commonly marketed as Tylenol.

Vicodin, a combination of hydrocodone and acetaminophen, is an effective painkiller because these drugs have different mechanisms of action in the body. Hydrocodone is a synthetic narcotic analgesic that is structurally related to morphine, a natural component of the poppy plant, *Papaver somniferum*. The pharmacological effects of hydrocodone include analgesia, respiratory depression, constricted pupils, reduced gastrointestinal motility, and euphoria. Chronic use or abuse of this class of drugs leads to tolerance (decreased responsiveness to the same dose of a drug over time) and physical dependence (the need to continue to take the drug in order to prevent the development of withdrawal symptoms). Withdrawal from this drug may include some or all of the following symptoms: mydriasis (dilation of the pupils), irritability, insomnia, vomiting, weight loss, dehydration, diarrhea, increased heart rate, and abdominal pain. Morphine and morphinelike drugs can cross the placenta; therefore, abuse of these drugs during pregnancy can produce neonatal dependence. Drugs from this class exert their effects through interaction with different classes of opioid receptors in the spinal cord and brain. The effects of hydrocodone last 4 to 6 hours, and overdose can be treated by intravenous infusion of the antagonist naloxone. Hydrocodone should not be given to alcoholics or patients suffering from respiratory depression.

Acetaminophen is a common household analgesic that is taken to relieve mild pain and fever. Its effects are similar to aspirin and ibuprofen. This drug is safe provided that the recommended dosage is not exceeded. In overdose, acetaminophen is dangerous, as it can cause severe liver and kidney damage. The initial sign of overdose is abdominal pain, though this may not occur until 24 to 48 hours after ingestion and tends to worsen within 72 to 96 hours. Gastric lavage (neutralizing the overdose with charcoal) may be necessary. Liver damage may be exacerbated by consumption of alcohol.

Of the 4 million Americans who admitted that they abused drugs in 2001, 65 percent reported misuse of prescription pain relievers. Of these, Vicodin is one of the most commonly abused combination analgesics. In 2002, 10 percent of twelfth grade students in the United States reported using Vicodin for illicit purposes. Vicodin has gained notoriety in recent years. It has become a common drug of abuse among celebrities, as it produces the same effects as drugs such as heroin but does not yet have the same social stigma. Vicodin should not be taken in combination with alcohol, antihistamines, barbiturates, benzodiazepines, or general anesthetics, all of which cause drowsiness and may impair respiration. Vicodin has been reported to cause anxiety or fear in patients and to precipitate panic attacks in predisposed patients.

J. G. Newell, S. M. J. Dunn

KEY FACTS

Classification
Schedule II (USA), Schedule I (Canada), Class A (UK), Schedule I (INCB). Opioid.

Street names
Vike, Watson-387 (name on generic tablet). Trade names: Hycodan, Lorcet, Lortab, Tylox.

Short-term effects
Euphoria, nausea, vomiting, drowsiness, confusion, and constipation

Long-term effects
Respiratory depression, liver damage, dependence

SEE ALSO:
Morphine • Narcotic Drugs • Opiates and Opioids • Prescription Drugs

Violence

Many people associate drug or alcohol use with aggressive or violent behavior. Research into other cultures' experiences of substance use suggests that such reactions may have more to do with expectations than physiological effects.

There is a common assumption that drugs and alcohol make people violent. Images of crack-crazed murderers and reports of alcohol-fueled violence are common in the mass media. That certain drugs, and alcohol in particular, make people violent is arguably a well-ingrained belief in modern Western societies. Indeed, when various statistics relating to the occurrence of violent events and alcohol and other drugs are examined, there are very strong statistical correlations between the two; that is, of those convicted of violent crimes, a high proportion will have evidence of alcohol or other drugs in their bodies and will have had so at the time of the crime. Two things commonly appearing in the same place, however, is not proof of one causing the other. Although alcohol and other drugs may be highly correlated with violent crime, there is a great deal of cross-cultural and other evidence that suggests that alcohol and other drugs do not cause such outcomes, and that violence occurs for other reasons.

There is no doubt that substance use and violence are highly correlated. Statistics differ, but research in 1997 estimated that up to 86 percent of homicide offenders, 37 percent of assault offenders, 60 percent of sexual offenders, and 57 percent of male-on-female marital violence offenders were under the influence of alcohol when the offense was committed. Some research evidence points toward a significant relationship between the use of drugs such as crack cocaine, amphetamines, and barbiturates, but figures for these and other substances are in fact fewer and far less reliable. With this in mind, this article will refer mainly to alcohol, as it is the substance most linked with causing violence and is itself a drug.

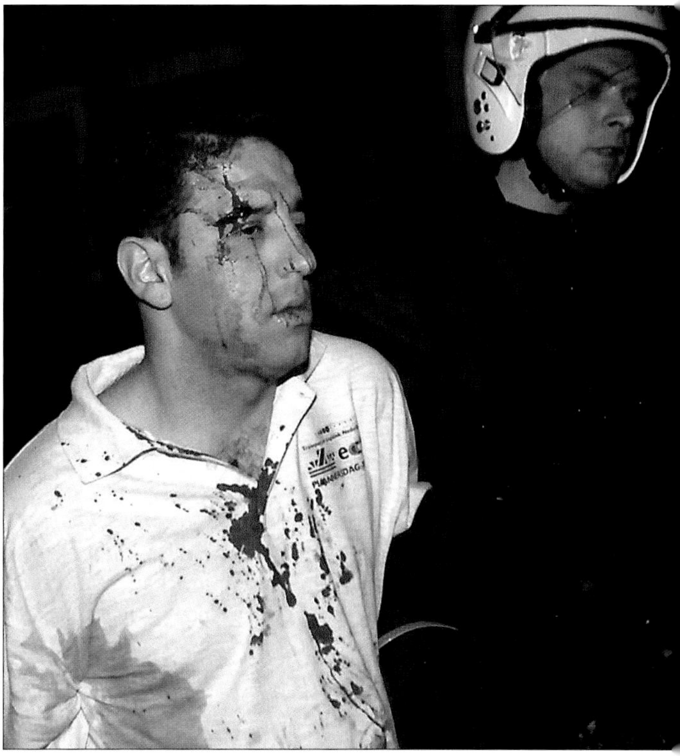

Images of European soccer hooligans seeking violent confrontation after drinking large amounts of alcohol would seem to support the assertion that alcohol promotes aggression. However, the lack of similar behavior at other sports events suggests that violence is an expectation of the participants rather than a symptom of alcohol's effects.

Cross-cultural evidence

Alcohol has fairly predictable physiological effects, depending on how much is consumed, on certain motor functions. It slows reactions and affects coordination, for example. Researchers find, however, when they consider the effects of drinking in different societies that alcohol does not have uniform or predictable effects on behavior.

In societies such as the United States, Australia, and the United Kingdom, alcohol use is strongly linked to aggressive, violent, and antisocial behavior. In many parts of South America and the Mediterranean, drinking is far less associated with such behaviors and in many cases is actually associated with peaceful and nonviolent behavior—despite, in some cases, extreme levels of intoxication.

The Camba of Bolivia in South America is one such group in which most of the behaviors associated with drinking in Western industrial societies are significantly absent. Despite drinking locally produced alcohol that, in terms of strength (the equivalent of 178 U.S. proof), is far more powerful than anything available in most other societies, and despite drinking in a type of ritualized binge that lasts until the alcohol runs out or participants fall asleep or unconscious, aggression or violence is not an outcome. One anthropologist who has spent nearly 50 years researching the Camba and their drinking describes it thus: "It was extremely rare that any Camba, drunk or sober, should show any aggression, whether verbal, physical, sexually suggestive, threatening, or of any other sort. No one acted particularly daring after drinking nor did they become unusually amicable or boisterous."

Although they are culturally distinct from the Camba, the Aritma in northern Colombia show similar characteristics, and research indicates that "regardless of the occasion and regardless of the degree of intoxication that is achieved 'the rigid mask of seriousness' remains firmly in place." Cross-cultural research of this kind not only demonstrates that alcohol, even when consumed to excess (often to an excess far greater than in the West), not only does not necessarily produce the expected stereotyped behavior but may in fact produce little variation in behavior from the social norm. Different relationships to alcohol and the evidence that it causes violence only in some cultures, not in others, may relate to the expectations of the kinds of behavior that surround it in different societies.

Expectation

That expectation has a great deal to do with drug effects is a well-established fact. Numerous experiments with alcohol, various drugs, and even placebos (substances that have no chemical effects but the user thinks they do) have demonstrated that researchers can manipulate the behavior (to varying degrees) of subjects involved in various ways. Thus, in some experiments, people have been fooled into believing that the drugs they have taken will increase aggressive or unusual behavior (although they do not), and such behavior often then emerges in the experimental subjects. In other experiments, people have been told they are taking a particular drug, and many then act according to what they think the drug's effects should be (for example, to make them feel drowsy or sleepy), even though the drug given does not produce these effects. In extreme cases people have been recorded as having gotten high on drugs that had no active drug present at all. Clearly, expectations of what a drug does to a person appear to be a powerful factor in what a user then experiences and how he or she behaves under the influence of a substance, or even a placebo. It can therefore be imagined that for any substance for which there is a strongly ingrained cultural belief in its link to aggression and violence, it will be difficult to separate out violence that results from belief from violence that results from the substance itself.

It is also worth referring to the admittedly scant experimental literature that has shown that, depending on which beverage is tested, differential results will occur. Thus, subjects given spirits (such as whiskey, gin, or vodka) will tend to display increased aggression under experimental conditions, whereas those given wine do not. Clearly such differences, given that the active ingredient (alcohol) is the same in each case, suggest that there are different expectations and expectational roles associated with different drugs, and that these expectations may result in increased aggression, as opposed to a simple chemical-induced behavior.

Situational violence (coupled with expectation)

Understanding the nature of an alcohol-fueled violent episode is important in further understanding the cross-cultural differences that can be observed. The picture of someone "out of control" is common. The alcohol is thought to have either dismantled the normal inhibitory mechanisms that stop us all from being violent all the time or to have "taken over" the individual. The idea that the alcohol (or a drug) is to blame and that there was nothing (once drunk) the drunken person could do about it is not uncommon. Such a perspective, however, is undermined by evidence that shows that drunken acts of violence, in which people are seemingly out of control, can be suddenly moderated when the assailant is confronted with choices about ending his or her violent behavior—suggesting flaws in the idea that a person is "taken over" by the substance involved. Men and women who commit acts of domestic violence often stop if interrupted, and also strategically injure their partners in places difficult for others to see—again hardly the act of uncontrolled violence. The fact that the violence appears to have very particular limits, within which it is effectively constrained, suggests that the degree of "disinhibition" experienced is influenced by the context (and the considered norms of drunken behavior) in which the drunken violence takes place. Consistent with this position, some of the more experimentally based research has shown that providing alcohol-intoxicated individuals with the choice of responding to aggression in a nonaggressive way (in which doing so does not involve losing face) in a potentially violent situation will often lead to a nonaggressive response, or a lessened one.

Disinhibition as "time out"

There is no doubt that many people experience alcohol- or drug-related behaviors as less inhibited, but, as has been shown, the idea that disinhibition occurs as a predictable effect of alcohol or other substance use is not supported by the cross-cultural literature. There are, however, good explanatory devices for understanding both how disinhibition occurs and its common association with alcohol or substance use. Two that are of importance are "time out" and ritual.

Study of drug use in various tribal and other groups has shown that highly ritualized approaches to drug use—in which individuals or groups partake in a range of preparations before drug use, carry out consistent behaviors (clothing, dance, chanting, and so on), and have a common idea of the visions they would like to see or the journey they would like to travel when under the influence of drugs—can produce predictable, desired outcomes (drug effects). This suggests that even with powerful hallucinatory drugs, the effects can be managed and brought under social control. The ritual is a powerful technique in managing both the drug-using environment and the required drug effect. In the West, ritualized drug use is much more muted but still present. Although the ritual surrounding alcohol is varied, encouragement of drinking is commonplace. Not only do many people want to drink, many want to do so with others, and intoxication (to varying degrees) is a common aim. Indeed, it could be argued that the overwhelming objective of alcohol (and much drug) consumption is to relax or "let go." Whether the aim is relaxation or intoxication, alcohol is being used to aid the individual to take time out from the stresses and strains of normal life. In other words, not only is alcohol used to aid relaxation, but the user is self-consciously aiming at letting go. Many of the things that constrain people are the norms and values of the society and culture in which they are immersed. Taking "time out" thus also means letting go of many of those inhibiting emotional and cultural behavioral constraints (be polite, do not talk too loud, stay in control). In such circumstances, ritual may be said to include the preparation of getting dressed up to go out, playing music to set the mood and relax, and talking to friends prior to the event. In other words, even before the first drink is consumed, the individual expects to become relatively disinhibited and partakes in rituals to aid the success of that expectation. When this expectation is combined with the belief that alcohol and other drugs chemically aid this process, while at the same time the physical experience of the substance begins to take effect (speech slurring, and so on), it can be seen how the two become inextricably associated to the point that one is believed to cause the other, at least in Western society.

Attribution of drug effects in historical perspective

Historically, different substances, including marijuana, tobacco, opium, heroin, cocaine, and others, have been attributed with the power to turn otherwise normal people into immoral savages, stripped of the ability to think reasonably and made to act in unreasonable ways, often with violent outcomes. Many of these attributions, however, are now discredited: marijuana is no longer demonized as likely to drive a person to insane violence (as was propagated in the United States in the 1940s and 1950s) and powder cocaine is no longer associated with giving men the power to withstand small caliber bullets or incite the rape of women (although nearly identical beliefs were subsequently transposed onto PCP). At different points in history or in different geographical locations, many substances have been believed to induce a range of behaviors—many of which are contradictory. Marijuana, for example, is now seen as a mellowing drug and in some research is associated with less aggressiveness than in nondrug users, while previously it was said to induce uncontrolled rage.

Many who have studied the history of drug control consistently point to the underlying prejudice or racism that accompanies and contributes to the perception of certain drugs. Although many middle-class white people used cocaine at the end of the nineteenth century, it was not considered to be particularly problematic for them. Where "cocainism," as it was known, was problematic was among prostitutes, gamblers, and other "dope-fiends" in the underworld, for cocaine was said to destroy the moral senses, turning women into prostitutes, boys into thieves, and men into hardened killers.

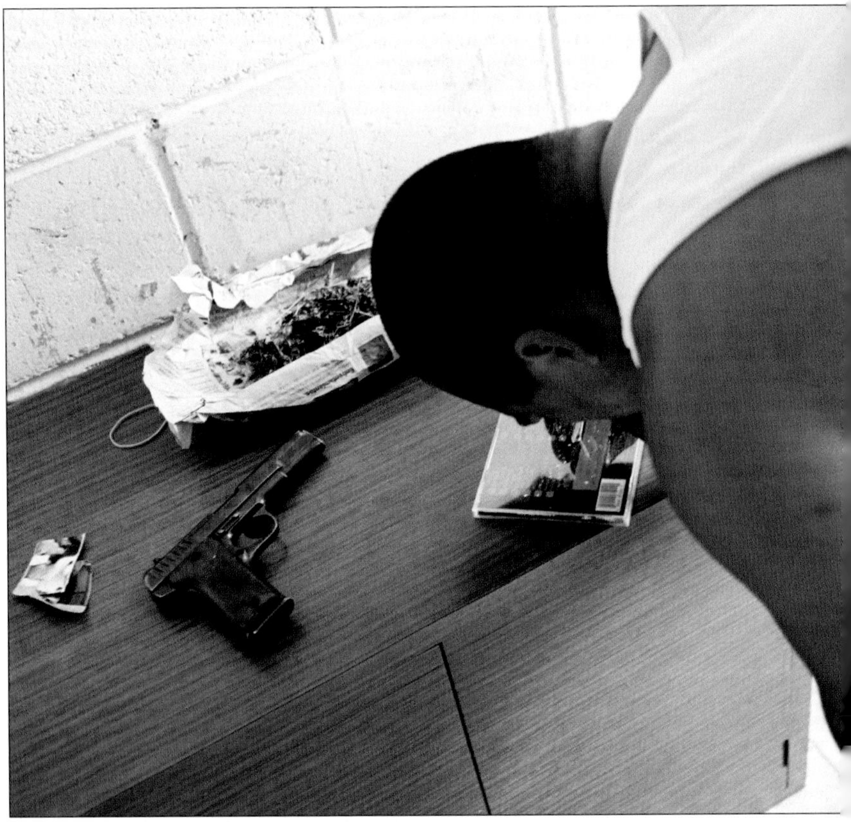

Much of the actual violence associated with drug use relates to the trade in drugs. Gangs and dealers are more likely to resort to extreme measures to protect their territory, particularly if they already have a history of violent behavior.

Others have related how the Chinese in the United States and United Kingdom were associated with immoral drug-related behavior as a consequence of their use of opium, while similar drug use by white people shouldered little criticism. Thus, the attribution to particular drugs of powerful destructive effects when used by particular groups (often immigrants, nonwhite groups, or others seen as deviant) is a common but flawed reaction to drug use. These fantasies, it has been argued, in fact characterized popular (usually white) fears, and provided one more reason for the repression of the groups (blacks, Chinese, Chicanos, and so on) upon which negative attention was already focused.

At least in part, these preexisting fears and anxieties about populations that were in some way different were given greater respectability if those fears were attributed to the use of drugs particular to them. These early attributions of drug effects—having the power to rob the individual of moral sensibilities—not only became prominent toward the end of the nineteenth century but have proved difficult to shift, even in changed circumstances.

Real drug-related violence

Statistics that report drug-related violence relate for the most part not to taking drugs but to the distribution of illegal drugs—to drug dealing and trafficking. The relationship with violence comes about as a result of the illicit nature of the commodity involved, the high level of demand, and the enormous sums of money the trade in drugs produces. It is important to note, however, that numerous factors also affect the levels of violence that do or do not attach themselves to the drug trade at any one moment in time. In the United States, for example, a great deal of drug trading has been managed by street gangs, and the violence that was often already endemic between gangs has been integrated into their drug distribution activities. In other countries or locations, this is not necessarily the case. While the level of violence does to some significant degree appear to depend on who is involved, that is, the degree to which people with a preexisting violent disposition decide to trade in drugs rather than some other form of violent crime, it also does appear to reflect the maturity of the market and how it operates. Emerging, immature markets, for example, with the early jousting for trade and the lack of working rules, appear more likely to be highly volatile than those that have matured or that are in decline. Likewise, open markets, where neither customers nor sellers are trusted and where there is minimal discretion about buyers and sellers, appear to be more fractious than closed markets, where access to the seller is more controlled and where an element of trust has been built up on both sides. Nonetheless, violence appears to be an increasing phenomenon in the trading of drugs, and the combination of heavy sentencing and policing and the possibility of making large profits appear to increase its likelihood. Real drug-related violence thus appears to have more to do with black market trading structures and the way it is policed than with the effects of the drugs themselves.

Predisposition to violence

Although the research is far from comprehensive, there appears to be more evidence to suggest that those committing drug-related violent crimes were already of a violent disposition before they were drug users or already had violent criminal records that preceded drug use. Indeed, some cross-cultural research on PCP (phencyclidine) use—a drug commonly associated with violence in the United States—showed that in those using groups with no history or tendency for aggression or violence, none was produced as a result of PCP use. However, in the groups that did present greater levels of aggression and violence, these were normal mechanisms for resolving conflict in those groups. Some research also suggests that certain individuals with a predisposition to aggression and violence may be more likely to choose substances they believe will enhance or complement that predisposition. Examples of this may include the use of alcohol by some in Western societies to bolster courage before taking part in a frightening activity, the use of opium before battle by warriors in ancient India, or the use of drugs such as PCP by violent criminals who believe the drug will imbue them with greater strength, pain resistance, and sufficient aggression to fulfill their self-conceived role.

Conclusion

While the belief that many substances—alcohol in particular—cause people to be aggressive and violent is widespread and popularly held, it is a view that is problematic in a number of significant ways. The cross-cultural evidence suggests that neither disinhibition, aggression, nor violence is a necessary or predictable outcome of alcohol or drug use, and that expectations about what the drug does, along with the context in which use takes place, are highly important factors. Coupled with the knowledge that much drug-related violence is in fact related to drug markets and that many of those with drug-related criminal histories also had predrug-use convictions for violence, evidence emerges that the relationship of chemical substances to violence is not a simple one. A historical understanding of the development of drug controls demonstrates that attributions of violence to some drugs have their roots not in an understanding of the drugs in question but in fears of various outsider groups. One overriding consequence, however, of the Western cultural belief that alcohol disinhibits or makes people violent is that this expectation will result in just that. Once the individual's expectations are fulfilled, then the belief is confirmed. Confirmation of the belief reinforces the belief, and so on. So, while it appears that it is unlikely that alcohol and other drugs chemically produce this disinhibited state, the overwhelming association of drugs and violence in Western societies effectively confirms their connection in practical terms.

R. COOMBER

SEE ALSO:
Binge Drinking • Crime and Drugs • Cultural Attitudes • Ethanol • Gangs • History of Drug Use • Homicide • Medical Care • Mortality Rates • Organized Crime • PCP • Placebos

Vulnerability

It is hard to say exactly what makes an adolescent vulnerable to the influence of drugs. Researchers are discovering that a wide mix of biological, sociological, and enviromental factors may all play a part in the addiction process.

Why can some people use drugs or alcohol recreationally, while others develop serious problems? Can we predict which young people are at most risk of developing drug- or alcohol-related disorders? These questions concerning vulnerability or susceptibility to substance abuse and addiction have been the focus of significant research for several decades. Traditionally, research on vulnerability has focused on identifying risk factors that increase the probability of developing a substance use problem. More recently, however, there has been growing interest in the role of protective factors, which reduce vulnerability to substance use disorders (SUD). However, it is important to realize that vulnerability is not simply the culmination of risk and protective factors, as there are many elements that potentially contribute to the development of SUD (including genes and proteins, neuronal circuits, behavior, and social networks). To this end, researchers have now identified an array of biopsychosocial factors that are all associated with vulnerability to SUD.

Children may be drawn into addiction by drug-using friends. Peer influence is one of the strongest factors in starting and maintaining drug use.

Genetic and neurobiological vulnerabilities

Epidemiological studies have demonstrated that young people with a family history of SUD are more vulnerable than peers without a family history to developing later substance abuse and addiction. The evidence appears strongest for alcoholism, although other SUDs also appear to have a heritable component. While researchers believe that there are specific sets of genes that directly contribute to SUD, inheritable behavioral, personality, and temperament traits are also associated with an increased risk of SUD (for example, antisocial personality disorder). The role of genetic factors has been further explored using animal models. These studies have shown that certain genes are responsible for an animal's preference for different drugs, as well as their pattern of use. For example, by manipulating certain genes using "knockout techniques," in which certain genes are removed from the genome of the animal, researchers have been able to make some animals compulsively self-administer drugs, while reducing use in others. As the functional significance of gene polymorphisms (variation in DNA structure) in behavior and their differential expression in addicted versus nonaddicted individuals is investigated more fully, we will better understand which genes are involved in vulnerability to substance abuse and addiction, and how they interact with neurobiology and behavior.

Another interesting area of neurobiological vulnerability is that of brain structure and function. We now know that a tremendous amount of structural and functional (cognitive and emotional) brain development takes place during the teenage years. In addition, animal studies have shown that the adolescent brain is more vulnerable to the neurotoxic effects of alcohol, and perhaps other drugs, than in adulthood. Studies in humans have shown that certain areas of the brain, particularly those in the frontal cortex (the areas involved in aspects of self-regulation, planning, complex attentional skills, impulse control) are still maturing during adolescence, and may be particularly susceptible to the long-term effects of alcohol and drugs. An arrest or disruption to the maturation of these brain regions and functions may in turn contribute to young people experiencing difficulties in regulating or ceasing substance use (as a result of problems with planning, attention, impulse control), particularly if they are already vulnerable (have a chronic mental illness, for example, or a strong family history of substance abuse). Studies investigating brain activity in children with a family history of alcoholism show abnormal electroencephalographic (EEG) activity, suggesting that brain processes are altered in at-risk individuals, although the significance of these results are yet to be fully determined. Finally, the rate and timing of puberty have also been implicated in SUD (through its influence on brain and social development), in which early puberty in girls and delayed puberty in boys are also identified as risk factors.

Cognitive and behavioral vulnerabilities

School-related behavioral and academic problems are also a major risk factor for SUD, with poor academic achievement, discipline problems, truancy, and school dropout all identified as risk factors. Young people with below average levels of intellectual functioning, or with language or other learning disorders, are also at risk. In fact, young people with a current SUD or who are at high risk of developing SUD have been found to have specific neuropsychological deficits on formal testing. These deficits in executive cognitive functioning (ECF) include tests of problem solving, attention, memory, and hypothesis generation. Lower ECF capacity is also a risk factor for SUD through its association with other behavioral risk factors, such as impulsive, aggressive, or antisocial behavior.

In terms of other behavioral risk factors, young people who have behavioral problems early (for example, a difficult temperament in infancy or oppositional, aggressive, or impulsive behaviors in childhood) are at increased risk of developing SUD, especially males. Childhood diagnoses of oppositional defiant disorder (ODD), conduct disorder (CD), and attention deficit hyperactivity disorder (ADHD) are also well-established risk factors for youth SUD, as is early use of substances. A history of childhood bereavement or major illness, teen pregnancy, or childhood sexual, emotional, or physical abuse are also significant risk factors. In addition, a number of mental health disorders are also associated with predisposition to problematic substance use. Disorders such as depression, anxiety, schizophrenia, bipolar disorder, and obsessive-compulsive disorder have high rates of comorbid substance use, although the mechanisms underlying this increased vulnerability are complex and multifaceted.

Emotional and personality vulnerabilities

A number of personality traits have also been identified as risk factors for SUD, including negative affectivity/neuroticism (NA/N) and disinhibition/impulsivity (DIS/IMP). NA/N is characterized by a general tendency to experience life negatively and a difficulty in controlling one's mood, while DIS/IMP is associated with impulsivity, irresponsibility, risk taking, and sensation seeking. There is growing evidence to suggest that adolescent substance misuse and SUD result either from an attempt to reduce negative affectivity (arising from an individual's general disposition to experience negative mood states or being less tolerant to stressful life events, that is, NA/N) or as a result of an individual's disinhibited behavior or impulsivity. Furthermore, at-risk individuals high in DIS/IMP have also been found to experience significant reductions in stress when intoxicated, suggesting they may also be more vulnerable to stress-induced drinking and drug use.

Finally, low self-esteem is also commonly cited as a risk factor for SUD, even though there is little research evidence to support such an association. However, self-esteem is a difficult construct to study, and it is likely that both low self-esteem and substance abuse are linked through other risk factors. For example, several factors related to how individuals see themselves (that is, their self-concept) are also important risk factors for SUD. These include self-efficacy (how confident you are that you will succeed at a specific task), self-belief (how optimistic or pessimistic you are about yourself and the future), self-control (for example, how you control any aggressive tendencies) and social confidence (how you believe you get along with others and whether you make friends easily).

Environmental vulnerabilities

Understanding SUD also requires a consideration of factors within the individual's environment, and how they interact with more individually specific risk factors as mentioned above.

In recent years, there has been increased recognition of the role of family environmental factors in risk for SUD. Parental substance use and parental beliefs and attitudes that are conducive to substance use are important risk factors for SUD in young people. Twin and adoptive studies have also indicated that parental divorce, death, or mental illness also increase the risk of SUD in young people. However, while parental characteristics are important, parenting style and other factors in the family environment may have a bigger impact on subsequent SUD. Such factors include inconsistent child-rearing practices, communicating in a negative style, and a lack of emotional support within the family. A lack of parental supervision and monitoring are particularly important risk factors for SUD. Finally, how families use substances are important in determining adolescent expectations and patterns of use, as overt parental use may teach children that alcohol or drug use is an appropriate means of coping with adversity.

Participation in family and social events, such as going to church, is a protective factor against drug use. Strong family bonds help increase the resiliency of adolescents to say no to drugs.

Peer factors

Peer variables have universally been identified as the single factor most likely to predict adolescent substance misuse. Young people are usually introduced to substances by their peers, and peer substance use has consistently been identified as the most robust predictor of SUD. Other peer variables, including positive peer attitudes toward substance use, peer pressure or encouragement to use, and low sanctions against using are also important. Affiliation with a deviant peer group also contributes to continued substance use, as individuals fail to develop attitudes and values consistent with society at large. However, it is difficult to determine whether the association between peer variables and risk of SUD is related to peer influences to use or a preference for drug-using peers. Nevertheless, there is clear evidence of the importance of peer variables in youth SUD, as they are not only the most potent predictor of SUD but also mediate the influence of other individual and environmental risk factors.

Neighborhood factors

Factors in the neighborhood environment of young people, including poverty, high crime rates, homelessness, and low numbers of religious and cultural institutions have also been found to influence substance use outcomes. However, these factors do not invariably result in SUD among young people in these environments, as many of these young people do not develop SUD. As such, it is likely that neighborhood variables influence youth SUD through their interaction with other factors, such as peer, family, and individual risk factors (for example, higher number of drug-using peers, limited youth-specific social venues, parental mental illness, poor academic performance, and easier access to illegal substances in socioeconomically deprived regions).

Cultural and sociopolitical factors

Cultural factors also have an important role in vulnerability to SUD. Cultural and subcultural attitudes toward specific substances, appropriate situations in which to use, and even acceptability of intoxication have been noted to be important risk factors. For example, in Jewish culture, where alcohol is introduced early in a ritualized fashion and drunkenness is frowned upon, community rates of alcohol dependence are low. In contrast, in Irish communities, where alcohol is a central feature of social interaction, rates of alcoholism are significantly higher. This sharing of cultural norms may explain why ethnicity has been found to be a powerful predictor of substance misuse.

Other subcultures that may affect rates of substance abuse include deviant youth groups and even some amateur sports clubs. In these latter settings, heavy alcohol use may be encouraged by the shared ideal that alcohol intake is a sign of masculinity. Certain occupations are also more vulnerable to substance abuse, largely as a result of increased accessibility and availability, such as alcoholism among bar owners or abuse of anesthetic gases among dentists and anesthetists. Similarly, availability (including access and price) affects the pattern and level of alcohol and drug use in the wider community. Other institutional factors that affect community substance use include legislation, advertising, and regulation of alcohol or drug access and supply. For example, there are lower levels of community smoking in industrialized nations compared with developing countries following the introduction of smoking bans in the workplace and social venues, higher taxes on tobacco, limited advertising, and enforced legislation that prevents the sale of cigarettes to adolescents.

Protective factors

Since the 1990s there has been growing interest in the identification of protective factors that reduce vulnerability to SUD. However, these variables are not simply the opposite of risk factors; they also act to increase the resiliency of young people. Factors associated with lowered risk of substance use have most commonly been identified in the family environment of young people. Family bonding, including strong parental support and involvement, have most consistently been identified as a protective factor for youth SUD. Parental monitoring and supervision have also been identified as important protective factors, and there is some evidence that involvement with spiritual or religious organizations is also protective. More recently, a large body of work has identified "connectedness," or a strong sense of connection and closeness to parents, family, or other adults from school or other community-based institutions, as a critical protective factor for youth SUD.

While neurobiological and genetic protective factors are yet to be fully determined, there are examples of physiological protective factors within distinct ethnic populations. For example, a particular variant of aldehyde dehydrogenase (an enzyme involved in the metabolism of alcohol) that is linked to an aversive "flushing response" after drinking alcohol is found in a high proportion of people from China and Japan, resulting in low levels of alcohol misuse. However, while potentially protective, these factors do not work in isolation and are influenced by a range of other relevant risk factors. It has been observed that Asians with the enzyme variant who live in the United States have rates of alcohol use that are similar to those of their local communities.

Conclusions

Research since the 1970s has established a number of important risk factors for SUD in youth. Such factors include individual (for example, being male, family history of substance-related problems, mental health or behavioral problems, personality difficulties, history of abuse), family (parental drug use, family dysfunction), peer (peer drug use, low sanctions against use), and sociocultural variables (drug availability, cultural acceptance, community support), as well as specific protective factors (family bonding, parental supervision, connectedness). However, while this research has assisted in the development of prevention programs that combat risk factors and promote protective factors, we are still yet to develop a comprehensive understanding of the underlying causes and vulnerabilities to SUD.

There is now an increased emphasis on the need to understand risk and protective factors at the individual level. The interaction between a young person and his or her environment requires clear elucidation so that more targeted prevention programs may be developed to identify high-risk youth promptly and provide early intervention strategies.

L. HIDES, D. I. LUBMAN, M. YÜCEL

SEE ALSO:
Biopsychosocial Theory of Addiction • Causes of Addiction • Family Environment • Parenting • Peer Influence • Protective Factors • Risk Factors

War and the Military

Like most employers, the military has strict rules against the use of illicit drugs by members of the services. However, in times of war there are some drugs that are sanctioned for use to keep troops alert.

Throughout the history of war and conflict, soldiers have fought both enemy and fatigue. Combat often demands alertness in life or death situations. At the same time, soldiers must perform physically strenuous activities while they experience extensive physical fatigue and exhaustion. Along with this, it is often difficult to get enough sleep due to physiological arousal, anxiety, crowded or noisy conditions, or lack of time.

Armies have consumed alcohol for thousands of years, partly because of the unreliability of water supplies and partly to imbue courage into the troops or to help them forget the horrors of war. The Duke of Wellington, fighting Napoleon's forces in the early 1800s, complained that British soldiers would drink themselves into unconsciousness as soon as they found a wine cellar in a captured town. Navies, too, would allow sailors a daily ration of grog or rum to reduce tensions among men cooped up on board ship for long periods.

To combat drunkenness among U.S. forces, Congress imposed limited prohibition in 1890 by banning intoxicating beverages at military bases. However, beer and light wines were considered acceptable until World War I (1914–1918), when restrictions were extended to cover overseas service and it became illegal to sell any intoxicating drinks to men in uniform. This restriction continued until 1953, when base commanders were given authority to control the sale and use of alcohol by troops.

Psychoactive drugs were less prevalent in early times, although invading Vikings reputedly ate amanita mushrooms to send themselves into a frenzy. The problem of addiction, rather than drunkenness, came with the discovery of morphine, which was used as a painkiller in treating injuries among troops on both sides during the American Civil War (1861–1865). Some soldiers became addicted and carried on their use after the war had ended.

Amphetamines were discovered in the late nineteenth century. By the 1930s their ability to stimulate the central nervous system made them popular as pep pills or diet pills, and they are also known as uppers or speed. Troops on all sides in World War II (1939–1945) were given amphetamines to enable them to go for long periods without sleep and give them energy to fight. As recently as the Iraq War in 2003, fighter pilots have also used amphetamines to fight fatigue and exhaustion. The flight surgeon can prescribe "go-go pills" in the form of dextroamphetamine (trade name, Dexedrine). Despite potentially dangerous side effects described by some, the U.S. Department of Defense (DoD) has insisted that amphetamine tablets are not only harmless but beneficial since they keep a combatant alert and awake. The air force position is that use is strictly voluntary; however, a pilot can be grounded for exercising his or her right not to use them. Being taken off flight status is very damaging to a pilot's career, and most pilots are understandably reluctant to risk such a possibility.

The drawbacks of amphetamines, including the feeling of being "wired," the need to take tranquilizers to fall asleep, and dependence, have led to the use by the military of another drug, modafinil, used to treat the sleep disorder narcolepsy. Although this drug is not addictive, clinicians have warned of the dangers of repeated sleep deprivation among troops.

The Vietnam War

In addition to the legitimized use of amphetamines, illegal drug use in the military occurs and reached its pinnacle during the Vietnam War. Marijuana was readily available in Vietnam and smoked by large numbers of soldiers. Efforts to stamp out use led troops to switch to an equally cheap and available drug—heroin. Once the commanders realized what was happening, the rules on marijuana were relaxed, but it was already too late to prevent some soldiers from becoming addicted to heroin. The subsequent crackdown on heroin pushed up the price, and soldiers began injecting rather than smoking the drug.

What was remarkable about the use of drugs during this war was that only a small percentage of

Drug use is forbidden in the armed services as it can make people unreliable when on active duty and can undermine morale. Personnel are screened regularly and warned of the consequences if they test positive.

those who used or became addicted to opiates while they were in Vietnam returned to drug use when they came home. Many of the ongoing users were men who had used narcotics before they joined the army.

Current drug use in the military

Use of illicit drugs by today's military violates the Uniform Code of Military Justice. The code lists offenses, which, if perpetrated by service personnel, are punishable by court martial. Article 112 refers to being drunk on duty, while Article 112a outlaws the knowing use or possession of any illegal drug in the military. The DoD also screens all applicants for military service for marijuana and cocaine use as mandated by the National Defense Authorization Act of 1988. Applicants who test positive for either drug are not eligible for military service for two years from the date of a second test. Those who test as cocaine-positive are not eligible for one year from the date of screening, and those confirmed as marijuana-positive are not eligible for military service for six months from the date of screening.

The DoD has periodically surveyed members of the military regarding prevalence of illegal drug use. In 1980 the DoD reported that close to 28 percent of military respondents admitted using an illegal drug within the 30 days prior to the study. This proportion fell to 3.4 percent in 2002, appreciably lower than the 12 percent found among civilians. Of the drugs used, marijuana was used the most and remains the most heavily used illegal drug within the military.

The large drop in drug use is the result of a concentrated effort by the DoD on both the supply and demand sides of drug use. The DoD works closely with the Drug Enforcement Administration to deter the flow of illegal drugs into the country. In terms of the demand for illegal drugs, the military uses education and deterrence as key methods for reducing such demand. Although the services do not take every case to court for illegal drug use, the individual is not allowed to remain on active duty. This practice creates a strong deterrent to violating rules against using drugs. Nevertheless, and despite the decline in drug use in the military between 1980 and 2002, concerns remain. Some 17,000 people were discharged from the military for drug use between 1999 and 2002.

In terms of alcohol use and heavy drinking in the military, a DoD survey indicated that the rate was 20.8 percent in 1980 and decreased to 18.1 percent in 2002. Hence, alcohol use is relatively constant, reflecting rates in society at large and the lack of severe consequences associated with its use. However, figures show that among military personnel aged 18 to 25 the rate of 27 percent is almost double that of the civilian population. Smoking rates are similar to civilian rates at 34 percent, down from 51 percent in 1980.

The military has policies on drug use and testing. Additionally, the military relies upon screening of potential recruits, and active duty service members must undergo a urine drug test annually. Recruiters explain the drug testing policy several times to potential enlistees. These enlistees are first tested when screened by physicians at regional processing centers. Marine recruits hear the drug policy again within the first five minutes of boot camp, and their urine is tested within their first 72 hours. If tested positive, they are sent home immediately. In boot camp, recruits also have a two-hour class on drug rules, the testing program, and the harm that drug use can cause. There are also several occasions for informal discussion of deterrence of drug use.

Testing schedules

As noted, active duty service members are tested annually and reserve component members (who make up close to half the military force) must be tested at least every two years. DoD laboratories are equipped to test for marijuana, cocaine, amphetamines (including Ecstasy), LSD, opiates (including morphine and heroin), barbiturates, and PCP. However, not all samples are tested for all of these drugs. Every sample gets tested for marijuana, cocaine, and amphetamines, but tests for other drugs are done at random on different schedules for each laboratory. Tests are becoming more sensitive, and more are being done on weekends and on Mondays because some popular drugs, such as Ecstasy, may be taken on a Saturday and are undetectable by Tuesday.

Most military branches randomly test about 10 percent of members each month. The marines administer close to four tests per capita each year. The air force tests the least in a year, less than one test per service member. The navy and marines also do unit-wide drug tests at least once a year. There is senior leader and commander discretion when confronted with drug use and random testing. For example, in 2001, a San Diego admiral doubled the drug tests for sailors on many ships.

The Pentagon instituted random drug testing in 1981. It is estimated that at the time approximately 40 percent of active duty military personnel used marijuana. Zero-tolerance policies were first instituted during the Reagan administration in the 1980s. Prior to the 1980s, drug users in the military were treated and kept in the service. The military adopted a zero-tolerance policy because drug use in a unit can interfere with military readiness. Troops who use drugs are more likely to make mistakes, react slowly in combat, negatively affect morale, and be vulnerable to blackmail. Despite this zero-tolerance policy, thousands of military members who test positive for drug use remain in the military because some senior leaders and commanders use their discretion and give first-time offenders a second chance. For example, in 2001, 8,948 army soldiers tested positive, but only 1,262 were removed.

In addition to education efforts to counteract illicit drug use, military policy includes potentially severe consequences for drug abuse associated with its zero-tolerance policy. Those who fail a random drug test can be dismissed through an administrative process or a series of discharges ranging from honorable to other-than-honorable discharge. The consequences of such dismissals may preclude reenlistment and candidacy for some federal and state jobs. Further, loss of veterans' benefits can occur as a consequence. When offenders are court-martialed, they can face fines, forfeiture of pay, prison, loss of rank, and a dishonorable or bad-conduct discharge. Additionally, depending upon the severity of the crime, they may have a misdemeanor or felony record.

J. L. JOHNSON

SEE ALSO:
Amphetamine Sulfate • Dependence • Drug Testing • Workplace

Withdrawal

Quitting some types of drugs can be difficult because of the physical symptoms that occur when the user stops taking the drug. This syndrome is called withdrawal and is a major obstacle in the difficult process of giving up drugs.

Some drugs induce a physical dependence, which is an adaptive state of the body produced by repeated drug administration. When a person becomes physically dependent on a drug, that person will experience intense averse physical disturbances, called withdrawal, when he or she stops taking the drug. In fact, the only way to measure physical dependence is to observe the degree of withdrawal symptoms. Generally, the effects of drug withdrawal are opposite from the effects of the drug itself. Most drugs of abuse produce a feeling of euphoria, thus withdrawal from these drugs produces a dysphoria, which is a feeling of anxiousness and misery.

The process and function of withdrawal is not well understood. However, it is generally agreed that a drug alters the preset levels, or homeostatic "set points," of a variety of systems in the body. These homeostatic set points maintain the functions of various systems of the body at an optimal level. If a drug alters a body system in one direction, the body then alters the system in the opposite direction in an attempt to maintain the homeostatic set point. This opposing action of the body is thought to result in drug tolerance, requiring that more of the drug must be taken in order to get the same effect. If the drug is abruptly discontinued, however, the body's response to the drug is now unopposed and the person experiences the opposite effects (withdrawal). The specific psychological and physiological symptoms of withdrawal depend on the specific drug that caused the dependency. Some drugs such as marijuana produce only a mild withdrawal syndrome, while other drugs such as the opiates and alcohol produce such a severe withdrawal that avoiding these effects is an important factor in the continuation of drug use. In fact, withdrawal from alcohol can be lethal.

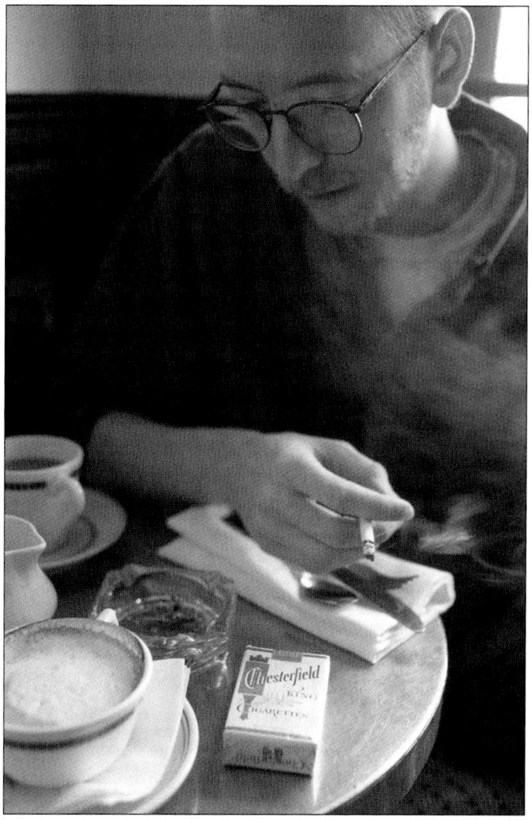

Nicotine in cigarettes and caffeine in coffee can both produce withdrawal symptoms if use is suddenly stopped. Nicotine is notoriously difficult to give up, as cravings can last for many months, but symptoms can be alleviated by nicotine patches or gum.

Mechanisms behind withdrawal

There appear to be various ways in which a body opposes the effects of a drug. It is these opposing effects that result in withdrawal when drug taking is abruptly stopped. The first mechanism involves modulation at a cellular level. There is a decrease in the production and release of the transmitter substances that the drug causes to be released. These transmitters activate certain molecules called receptors. These receptors are on nerve cells, and it is the activation of these receptors that results in the effects of the drug. In addition to decreasing the amount of neurotransmitters, the body also decreases the number of receptors. Both of these actions decrease the effect of the drug.

Withdrawal also involves a type of learning called behavioral conditioning. When a neutral stimulus is regularly followed by a stimulus that causes a response, the previously neutral stimulus begins to cause the same response by itself. Behavioral conditioning was established by Russian scientist Ivan Pavlov. Using dogs as experimental animals, Pavlov rang a bell just before showing food to the dogs. Over time, the dogs began to salivate at the sound of the bell itself, even without the presence of food. When a person takes a drug, the drug produces its effects on the body, which in turn cause the body to evoke its own compensatory response to the drug. Any environmental stimuli that are paired with the drug begin to be associated with the drug. This can include the room in which the drug is taken (for example, a bar) and the drug paraphernalia (such as shot glasses, rolling papers, a needle, and so on). This environmental stimuli is akin to the bell in Pavlov's experiment. Thus, over time, the compensatory effects of the body to oppose the effects of the drug are elicited not only by the drug itself but also by the environmental stimuli. If a heroin addict enters a room where he or she normally takes the drug, these environmental cues will quickly cause withdrawal symptoms such as agitation, cramping, and dysphoria. The only way to get rid of these withdrawal effects is to wait for them to fade or to take more of the drug.

TYPICAL WITHDRAWAL PERIODS

Alcohol
Mild symptoms peak within 12 to 24 hours and have largely subsided after 48 hours. Severe and potentially life threatening late withdrawal occurs between 72 and 96 hours after last drink.

Benzodiazepines
Symptoms can appear within hours, depending on half-life of drug, and can persist for several days. Untreated rebound symptoms may persist for months.

Opioids
Symptoms appear between 12 to 24 hours, peak after 4 days, and begin to subside after 7 days. Some withdrawal symptoms may persist for weeks or months afterward.

Stimulants
Binge use leads to exhaustive crash and intense cravings that may last 9 hours to 4 days. Withdrawal is mild but may be protracted, varying from 1 to 10 weeks, accompanied by craving.

Nicotine
Strong symptoms in first few days of withdrawal that usually diminish within a month. Some smokers may continue to feel symptoms for several months.

Withdrawal symptoms

The magnitude and type of withdrawal symptoms vary, depending on the drug taken. One of the important factors is the rate of disappearance of the drug from the body. Long-acting drugs take longer to leave the body, hence withdrawal from long-acting drugs has a delayed onset and is fairly mild. In contrast, shorter-acting drugs cause a withdrawal that is more intense but comparatively brief. After a person has become physiologically dependent on a drug, that person's body has responded by making adaptations that are directly opposite the effects of that drug. After the drug itself is removed, the withdrawal symptoms are also then directly opposite to the effects of the drug.

The effects of withdrawal from depressants of the nervous system are generally quite similar. These include alcohol, sedative-hypnotics such as barbiturates and benzodiazepines (including Nembutal and Valium), anxiolytics such as Xanax, anesthetics such as ether or nitrous oxide, and also substances that are inhaled, for example, glue and paint thinners. These drugs are used or abused for similar reasons: to decrease tension, reduce anxiety, and produce sedation. These drugs all depress the activity of the central nervous system (the brain and spinal cord). These drugs also have an additive effect with one another, and becoming dependent on one, for example, heroin, will cause cross-tolerance with other drugs in the same class, such as morphine or codeine. The withdrawal syndrome from general depressants is far more dangerous than that of other drugs and can even be fatal. Generally, symptoms appear within 24 hours after the drug is

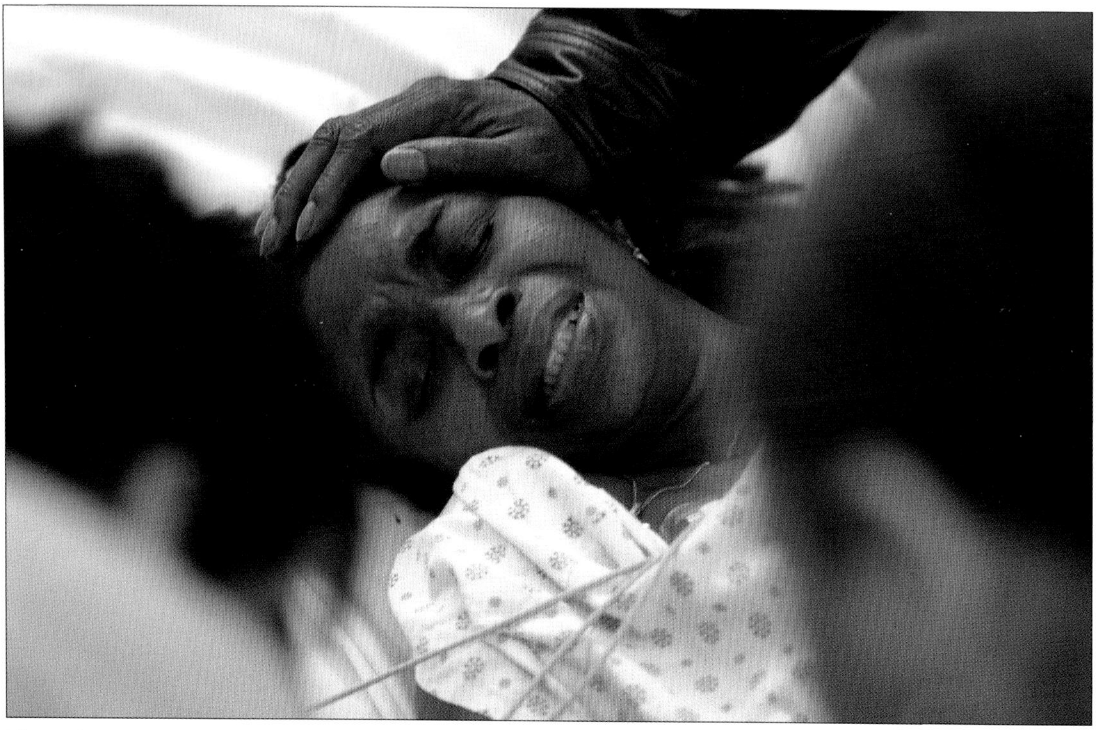

Planned or sudden withdrawal from heroin can be traumatic because symptoms begin as soon as a dose is missed and intensify over the following days. Administration of another opioid can help reduce symptoms, but this process must be carefully monitored, since the replacement may itself produce withdrawal.

discontinued, peak in 2 to 3 days, and last 7 to 14 days. The first few days of withdrawal from depressants are characterized by insomnia, headaches, anxiety, involuntary muscle twitching and tremor, sweating, intense dreaming, and nausea and vomiting. A few strongly dependent people go on to show later withdrawal symptoms in the following few days (these are called delirium tremens, or the DTs). People suffering from the DTs will have increasing agitation, general confusion and delirium, fever, vivid visual hallucinations (these are quite terrifying and often involve small animals such as rats, bats, or insects), and even seizures. The DTs are often fatal when they are not treated. Generally, treatment includes supportive care and administration of a long-acting depressant such as Valium. If this seems paradoxical, recall that the magnitude of withdrawal depends on the rate of drug disappearance from the body. Since all of the depressants cause cross-tolerance, a faster-clearing depressant such as alcohol is generally more dangerous, and the withdrawal syndrome can be controlled at a slower, less dangerous rate with a longer-acting depressant such as Valium. Supportive care includes reassurance, keeping the patient warm, preventing dehydration, and reducing sensory stimulation by keeping the patient in a quiet, dimly lit room. Sometimes an antipsychotic is also prescribed to combat the hallucinations.

Drugs in the opioid class include morphine, codeine, heroin, and synthetic opioids such as meperidine (Demerol). Like the depressants, these drugs all cause a similar withdrawal syndrome, and cross-tolerance occurs among them. Hence, they can be freely substituted with each other to prevent or lessen the withdrawal syndrome. Withdrawal from opioids begins shortly after the next scheduled dose is missed, becomes more intense over the next few days, and then lessens over the next 7 to 10 days. Opioid withdrawal is similar to withdrawal from depressants, although this is not as severe. Symptoms include anxiety, irritability, restlessness, muscle aches, insomnia, sweating and flushing, nausea and vomiting, and fever. Treatment for opioid withdrawal usually includes giving another opioid, although this is not necessary, since this type of withdrawal is not as severe and is never fatal. Supportive care is helpful, however, and is similar to that for the depressants. It should be pointed out that withdrawal syndrome can be caused by giving an opioid antagonist such as naloxone or naltrexone (antagonists will bind to the active area on cells but not activate them, thus they compete with and can block the actions of opioids). This type of withdrawal is immediate, peaks in a half hour, and is much more severe.

Stimulant withdrawal

Drugs in the stimulant class include amphetamines, cocaine, and caffeine. Unlike the other classes, withdrawal from these drugs varies, depending on the specific drug. First, these drugs vary in their ability to produce a physiological dependence (although they all can cause a strong psychological dependence). Amphetamines (including Ecstasy) and cocaine do not really cause a physiological dependency, hence there is not a strong withdrawal syndrome with these drugs. It should be pointed out, however, that there are rebound effects to the stimulatory nature of these drugs. These effects can include a psychological and physical depression, lethargy, and a period of prolonged sleep, especially for amphetamine, which causes long-lasting wakefulness. In contrast to the amphetamines and cocaine, people can become physiologically dependent on caffeine, which can cause a withdrawal syndrome when it is discontinued. The most common caffeine withdrawal symptom is headache. Other symptoms include drowsiness, decreased energy and fatigue, impaired concentration, irritability, and decreased motivation. Caffeine withdrawal begins within 12 to 24 hours, peaks at 1 to 2 days, and can persist as long as a week. It is interesting to point out that caffeine withdrawal is an important issue when people have to undergo procedures where fasting is required, such as operations or various laboratory testing. It also is probably a factor when people are grouchy in the morning until they have had their tea or coffee. It probably even contributes to headaches and illness that people experience on holidays or weekends when their normal caffeine intake is altered.

Nicotine, marijuana, and psychedelics

Nicotine dependence comes on more slowly than dependence on other drugs, and its withdrawal syndrome varies in intensity among different people. However, while withdrawal from nicotine is not as physically severe as that from heroin, it is just as psychologically stressful. Many ex-heroin addicts who also quit smoking have said it was actually easier to give up heroin than nicotine. Withdrawal from nicotine usually includes increased eating (leading to weight gain), decreased heart rate, lack of concentration, lighter patterns of sleep or insomnia, anxiety, aggression, depression, and intense cravings for nicotine. Most of these symptoms disappear within a month, although the craving and weight gain continue longer, often as long as 6 months or occasionally longer. These symptoms can be relieved by exposure to nicotine, and different administrative routes of nicotine are helpful in quitting, including nicotine patches and gum. The symptoms can even be relieved temporarily by the taste or smell of tobacco. Unlike other drugs, withdrawal from nicotine is not directly related to dose. Heavy and light smokers both report equally severe withdrawal effects.

Unlike many other drugs, no marked withdrawal takes place from marijuana or psychedelics such as LSD. Withdrawal has only been seen after high, prolonged use of marijuana, and even then it is slight. The symptoms of withdrawal in a high-dose study using volunteers included a report by the subjects of "inner unrest," irritability, sweating, and restlessness. However, in a study where subjects were required to smoke only one marijuana cigarette per day for 28 days, no withdrawal symptoms were reported.

As a final note, it should be pointed out that drug withdrawal can be a factor in newborn babies of drug-dependent mothers. These babies will have the same symptoms as adults do and must be treated carefully to ease their withdrawal symptoms, which can persist for 4 to 6 months after birth.

J. JAWORSKI

SEE ALSO:
Addiction • Alcoholism Treatment • Detoxification • Heroin Addiction Treatment • Medical Care • Pregnancy and Fetal Addiction • Tolerance • Treatment

Women and Drugs

Women who use substances, including alcohol, face more physical and psychiatric consequences than men. In addition, a mother's substance use affects children before and after birth.

Approximately 17.9 percent of females aged 15 to 24 in the United States have, at some point in their lifetime, suffered from a substance use disorder. The problem of substance use among women has only recently received much attention; the first programs and therapies that were designed to treat addiction were developed for men. Recent investigations in the area of women and addiction have focused on women's reasons for substance use, the types of substances women use, aspects of physiology and biology that affect women's substance use, the consequences of substance use on women's lives, and treatment approaches. Each of these areas will be briefly reviewed in the following sections.

Reasons for substance use among women

Men and women are motivated to use substances for different reasons. Research involving adult participants shows that women are more likely than men to use substances as the result of a specific symptom, such as depression, low self-esteem, anxiety, or shyness, or following the experience of a stressful or traumatic event, such as an assault or a serious car accident. Men, on the other hand, are more likely to experience stressful or traumatic events and develop psychiatric symptoms as the result of alcohol or drug use. Thus, men tend to first develop an addiction, which then puts them at risk for exposure to traumatic life events, which could include serious injury or accident due to being under the influence of substances as well as psychiatric symptoms, for example, depressive symptoms from losing a job or family because of addiction.

The way that men and women are introduced to substances is also different. Girls and women are more often introduced to substances by a female friend or male partner. In addition, women often report continuing to use substances in order to maintain a relationship with their substance-using partner. Men more often than women report initiating use because of curiosity about the drug or to gain peer acceptance.

One of the largest studies examining the reasons that girls and young women use substances was conducted by the National Center for Addiction and Substance Abuse (CASA) at Columbia University in 2003. The participants of the study were approximately 1,220 females aged 8 to 22. The findings demonstrate that young women use substances to improve their mood, increase self-confidence, lose weight, cope with problems, or enhance sexual activity. Boys and young men tend to use substances because of curiosity and sensation seeking reasons.

Types of substances women use

The CASA study found that high school girls reported lifetime use of alcohol (45 percent), cigarettes (28 percent), marijuana (20 percent), inhalants (4 percent), and cocaine (4 percent). Among adults, men and women appear to be equally likely to develop dependence on cocaine, heroin, hallucinogens, tobacco, and inhalants. Women, however, are more likely than men to become dependent on sedatives, anti-anxiety medications, and sleep medications. Men are more likely than women to abuse alcohol and marijuana. Data from CASA also indicate that it is easier for girls to purchase substances. When buying cigarettes, for example, girls are less likely to be asked to show identification and proof of age than boys.

Gender differences and women's substance use

There are a number of important physiological differences between men and women that impact the way that their bodies react to alcohol and drugs. Women become tolerant and dependent on substances at a faster rate than men, even though women may use less of the substance. In addition, women develop substance-related problems, for example, cirrhosis of the liver, at a faster rate than men. This phenomenon is known as telescoping. Gender differences in physiology may help explain the process of telescoping. On average, women have more body fat and less body water than men. Alcohol absorbed through the gastrointestinal tract is distributed into total body water. Thus, because women have less body water, they will have higher concentrations of alcohol. When given equal amounts of alcohol, therefore, women reach higher blood alcohol concentration levels faster than men. The different body fat composition in women will also result in longer half-lives of fat-soluble drugs, such as diazepam and oxazepam. Women also have lower levels of the enzyme alcohol dehydrogenase, which is responsible for the metabolism of alcohol. Because of this, women absorb more of the alcohol that they consume. Generally, one alcoholic drink has the impact on a woman that two drinks have on a man.

Consequences of substance use on women

Substance use has serious consequences on women's physical health, mental health, social and occupational functioning, and economic status. For a substantial proportion of women, substance use will even result in death. The average life span for alcohol-dependent women is decreased by approximately 15 years, and the risk for mortality is higher for addicted women than for addicted men.

Common medical problems among addicted women include cirrhosis of the liver, hypertension, anemia, malnutrition, gastrointestinal hemorrhage, peptic ulcers, and brain damage. Telescoping, as previously mentioned, leads to an accelerated rate of medical problems among women. For example, in comparison with men, women are twice as likely to develop cirrhosis of the liver from alcohol use, they have more lung damage from smoking, they suffer more alcohol-induced brain damage, and they are more likely to be admitted to the hospital because of poisoning from substances. The use of Ecstasy is also more likely to result in brain damage, sleep disorders, memory problems, and other forms of cognitive impairment among girls than boys. Thus, women are at greater risk than men for developing physical health problems more quickly. Telescoping occurs even at a lower level of use; women can drink less than men but still be at a higher risk of developing medical problems.

In addition to higher rates of medical problems, addicted women also suffer from higher rates of psychiatric problems when compared with addicted men. In particular, addicted women are more likely than addicted men to have co-occurring eating disorders, major depression, and post-traumatic stress disorder. Among women, psychiatric disorders usually develop after substance use and may, therefore, be the direct result of the substance or the effect of the substance on the brain chemistry, or the problems that result from substance use, or both.

HIV (human immunodeficiency virus), AIDS (acquired immunodeficiency syndrome), and other sexually transmitted diseases, such as gonorrhea, genital warts, and herpes, are also a serious concern among substance-using women. AIDS is the fourth leading cause of death among women aged 15 to 44. Most women who have HIV acquired the virus through substance-related activity, including using a needle for injecting drugs, and exchanging sex for drugs. When under the influence of alcohol or drugs, judgment and decision-making skills are impaired, leaving women vulnerable to unprotected sex. Prostitution is a major problem, particularly among drug-using women. Crack cocaine and heroin users may trade sex for money or drugs, thus increasing the risk of sexually transmitted diseases and pregnancy.

Chronic alcohol or drug use can seriously impair women's reproductive functioning. Over time, alcohol use can result in the inhibition of ovulation, infertility, and loss of orgasmic function. Use of cocaine, amphetamines, or heroin have similar effects. These findings are contrary to cultural myths that portray alcohol and drugs as aphrodisiacs that stimulate sexual desire and ability, when in fact they suppress sexual desire and responsiveness over time.

Substance use of any kind during pregnancy can result in intractable, lifelong defects in the child. Fetal alcohol syndrome, mental retardation, vision and hearing impairments, and low birth weight are some of the complications found in babies born to mothers using substances during pregnancy. The risk of miscarriage is increased by substance use during pregnancy. No amount of alcohol or drugs (including cigarettes) is safe during pregnancy.

Sociocultural attitudes, beliefs, and stereotypes about addicted women can lead to serious consequences for women substance users. Women who use alcohol or drugs are often stigmatized as being promiscuous. Thus women substance users are at greater risk of sexual assault, date rape, spousal abuse,

Young women who smoke and drink alcohol could be laying the foundation for health problems later in life.

and other violent crimes. Women who are assaulted while intoxicated are more likely to be blamed for the crime than women who are sober.

Addiction and its related problems also make it difficult for girls to adopt adult roles as women. Substance use affects girls' ability to succeed academically, seek and obtain employment, have a healthy marriage, and raise healthy children.

Treatment approaches for women

Given the sociocultural factors mentioned in the previous section, it is no surprise that women are less likely than men to seek treatment for addiction, and they are more likely to drop out of treatment after the first visit. One study found that less than 14 percent of addicted women were in treatment. In general, addicted women seek treatment services for marital or emotional problems or physical health rather than addiction. On average, women present for treatment after five years of substance use. Men usually present for treatment after an average of eight years of substance use. This difference is thought to be related to the phenomenon of telescoping, since women become dependent on and develop substance-related problems faster than men.

Pregnant women who seek addiction treatment may have fears regarding the legal implications of their substance use. In some states, if a pregnant woman has a positive urine drug-screen test result, this can lead to the automatic removal of the child at birth. Some authorities cite prenatal child abuse as a result of pregnant women using substances. Many believe that these policies only further decrease the likelihood that an addicted woman will seek and receive appropriate and helpful addiction treatment.

Gender specific treatments

Once women enter treatment, there is little research to guide the treatment focus. New investigations are being conducted to test whether treatments designed specifically for women are more effective than treatments designed for either men or women. As mentioned earlier, most of the treatments have been designed to treat addicted men. It is not clear

RISK AND PROTECTIVE FACTORS FOR GIRLS AND YOUNG WOMEN

The following factors put girls and young women at high risk for using substances: early puberty, depression and suicidal tendencies, a history of physical or sexual abuse, having an older sibling who uses substances, and frequent moves. Girls who engage in unhealthy dieting, are overly concerned about their weight, or are dissatisfied with their weight or shape are also at high risk for using alcohol and drugs. Many girls are unaware that alcohol contains high calories and increases weight, and some use cocaine or other stimulants as a means of appetite suppression.

The ages of 18 to 25 appear to be a time of particularly high risk for young women. During this period, they are at high risk for binge drinking, that is, consuming five or more drinks on one occasion, and heavy drug use. It is notable that the ages of 18 to 25 signify important developmental transitions for women, for example, moving out of the home and away from their parents, beginning college or work, and dating and sexuality. These transitions may be related to the increased risk of substance use during that period of time.

The following have been shown to serve as protective factors against substance use for girls and young women: engagement in religious services, strong identification with one's racial and ethnic background, parental monitoring, conversations with parents about substances, and the support of extended family members, for example, aunts, uncles, or grandparents.

whether this generic approach is helpful. The essential elements of treatment for men may or may not be what women need. Several early studies examining addiction treatments designed for women have shown promising results.

These studies consider certain factors to be important in the treatment of addicted women: assessment of other psychiatric disorders, such as depression and anxiety; attention to history of sexual and physical abuse; assessment of prescription drug abuse; comprehensive physical examination; education regarding substance use during pregnancy; child care services; parenting education; evaluation and treatment of male partners; positive female role models among the treatment staff; attention to issues of guilt, shame, and assertiveness; attention to the effects of sexism in the areas of employment, education, financial resources, feelings of power and control; and special attention to the needs of minority women, lesbians, and women in the criminal justice system. Many women having treatment will be unemployed or underemployed and will need rehabilitation. Gaining work skills and a job can help increase feelings of self-competence, control, and power, which will help in recovery.

Another issue of importance for addicted women is concern about weight and body shape. Compared with men, women tend to be more concerned about their weight and body shape and tend to use cigarettes, cocaine, and amphetamines as a way of controlling their weight or appetite. New treatment approaches are being specifically designed to help women develop healthier perceptions of their bodies, to help in their recovery from addiction.

Most people relapse on the path to abstinence. Men and women relapse for different reasons; women relapse as a result of negative emotions and personal problems, while men relapse due to positive emotions such as getting a job and wanting to celebrate.

Alcoholics Anonymous (AA) has women-only meetings. Al-Anon, Narcotics Anonymous, Cocaine Anonymous, Narc-Anon, Alateen, and other self-help community organizations such as Women for Sobriety can be helpful for addicted women and their families.

S. E. BACK

SEE ALSO:
Abstinence • Adolescents and Substance Abuse • Alcoholism • Hormonal Effects • Pregnancy and Fetal Addiction • Prostitution • Rape • Treatment

Workplace

The use of drugs in the workplace is an issue for many employers. Substance abuse has costs in terms of productivity and performance of employees, but workplace support can help many workers in overcoming their problems.

A significant amount of illegal substance abuse takes place in the workforce, and some of this abuse occurs while at work or just prior to going to work. The belief that most people who use illicit drugs are unemployed and concentrated in impoverished parts of inner cities is a myth. A large-scale nationally representative study in the United States—*Worker Drug Use and Workplace Policies and Programs: Results from the National Household Survey on Drug Abuse*—shows that in 1997, 70 percent of the 9 million persons between the ages of 18 and 49 years who admitted using illicit drugs in the preceding month were full-time workers. It also shows that the overall rate of current illicit drug use among full-time employees has fallen from 17.5 percent in 1985 to a low point in 1992 of 7.4 percent and stayed at a steady rate of about 7 to 8 percent through 1997. One-third of full-time workers are smokers, more than one-fifth reported binge drinking in the past month, and approximately 12 percent say they used illicit drugs during the past year. Among full-time workers aged 18 to 49, there were an estimated 6.3 million current illicit drug users and an estimated 6.2 million heavy alcohol users (drinking five or more drinks on one occasion five or more days in the past 30 days). Included in this number were 1.6 million people who abused both illicit drugs and were heavy alcohol users, for a total of 10.9 million people who were heavy alcohol users, illicit drug users, or both. Workers are three times more likely to report a dependence on alcohol than on illicit drugs. Male workers are twice as likely to be current illicit drug users and four times as likely to be heavy alcohol users as female workers. Substance abuse is more common in certain occupations and industries. Heavy alcohol and illicit drug use is highest among construction workers and food preparers. Auto mechanics, laborers, and light-truck drivers are among those more susceptible to alcohol use. In addition, tobacco use is more common among blue-collar workers than among white-collar workers.

Economic cost

Substance abuse can create hazards, not only for employees, but also for co-workers and the public. Substance abuse among transportation workers, for example, can endanger the lives of passengers and bystanders.

In 1997 workers who reported current illicit drug use were more likely than those who did not report illicit drug use to have worked for three or more employers (9 percent versus 4 percent), to have voluntarily left an employer in the past year (25 percent versus 15 percent), and to have skipped one or more days of work in the past month (13 percent versus 5 percent). Workers who reported heavy alcohol use were about twice as likely as those who did not report such use to have worked for three or more employers in the past year (8 percent versus 4 percent) and to have skipped one or more days of work in the past month (11 percent versus 5 percent).

It is hard to measure the full economic burden of substance abuse on the workplace alone because of the society-wide spread of substance abuse. In general, the impact of substance abuse on the material welfare of a society can be estimated by examining the social and financial costs of law enforcement, lost productivity, treatment, prevention, and research, plus some measure of the quality of life-years lost, relative to a hypothetical scenario in which there is no substance abuse.

Employers' policies on drug use

Employers can help their own bottom line, while at the same time reducing substance abuse, by clearly setting out in writing their policies regarding drug and alcohol abuse and encouraging substance abusers to enter treatment. The U.S. Congress expressed in the Drug-Free Workplace Act of 1998 that businesses should adopt drug-free workplace programs and that states should consider incentives to encourage businesses to adopt drug-free workplace programs. Many workplaces provide information regarding the use of alcohol or drugs. Some workplaces have a written policy regarding employee use of alcohol or drugs, and some provide access to employee assistance programs (EAPs) or some other type of counseling program for employees with alcohol or drug-related problems.

Testing in the workplace

In 1981, following a U.S. Department of Defense survey and precipitated by the crash of a navy plane on the deck of the aircraft carrier *Nimitz,* the U.S. Navy initiated a policy of zero tolerance to drugs and instituted a Navy-wide testing program. On September 15, 1986, President Ronald Reagan signed Executive Order 12564, which required each executive agency to establish a program to test federal employees in "sensitive positions" (broadly defined) for use of illegal drugs and to offer voluntary testing. The order also authorized testing for cause, as follow-up to counseling or rehabilitation, and at the pre-employment stage. The Drug-Free Workplace Act of 1988 requires federal government contractors to maintain drug-free workplaces. Urine is collected for federally regulated workplace drug-testing programs and for most private sector programs. In all, an estimated 33 million workplace drug tests are carried out each year for U.S. employers. Aiming at improving precision in drug screening and making it harder for workers to cheat on urine tests, the U.S. Department of Health and Human Services' Substance Abuse and Mental Health Services Administration (SAMHSA) intends to issue revised rules that set specifications for alternatives to traditional lab-based urine tests, including lab testing of hair, saliva, and perspiration.

Current illicit drug users were more likely to report that their workplaces tested at hiring, randomly,

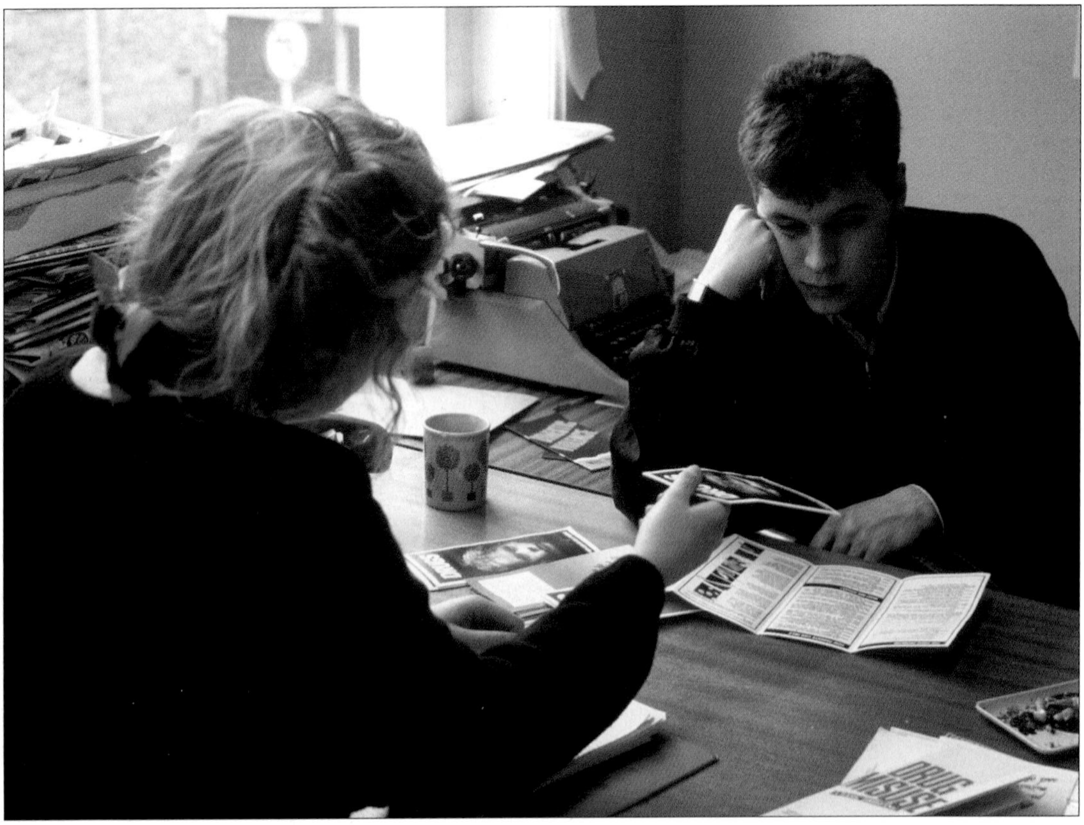

Many employers have strict policies about drug use among their workers. These may include mandatory or random drug testing to deter use or identify people who need help. Employee assistance programs are often used to provide counseling and support and advice on how to access treatment services.

upon suspicion, and post-accident in 1997 than in 1994 (24 percent versus 36 percent at hiring; 12 percent versus 21 percent randomly; 23 percent versus 33 percent upon suspicion; and 19 percent versus 30 percent post-accident). Despite its widespread use, drug testing has led to some controversy regarding reliability and validity, its effect on job applicants and current employees, and its legal status. The full range of costs and outcomes of these programs remains to be examined. Drug testing may have a deterrent effect, but this often comes at a high cost in the form of drug-testing expenses, employee turnover, and additional recruitment efforts.

Increasingly, illicit drug users have become much more accepting of drug testing in medium (25 to 499 employees) or large (500 or more employees) workplaces. For example, in 1994, 31 percent of current illicit drug users in medium establishments and 29 percent in large establishments said they would be less likely to work for an employer who tests for drugs at hiring, while in 1997 only 15 percent in medium establishments and 7 percent in large establishments said they would. In 1994, 41 percent of illicit current drug users in medium establishments and 48 percent in large establishments said they would be less likely to work for an employer who tests for drugs randomly, while in 1997 only 25 percent in medium establishments and 13 percent in large establishments said they would. Workers' attitudes toward workplace drug testing differ according to their drug-use status. In 1997, as in 1994, a larger percentage of current illicit drug users than nonusers said they would be less likely to work for an employer who tests for drug use upon hiring (22 percent versus 4 percent), randomly (29 percent versus 6 percent), upon suspicion (24 percent versus 10 percent), or after an accident (13 percent versus 4 percent).

Employee assistance programs

Employee assistance programs (EAPs) have been used for three decades to reduce absenteeism, promote recovery, minimize relapse, cut treatment costs, and improve productivity among drug-using workers. Larger establishments were more likely to provide an EAP regarding drug and alcohol use. Three-fourths of those working in large establishments reported that their workplace had such a program, while only about one-fourth of the workers in small businesses said they had access to such a program. Of workers in mid-sized businesses, slightly more than half reported access to assistance programs. Belief in the efficacy of EAPs directly increased the likelihood of seeking help at an EAP. Greater perceived social support and supervisor encouragement increased the likelihood of going to an EAP both directly and indirectly.

Prevention and treatment in the workplace

Workplace drug testing is regarded as an essential demand-reduction component of a prevention program because it serves as a deterrent to continued use of illicit substances; provides a means to detect and, thereby, identify employees or job applicants who are using illicit substances; and assists employees in recognizing and admitting their abuse problems so that they may obtain the necessary treatment.

Workplace drug treatment is a critical way to reach those who need help. Increasingly, it is considered desirable that drug treatment should be covered at the same benefit level as other chronic relapsing disorders. In the United States, the Center for Substance Abuse Prevention (CSAP) offers a toll-free telephone consulting service through its Workplace Help line.

Workers' attitudes toward various drug-testing programs have changed over time. Although some controversial issues surrounding alcohol and drug testing at the workplace still exist, overall, the vast majority of workers worldwide would be willing to work for an employer who has a drug-testing program. While future workplace intervention programs may benefit from this general attitude change, prevention and treatment efforts should attempt to engage in customized and effective communications during implementation of the program, taking into account the variations in the different groups, such as the size of the workplace and the occupations involved.

Z. ZHANG

SEE ALSO:
Counseling • Driving While Impaired • Drug Testing • Economic Costs of Addiction • Employee Assistance Programs

World Health Organization (WHO)

The World Health Organization deals with all types of health issues, including that of substance abuse and dependence. It collates statistics from its member states that can be used by health workers all over the globe.

The World Health Organization (WHO) was founded in 1948 by the United Nations as its specialized agency for health. It is governed by 192 member states, representatives of which form the World Health Assembly. The Health Assembly makes WHO's major policy decisions and approves budgets. WHO's constitution states that health is not only the absence of disease or infirmity but is also the state of complete physical, mental, and social well-being. In the area of substance abuse, WHO's mandate includes: prevention and reduction of the negative health and social consequences of psychoactive substance use; reduction of the demand for nonmedical use of psychoactive substances; assessment of psychoactive substances so as to advise the United Nations with regard to their regulatory control. WHO is the only international agency that deals with all psychoactive substances, regardless of their legal status.

A number of different departments and bodies within WHO are responsible for achieving these aims. The Expert Committee on Drug Dependence, for example, advises the United Nations on regulatory control of psychoactive substances. The advice of this committee is given to the United Nations Commission on Narcotic Drugs, which then votes on whether a drug should be added to one of the lists of internationally controlled drugs, transferred to another list, or removed altogether.

The Department of Mental Health and Substance Dependence is concerned with the management of problems related to the use of psychoactive drugs. The tasks of this department are broken down into specific areas, such as the epidemiology of alcohol and drug use, substance use and HIV/AIDS, and the neuroscience of substance use and dependence. One of its key publications is its contribution to the *International Classification of Diseases and Related Health Problems* (ICD-10). Chapter V deals with the diagnosis of more than 300 mental and behavioral disorders, including those that relate to substance abuse. These classifications are used throughout the world as a means of assessing whether a person has developed a dependence on drugs as well as any other comorbid mental or behavioral symptoms that may relate to the problem.

WHO recognizes the importance of developing accurate and detailed sources of information on the epidemiology of drug use, particularly in developing countries where information may be limited. Extensive research carried out in many countries is used to create a thorough body of knowledge, which may then be consulted by policy makers and health professionals. In the case of the epidemiology of alcohol and drug use, for example, the *Global Status Report on Alcohol* presents data on alcohol consumption in 173 member states, while the *Guide to Drug Abuse Epidemiology*, produced in collaboration with the U.S. National Institute on Drug Abuse (NIDA), provides information on measures and methods that aid the assessment of national trends in drug taking. This guide is designed so that it may be adapted to a wide range of circumstances, including the limited medical resources and expertise that may be found in developing countries.

WHO works closely with a number of other organizations to improve existing knowledge on substance use. Research carried out, for example, with the Cochrane Collaborative Review Group on Drug and Alcohol Addiction aims to provide regularly updated information on the effects of prevention and treatment methods for psychoactive substances. Other activities of WHO include the exchange and dissemination of information through a variety of books, reports, and events, including conferences that target particular areas of concern and global awareness days.

P. G. THOMPSON

SEE ALSO:
International Cooperation • International Narcotics Control Board (INCB) • National Institute on Drug Abuse (NIDA) • United Nations Office on Drugs and Crime (UNODC)

Youth Culture

Growing up is a time of experimentation for adolescents in which they seek to define themselves and their place in the world. Taking risks and undertaking activities their parents would not approve are part of this process.

"Loud music, drugs, different clothes, crazy haircuts, always challenging authority—what's wrong with young people today?" This question has probably been posed countless times by numerous adults over the years. Why do young people need to assert themselves differently, and what is the role of such behavior? Why do some young people need a specific youth culture to identify with, and what is its relationship with adolescence? To answer these questions we must explore the psychological processes relevant to adolescent development and consider the expectations of young people within contemporary society.

Adolescence is a period of significant change, encompassing physical, emotional, intellectual, and social growth. It is characterized by a shift from total dependence to evolving independence, through a process of increasing identification with friends and peers. Attitudes and values of other young people become increasingly important as the young person begins to question who he or she is and how he or she fits into the world.

These questions are characteristic of the developmental changes occurring throughout adolescence. Not only must a young person come to terms with his or her changing physical appearance, but he or she must also develop a sense of personal identity. Eric Erikson, perhaps the most famous psychologist associated with development across the life cycle, suggested that adolescence was a key period of identity formation (figuring out who exactly one is, where one is going, and how one might get there). In tackling this developmental stage, he suggested that young people become preoccupied with appearance,

Adolescence is a time when establishing one's own identity through fashion, attitudes, and belonging to a particular group plays an increasingly important role in becoming independent of parental control.

hero worship, and ideology, and develop a strong group identity with their peers.

Over the past century, there have been significant changes within the social, moral, and political spheres of contemporary societies. The responsibilities and expectations of young people within industrialized nations have also been changing rapidly, with young people increasingly turning to their peers for direction and support. Increasing urbanization and geographic mobility within many industrialized countries has contributed to this process, as the influence of extended families and communities have been significantly eroded. This change in the structure of Western society led to the development of a specific youth culture over the latter half of the twentieth century, which allowed young people a forum to master developmental tasks and explore new identities and roles.

What exactly is youth culture in today's world? In contemporary society, youth culture includes a focus on leisure rather than work—a culture of consumerism and freedom of choice. What the young person buys, wears, and does is very important, reflecting the heightened importance of the peer group. Particular styles of clothing, music, behavior, or activities are very important and help young people explore new identities or distinguish themselves from differing groups. These pursuits may seem trivial to the parent, but for the adolescent, they offer a sense of belonging and a cultural identity that is clearly distinguishable from adults. Criticism of existing social, political, or religious systems is also common, as is a passionate concern for humanity and the environment. However, youth culture is not and cannot be a singular entity but is reflective of the ethnicity, socioeconomic status, educational, and political backgrounds of the young people of the day.

Rites and rituals of growing up

In many so-called primitive societies, the privileges and duties of different age groups are clearly elucidated, and specific rites of passage are conducted to recognize a young person's transition to adulthood. In some societies, adolescents may be expected to undergo an initiation experience to mark this important milestone. For women, this may be the time of their first period (menses), as the loss of blood provides a symbolic marker of the end of childhood and entry into the adult world (with the capacity to bear children). For men, initiations may include the loss of a tooth, circumcision, making a scar, or other experiences symbolic of becoming a man.

However, in contemporary society, there is no such clear delineation of a young person's role or rites of passage, and significant differences exist across cultures, communities, and nations in the expectations and restrictions of young people (for example, age allowed to drive, drink, marry, vote). Instead, youth culture may be seen as providing a contemporary set of symbolic markers for young people, where conformity to peer group standards is of primary importance. In this context, experimentation with alcohol or drugs may be seen as a symbol of increasing independence or a modern rite of passage, since recreational use of certain substances (such as alcohol) is associated with an adult role within most Western societies.

Natural rebellion

Despite being an important developmental stage, youth culture is often portrayed as being oppositional or subversive, challenging mainstream opinion, or parental or cultural values. However, this rebellion may be considered a normal part of adolescent development, reflecting changes in cognitive ability. The Swiss psychologist Jean Piaget labeled this stage of cognitive development "formal operational thinking," characterizing it by the ability to think abstractly, reason deductively, and define concepts and probabilities. Although some may never reach this stage fully, the developing young person becomes able to think in a more objective and abstract fashion, and begins to see a new world of possibilities. This change in thinking means that previously accepted values and opinions are no longer accepted blindly but are reevaluated and challenged and alternative viewpoints proposed. This new inquisitive approach means that young people may begin experimenting with new behaviors (such as drinking alcohol) that were previously taboo. As a result, this natural rebellion frequently results in negative perceptions of young people and their choices. This is especially true when young people choose to express and define themselves in ways that are unknown or uncomfortable to adults. Moral and ethical ideas that are held as important to many

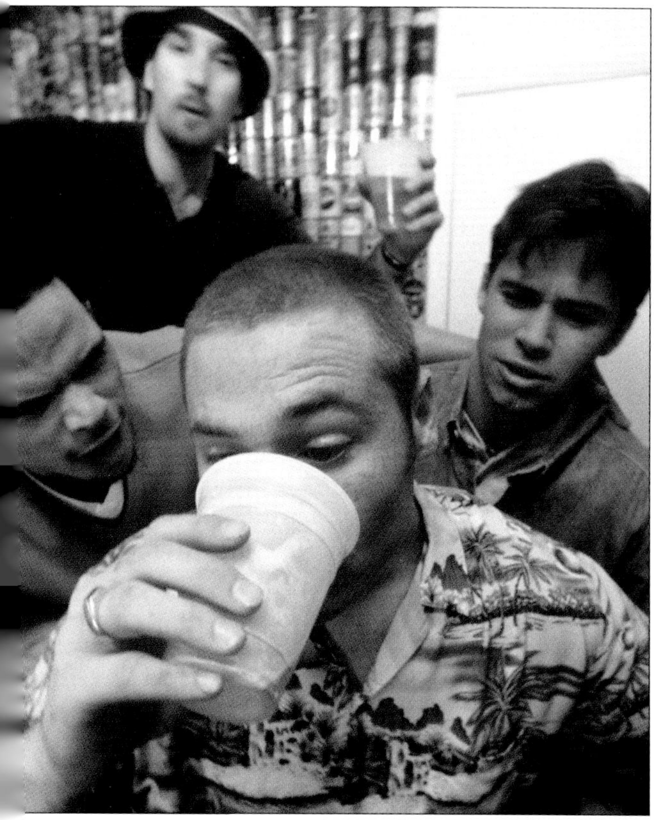

The ability to drink large quantities of alcohol is often regarded by young adults as proof that they are grown up enough to handle liquor. The risks of binge drinking are usually overlooked or dismissed as unlikely.

adults and mainstream cultures (such as abstinence from drugs) are often challenged by youth cultures and this can make them particularly threatening. However, natural rebellion must be acknowledged as an important and natural part of adolescent development that allows the young person the opportunity to broaden his or her skills base and assert a more independent identity.

Positive and negative influences

In order to successfully master the developmental tasks of adolescence, young people require the support and understanding of their parents, peers, and social or religious institutions. In fact, parents play the most significant role in helping young people cope with the developmental demands of adolescence, even though adolescent-parental conflicts are common. Challenging values and rules are a reflection of changes in mental capacity and the increased social power and control individuals develop as they become independent. However, despite growing independence, adolescents, like children, need loving and caring parents whom they can trust. Parental hostility, rejection, or neglect affects the young person's developing self-esteem and sense of identity, which can manifest as academic or behavioral problems, impaired social relationships with peers and adults, significant drug use, or personality problems. Authoritarian parental attitudes are problematic and may result in significant rebellion. Instead, young people need to be heard and supported, with encouragement to develop age-appropriate and independent skills.

Peer influences are also important, and approval and acceptance by the peer group allow for the development of self-confidence and a strong sense of identity. Unpopular adolescents or those with significant issues are likely to be emotionally troubled and to lack a secure personal identity. This identity confusion leads some adolescents to choose an alternate negative identity characterized by delinquent behavior and problematic drug use, in which a lack of social achievement is embraced. These young people readily identify with alternate subcultures, such as deviant peer groups, who support their negative self-image.

Other important influences for young people include the degree of support and understanding provided by schools or religious institutions, the interest of adults outside the family (such as teachers, ministers, athletic coaches, friends), and the general climate of society as a whole (degree of discrimination, poverty, violence, unemployment), including its attitude toward young people and their views.

Attitudes toward drugs and alcohol

Despite the constant association between substance use and youth culture in the media, it is important to emphasize that drugs in general are widely accepted within contemporary society, and a multitude of licit and illicit substances are readily available and accessible to young people. Drugs are prescribed for a multitude of medical conditions, and contemporary society openly endorses drug use for a range of physical and psychological ailments. Drinking alcohol is also widely condoned within Western societies and its use associated with both religious ceremonies and societal celebrations. Thus, alcohol and drug use are somewhat normalized within contemporary society, although changes in the political and cultural climate determine which substances are considered acceptable. Consequently, experimentation with substances is common among adolescents, who are curious about new experiences, openly challenge mainstream views, and are more inclined to take risks than adults. The choice of substances, however, is largely determined by availability, making alcohol, tobacco, marijuana, and inhalants the most likely substances to be used by this population.

Young people may also experiment with drugs because of peer group influences. In fact, research suggests that the best predictor of adolescent drug involvement is peer attitude toward drugs and current use. Alternatively, taking drugs, especially illegal drugs, can be an effective method of rebelling against parents and social attitudes. Because most parents and communities disagree with illicit drug use, acting in opposition to these views helps young people show how they are different from their parents and are developing their own ideas and approaches to life as they become more independent. Such activities should be considered on the spectrum of natural rebellion, although serious use is more likely to be a reflection of problematic relationships with parents, alienation, a history of abuse, negative life events, or other emotional disturbances.

Sensation seeking and risk taking

Connected to experimentation with drug use is the need by young people to undertake what many adults would consider sensation-seeking or risk-taking activities. This change in behavior is common to adolescents across animal species, and corresponds to changes within brain structure and function during this developmental period. As such, risk taking may be considered of evolutionary importance for an animal required to rapidly develop the skills necessary for independent living and possible expulsion from its social group.

Sensation-seeking and risk-taking behaviors also provide important opportunities for young people to grow, learn, and discover individual likes and dislikes. They provide opportunities to experience strong sensations and discover how these feel. In contrast to adolescents, who have a reduced perception of risk, many adults are particularly fearful and concerned about risk-taking activities in young people. This is partly because parents fear their son or daughter will be hurt in some way. However, perhaps more important is the fact that adults have generally completed this phase of their own development and would find it particularly difficult and anxiety provoking to experience new scenarios in the same way that adolescents do.

Reconnection programs

Reconnection programs designed to address alcohol and other drug abuse are based on the idea that community involvement through educational, vocational, social, and recreational activities can reduce the harms associated with drug use, building both self-esteem and a positive sense of identity. They provide a meaning and purpose to life by a connection to the wider community. As such, these programs are designed to assist individuals in developing age-appropriate skills, contacts, and opportunities that allow participation in local community activities.

Reconnection programs also frequently provide education and information to young people about the problems and harms associated with substance use, and can provide a supportive nonjudgmental and nonconfrontational environment in which to take time out from ongoing negative drug-using experiences. They can also help individuals learn new ways of coping with problems that may have precipitated their substance use disorder or contribute to their ongoing use, for example, relaxation techniques for anxiety disorders or assertion skills to build self-esteem.

N. ROGERS, D. I. LUBMAN

SEE ALSO:
Addictive Behavior • Adolescents and Substance Abuse • Children • Cultural Attitudes • Drug Use Subcultures • Gangs • Parenting • Peer Influence • Prevention • School and Drugs • Self-Esteem • Vulnerability

Resources for Further Study

BIBLIOGRAPHY

Reference Works

Bonnie, Richard J., and Charles H. Whitebread. 1999. *The Marijuana Conviction: A History of Marijuana Prohibition in the United States.* New York: Lindesmith Center.

Carroll, Marilyn. 1994. *Cocaine and Crack.* Hillside, N.J.: Enslow Publishers.

Carson-DeWitt, R., ed. 2001. *Encyclopedia of Drugs, Alcohol, & Addictive Behavior.* 2nd ed. Farmington Hills, Mich.: Macmillan Reference USA.

Cherniske, Stephen. 1998. *Caffeine Blues: Wake Up to the Hidden Dangers of America's #1 Drug.* New York: Warner Books.

Clayton, Lawrence. 2001. *Barbiturates and Other Depressants.* Rev. ed. New York: Rosen Pub. Group.

Clayton, Lawrence. 1994. *Designer Drugs.* New York: Rosen Pub. Group.

Debenedette, Valerie. 1996. *Caffeine.* Springfield, N.J.: Enslow Publishers.

Fernandez, Humberto. 1998. *Heroin.* Center City, Minn.: Hazelden.

Flynn, John C. 1991. *Cocaine: An In-Depth Look at the Facts, Science, History and Future of the World's Most Addictive Drug.* New York, N.Y.: Carol Pub. Group.

Furst, Peter E. 1986. *Mushrooms: Psychedelic Fungi.* New York: Chelsea House Publishers.

Gahlinger, Paul M. 2004. *Illegal Drugs: A Complete Guide to Their History, Chemistry, Use, and Abuse.* Rev. ed. New York: Plume.

Goodwin, William. 2002. *Marijuana.* San Diego, Calif.: Lucent Books.

Griffith, H. Winter, et al. 1999. *Complete Guide to Prescription and Nonprescription Drugs.* New York: Berkley Publishing Group.

Iversen, Leslie. 2001. *Drugs: A Very Short Introduction.* New York: Oxford University Press.

Kehner, George B. 2004. *Date Rape Drugs.* Philadelphia: Chelsea House Publishers.

Kuhn, Cynthia, et al. 2003. *Buzzed: The Straight Facts about the Most Used and Abused Drugs from Alcohol to Ecstasy.* 2nd ed. New York: W. W. Norton.

Lenson, David. 1995. *On Drugs.* Minneapolis: University of Minnesota Press.

Perrine, Daniel M. 1996. *The Chemistry of Mind-Altering Drugs: History, Pharmacology, and Cultural Context.* Washington, D.C.: American Chemical Society.

Rudgley, Richard. 1999. *The Encyclopaedia of Psychoactive Substances.* New York: St. Martin's Press.

Schuckit, Marc A. 1998. *Educating Yourself about Alcohol and Drugs: A People's Primer.* Rev. ed. New York: Plenum Trade.

Smith, Sandra L. 1999. *Marijuana.* Rev. ed. New York: Rosen Pub. Group.

Weil, Andrew, and Winifred Rosen. 2004. *From Chocolate to Morphine: Everything You Need to Know about Mind-Altering Drugs.* Rev. ed. Boston, Mass.: Houghton Mifflin.

Weiss, Roger D., Steven M. Mirin, and Roxanne Bartel. 1994. *Cocaine.* 2nd ed. Washington, D.C.: American Psychiatric Press.

Williams, Mary E., ed. 2005. *Hallucinogens.* San Diego, Calif.: Greenhaven Press.

Human Physiology and Health

American Psychiatric Association (APA). 2000. *Diagnostic and Statistical Manual of Mental Disorders.* 4th ed. Washington, D.C.: APA.

Bellenir, Karen, ed. 2002. *Drug Information for Teens: Health Tips about the Physical and Mental Effects of Substance Abuse.* Detroit: Omnigraphics.

Brick, John, and Carlton K. Erickson. 1998. *Drugs, the Brain, and Behavior: The Pharmacology of Abuse and Dependence.* New York: Haworth Medical Press.

Brick, John, ed. 2004. *Handbook of the Medical Consequences of Alcohol and Drug Abuse.* New York: Haworth Press.

DuPont, Robert L. 2000. *The Selfish Brain: Learning from Addiction.* Center City, Minn.: Hazelden.

Frances, Richard J., Sheldon I. Miller, and Avram H. Mack. 2005. *Clinical Textbook of Addictive Disorders.* 3rd ed. New York: Guilford Press.

Karch, Steven B. 2002. *Karch's Pathology of Drug Abuse.* 3rd ed. Boca Raton, Fla.: CRC Press.

Liska, Ken. 2004. *Drugs and the Human Body.* 7th ed. Upper Saddle River, N.J.: Prentice Hall.

McKim, William A. 2003. *Drugs and Behavior: An Introduction to Behavioral Pharmacology.* 5th ed. Upper Saddle River, N.J.: Prentice Hall.

Miller, Norman S., ed. 1991. *Comprehensive Handbook of Drug and Alcohol Addiction.* New York: Dekker.

Piasecki, Melissa P., and Paul Newhouse, ed. 2000. *Nicotine in Psychiatry: Psychopathology and Emerging Therapeutics.* Washington, D.C.: American Psychiatric Press.

Spence, Richard T., et al. 2001. *Neurobiology of Addictions: Implications for Clinical Practice.* New York: Haworth Social Work Practice Press.

Twerski, Abraham J. 1997. *Addictive Thinking: Understanding Self-Deception.* 2nd ed. Center City, Minn.: Hazelden.

Drug Abuse, Addiction, and Treatment

Burns D. 1999. *Feeling Good: The New Mood Therapy.* Rev. ed. New York: Avon.

Coombs, Robert H. 1997. *Drug Impaired Professionals.* Cambridge, Mass.: Harvard University Press.

Dodes, Lance M. 2002. *The Heart of Addiction.* New York: HarperCollins.

DuPont, Robert L. 1984. *Getting Tough on Gateway Drugs: A Guide for the Family.* Washington, D.C.: American Psychiatric Press.

DuPont, Robert L., and John P. McGovern. 1994. *A Bridge to Recovery: An Introduction to 12-Step Programs.* Washington, D.C.: American Psychiatric Press.

Estroff, Todd Wilk, ed. 2001. *Manual of Adolescent Substance Abuse Treatment.* Washington, D.C.: American Psychiatric Press.

Fisher, Gary L., and Thomas C. Harrison. 2005. *Substance Abuse: Information for School Counselors, Social Workers, Therapists, and Counselors.* 3rd ed. Boston, Mass.: Pearson/Allyn and Bacon.

Galanter, Marc, and Herbert D. Kleber, ed. 2004. *The American Psychiatric Publishing Textbook of Substance Abuse Treatment.* 3rd ed. Washington, D.C.: American Psychiatric Publishers.

Gitlow, Stuart. 2000. *Substance Use Disorders: A Practical Guide.* Philadelphia: Lippincott Williams and Wilkins.

Goldstein, Arnold P., Kenneth W. Reagles, and Lester L. Amann. 1990. *Refusal Skills: Preventing Drug Use in Adolescents.* Champaign, Ill.: Research Press.

Gorski, Terence T., and Merlene Miller. 1986. *Staying Sober: A Guide for Relapse Prevention.* Independence, Mo.: Independence Press.

Hanson, David J. 1996. *Alcohol Education: What We Must Do.* Westport, Conn.: Praeger Publishers.

Henderson, Elizabeth Connell. 2000. *Understanding Addiction.* Jackson, Miss.: University Press of Mississippi.

Hogan, Julie, et al. 2003. *Substance Abuse Prevention: The Intersection of Science and Practice.* Boston, Mass.: Allyn and Bacon.

Jaffe, Steven L. 1990. *Step Workbook for Adolescent Chemical Dependency Recovery: A Guide to the First Five Steps.* Washington, D.C.: American Academy of Child and Adolescent Psychiatry.

Keene, Jan. 1996. *Drug Misuse: Prevention, Harm Minimization and Treatment.* New York: Singular Publishing Group.

Khantzian, Edward J. 1999. *Treating Addiction as a Human Process.* Northvale, N.J.: Jason Aronson.

Knowles, Cynthia R. 2001. *Prevention That Works: A Guide for Developing School-based Drug and Violence Prevention Programs.* Thousand Oaks, Calif.: Corwin Press.

Kurtz, Ernest. 1979. *Not-God: A History of Alcoholics Anonymous.* Center City, Minn.: Hazelden Educational Services.

Landry, Mim J. 1994. *Understanding Drugs of Abuse: The Processes of Addiction, Treatment, and Recovery.* Washington, D.C.: American Psychiatric Press.

Lowinson, Joyce H., et al. 2004. *Substance Abuse: A Comprehensive Textbook.* 4th ed. Philadelphia: Lippincott Williams and Wilkins.

Mack, Avram H., John E. Franklin, and Richard J. Frances. 2001. *Concise Guide to Treatment of Alcoholism and Addictions.* 2nd ed. Washington, D.C.: American Psychiatric Press.

Massing, Michael. 1998. *The Fix.* New York: Simon & Schuster.

McCance-Katz, Elinore F., and Thomas R. Kosten, eds. 1998. *New Treatments for Chemical Addictions.* Washington, D.C.: American Psychiatric Press.

Milhorn, H. Thomas. 1994. *Drug and Alcohol Abuse: The Authoritative Guide for Parents, Teachers, and Counselors.* New York: Plenum Press.

Miller, Geri. 2005. *Learning the Language of Addiction Counseling.* 2nd ed. New York: John Wiley.

Miller, Norman S., ed. 1997. *The Integration of Pharmacological and Nonpharmacological Treatments in Drug/Alcohol Addictions.* New York: Haworth Medical Press.

Mooney, Al J., Arlene Eisenberg, and Howard Eisenberg. 1992. *The Recovery Book.* New York: Workman Pub.

Narcotics Anonymous. 1998. *The Narcotics Anonymous Step Working Guides*. Chatsworth, Calif.: Narcotics Anonymous World Services.

Peele, Stanton, and Archie Brodsky. 1991. *The Truth about Addiction and Recovery: The Life Process Program for Outgrowing Destructive Habits*. New York: Simon & Schuster.

Perkins, H. Wesley, ed. 2003. *The Social Norms Approach to Preventing School and College Age Substance Abuse: A Handbook for Educators, Counselors, and Clinicians*. San Francisco: Jossey-Bass.

Pinsky, Drew. 2003. *Cracked: Putting Broken Lives Together Again*. New York: ReganBooks.

Ruden, Ronald A. 2000. *The Craving Brain: A Bold New Approach to Breaking Free from Drug Addiction, Overeating, Alcoholism, Gambling*. 2nd ed. New York: HarperCollins.

Shavelson, Lonny. 2001. *Hooked: Five Addicts Challenge Our Misguided Drug Rehab System*. New York: New Press.

Washton, Arnold M. 1989. *Cocaine Addiction: Treatment, Recovery, and Relapse Prevention*. New York: Norton.

White, William. 1993. *Critical Incidents: Ethical Issues in Substance Abuse Prevention and Treatment*. Bloomington, Ill.: Lighthouse Training Institute.

White, William. 1998. *Slaying the Dragon: The History of Addiction Treatment and Recovery in America*. Bloomington, Ill.: Chestnut Health Systems/Lighthouse Institute.

Drugs and Society

Abbey, Edward, and Douglas Brinkley. 2000. *The Monkey Wrench Gang*. New York: Perennial Classics.

Asken, Michael J. 1988. *Dying to Win: The Athlete's Guide to Safe and Unsafe Drugs in Sports*. Washington, D.C.: Acropolis Books.

Bayer, Linda N., and Austin Sarat. 2001. *Drugs, Crime, and Criminal Justice*. Philadelphia, Pa.: Chelsea House Publishers.

Belenko, Steven R., ed. 2000. *Drugs and Drug Policy in America: A Documentary History*. Westport, Conn.: Greenwood Press.

Bugliosi, Vincent T. 1996. *The Phoenix Solution: Getting Serious about Winning America's Drug War*. Beverley Hills, Calif.: Dove Books.

Burris-Kitchen, Deborah. 1997. *Female Gang Participation: The Role of African-American Women in the Informal Drug Economy and Gang Activities*. Lewiston, N.Y.: Edwin Mellen Press.

Cagin, Seth, and Philip Dray. 1984. *Hollywood Films of the Seventies: Sex, Drugs, Violence, Rock 'N' Roll & Politics*. New York: Harper & Row.

Cohen, Peter J. 2004. *Drugs, Addiction, and the Law: Policy, Politics, and Public Health*. Durham, N.C.: Carolina Academic Press.

Derthick, Martha A. 2004. *Up in Smoke: From Legislation to Litigation in Tobacco Politics*. 2nd ed. Washington, D.C.: CQ Press.

Donohoe, Tom, and Neil Johnson. 1987. *Foul Play: Drug Abuse in Sports*. New York: B. Blackwell.

Escohotado, Antonio. Trans. Kenneth A. Symington. 1999. *A Brief History of Drugs: From the Stone Age to the Stoned Age*. Rochester, Vt.: Park Street Press.

Finley, Laura, and Peter Finley. 2005. *Piss Off!: How Drug Testing and Other Privacy Violations Are Alienating America's Youth*. Monroe, Me.: Common Courage Press.

Gerber, Jurg, and Eric L. Jensen, eds. 2001. *Drug War, American Style: The Internationalization of Failed Policy and Its Alternatives*. New York: Garland Pub.

Gerdes, Louise, ed. 2001. *Legalizing Drugs*. San Diego, Calif.: Greenhaven Press.

Goldstein, Avram. 2001. *Addiction: From Biology to Drug Policy*. 2nd ed. New York: Oxford University Press.

Gottfried, Ted. 2000. *Should Drugs Be Legalized?* Brookfield, Conn.: Twenty-First Century Books.

Gray, James P. 2001. *Why Our Drug Laws Have Failed and What We Can Do about It: A Judicial Indictment of the War on Drugs*. Philadelphia, Pa.: Temple University Press.

Gray, Mike. 1998. *Drug Crazy: How We Got into This Mess and How We Can Get Out*. New York: Random House.

Haley, James, and Tamara L. Roleff. 2003. *Performance Enhancing Drugs*. San Diego, Calif.: Greenhaven Press.

Hanson, David J. 1995. *Preventing Alcohol Abuse: Alcohol, Culture and Control*. Westport, Conn: Praeger Publishers.

Hyde, Margaret O. 1995. *Kids in and out of Trouble*. New York: Cobblehill Books.

Kleiman, Mark A.R. 1992. *Against Excess: Drug Policy for Results*. New York: BasicBooks.

Kuhn, Cynthia, et al. 2000. *Pumped: Straight Facts for Athletes about Drugs, Supplements, and Training*. New York: W.W. Norton & Co.

Lee, Gregory D. 2005. *Conspiracy Investigations: Terrorism, Drugs and Gangs*. Upper Saddle River, N.J.: Prentice Hall.

Lusane, Clarence. 1991. *Pipe Dream Blues: Racism and the War on Drugs*. Boston, Mass.: South End Press.

MacCoun, Robert J., et al. 2001. *Drug War Heresies: Learning from Other Vices, Times, and Places*. New York: Cambridge University Press.

Marez, Curtis. 2004. *Drug Wars: The Political Economy of Narcotics*. Minneapolis, Minn.: University of Minnesota Press.

McCollum, Bill, ed. 1999. *Taking the Profit out of Drug Trafficking: The Battle against Money Laundering*. Washington: U.S. G.P.O.

Miller, Joel. 2004. *Bad Trip: How the War against Drugs Is Destroying America*. Nashville, Tenn.: WND Books.

Monaghan, Lee F. 2001. *Bodybuilding, Drugs, and Risk*. New York: Routledge, 2001.

Mottram, David R., ed. 2003. *Drugs in Sport*. 3rd ed. New York: Routledge.

Musto, David F. 1999. *The American Disease: Origins of Narcotic Control*. 3rd ed. New York: Oxford University Press.

Nielsen, James Robert. 1992. *Handbook of Federal Drug Law*. 2nd ed. Philadelphia, Pa.: Lea and Febiger.

Ringhofer, Kevin R., and Martha E. Harding. 1996. *Coaches Guide to Drugs and Sport*. Champaign, Ill.: Human Kinetics.

Roleff, Tamara L., ed 2004. *The War on Drugs: Opposing Viewpoints*. San Diego, Calif.: Greenhaven Press.

Rudgley, Richard. 1993. *Essential Substances: A Cultural History of Intoxicants in Society*. New York: Kodansha International.

Schivelbusch, Wolfgang. Trans. David Jacobson. 1993. *Tastes of Paradise: A Social History of Spices, Stimulants, and Intoxicants*. New York: Vintage Books.

Schlaadt, Richard G., 1992. *Drugs, Society, and Behavior*. Guilford, Conn.: Dushkin Pub. Group.

Shapiro, Harry. 2003. *Waiting for the Man: The Story of Drugs and Popular Music*. New York: Morrow.

Shapiro, Harry. 2004. *Shooting Stars: Drugs, Hollywood, and the Movies*. New York: Serpent's Tail.

Shulgin, Alexander T. 1992. *Controlled Substances: A Chemical and Legal Guide to the Federal Drugs Laws*. 2nd ed. Berkeley, Calif.: Ronin Pub.

Simon, David, and Edward Burns. 1998. *The Corner: A Year in the Life of an Inner-City Neighborhood*. New York: Broadway Books.

Szasz, Thomas. 2003. *Ceremonial Chemistry: The Ritual Persecution of Drugs, Addicts, and Pushers*. Rev. ed. Syracuse, N.Y.: Syracuse University Press.

Taylor, Carl S. 1993. *Girls, Gangs, Women, and Drugs*. East Lansing, Mich.: Michigan State University Press.

Taylor, Lawrence, and Steve Serby. 2003. *LT: Over the Edge: Tackling Quarterbacks, Drugs, and A World beyond Football*. New York: HarperCollins.

Tracy, Sarah W., and Caroline Jean Acker. 2004. *Altering American Consciousness: The History of Alcohol and Drug Use in the United States, 1800–2000*. Amherst, Mass.: University of Massachusetts Press.

Tricker, Ray, and David L. Cook, ed. 1990. *Athletes at Risk: Drugs and Sport*. Dubuque, Iowa: W. C. Brown.

United Nations Office for Drug Control and Crime Prevention. 2003. *Alcohol and Drug Problems at Work: The Shift to Prevention*. Geneva: ILO.

Valentine, Douglas. 2004. *The Strength of the Wolf: The Secret History of America's War on Drugs*. New York: Verso.

Waddington, Ivan. 2000. *Sport, Health, and Drugs: A Critical Sociological Perspective*. New York: E & FN Spon.

Webb, Margot. 1998. *Drugs and Gangs*. Rev. ed. New York: Rosen Pub. Group.

Weir, William. 1995. *In the Shadow of the Dope Fiend: America's War on Drugs*. North Haven, Conn.: Archon Books.

Williams, Stanley, and Barbara Cottman Becnel. 1996. *Gangs and Drugs*. New York: PowerKids Press.

Woodland, Les. 2003. *The Crooked Path to Victory: Drugs and Cheating in Professional Bicycle Racing*. San Francisco, Calif.: Van der Plas Publications.

Yablonsky, Lewis. 1997. *Gangsters: Fifty Years of Madness, Drugs, and Death on the Streets of America*. New York: New York University Press.

Periodicals and Journals

Addiction Biology. Abingdon, Oxfordshire, England: Taylor & Francis Ltd.

The Addiction Letter. Reston, Va: Manisses Communications Group.

Addiction Research. New York: Harwood Academic Publishers.

Addiction Research & Theory. Amsterdam: Harwood Academic Publishers.

Administration and Policy in Mental Health. New York: Human Sciences Press.

Alcohol Health and Research World. Rockville, Md.: U.S. Dept. of Health, Education, and Welfare, Public Health Service, Alcohol, Drug Abuse, and Mental Health Administration.

Alcohol Research & Health: The Journal of the National Institute on Alcohol Abuse and Alcoholism. Rockville, Md.: Public Health Service, National Institutes of Health.

American Journal of Drug and Alcohol Abuse. New York: Marcel Dekker.
American Journal of Health Behavior. Star City, W. Va.: PNG Publications.
American Journal of Health Education. Reston, Va.: American Alliance for Health, Physical Education, Recreation, and Dance.
American Journal of Health Studies. Tuscaloosa, Ala: Program in Health Studies in the College of Education at the University of Alabama.
American Journal of Psychiatry. Washington: American Psychiatric Association.
American Journal of Public Health. New York: American Public Health Association.
American Journal of Sociology. Chicago: University of Chicago Press.
The American Journal on Addictions. Washington, D.C.: American Psychiatric Press.
Behavioral Health Management. Cleveland, Ohio: Medquest Communications.
British Journal of Addiction. Abingdon, Oxfordshire, UK: Carfax Pub. Co.
Brown University Digest of Addiction Theory and Application: DATA. Providence, R.I.: Manisses Communications Group.
Clinical Research and Regulatory Affairs. New York: Dekker.
Community Mental Health Journal. New York: Human Sciences Press.
Contemporary Drug Problems. New York, Federal Legal Publications.
CrossCurrents: The Journal of Addiction and Mental Health. Toronto, Ontario.: Communications, Education and Community Health Department, Centre for Addiction and Mental Health.
Drug and Alcohol Dependence. Lausanne: Elsevier Science.
Drug and Chemical Toxicology. New York: Marcel Dekker
International Journal of Rehabilitation and Health. New York: Plenum Pub. Corp.
International Journal on Drug Policy. Liverpool, England: International Journal on Drug Policy.
The Journal. Toronto: Addiction Research Foundation.
Journal of Addictions & Offender Counseling. Alexandria, Va.: International Association of Addictions and Offender Counselors.
Journal of Adolescent Health Care: Official Publication of the Society for Adolescent Medicine. New York: Elsevier North Holland.
Journal of Alcohol and Drug Education. Lansing, Mich.: North American Association of Alcoholism Programs.
Journal of American College Health: Washington, D.C.: Helen Dwight Reid Educational Foundation.
Journal of Drug Issues. Tallahassee, Fla.: Journal of Drug Issues.
Journal of Health Politics, Policy, and Law. Durham, N.C.: Duke University Press.
Journal of Psychiatric and Mental Health Nursing. Boston, Mass.: Blackwell Scientific Publications.
Journal of Psychology and the Behavioral Sciences. Madison, N.J.: Fairleigh Dickinson University.
Journal of Toxicology: Clinical Toxicology. New York: Marcel Dekker.
Journal of Toxicology: Toxin Reviews. New York: Marcel Dekker.
Psychology & Health. New York: Harwood Academic Publishers.
Psychology, Health & Medicine. Cambridge, Mass.: Carfax.
Social Science. Chapel Hill, N.C.: Institute for Research in Social Science, University of North Carolina.
Social Work in Health Care. Binghamton, N.Y.: Haworth Press.
Substance Use & Misuse. New York: Marcel Dekker.
WHO Drug Information. Geneva: World Health Organization.

Selected Surveys and Research

Armstrong, T. D., and E. J. Costello. 2002. Community Studies on Adolescent Substance Use, Abuse, or Dependence and Psychiatric Comorbidity. *Journal of Consulting and Clinical Psychology* 70:1224–1239.
Blow, Frederic C. 1998. Substance Abuse among Older Adults. Treatment Improvement Protocol Series 26. Rockville, Md. U.S. Department of Health and Human Services Publication No. (SMA) 98-3179.
Carlisle Maxwell, J. 2003. The Response to Club Drug Use. *Current Opinion in Psychiatry* 16:279–289.
Cloninger, C. R., S. Sigvardsson, and M. Bohman. 1996. Type I and Type II Alcoholism: An update. *Alcohol Health and Research World* 20:18–24.
Cone, Edward J. 1997. New Developments in Biological Measures of Drug Prevalence. Monograph 167. National Institute on Drug Abuse, Baltimore, Md. www.nida.nih.gov/pdf/monographs/monograph167/108-129_Cone.pdf).
Del Boca, F. K., and M. N. Husselbrock, 1996. Gender and Alcohol Subtypes. *Alcohol Health and Research World* 20:56–63.
Drug Abuse Warning Network Report, June 2003. Office of Applied Studies, Substance Abuse, and Mental Health Services Administration.

Egley, A. 2002. National Youth Gang Survey Trends from 1996 to 2000. OJJDP Fact Sheet. www.ncjrs.org/pdffiles1/ojjdp/fs200203.pdf

Gordis, Enoch. 1998. Alcohol and Aging. *Alcohol Alert No. 40.* U.S. Department of Health and Human Services. Rockville, Md.

Grant, B., et al. 1994. Epidemiologic Bulletin No. 35: Prevalence of DSM-IV Alcohol Abuse and Dependence, United States 1992. *Alcohol Health and Research World* 18:243–248

Grant, B. F., and D. A. Dawson. 1999. Age of Onset of Alcohol Use and Its Association with DSM-IV Alcohol Abuse and Dependence: Results from the National Longitudinal Alcohol Epidemiologic Survey, *Journal of Substance Abuse* 9:103–110.

Homanics, G. E., and S. Hiller-Sturmhofel. 1997. New Genetic Technologies in Alcohol Research. *Alcohol Health & Research World* 21:298–308

Howell, J., and S. Decker. 1999. The Youth Gangs, Drugs, and Violence Connection. *Juvenile Justice Bulletin.* www.ncjrs.org/pdffiles1/93920.pdf

Huddleston, C. West. 1998. Drug Courts and Jail-based Treatment: Jail Setting Poses Unique Opportunity to Bridge Gap between Courts and Treatment Services. *Corrections Today,* 98–101.

Inter-University Consortium for Political and Social Research. 2001. Arrestee Drug Abuse Monitoring in the United States. www.icpsr.umich.edu:8080/ICPSR-STUDY/03688.xml)

Jensen, Gary. 2000. Prohibition, Alcohol, and Murder. *Homicide Studies* 4:18–36.

Johnston, L. D., P. M. O'Malley, and J. G. Bachman. 2004. Monitoring the Future Study. National Results on Adolescent Drug Use: Overview of Key Findings, 2003. University of Michigan Survey Research Center, Michigan. www.monitoringthefuture.org/

Liptzin, Benjamin. 1995. Epidemiology of Substance Abuse in the Elderly. *Psychiatric Times.* www.mhsource.com/edu/psytimes/p950131.html)

Marzo, V. D., and D. Piomelli. 1994. Formation and Inactivation of Endogenous Cannabinoid Anandamide in Central Neurons. *Nature* 372:686.

Miller, W. R. 1985. Motivation for Treatment: A Review with Special Emphasis on Alcoholism. *Psychological Bulletin* 98:84–107.

The National Center on Addiction and Substance Abuse at Columbia University. 2000. No Place to Hide: Substance Abuse in Mid-size Cities and Rural America. www.casacolumbia.org/usr_doc/23734.PDF. Columbia NY

National Institute of Justice. 2003. 2000 Arrestee Drug Abuse Monitoring: Annual Report. www.ojp.usdoj.gov/nij/adam/welcome.html)

National Institute of Justice, International. I-ADAM: Measuring Drug Prevalence among Arrestees in Other Countries. www.ojp.usdoj.gov/nij/international/programs/iadam.html

National Institute on Drug Abuse. 2003. Preventing Drug Use among Children and Adolescents: A Research-based Guide for Parents, Educators, and Community Leaders, 2nd Edition, Baltimore, Md.

National Institute on Drug Abuse. 2002. Principles of HIV Prevention in Drug-Using Populations: A Research-based Guide. www.165.112.78.61/POHP/index.html

National Institute on Drug Abuse. 2001. Prescription Drugs Abuse and Addiction. NIDA Research Report. www.nida.nih.gov/ResearchReports/Prescription/Prescription.html

NIDA InfoFacts—Pregnancy and Drug Use Trends. www.drugabuse.gov/Infofax/pregnancytrends.html

Office of Juvenile Justice and Delinquency Prevention.1999. 1997 National Youth Gang Survey. www.ncjrs.org/html/ojjdp/97_ygs/summary.html

The Right Start for America's Newborns: A Decade of City and State Trends (1990–2000). 2003. Annie E. Casey Foundation, Baltimore, Md. www.aecf.org/kidscount/rightstart2003/

Robinson, Jerome J., and J. W. Jones. 2000. Drug Testing in a Drug Court Environment: Common Issues to Address. Washington, D.C.: U.S. Department of Justice, Office of Justice Programs.

Spear, L. P. 2002. The Adolescent Brain and the College Drinker: Biological Basis of Propensity to Use and Misuse Alcohol. *Journal of Studies on Alcohol* 63:(Suppl. 14) 71–81.

State of Delaware Statistical Analysis Center. 2002. Sentencing Trends and Correctional Treatment in Delaware. www.surj.org/finalreport.pdf

Substance Abuse & Mental Health Services Administration. 2003. National Survey on Drug Use and Health (NSDUH). Rockville, Md. www.oas.samhsa.gov/nhsda.htm

Swartz, James A. 1998. Program Finds High Rates of Drug Use among People Who Have Been Arrested. Illinois Criminal Justice Information Authority, *The Compiler* 14–16.

Tomaso, E. D., M. Beltramo, and D. Piomelli. 1996. Brain cannabinoids in chocolate. *Nature* 382:677.

UNAIDS Information Centre, 2004. Aids Epidemic Update 2004. Geneva, Switzerland. www.unaids.org/en/resources/publications.asp

Warren, K. R., and L. L. Foudin. 2001. Alcohol-related Birth Defects, the Past, Present and Future. *Alcohol Research & Health* 25:15–158. www.niaaa.nih.gov/publications/arh25-3/153-158.html

Wechsler, H., and T. F. Nelson. 2001. Binge Drinking and the American College Student: What's Five Drinks? *Psychology of Addictive Behaviors* 15:287–291. www.hsph.harvard.edu/cas/Documents/Five_Drinks

World Health Organization. 1992. International Classification of Diseases and Related Health Problems (10th revision). ICD-10. Geneva: Switzerland.

Selected Fiction

Anonymous. 1998, 1971. *Go Ask Alice*. New York: Aladdin Paperbacks.

August, Edmund, ed. 2004. *Tobacco: A Literary Anthology*. Nicholasville, Ky.: Wind Publications.

Burgess, Melvin. 1999. *Smack*. New York: Holt.

Burroughs, William S. 2003, 1959. *Naked Lunch*. New York: Grove Press.

Dick, Philip K. 1999, 1977. *A Scanner Darkly*. London: Gollancz.

Draper, Sharon M. 1994. *Tears of A Tiger*. New York: Atheneum Books for Young Readers.

Fisher, Carrie. 1987. *Postcards from the Edge*. New York: Simon and Schuster.

Hopkins, Ellen. 2004. *Crank*. New York: Simon Pulse.

Huxley, Aldous. 2004, 1963. *The Doors of Perception and Heaven and Hell*. New York: Perennial.

Huxley, Aldous. 2004. *Brave New World*. London: Vintage Books.

Jay, Mike, ed. 1999. *Artificial Paradises: A Drugs Reader*. New York: Penguin Books.

Rudgley, Richard. 2001. *Wildest Dreams: An Anthology of Drug-related Literature*. London: Abacus.

Selby, Jr., Hubert. 2000, 1978. *Requiem for a Dream*. New York: Thunder's Mouth Press.

Shannonhouse, Rebecca, ed. 2003. *Under the Influence: The Literature of Addiction*. New York: Modern Library.

Welsh, Irvine. 1994. *Trainspotting*. London: Minerva.

Wolfe, Tom. 1968. *The Electric Kool-Aid Acid Test*. New York: Farrar, Straus, and Giroux.

Zola, Émile. 1998, 1877. *L'Assommoir*. Oxford: Oxford World Classic Paperbacks.

TREATMENT CENTERS

Betty Ford Clinic
www.bettyfordcenter.org
Tel: 800-854-9211
E-mail: admissions@bettyfordcenter.org

Daytop Village
www.daytop.org/index.html
Tel: 212-354-6000

Gateway Foundation
www.gatewayfoundation.org
Tel: 312-663-1130
E-mail: webmaster@gatewayfoundation.org

Hazelden Foundation
www.hazelden.org/servlet/hazelden/go/home
Tel: 800-257-7810
E-mail: info@hazelden.org

Institute on Black Chemical Abuse
www.aafs.net/ibca/ibca.htm
E-mail: contact@aafs.net

JACS (Jewish Alcoholics, Chemically Dependent Persons)
www.jacsweb.org
Tel: 212-397-4197
E-mail: jacs@jacsweb.org

Marathon House
www.state.vt.us/adap/marathonhouse.htm
Tel: 603-563-8501

Operation PAR
www.operationpar.org
Tel: 888-PAR-NEXT

Oxford House
www.oxfordhouse.org
Tel: 800-689-6411
E-mail: info@oxfordhouse.org

Phoenix House
www.phoenixhouse.org

Walden House
www.waldenhouse.org
Tel: 415-554-1100
E-mail: editor@waldenhouse.org

HOTLINES

- 800-COCAINE: 1-800-262-2463
- 888-MARIJUANA: 1- 888-627-4582
- The Alcohol Hotline: 1-800-ALCOHOL
- Al-Anon/Alateen Family Group Headquarters: 1-800-344-2666
- Drug and Alcohol Treatment Referral National Hotline: 1-800-662-HELP
- Marijuana Anonymous: 1-800-766-6779
- Narcotics Anonymous World Service Line: (818) 773-9999
- National AIDS Hotline: 1-800-342-AIDS
- National Institute on Drug Abuse Hotline: 1-800-622-HELP

WEB RESOURCES

The following World Wide Web sources feature information useful for students, teachers, and health care professionals. By necessity, this list is only a representative sampling; many government bodies, charities, and professional organizations not listed have Web sites that are also worth investigating. Other Internet resources, such as newsgroups, also exist and can be explored for further research. Please note that all URLs have a tendency to change; addresses were functional and accurate as of January 2005.

Academic, Research, and Professional Organizations

Addiction Treatment Forum
www.atforum.com
A site that reports on substance abuse and addiction research, therapies, and news of interest to both professionals and patients. The focus is on the science of methadone used in opioid addiction treatment, but many other treatment options and topics of concern are presented.

American Academy of Addiction Psychiatry
www.aaap.org/home.htm
The Academy was formed to promote high quality treatment, educate the public and professionals on addiction, and encourage research.

American Society of Addiction Medicine
www.asam.org
An association of physicians dedicated to promoting research, educating health care workers, and improving the treatment of individuals suffering from alcoholism and other addictions.

Canadian Society of Addiction Medicine
csam.org
Click on "CSAM Policy Statements" to read national policies and "CSAM Bulletins" to read archives of the professional journal *Canadian Addiction Medicine Bulletin.*

Center for Education and Drug Abuse Research
cedar.pharmacy.pitt.edu
Based at the University of Pittsburgh School of Pharmacy, Cedar's mission is to carry out long-term research into substance abuse. The research encompasses both genetic and environmental factors in abuse.

Center for Treatment Research on Adolescent Drug Abuse
www.miami.edu/ctrada/
CTRADA was established to conduct research on the treatment of adolescent drug abuse. It evaluates different treatments to develop a greater understanding of successful treatment factors.

College on Problems of Drug Dependency
www.cpdd.vcu.edu
The CPDD is the longest-standing group in the United States addressing the problems of drug dependence and abuse. Download policy statements, reports, and fact sheets at *www.cpdd.vcu.edu/pages/statements.html*

International Society of Addiction Medicine
www3.sympatico.ca/pmdoc/ISAM
An international fellowship of physicians who consider addiction a treatable disease. The ISAM aims to enhance the physician's role in treatment and establish practice guidelines. Access ISAM's e-journal at *www3.sympatico.ca/pmdoc/ISAM/main.html*

National Association of Alcoholism and Drug Abuse Counselors
www.naadac.org
The largest professional membership organization for counselors who specialize in addiction treatment.

National Center on Addiction and Substance Abuse
www.casacolumbia.org
CASA is based at Columbia University. It is the only national organization that brings together the professional disciplines needed to study and combat abuse of alcohol, nicotine, and illegal, prescription, and performance-enhancing drugs.

The Office of Juvenile Justice and Delinquency Prevention
www.strengtheningfamilies.org
An overview of research that seeks to understand, prevent, or treat juvenile delinquency. It assesses the best practice and provides links to individual programs.

Treatment Research Institute
www.tresearch.org
TRI is a not-for-profit organization dedicated to reducing the effects of alcohol and other drug abuse on individuals, families, and communities by employing scientific methods and disseminating evidence-based information. Find out about TRI's Addiction Severity Index at *www.tresearch.org/ASI2.htm*

Government Agencies

Brookhaven National Laboratory Addiction Research
www.bnl.gov/bnlweb/addiction.html
Brookhaven is one of ten national laboratories funded by the U.S. Department of Energy. Brookhaven conducts research in the physical, biomedical, and environmental sciences.

Canadian Center on Substance Abuse
www.ccsa.ca
CCSA is Canada's national addictions agency. It provides information and advice to help reduce the harm associated with substance abuse and addictions. There is a list of recommended reading to download on the topic of young people and drugs at *www.ccsa.ca/index.asp?ID=10*

Center for Substance Abuse Treatment
csat.samhsa.gov/
CSAT's mission is to expand the availability of effective treatment and recovery services for alcohol and drug problems. It aims to improve the lives of individuals and families affected by alcohol and drug abuse by ensuring access to clinically sound, cost-effective addiction treatment that reduces the health and social costs to communities and the nation.

Drug Enforcement Administration
www.usdoj.gov/dea
News bulletins, briefings, and background reports on a wide range of issues about illegal drugs. Find out about the DEA's new museum "Target America: Traffickers, Terrorists, and You" at *www.targetamerica.org*

Food and Drug Administration
www.fda.gov
The FDA approves drugs for legal use in the United States. Information on over-the-counter, prescription, and generic drugs as well as the illegal use and trafficking of controlled drugs is available on their Web site.

National Clearing House for Alcohol & Drug Information
www.health.org/calendar
A Department of Health and Human Services and SAMHSA site. Look up information by drug name, user groups, or issues, or search the online databases.

National Institute on Alcohol Abuse and Alcoholism
www.niaaa.nih.gov
NIAAA conducts and publishes research on alcohol abuse and alcoholism. Click on "databases" to access: APIS (Alcohol Policy Information System; *alcoholpolicy.niaaa.nih.gov*), which provides information on the effectiveness of alcohol-related policies in the United States; NESARC (National Epidemiologic Survey on Alcohol and Related Conditions; *niaaa.census.gov*), the primary source for data on alcohol and drug abuse within the U.S. adult population; and the Alcohol and Alcohol Problems Science Database (*etoh.niaaa.nih.gov*).

National Institute on Drug Abuse
www.nida.nih.gov
This site provides information on particular drugs as well as statistics on drug use, treatment advice, and research.

Prevention Among Injection Drug Users
www.cdc.gov/idu/default.htm
Provides materials and resources to assist HIV, STD, and TB prevention providers working with injection drug users (IDUs) and their partners.

Substance Abuse and Mental Health Services Administration
www.samhsa.gov
SAMHSA's Web site is an important resource for data, briefings, and reports. SAMHSA's Office of Applied Studies (*oas.samhsa.gov*) provides national data on drug-abuse issues.

Substance Abuse Treatment Facility Locator
findtreatment.samhsa.gov
This searchable directory of treatment programs shows the location of facilities around the country that treat alcohol and drug abuse problems.

Treatment Improvement Exchange
www.treatment.org
Sponsored by the Center for Substance Abuse Treatment (CSAT), this Web site allows for an information exchange between CSAT staff and alcohol and substance abuse agencies, both state and local. Click on "online resources" or "special topics" for briefings, reports, latest news, and links to topics such as dual disorders and health care reform.

White House Office of National Drug Control Policy (ONDCP)
www.whitehousedrugpolicy.gov/drugfact/index.html
Federally sponsored drug-related statistics, links, presentations, and resources. The principal purpose of ONDCP is to establish policies, priorities, and objectives for the nation's drug control program. The goals of the program are to reduce illicit drug use, manufacturing, and trafficking, drug-related crime and violence, and drug-related health consequences.

Nongovernmental Organizations and Charities

Advocates for Recovery
www.advocatesforrecovery.org
With a focus on the importance of recovery, this Web site aims to educate the public about addiction, the consequences of untreated addiction, and the process of recovery. A useful database of facts can be accessed by typing in a keyword.

Al-Anon
www.al-anon.org
Al-Anon helps the families and friends of alcoholics. It focuses on the importance of recovery and explains how to cope with the effects of problem drinking.

Alcoholics Anonymous
www.alcoholics-anonymous.org
A fellowship of men and women who share experiences to help solve their common problems. The aim is to help other alcoholics achieve sobriety.

DrugStory
www.drugstory.org/index.asp
This Web site is aimed at writers and journalists. DrugStory has links to Web sites that offer detailed content on specific drugs and drug-related issues. Specific questions can be e-mailed to a select list of drug experts.

Hazelden
www.hazelden.org/servlet/hazelden/go/home
A not-for-profit organization, Hazelden helps those addicted to alcohol and other drugs. It provides treatment and care services, education, research, and publishing products.

National Council on Alcoholism and Drug Dependence, Inc.
www.ncadd.org
The NCADD provides education, information, and help to the public. This Web site has statistics, interviews with experts, and recommendations about drinking from leading health authorities. A nationwide network of affiliates can be accessed through the site.

National Families in Action
www.nationalfamilies.org
The mission of National Families in Action is to help families and communities prevent drug use among children and promote policies based on science.

The National Youth Anti-Drug Media Campaign
www.mediacampaign.org
Many different media are used to put across the Campaign's antidrug message. Look in the Gallery to view or download the latest television, print, radio, and banner advertisements. Fact sheets for parents and young people and marijuana awareness kits are also downloadable.

Mothers Against Drunk Driving
www.madd.org/home/
MADD's mission is to stop drunk driving, support victims of this crime, and prevent underage drinking. This Web site has the latest statistics on the impact of drunk driving, plus information on the laws, underage drinking research, and other issues related to MADD's mission.

National Inhalant Prevention Coalition
www.inhalants.org
NIPC promotes awareness and recognition of the problem of inhalant use. It campaigns on the issue, promotes the latest research, and can advise on individual local programs.

Partnership for a Drug-Free America
www.drugfreeamerica.org
This Web site helps children and teens reject substance abuse by influencing attitudes through persuasive information. View commercials by category—such as drug, message, agency, audience, or medium.

Sober Recovery
soberrecovery.com
SoberRecovery lists hundreds of drug treatment centers in the United States, Canada, and overseas. It offers information on different treatments available, such as rapid detox, long-term drug treatment centers, teen boot camps, wilderness programs, outpatient programs, sober houses, and halfway houses.

The United States Anti-Doping Agency
www.usantidoping.org
USADA is dedicated to stamping out drugs in sports. Find out about drug tests, the consequences of using prohibited substances, and the rights and responsibilities of athletes.

Other Web Resources

United Nations Office on Drugs and Crime
www.unodc.org/unodc/index.html
The UNODC is a global leader in the fight against illicit drugs and international crime. The organization's Web site provides information on the fight against illegal drugs, including legislation passed by the United Nations. Analyses, reports, and statistics are at *www.unodc.org/unodc/en/analysis_and_statistics.html*

Addiction Search
www.addictionsearch.com
This site offers links to the latest information from well-respected, reliable sources. The focus is on research, especially the kind that gives an overview of a key area.

Alcohol Problems and Solutions
www2.potsdam.edu/alcohol-info/index.html
Fun facts and serious information on alcohol. Explains the legal position on underage drinking and driving, with links to the legal codes in each state.

The Antidrug
www.theantidrug.com
This Web site was created by the National Youth Anti-Drug Media Campaign to equip parents with the tools they need to raise drug-free kids. It has helpful articles, advice from experts, and the latest scientific news. Parents can find support from other parents in the same situation, plus perspectives from teens themselves.

CHEMystery
library.thinkquest.org/3659
An interactive guide to chemistry.

Common Sense Drug Policy
www.csdp.org
This nonprofit organization is dedicated to expanding discussion on drug policy. Find educational material at *www.csdp.org/about.htm*

Compass Point Addiction Foundation
www.addictionresearch.com
Formerly the American Foundation for Addiction Research (AFAR), Compass Point is dedicated to fostering scientific research and disseminating information about the causes and nature of addiction disorders. Access addiction news, Web links, and articles at *www.addictionresearch.com/resources.cfm*

Daily Dose
www.dailydose.net
Updated daily, this Web site contains links to news and reports concerning drug and alcohol use and misuse.

How Stuff Works—The Drugs Channel
health.howstuffworks.com/drugs-channel.htm
Find out how drugs from aspirin to nicotine and performance-enhancing drugs work. Search for articles on addiction, how the brain and neurotransmitters work, and other physiology topics at the main site: *www.howstuffworks.com*

Law for Kids
www.lawforkids.org/laws/browse.cfm?topic=ILLEGAL_SUBSTANCES
Sets out the legal position on alcohol, tobacco, and illegal drugs in language that is clear and easy to understand.

Legal Information Institute
www.law.cornell.edu/topics/alcohol_tobacco.html
Gives information on the legal position regarding alcohol sales.

Marijuana Policy Project
www.mpp.org
The Marijuana Policy Project works to minimize the harm associated with marijuana—in particular, by campaigning against the laws that are intended to prohibit its use. MPP focuses on removing criminal penalties for marijuana use, with the emphasis on making marijuana available medically, on prescription from a doctor.

Medem
www.medem.com
A health information Web site set up by the American Medical Association and several other physician groups. Visit Medem's medical library on substance abuse and addiction for briefings, reports, and research.

National Association of Teen Institutes
http://www.teeninstitute.org/
A national organization that runs education and training programs for young people. The aim is to help teenagers recognize and reduce high-risk behaviors that may lead to drug, alcohol, and tobacco abuse.

Nicotine and Tobacco Research
www.ntrjournal.org
Official journal of the Society for Research on Nicotine and Tobacco (*www.srnt.org*). Download pdf summaries of topics in each issue at *www.ntrjournal.org/summaries.html*

Psychotropics
www.psychotropics.dk
The Lundbeck Institute's comprehensive guide to central nervous system compounds and products.

Science Daily
www.sciencedaily.com
Access the latest research news on a variety of scientific topics, including neuroscience and drugs.

Street Drugs
www.streetdrugs.org
Information for students, parents, teachers, and health professionals on the signs of drug use and a list of street drugs and their effects.

Tobacco Free Kids
www.tobaccofreekids.org
This site offers news, research, and facts to discourage children from smoking. It presents the latest federal and state initatives and provides facts and figures on young smokers in each state.

University of Michigan Documents Center
www.lib.umich.edu/govdocs
A central reference point for government information: local, state, federal, and international. Includes news and statistics.

Web of Addictions
www.well.com/user/woa/index.html#return_point
The Web of Addictions is dedicated to providing accurate information about alcohol and other drug addictions, with links to many other sites. It provides a resource for teachers, students, and others who need factual information about abused drugs.

World Health Organization
www.who.int
The World Health Organization offers support to countries to prevent and reduce drug abuse. It presents recommendations to the United Nations about which psychoactive substances should be regulated. Information about substance abuse, including WHO projects, activities, and publications, is available at www.who.int/substance_abuse. The WHO drug and narcotic control Web page (*www.who.int/topics/drug_narcotic_control/en/*) links WHO offices working on drug control. Find descriptions of activities, reports, news and events, as well as contacts.

RESOURCES FOR YOUNGER READERS

Every effort has been made by the editors to ensure that the Web sites in this list are suitable for children, that they are of the highest educational value, and that they contain no offensive or inappropriate material. However, because of the nature of the Internet, it is impossible to guarantee that the contents of these sites will not be altered. We strongly advise that Internet access be supervised at all times by a responsible adult.

Books

Bellenir, Karen. 2002. *Drug Information for Teens: Health Tips about the Physical and Mental Effects of Substance Abuse.* Detroit: Omnigraphics.

Carroll, Marilyn. 1985. *PCP: The Dangerous Angel.* New York: Chelsea House.

Chiu, Christina. 1998. *Teen Guide to Staying Sober.* New York: Rosen Pub. Group.

Clayton, Lawrence. 1997. *Drugs, Drug Testing, and You.* New York: Rosen Pub. Group.

DeStefano, Susan. 1991. *Drugs and the Family.* Frederick, Md.: Twenty-First Century Books.

Dudley, William, ed. 2002. *Drugs.* San Diego, Calif.: Greenhaven Press.

Fleming, Martin. 1992. *101 Support Group Activities for Teenagers Affected by Someone Else's Alcohol/Drug Use.* Minneapolis: Johnson Institute.

Gottfried, Ted. 2005. *The Facts about Alcohol.* New York: Marshall Cavendish.

Gottfried, Ted. 2005. *The Facts about Marijuana.* New York: Marshall Cavendish.

Hornik-Beer, Edith. 2001. *For Teenagers Living with a Parent Who Abuses Alcohol/Drugs.* Lincoln, Nebr: iUniverse.com.

Houle, Michelle M. 2000. *Tranquilizer, Barbiturate, and Downer Drug Dangers.* Berkeley Heights, N.J.: Enslow.

Hyde, Margaret T., and Susan Greenskin. 1990. *Know about Drugs.* 3rd ed. New York: Walker.

Lawler, Jennifer. 1999. *Drug Legalization: A Pro/Con Issue.* Berkeley Heights, N.J.: Enslow.

Levert, Suzanne. 2005. *The Facts about Ecstasy.* New York: Marshall Cavendish.

Levert, Suzanne. 2005. *The Facts about Steroids.* New York: Marshall Cavendish.

Littell, Mary Ann. 1999. *Heroin: Drug Dangers.* Springfield, N.J.: Enslow Publishers.

Littell, Mary Ann. 1999. *Speed and Methamphetamine: Drug Dangers.* Berkeley Heights, N.J.: Enslow.

Madison, Arnold. 1990. *Drugs and You.* Rev. ed. Englewood Cliffs, N.J.: J. Messner.

Menhard, Francha. 2005. *The Facts about Inhalants.* New York: Marshall Cavendish.

Mitchell, Siobhan, E., et al. 2004. *Antidepressants.* Philadelphia: Chelsea House Publishers.

Mohun. Janet. 1988. *Drugs, Steroids, and Sports.* New York: Franklin Watts.

Newman, Susan. 1986. *You Can Say No to a Drink or a Drug: What Every Kid Should Know.* New York: Putnam.

Newman, Susan. 1987. *It Won't Happen to Me: True Stories of Teen Alcohol and Drug Abuse.* New York: Perigee Books.

Ojeda, Auriana, ed. 2002. *Drug Trafficking.* San Diego, Calif.: Greenhaven Press.

Olive, M. Foster. 2004. *Designer Drugs.* Philadelphia: Chelsea House Publishers.

Petechuk, David. 2005. *LSD.* Farmington Hills, Mich.: Lucent Books.

Robbins, Paul R. 1999. *Crack and Cocaine Drug Dangers.* Springfield, N.J.: Enslow Publishers.

Roza, Greg. 2001. *The Encyclopedia of Drugs and Alcohol.* New York: Franklin Watts.

Schroeder, Brock E., et al. 2004. *Ecstasy.* Philadelphia: Chelsea House Publishers.

Super, Gretchen. 1990. *Drugs and Our World.* Frederick, Md.: Twenty-First Century Books.

Super, Gretchen. 1990. *You Can Say No To Drugs.* Frederick, Md.: Twenty-First Century Books.

Talmadge, Katherine S. 1991. *Drugs and Sports.* Frederick, Md.: Twenty-First Century Books.

Uschan, Michael V. 2002. *Alcohol.* San Diego, Calif.: Lucent Books.

Youngs, Bettie B., and Jennifer Leigh Youngs. 2003. *A Teen's Guide to Living Drug Free.* Deerfield Beach, Fla.: Health Communications.

Web Sites

Alateen
www.al-anon.org/alateen.html
Alateen is part of Al-Anon, which helps families and friends of alcoholics recover and cope with the effects of problem drinking.

Alcoholics Anonymous—Message to Teenagers
www.alcoholics-anonymous.org/default/en_about_aa.cfm?pageid=11
Alcoholics Anonymous is a fellowship of people who share their experiences to achieve sobriety. They stress that alcoholism is an illness that can hit anyone, young or old. This site asks teenagers 12 questions about their drinking to help them decide if they have a problem.

Check Yourself
CheckYourself.com
Aimed at older teens, this Web site invites young people to consider whether their use of drugs or alcohol is turning into a problem. Visitors can answer questions about their lifestyle, read first-person stories, communicate with other teens, and play decision games to see how they might act. The site answers questions about drug abuse and gives information on counseling and treatment facilities. Six teens currently in treatment for drug use are ongoing columnists who share their life experiences with others.

Children of Alcoholics Foundation
www.coaf.org
COAF helps children and adults from alcoholic and substance-abusing families. It helps children cope with their emotions and understand their parents' behavior. Practical information is at *www.coaf.org/family/childteen/children%20and%20tenns%20main.htm*

The Cool Spot
www.thecoolspot.gov
This government-sponsored interactive site provides facts on underage drinking and effective ways to avoid alcohol, with strategies to resist peer pressure. The "Reality Check" quiz is a fun way to learn some facts about underage drinking.

Girl Power
www.girlpower.gov
Government-sponsored Web site for 9- to13-year-old girls. Visit *www.girlpower.gov/girlarea/activity/younger/toughdecision.htm* if you need advice on resisting peer pressure to drink alcohol, smoke, or use drugs.

Heads Up
http://teacher.scholastic.com/scholasticnews/indepth/headsup/intro/index.asp?article=welcome
This drug education site explains the latest thinking on the effects drugs can have on the brain and the body. Discover the ins and outs of the workings of the brain, and how drugs interfere with its normal functioning. Plus, read the true stories of teens who have abused drugs.

I-Count Advisors
www.icountadvisors.com/login_net.htm#
I-Count Advisors are 9- to 18-year-olds who voice their opinions on the programs developed by the National Youth Anti-Drug Media Campaign. By providing feedback and ideas, they help their peers stay healthy and drug free. People can apply to become an I-Count Advisor at this site, too.

Media Campaign
www.mediacampaign.org/getinvolved/index.html
This interactive Web site lets you create your own antidrug stickers and other materials.

National Association for Children of Alcoholics
www.nacoa.org/kidspage.htm
Helps children feel safer and find new ways to deal with problems at home. It showshow to find hope, even if parents do not change.

NIDA for Teens
teens.drugabuse.gov
This Web site is linked to the National Institute on Drug Abuse (NIDA). There are sections on the brain's response to different drugs, real-life stories, and a quiz to see how much a person knows. Common questions about drugs are answered by a physician.

Partnership for a Drug-Free America
www.drugfreeamerica.org/Kids_Teens
Read the real life stories of teenagers and discover the impact drugs and alcohol have had on their lives.

Planet Know
www.planet-know.net/first.htm
This colorful Web site presents facts and statistics on drugs. It explains how drugs affect the brain and shows short films. You can also take a quiz to test your general knowledge of drugs.

The Reconstructors
reconstructors.rice.edu
This problem-based adventure game engages the player in the role of scientist, historian, geographer, and detective. Several consecutive episodes each have their own learning objectives. The knowledge gained from each episode will help the player make better, more informed health choices when it comes to avoiding drugs of abuse.

¡Soy Unica! ¡Soy Latina!
www.soyunica.gov
A Web site to help Hispanic girls aged 9 to 14 avoid the harmful consequences of alcohol, tobacco, and illegal drug use.

Tobacco Information and Prevention Source (TIPS)
www.cdc.gov/tobacco/tips4youth.htm
In this government-run site you can learn exactly what is in a cigarette, watch a video, catch up with the latest news, download posters, test your knowledge in a quiz, and find out what celebrities think of smoking.

Too Smart to Start
www.toosmarttostart.samhsa.gov
An alcohol-use prevention initiative for parents, caregivers, and their 9- to 13-year-old children. Information for children can be found at *www.toosmarttostart.samhsa.gov/youth.html* and includes advice from teen columnists and a puzzle about the effects of alcohol. There is also a section that shows how alcohol can affect the body's organs.

Glossary

acetylcholine Neurotransmitter that occurs throughout the brain and at the junction between motor neurons and muscle fibers, causing the fibers to contract. Cholinergic neurons are those that release acetylcholine at the synapse when stimulated. See encyclopedia entry.

action potential A rapid change in the electrical potential between the inside and outside of a neuron, resulting in the cell "firing" and a nerve impulse traveling along the axon.

addiction Problematic dependence on, and craving for, a drug or activity. Addictions can cause physiological changes (as in alcoholism) or have a solely psychological basis (as in gambling). See encyclopedia entry.

adrenergic Neurons that release epinephrine when stimulated. Adrenergic pathways are made up of adrenergic neurons.

adrenoceptor An adrenergic receptor; that is, a receptor that uses epinephrine or norepinephrine as the neurotransmitter.

adverse reaction (ADR) Negative side effects of drugs (prescribed or otherwise). See encyclopedia entry.

affect Used by psychologists to mean emotion, feeling, or mood. Adjective: affective.

agonist A drug that has a stimulating effect on physiological activity, increasing the effect of a natural hormone or neurotransmitter, or of another drug. See encyclopedia entry.

AIDS Acquired immune deficiency syndrome. The condition caused by the human immunodeficiency virus (HIV). See encyclopedia entry.

alcoholism Addiction to alcohol, taking the form of the habitual consumption of excessive amounts of alcoholic drinks. See encyclopedia entry.

alkaloid A group of organic (carbon-based) compounds containing nitrogen and produced by various flowering plants. Many alkaloids, including caffeine, nicotine, and quinine, have physiological effects.

allele One form of a specific gene. Many genes occur in a variety of different forms depending on the precise DNA sequence. People inherit two copies of most genes and can therefore have similar or different alleles of any gene.

allostasis Maintaining stability through change, as when the body adapts to a challenging or stressful situation. While this adaptation is helpful in the short term, allostatic loading occurs if the stress response continues, with potentially damaging effects on the brain, immune system, and cardiovascular system.

amphetamine A class of drugs that act as stimulants. Amphetamines suppress appetite and increase pulse rate and blood pressure, in addition to causing psychological effects. See encyclopedia entry.

anabolic steroid A steroid drug chemically related to male sex hormones, used to enhance the build-up of muscle tissue. See encyclopedia entry.

analgesic A substance that has a painkilling or pain-relieving effect. In contrast to anesthesia, the sense of touch is maintained during analgesia.

analog A substance that has a similar chemical structure to another substance, and which therefore has a similar chemical action or physiological effect. See encyclopedia entry.

anesthetic A substance that produces a lessening or complete loss of sensation, usually temporarily. General anesthetics cause the temporary loss of conscious awareness, while the effect of local anesthetics is limited to a particular body area.

anion A negatively charged ion, chemical group, or molecule. Adjective: anionic.

antagonist A drug that has an opposing effect, decreasing the effect of another drug or blocking the action of a natural hormone or neurotransmitter.

antidepressant drug A prescribed drug that alleviates the symptoms of depression. Classes of antidepressant drugs include MAOIs, tricyclics (such as imipramine), and SSRIs (such as fluoxetine, marketed as Prozac). See encyclopedia entry.

aphrodisiac drug A drug intended or with the actual effect of increasing sexual desire or enhancing sexual performance, for example, by facilitating erection. See encyclopedia entry.

arrhythmia An abnormal heart rhythm.

autoreceptor A receptor on a presynaptic neuron that acts as a feedback control to prevent excessive release of its corresponding neurotransmitter.

aversion A dislike or fear of something. Aversion therapy is a behavior modification technique that aims to treat those affected by pairing the addictive substance or habit with an unpleasant experience, thus building up an aversion to the addictive substance or habit. See encyclopedia entry.

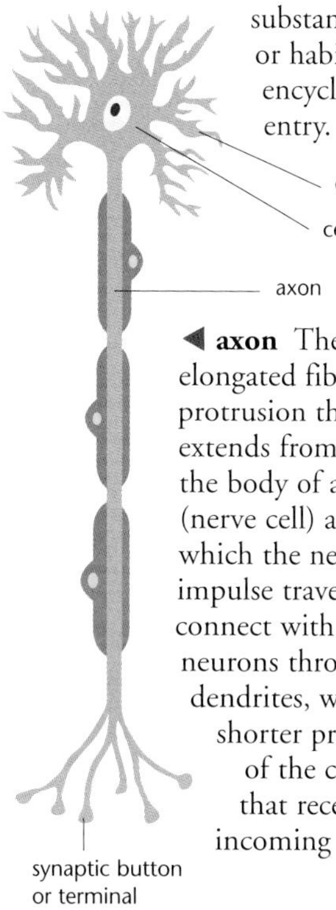

◀ **axon** The elongated fiberlike protrusion that extends from the body of a neuron (nerve cell) and along which the nerve impulse travels. Axons connect with other neurons through the dendrites, which are shorter protrusions of the cell's body that receive the incoming signal.

barbiturate A large class of drugs with a sedative effect, formerly prescribed as sleeping pills and still used in anesthesia. Barbiturate drugs are highly addictive. See encyclopedia entry.

benzodiazepine A group of tranquilizer drugs (for example, diazepam, marketed as Valium) used in the treatment of anxiety and stress and to help sleeping. These drugs were, in the past, prescribed liberally but are far less used today because of problems associated with discontinuing their use. See encyclopedia entry.

bioconversion *See* biotransformation

biopsychosocial Refers to a combination of biological, psychological, and social factors that may influence drug abuse and efforts to treat it.

biotransformation The chemical changes undergone by a substance within the the body as the substance is metabolized.

blood-brain barrier The means by which many toxic substances circulating in the bloodstream are inhibited from entering brain tissues. The walls of the capillaries in the brain are less permeable to some substances than capillaries elsewhere in the body. See encyclopedia entry.

cannabinoid Any chemical (including tetrahydrocannabinol, THC, the active ingredient of marijuana) that activates the body's cannabinoid receptors. Herbal cannabinoids occur in the cannabis plant; endogenous cannabinoids are those produced naturally in the body; synthetic cannabinoids are produced in the laboratory. See encyclopedia entry.

cannabis The plant known formally as *Cannabis sativa,* or hemp. Also, any of the psychoactive preparations (such as marijuana or hashish) or chemicals (THC) that are derived from the plant.

catalyst Anything that triggers, speeds up, or slows down a chemical reaction without itself being altered by that reaction. Enzymes are biological catalysts within the human body.

cation A positively charged ion, chemical group, or molecule. Adjective: cationic.

central nervous system (CNS) ▼ The brain and the spinal cord. Only vertebrate animals have a central nervous system, which is responsible for higher functions such as thinking and reasoning, and for integrating incoming sensory information and producing appropriate responses. The spinal cord is a bundle of nerves that conducts nerve impulses from brain to body and vice versa; it is protected by vertebrae (units of bone that make up the spine). See encyclopedia entry.

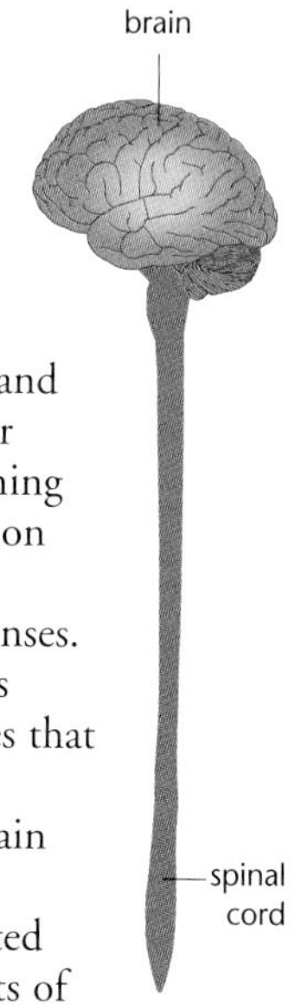

cerebral cortex The surface layer of the brain, also known as gray matter, where the brain's higher functions (such as language, thinking, and reasoning) take place and perceptual information is processed.

characteristic A specific inherited feature of an individual. A characteristic is a particular value or version of a trait: for example, the characteristic of having blue eyes is one version of the eye color trait.

cholinergic Relating to the neurotransmitter acetylcholine. Cholinergic neurons are those that release acetylcholine;

acetylcholine is the neurotransmitter within cholinergic neural pathways

club drug Any drug commonly used recreationally at nightclubs or other similar social events. See encyclopedia entry.

CNS *See* central nervous system

cognition Thinking; including mental functions such as memory, problem solving, language use, deliberation, reflection, and so on, which are often described as cognitive processes. Cognitive psychology focuses on how information is processed within the mind, constructing theoretical models to describe mental processing, including unconscious processes such as perception.

comorbidity Refers to diseases or disorders occurring together, such as alcoholism with depression. Adjective: comorbid.

conditioning Learned associations (in animals and humans) induced, deliberately or otherwise, by repetition of paired events. Classical or Pavlovian conditioning involves the pairing of an "unconditional" stimulus that has an obvious beneficial or harmful value (such as food or an electric shock) with a neutral stimulus (such as a ringing bell). In time, the neutral stimulus comes to be associated with the unconditioned stimulus and to elicit the same behavior or physiological effects (such as salivation). Instrumental (or operant) conditioning results when specific behaviors are reinforced or inhibited by being paired with reward or punishment. See encyclopedia entry.

conjugation Modification of a (natural or synthetic) chemical by enzymes, usually to make it more soluble in water and thus more easily excreted.

contractility A measure of the ability to contract, for example, like muscle fibers. Adjective: contractile.

counterculture movement Any social (often also political and artistic) movement that questions society's established conventions. A highly influential movement developed in the United States and Europe during the late 1960s.

cross-sensitization The process by which a sensitivity to one drug can produce an accelerated response to another drug.

cross-tolerance The transfer of tolerance from one drug to another drug within the same family. For example, prolonged use of heroin produces tolerance to all other opiate drugs, as well as to heroin itself.

delirium Mental confusion that can result from a variety of causes, including intoxication. Symptoms of delirium include disorientation, hallucinations, drowsiness, and fear of imaginary disasters.

dementia Loss of mental capacity, usually progressive, to the extent that normal social and intellectual functions (memory, reasoning, and so on) can no longer be carried out. Dementia has many causes, including severe alcoholism, strokes, and Alzheimer's disease.

dependence State in which an individual has a compelling desire to take a drug, drink alcohol, or indulge in a particular behavior despite the harm it is causing to the individual and the people around the individual.

depolarization ▶ The reduction of the electrical potential across the membrane of a neuron, such as occurs during a nerve impulse. When a neuron "fires," a wave of depolarization travels along the axon. Verb: depolarize.

depressant An agent that reduces a bodily functional activity or an instinctive desire (like appetite). A drug that has a depressant, rather than stimulating, effect, generally causes relaxation. The most commonly used depressant is alcohol. Adjective: depressant.

depression A common mood disorder in which the affected person typically feels sad and pessimistic and is unable to be normally active and interested in what is usually pleasurable. Bipolar depression is a clinically separate disorder from the more common unipolar depression. As well as depressive phases, bipolar depression includes phases of abnormally high activity and excitement, called mania. See encyclopedia entry.

designer drug A chemically modified version of an illegal recreational drug, designed to have similar effects but to avoid the problems of illegality through its distinct chemical identity.

detoxification The process of treatment for the physiological damage caused by drug abuse, involving medication, rest, and other procedures. See encyclopedia entry.

Diagnostic and Statistical Manual of Mental Disorders Standard reference work used by clinicians to classify, diagnose, and treat psychiatric and other mental disorders. First published in 1952, the manual is updated frequently to reflect changing medical and social opinion. Editions are signified by the use of Roman numerals after the book's acronym; for example, DSM IV refers to the current, fourth edition.

diathesis Medical term for a predisposition (usually inherited) to specific disorders.

dilation of pupils The enlargement of the pupil. Dilation of pupils occurs under the influence of certain drugs.

dopamine A neurotransmitter that plays an important role in movement. Dopamine deficiency produces the tremors and movement difficulties of Parkinson's disease, and there is evidence that some symptoms of schizophrenia are caused by excessive dopamine. See encyclopedia entry.

drug courts Courts established for the purpose of dealing with offenses that stem from drug use. Rather than punishment, drug courts emphasize treatment for drug addiction and monitoring to guard against further drug use, with the goal of rehabilitating the defendant. See encyclopedia entry.

DSM or **DSM IV** *See* Diagnostic and Statistical Manual of Mental Disorders

dysfunction Impairment in normal functioning of any kind, whether social, psychological, or physiological.

dysphoria The opposite of euphoria. Dysphoria is an inappropriately negative mood or feeling, often associated with anxiety or depression.

dysregulation The changes that occur in the central nervous system and body generally in response to the long-term use of drugs. Normally, systems of the body are regulated to stay at an optimal value. Prolonged drug use causes disturbances in this balance, and regulatory systems respond by producing compensation effects.

endocytosis The process by which material, including fluids and particles, is taken into a cell. Certain specific molecules can gain entry to the cell by initiating endocytosis when they attach to receptors on the cell's surface.

enzyme A specific molecule that has a particular function in cells or in the body generally, from digestion to DNA synthesis. Enzymes are proteins, and their structure enables them to attach with great specificity to other molecules and act as biological catalysts by bringing the reactant molecules together.

epidemiology The study of the incidence and spread of diseases within a population. Epidemiologists use statistical methods to identify possible causes for diseases by examining a great deal of data obtained over time. For example, epidemiology was used to identify smoking as a major cause of lung cancer.

euphoria A sense of extreme elation and optimism. In addition to such positive feelings, euphoria can sometimes be accompanied by delusional states of mind.

excitation, neuronal ▶ The state of a neuron resulting from its stimulation. Neuronal excitation occurs when incoming excitatory signals from neighboring neurons build up, eventually resulting in a nerve impulse traveling along the axon. Incoming signals can be excitatory or inhibitory, so the degree of neural excitation depends on the balance of these opposing effects.

exocytosis The expulsion of substances from inside a cell.

extinction In behavioral conditioning, the elimination of a behavior by withholding the stimulus or event that maintains the behavior. In Pavlov's classical conditioning experiment, presenting the bell without the food would result in extinction of the association. Learned responses can similarly be extinguished through withdrawal of the reward.

fetal alcohol syndrome (FAS) Physical and mental abnormalities in a baby resulting from the mother's alcohol intake during pregnancy.

EXCITATION AND DEPOLARIZATION OF A NEURON

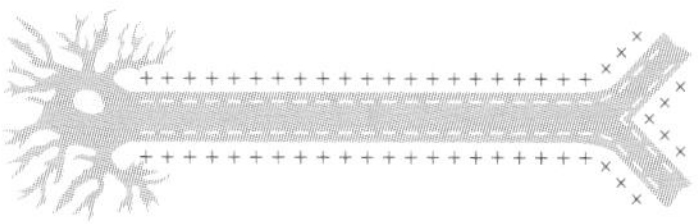

An "unexcited" neuron during the resting stage. The neuron has a slight negative charge on the inside of the cell and a positive charge on the outside.

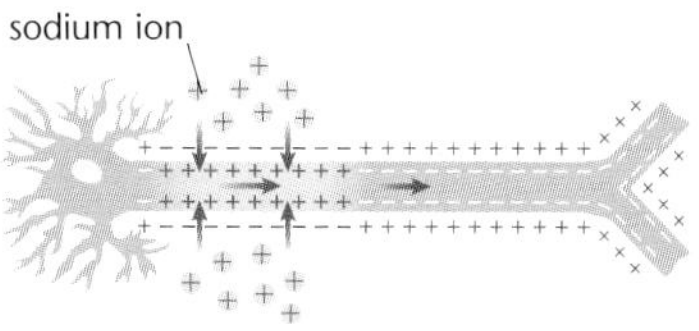

Excitatory signals build up (sodium ions flood into the cell), reversing the local polarity (charge). This is depolarization.

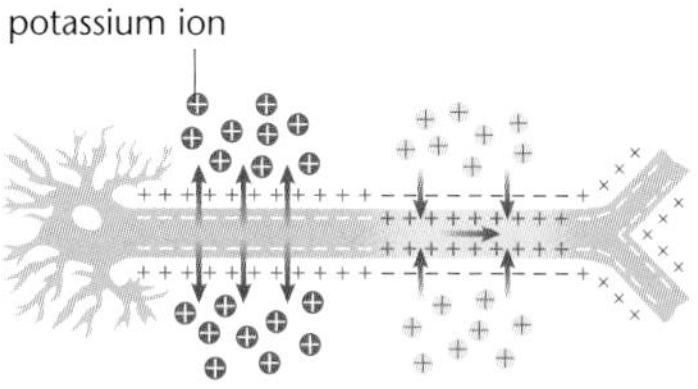

A nerve impulse travels along the axon as a wave of depolarization. Meanwhile, potassium ions flood out of the cell, repolarizing the interior of the cell and making it negative again.

functional group Chemical groups such as methyls, ethyls, and amides that determine the classification of organic (carbon-based) molecules. For example, hydrocarbon chain molecules with one or more hydroxyl (OH) group are classed as alcohols. Organic molecules often have more than one functional group.

GABA An amino acid (full name: gamma-aminobutyric acid) that acts as an inhibitory neurotransmitter in the central nervous system. GABA imbalances are thought to play a role in anxiety disorders. See encyclopedia entry.

gateway drug A controversial designation for drugs believed to open the way to the use of other, more damaging drugs. For example, according to this theory, use of marijuana is likely to lead to the use of "hard" drugs such as cocaine and heroin. See encyclopedia entry.

gene A unit of hereditary information comprising a segment of DNA. A single gene contains the information for producing a single substance used in the cell, usually a polypeptide (protein). Many genes take a variety of forms, called alleles.

genetics The study of heredity in living organisms based originally on abstract concepts such as genes, dominance, and inheritance. Many of these concepts are still used in modern genetics, which is based on an understanding of genes at the molecular, or DNA, level.

glutamate An amino acid that functions as a neurotransmitter; also known as glutamic acid.

habituation A reduction in a person's response to a stimulus due to repeated exposure to it. In terms of drug use, repeated use causes habituation in the form of desensitization and, eventually, dependence.

hallucinogen Any substance that induces hallucinations, which are sensory experiences (typically visual or auditory) that appear real but which are not produced by external reality. Some drugs are mildly hallucinogenic, while others (such as LSD) are strongly hallucinogenic. See encyclopedia entry.

heritability Also known as the "heritability ratio," the proportion of the variation of a particular trait in a population that can be traced to inherited factors. The term is a technical one and is not equivalent to the degree to which variation in a trait has a genetic, as opposed to environmental, origin.

hippocampus A structure within the limbic system of the brain that has a key role to play in many brain functions, including long-term memory, learning, and emotion.

HIV Human immunodeficiency virus; the virus that causes AIDS. HIV is a retrovirus: its genetic information is copied and incorporated into that of the host cell (the cell it infects).

homeostasis The regulation and maintenance of stability in biological systems, such as a stable internal environment in the body maintained by regulation of temperature and concentration of glucose, water, and oxygen.

hormone A protein that acts as a messenger substance within the human body. Hormones are secreted into the bloodstream and may act on several organs. Examples of hormones include epinephrine, insulin, testosterone, and estrogen.

hyperpolarization An increase in the electrical potential across the membrane of a neuron, inhibiting a nerve impulse. Verb: hyperpolarize.

hypnotic drug Drugs that depress the central nervous system, either acting as sedatives or inducing sleep, depending on the drug and its dose. See encyclopedia entry.

hypothalamus A structure situated at the base of the brain that plays an important role in controlling many aspects of body regulation and behavior, including thirst, hunger, sleep, growth, and sexual behavior.

immunoassay Method for determining the amount of a specific antigen (substance that generates an immune response). Immunoassays are used for clinical testing; for example, in pregnancy tests.

INCB International Narcotics Control Board, an organization within the United Nations that oversees the implementation of international treaties limiting the availability of controlled drugs.

incentive salience The extent to which an incentive is noticed and desired by an individual; in other words, its value as an incentive. Salience is a matter of the individual's response and therefore varies over time and between individuals.

inhalant Any substance that is used as a mind-altering drug by being inhaled. Inhalants are vapor-producing substances such as solvents, and the abuse of these substances can cause serious harm. See encyclopedia entry.

inhibition, neuronal Reduction in the likelihood of a nerve cell firing. Neuronal inhibition occurs when an inhibitory neurotransmitter (such as GABA) reaches the postsynaptic (message-receiving) membranes of a neuron, causing an increase in the electrical potential across the membrane. In contrast, excitatory neurotransmitters (such as acetylcholine or glutamate) cause a decrease in electrical potential and increase the likelihood of a nerve impulse being transmitted.

intercellular Occurring between cells. For example, intercellular fluid is the fluid that surrounds body cells.

intervention Any treatment or procedure for a specific purpose. For example, antidepressant medication and cognitive therapy are both possible interventions in the treatment of depression. See encyclopedia entry.

intoxication The effect of an intoxicating substance, usually alcohol but also caffeine, amphetamines, and other drugs. Literally, intoxication means having been poisoned. Adjective: intoxicated.

intracellular Occurring within a cell. For example, the nucleus and mitochondria are intracellular structures.

ionotropic receptor ▶ A receptor site that is triggered by molecules of neurotransmitter binding to its surface, which changes the shape of the receptor and opens the channel, allowing ions to pass through and trigger an action potential. Ionotropic receptors are the direct, faster-acting of the two main classes of receptor (compare with metabotropic receptors). See encyclopedia entry "Drug Receptors."

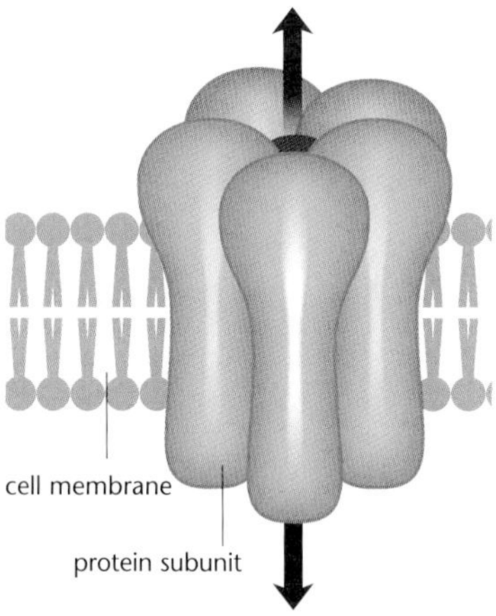

Ligand-gated receptors are composed of five structurally similar protein subunits that assemble to form a central channel through which ions can pass.

ligand-gated channel ▲ Channel associated with an ionotropic receptor within a cell membrane that opens in response to a ligand (a chemical group that donates electrons), in contrast to voltage-gated channels. The neurotransmitters serotonin, acetylcholine, and GABA operate by activating ligand-gated channels in the neuronal membrane. See encyclopedia entry "Drug Receptors."

maladaption A behavior pattern that is unlikely to be beneficial to the person displaying it. Describing behavior as maladaptive avoids the issue of whether psychiatric conditions are physiological illnesses. Adjective: maladaptive.

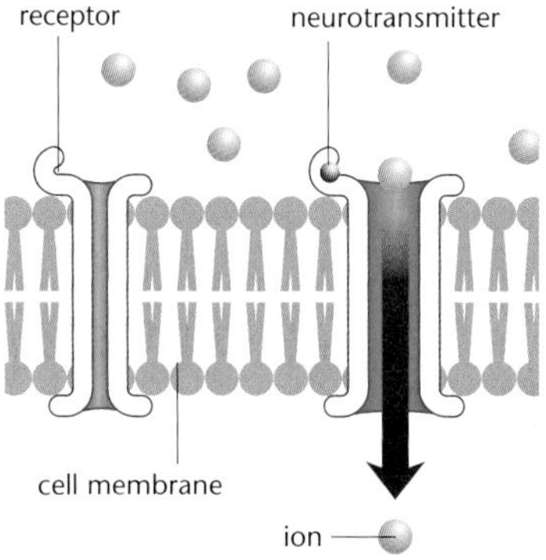

MAO Monoamine oxidase; an enzyme that breaks down substances called amines, some of which (such as dopamine, epinephrine, and serotonin) act as neurotransmitters. See encyclopedia entry.

MAOI Monoamine oxidase inhibitor; a group of substances that work by inhibiting the action of the enzyme monoamine oxidase. Because this enzyme breaks down amines, the effects of MAOIs are to increase the amounts of amine neurotransmitters, including dopamine, epinephrine, and serotonin. See encyclopedia entry "MAOs and MAOIs."

MDMA 3,4 methylenedioxy-methamphetamine, better known as Ecstasy, a commonly used illegal recreational drug. Ecstasy generates feelings of euphoria but can have dangerous side effects, including loss of control of body temperature and increased heart rate. See encyclopedia entry "Ecstasy."

mesocorticolimbic dopaminergic system *See* mesolimbic dopaminergic system.

mesolimbic dopaminergic system An important dopamine-secreting system within the brain, extending from the pons through the limbic system to the cortex.

metabolism The various vital processes by which substances are chemically converted in the body, including both the building up and breaking down of complex molecules such as proteins, and the use and production of energy. A metabolite is any substance involved in a metabolic process. See encyclopedia entry.

metabotropic receptor ▼ A receptor that influences the activity of a cell indirectly by first initiating a metabolic change in the cell. This metabolic change may ultimately affect the opening or closing of an ion channel or may alter some other activity of the cell, such as protein transcription. Metabotropic receptors are the slower acting of the two main classes of receptor, with longer-term effects (compare with ionotropic receptors). See encyclopedia entry "Drug Receptors."

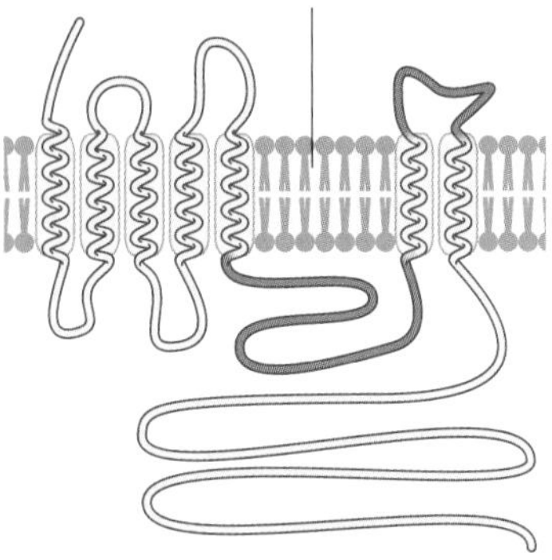

Metabotropic receptors are long proteins that pass in and out of the cell membrane seven times. Binding of a neurotransmitter causes a change in shape that allows the receptor to interact with a protein.

monoamine An amine with a single amino (NH_2) group. Monoamines include some hormones, proteins, and neurotransmitters.

Motivational Enhancement Therapy (MET) A form of one-on-one psychotherapy that aims to help people to reduce or eliminate their harmful use of a particular drug. Motivational Enhancement Therapy seeks to evoke a person's own motivation for change as a personal decision and to support that decision, using a technique called motivational interviewing.

narcotic drug Any drug that has both sedative and analgesic effects. Strictly, the term should be used to refer only to opioid drugs such as morphine and heroin, but sometimes it is also used for other psychoactive drugs, such as cocaine and marijuana. See encyclopedia entry.

neuron A nerve cell. The nervous system is made up of billions of neurons, each comprising a cell body, a long fiber called an axon, and several shorter projections, or dendrites. There are three main types of neurons: sensory neurons transmit information from sense receptors toward the brain; motor neurons transmit signals toward muscles and glands; and interneurons transmit signals within the central nervous system. Adjective: neuronal.

neuroplasticity The ability of groups of neurons to adapt their function. Neuroplasticity allows an infant's brain to learn and develop and also allows recovery after neural damage caused by strokes. Adjective: neuroplastic.

neurotoxin A substance that is toxic (poisonous) to nerve tissue, including the central nervous system.

neurotransmission ▶ The sending of signals within the nervous system. Transmission takes place between neurons using chemical messengers emitted by nerve cells that trigger an impulse in neighboring cells, thus transmitting the signal. See encyclopedia entry.

norepinephrine A neurotransmitter that occurs in the central nervous system and sympathetic nervous system. Alternative name: noradrenaline. See encyclopedia entry.

opiate, opioid Drugs such as the natural opiates opium, morphine, and codeine; or synthetic versions (heroin, fentanyl) that have a similar effect. Opioid drugs have both sedative and analgesic effects. See encyclopedia entry.

oxidase Enzymes that have the function of producing chemical oxidation—that is, the removal of hydrogen atoms—in the substances on which they act.

paranoia A psychiatric disorder characterized by jealousy, suspicion, and delusions of persecution. People with paranoia usually function well intellectually, so their beliefs may be internally coherent although delusional.

parasympathetic nervous system Part of the autonomic nervous system, which controls involuntary actions, particularly digestion and excretion. Nerves of the parasympathetic nervous system release the neurotransmitter acetylcholine, while those of the sympathetic nervous system release epinephrine.

peripheral nervous system (PNS) The part of the nervous system that extends from the central nervous system to the rest of the body, within the head and trunk and along the limbs to skin, muscles, and internal organs.

pharmacokinetics The study of the chemical mechanisms by which drugs act within the body, including the bodily absorption, distribution, metabolism, and excretion of drugs. See encyclopedia entry.

pharmacology The scientific study of drugs and their actions. See encyclopedia entry.

pharmacophores The physiologically active parts of the molecules of a drug substance that produce the drug's effect.

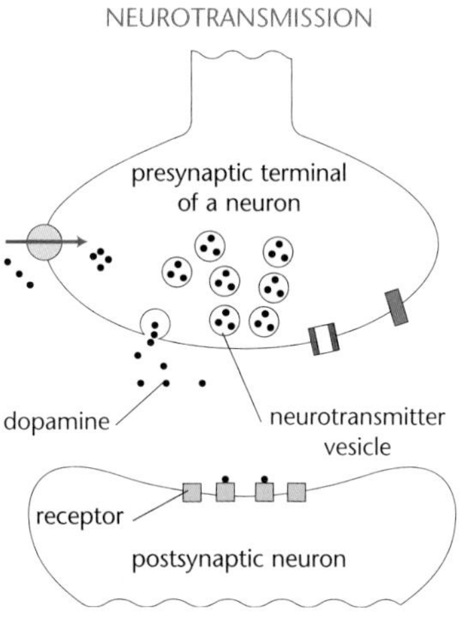

A neuron releases neurotransmitters such as dopamine to trigger a response in a neighboring neuron.

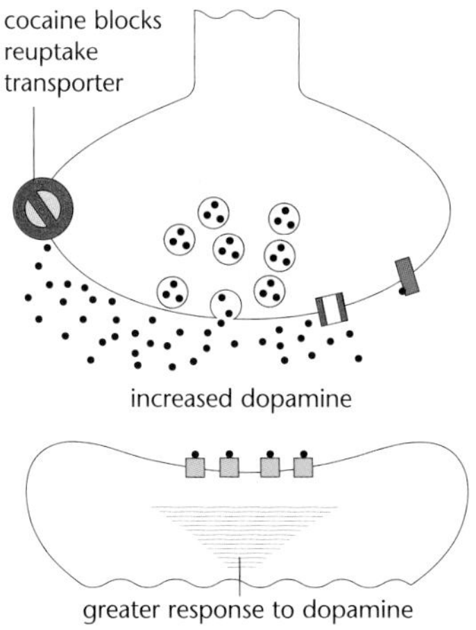

Cocaine blocks a presynaptic control point (the reuptake transporter) that removes excess dopamine (above). Prolonged cocaine use causes tolerance (below).

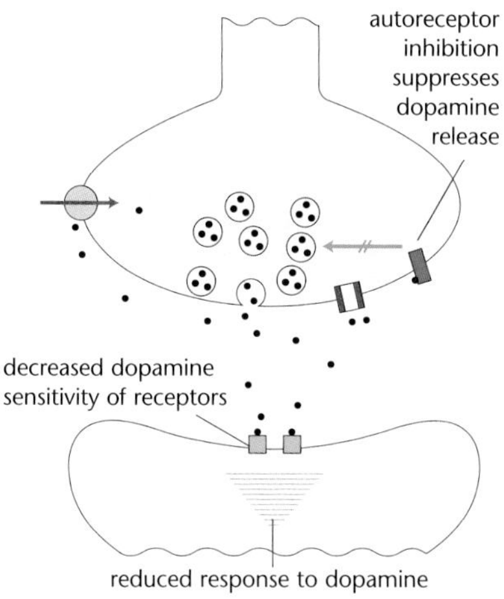

pharmacy drug An over-the counter drug bought without a prescription. Common painkillers such as paracetamol and aspirin, as well as some mild sedative drugs, are available in this way. See encyclopedia entry.

phenethylamines Chemicals derived from phenylethylamine, $C_8H_9NH_2$. Phenethylamines occur widely in nature, in plants as well as in the body. Dopamine, epinephrine, and norepinephrine are phenethylamines, as are some drugs, including Ecstasy and the amphetamines. See encyclopedia entry.

polar compound A chemical compound in which the molecules have a distinct electrical charge at one end in relation to the other. Water (H_2O) is a polar compound, since electrons are drawn to the oxygen atom, which thus has a negative charge with respect to the hydrogen atoms. Many organic (carbon-based) compounds in the body are nonpolar and have a relatively even charge distribution.

polysubstance dependence Term used by psychiatrists to describe multiple addictions involving three or more substances as a group, not including caffeine or nicotine, over a 12-month period.

postsynaptic After the synapse (the junction between one neuron's axon and the next neuron's dendrite). Nerve impulses are passed from a presynaptic neuron to a postsynaptic neuron.

post-traumatic stress disorder Disorder resulting from a traumatic event that causes the sufferer to experience a variety of psychologically distressing phenomena, such as recurrent and distressing dreams in which the traumatic event is re-experienced.

presynaptic Before the synapse (the junction between one neuron's terminal button and the next neuron). Nerve impulses are passed from a presynaptic neuron to a postsynaptic neuron.

prohibition The legal prohibition of the sale, manufacture, or use of a drug. See encyclopedia entries on prohibition of alcohol and of drugs.

proteomics The study of proteins. Proteins are large, carbon-based molecules that are extremely important in cells and the body as a whole, both structurally and functionally.

psychoactive The ability of a substance to produce a psychological effect, particularly on mood, consciousness, experience, and so on. Although common painkillers and other mild drugs could be said to affect consciousness in a limited sense, the term is generally used to indicate a more marked effect.

psychopharmacology The scientific study of the action of drugs on the mind and brain. Psychopharmacology includes both the endeavor to design drugs with desired psychological effects (such as antidepressants) and to understand why particular substances have their observed effects.

psychosis Any psychiatric disorder in which the person affected has beliefs that are grossly inappropriate and disconnected with external reality, involving delusions or hallucinations. Psychotic disorders include schizophrenia and bipolar depression

psychotropic drug Any mind-altering psychoactive drug, including hallucinogens, tranquilizers, and antipsychotic drugs. See encyclopedia entry.

receptor Any nerve cell that responds to sensory stimuli by producing a nerve impulse, for example, light-sensitive cells in the retina. The term also refers to receptor sites; that is, regions on the surface of a cell that bind specifically to particular molecules such as neurotransmitters and hormones, triggering characteristic changes in the cell. See encyclopedia entry "Drug Receptors."

reinforcement ▶ Any stimulus or event that rewards a particular action and thus makes that action more likely to happen again. In instrumental conditioning, for example, presentation of a food reward acts as a reinforcement for a rat's lever press.

reinstatement Restoration to a previous, often satisfactory, state. In the biological context, reinstatement can refer to a return to normal physiological or psychological functioning—for example, reinstatement of normal brain function after withdrawal from drug abuse.

relapse A worsening of any medical condition after previous improvement. In the addiction context, a relapse occurs if an addicted person returns to drug abuse after a period of reducing or eliminating the abusive behavior. See encyclopedia entry.

retrovirus A type of virus with RNA as the genetic material and that uses an enzyme (reverse transcriptase) to produce DNA from the RNA, with the viral DNA then being incorporated into the host cell's DNA. HIV is an example of a retrovirus.

reuptake The reabsorption of a neurotransmitter by the neuron after the neurotransmitter has been released into the synaptic gap (or cleft).

reward ▼ A pleasurable event or object obtained after a specified task or action has been carried out. See encyclopedia entry.

REINFORCEMENT BY REWARD
A rat learns to press the lever that delivers food, water, or a drug.

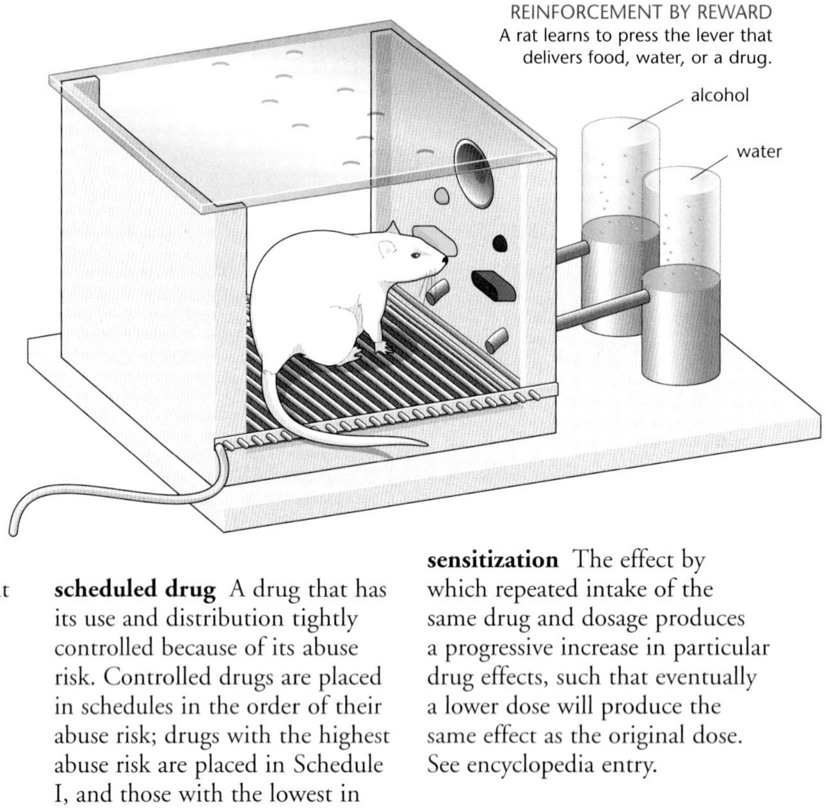

scheduled drug A drug that has its use and distribution tightly controlled because of its abuse risk. Controlled drugs are placed in schedules in the order of their abuse risk; drugs with the highest abuse risk are placed in Schedule I, and those with the lowest in Schedule V.

schizophrenia A group of psychiatric disorders in which thinking, emotions, and behavior are disrupted and often delusional. One characteristic of schizophrenia is hallucinations, often auditory ("hearing voices") rather than visual. Paranoid schizophrenia involves delusions of persecution.

sedative A drug that produces sedation—that is, drowsiness and a reduction in anxiety or aggression. Sedatives are most commonly used as sleeping pills. See encyclopedia entry.

self-medication The self-treatment of health problems by individuals without medical supervision. Medicines for self-medication are available without a doctor's prescription through pharmacies.

sensitization The effect by which repeated intake of the same drug and dosage produces a progressive increase in particular drug effects, such that eventually a lower dose will produce the same effect as the original dose. See encyclopedia entry.

serotonin A neurotransmitter found in the central nervous system; also known as 5-HT. See encyclopedia entry.

signal transduction The transformation of a signal from one form to another. For example, a signal meeting a sensory receptor (such as light meeting a light-sensitive retinal cell) is transduced (transformed) into a nerve impulse.

SNRI Serotonin norepinephrine reuptake inhibitor. This class of drugs is thought to act by limiting the reabsorption of serotonin and norepinephrine by neurons in the brain.

sobriety The state of being sober—that is, not under the effect of any drug, particularly alcohol.

speedball A combination of heroin with cocaine, amphetamine, or other stimulating drug injected directly into the bloodstream.

SSRI Selective serotonin reuptake inhibitor. SSRIs are a relatively new class of antidepressant drugs, of which one of the best known is fluoxetine (Prozac). These drugs increase the amount of the neurotransmitter serotonin by inhibiting its reuptake. See encyclopedia entry.

standard drink The amount of an alcoholic drink that contains the alcoholic equivalent of 14.7 ml of pure ethanol.

step program A strategy for overcoming dependence, involving graduated aims and the approach of taking "one step at a time." The original twelve-step program was developed by the organization Alcoholics Anonymous to help people overcome alcoholism. See encyclopedia entry.

stimulant A drug that produces a stimulating effect by activity in the central nervous system. Amphetamines, which increase alertness and raise levels of norepinephrine, are stimulants.

synapse The junction between two neighboring neurons, formed where the terminal button on the axon of one neuron meets a neighboring neuron. There is no direct physical contact between neurons at the synapse, and signals pass by means of chemical neurotransmitters.

synaptic cleft The gap between two adjacent neurons at the synapse, which is bridged by the release of neurotransmitters.

syndrome A collection of symptoms that tend to occur together, indicating a specific disorder.

synthesize To produce a particular substance by building it up from smaller components. For example, proteins are synthesized in the body from amino acids.

tachycardia An abnormally fast heartbeat; that is, a pulse rate of more than 100 beats per minute in a resting adult.

telescoping A phenomenon in which something develops at a faster rate than usual, such as the faster progression from alcohol use to alcohol abuse that some studies have found in women compared with men.

tetrahydrocannabinol (THC) The main psychologically active ingredient in marijuana.

thalamus A pair of structures in the center of the brain that function as a relay station between sensory information and the cortex, where the information is processed, resulting in the perception of sensations.

tolerance A reduced response to a drug due to repeated exposure to it, and a corresponding need to take larger and larger doses to achieve the previous effect. See encyclopedia entry.

toxicity The potency of a substance such as a toxin (poison). Adjective: toxic. See encyclopedia entry.

trait In genetics, a genetically determined variable. For example, height is a trait (in contrast, a particular person being tall or short is a characteristic).

transduction *See* signal transduction

tryptamine An organic (carbon-based) chemical, formula $C_{10}H_{12}N_2$. Tryptamine is formed in plant and animal tissues from the amino acid tryptophan and is an intermediate in various metabolic processes. Tryptamine derivatives include the neurotransmitter serotonin and the hallucinogenic drug DMT (dimethyltryptamine). See encyclopedia entry.

urinalysis Tests on a sample of urine to detect drugs.

ventral tegmental area (VTA) Region of the brain containing dopamine-secreting neurons; thought to be important in arousal.

voltage-gated channel Channel within a cell membrane that is opened by a change in electrical potential, rather than by the presence of a particular chemical. Compare with ligand-gated channels. See encyclopedia entry "Drug Receptors."

withdrawal The process of discontinuing the use of a drug or substance by a person who is dependent on it. Unpleasant physical and mental symptoms often accompany withdrawal. See encyclopedia entry.

Drug Table

Names in **boldface** indicate the most closely related articles in the encyclopedia. For additional street and alternate names, see Index of Drugs, pages 912–916.

COMMON NAME OR TRADE NAME	CHEMICAL, GENERIC, OR BOTANICAL NAME	STREET NAMES AND OTHER NAMES	TYPE OF DRUG
2C-T-7		Blue mystic, 7-up, beautiful, tripstasy	**Phenethylamine**
Acetorphine and etorphine		Elephant juice, M99	Opioid
Amyl nitrate		Aimies, boppers, pearls, poppers	**Inhalant**
Amytal	**Amobarbital**	Blues, blue heavens	Barbiturate
Ativan	Lorazepam		**Benzodiazepine**
Atropine			**Belladonna alkaloid**
Benzedrine	**Amphetamine sulfate**	Speed, bennies, amp	Amphetamine
Bufotenine	5-HO-DMT (5-hydroxy-dimethyltryptamine)		Tryptamine
Caffeine			Stimulant
Chloroform			**Sedative/Inhalant**
Cocaine	Cocaine hydrochloride	Coke, snow, blow, Bolivian marching powder, Charlie, big C, nose candy	Stimulant
Coca leaf	*Erythroxylon coca*	Coca	Stimulant
Codeine	methyl morphine		Opiate
Crack cocaine		Smack, rock	Stimulant
Demerol	**Meperidine, pethidine**		Opioid
DET	Diethyltryptamine		**Tryptamine**
Dexedrine	Dextroamphetamine (**amphetamine sulfate**)	Dexies	Amphetamine
Dilaudid	Hydromorphone	Hospital heroin	**Opioid**
DMT	Dimethyltryptamine	Businessman's LSD, Fantasia, 45-minute psychosis	Tryptamine
DOB	Brolamphetamine		**Amphetamine**
Doriden	**Glutethimide**		Sedative
Ecstasy	MDMA (3,4 methylene-dioxymethamphetamine)	XTC, love drug, Adam	Amphetamine
Ephedrine			Amphetamine
Equanil, Miltown	**Meprobamate**		Sedative
Erythropoietin		EPO	Hormone
Ethanol	Ethyl alcohol		Alcohol
Ether			Anesthetic/**Inhalant**
Ethyltryptamine	3-(2-aminobutyl)indole	ET, alpha-ET, love pearls, love pills	**Tryptamine**
Eticyclidine	PCE		**PCP analog**
Fentanyl		Jackpot, China white, TNT, friend, goodfellas	Opioid
GBL	Gamma-butyrolactone	Lactone, firewater, revivarant	Depressant/*see* **GHB**
GHB	Gamma-hydroxybutyrate	GBH, Georgia Home Boy, jib,liquid E (or X), organic quaalude, sleep	Depressant
Halcion	Triazolam		**Benzodiazepine**
Harmine and harmaline	*Banisteriopsis caapi*	Ayahuasca	Hallucinogen
Hashish	**Marijuana**	Gram, hash, soles, pollen	Hallucinogen
Heroin	Diacetylmorphine/ diamorphine	Antifreeze, brown sugar, China white, gold, H, horse, shit, stuff	Opioid
HGH	**Human growth hormone**		Hormone
Ibogaine	*Tabernanthe iboga*		Hallucinogen
Isobutyl nitrate		Aroma of men, bullet, locker room, snappers	**Inhalant**
Jimsonweed	*Datura stramonium*		Belladonna alkaloid
Ketamine		Special K, cat Valium, jet, kit-kat, vitamin K	Dissociative
Khat	Cathine/cathinone	Somali tea, African salad	Stimulant

COMMON NAME OR TRADE NAME	CHEMICAL, GENERIC, OR BOTANICAL NAME	STREET NAMES AND OTHER NAMES	TYPE OF DRUG
Klonopin	Clonazepam		**Benzodiazepine**
Laudanum			Opioid
Levorphanol	(-)-3-hydroxy-N-methylmorphinan		Opioid
Librium	Chlordiazepoxide		Benzodiazepine
LSD	Lysergic acid diethylamide	Acid	Hallucinogen
Magic mushrooms	**Psilocybin and psilocin**	Musk, mushrooms, shrooms, Simple Simon	Tryptamine
Marijuana	*Cannabis sativa*	Pot, weed, grass, hashish	Hallucinogen
MDA	3,4 methylenedioxy amphetamine	Eve	**Amphetamine/ Ecstasy analog**
Mecloqualone	3-(o-chlorophenyl)-2-methyl-4(3H)-quinazolinone		Sedative/*see* **Methaqualone**
Mescaline	3,4,5-trimethoxy-phenethylamine	Buttons, cactus, mescal, peyote	Phenethylamine
Methaqualone	2-methyl-3-o-tolyl-4(3H)-quinazolinone	Quaaludes, ludes, 714s, sporos	Sedative
Methanol	Methyl alcohol	Meths	Alcohol
Methamphetamine		Crank, crystal, ice, meth, redneck cocaine, ya-ba	Amphetamine
Methcathinone	2-(methylamino)-1-phenylpropan-1-one	Cat, Jeff, ephedrone, bathtub speed	Stimulant
Morphine		God's drug, Miss Emma, morf, unkie	Opiate
4-MTA	4-methylthioamphetamine	Flatliner, golden eagle	**Amphetamine**
Nembutal	**Pentobarbital**	Yellow jackets	Barbiturate
Nexus	2-CB, BDMPEA	Bromo, spectrum, toonies, Venus	Phenethylamine
Nicotine			Stimulant
Nitrous oxide	N_2O	Laughing gas, buzz bomb, whippets	Inhalant
Noctec	**Chloral hydrate**	Mickey Finn, knockout drops	Sedative
Opium	*Papaver somniferum*	Poppy, Auntie, big O, Chinese tobacco, God's medicine, midnight oil, zero	Opioid
OxyContin	**Oxycodone** (14-hydroxy-dihydrocodeinone)	Oxy 40s/80s, hillbilly heroin, kicker, oxycotton	Opioid
Parahexyl			Depressant/**Marijuana**
Paraldehyde			Depressant
PCP	Phencyclidine	Angel dust, crazy coke, mad dog, ozone, rocket fuel	Dissociative
Prozac	Fluoxetine		SSRI
Restoril	Temazepam		**Benzodiazepine**
Ritalin	Methylphenidate	MPH, vitamin R, west coast	Stimulant
Robitussin	**DXM (dextromethorphan)**	Robo, Velvet, DXM	Dissociative/opioid
Rohypnol	Flunitrazepam	Forget-me drug, pingus, roofies, roaches, rope	Benzodiazepine
Rolicyclidine	PHP, PCPy		Dissociative/**PCP analog**
Scopolamine			**Belladonna alkaloid**
Serax	Oxazepam		**Benzodiazepine**
Talwin	**Pentazocine**		Opioid
Toluene		Tolly	**Inhalant**
TCP	Tenocyclidine		Dissociative/**PCP analog**
Thorazine	**Chlorpromazine**		Sedative
Valium	Diazepam		Benzodiazepine
Versed	Midazolam		**Benzodiazepine**
Vicodin	Hydrocodone		Opioid
Xanax	Alprazolam		**Benzodiazepine**

Subject Indexes

Page numbers in *italic* refer to illustrations. Page numbers in **boldface** refer to main articles on a subject. **Boldface** numbers preceding colons are volume numbers. The comprehensive index begins on page 933.

Drugs

A

B

C

D

E

F

G

Page numbers in *italic* refer to illustrations. Page numbers in **boldface** refer to main articles on a subject. **Boldface** numbers preceding colons are volume numbers.

N

O

P

Q

Page numbers in *italic* refer to illustrations. Page numbers in **boldface** refer to main articles on a subject. **Boldface** numbers preceding colons are volume numbers.

Human Physiology

A

B

C

Page numbers in *italic* refer to illustrations. Page numbers in **boldface** refer to main articles on a subject. **Boldface** numbers preceding colons are volume numbers.

D

E

F

G

H

Page numbers in *italic* refer to illustrations. Page numbers in **boldface** refer to main articles on a subject. **Boldface** numbers preceding colons are volume numbers.

Drug Manufacturing and Trade

Page numbers in *italic* refer to illustrations. Page numbers in **boldface** refer to main articles on a subject. **Boldface** numbers preceding colons are volume numbers.

Abuse, Addiction, and Treatment

A

Page numbers in *italic* refer to illustrations. Page numbers in **boldface** refer to main articles on a subject. **Boldface** numbers preceding colons are volume numbers.

Page numbers in *italic* refer to illustrations. Page numbers in **boldface** refer to main articles on a subject. **Boldface** numbers preceding colons are volume numbers.

T

U

V

W

Page numbers in *italic* refer to illustrations. Page numbers in **boldface** refer to main articles on a subject. **Boldface** numbers preceding colons are volume numbers.

Social and Legal Issues

A

B

C

Page numbers in *italic* refer to illustrations. Page numbers in **boldface** refer to main articles on a subject. **Boldface** numbers preceding colons are volume numbers.

Page numbers in *italic* refer to illustrations. Page numbers in **boldface** refer to main articles on a subject. **Boldface** numbers preceding colons are volume numbers.

Comprehensive Index

Page numbers in *italic* refer to illustrations. Page numbers in **boldface** refer to main articles on a subject. **Boldface** numbers preceding colons are volume numbers. Individual subject indexes appear on pages 912–932.

Page numbers in *italic* refer to illustrations. Page numbers in **boldface** refer to main articles on a subject. **Boldface** numbers preceding colons are volume numbers.

Page numbers in *italic* refer to illustrations. Page numbers in **boldface** refer to main articles on a subject. **Boldface** numbers preceding colons are volume numbers.

Page numbers in *italic* refer to illustrations. Page numbers in **boldface** refer to main articles on a subject. **Boldface** numbers preceding colons are volume numbers.

C

Page numbers in *italic* refer to illustrations. Page numbers in **boldface** refer to main articles on a subject. **Boldface** numbers preceding colons are volume numbers.

Page numbers in *italic* refer to illustrations. Page numbers in **boldface** refer to main articles on a subject. **Boldface** numbers preceding colons are volume numbers.

E

Page numbers in *italic* refer to illustrations. Page numbers in **boldface** refer to main articles on a subject. **Boldface** numbers preceding colons are volume numbers.

Page numbers in *italic* refer to illustrations. Page numbers in **boldface** refer to main articles on a subject. **Boldface** numbers preceding colons are volume numbers.

Page numbers in *italic* refer to illustrations. Page numbers in **boldface** refer to main articles on a subject. **Boldface** numbers preceding colons are volume numbers.

Page numbers in *italic* refer to illustrations. Page numbers in **boldface** refer to main articles on a subject. **Boldface** numbers preceding colons are volume numbers.

N

Page numbers in *italic* refer to illustrations. Page numbers in **boldface** refer to main articles on a subject. **Boldface** numbers preceding colons are volume numbers.

Page numbers in *italic* refer to illustrations. Page numbers in **boldface** refer to main articles on a subject. **Boldface** numbers preceding colons are volume numbers.

Q

R

S

Page numbers in *italic* refer to illustrations. Page numbers in **boldface** refer to main articles on a subject. **Boldface** numbers preceding colons are volume numbers.

Page numbers in *italic* refer to illustrations. Page numbers in **boldface** refer to main articles on a subject. **Boldface** numbers preceding colons are volume numbers.

T

Page numbers in *italic* refer to illustrations. Page numbers in **boldface** refer to main articles on a subject. **Boldface** numbers preceding colons are volume numbers.